School Social Work

To the memory of Stephen Gold and Lenny Lehrer, and all the students I served in my professional capacity as school social worker.

School Social Work
A Direct Practice Guide

JoAnn Jarolmen

Former professor of social work and a public school social worker

Los Angeles | London | New Delhi
Singapore | Washington DC

Los Angeles | London | New Delhi
Singapore | Washington DC

FOR INFORMATION:

SAGE Publications, Inc.
2455 Teller Road
Thousand Oaks, California 91320
E-mail: order@sagepub.com

SAGE Publications Ltd.
1 Oliver's Yard
55 City Road
London EC1Y 1SP
United Kingdom

SAGE Publications India Pvt. Ltd.
B 1/I 1 Mohan Cooperative Industrial Area
Mathura Road, New Delhi 110 044
India

SAGE Publications Asia-Pacific Pte. Ltd.
3 Church Street
#10-04 Samsung Hub
Singapore 049483

Acquisitions Editor: Kassie Graves
Editorial Assistant: Elizabeth Luizzi
Production Editor: Stephanie Palermini
Copy Editor: Deanna Noga
Typesetter: C&M Digitals (P) Ltd.
Proofreader: Sally Jaskold
Indexer: Naomi Linzer
Cover Designer: Candice Harman
Marketing Manager: Lisa Brown
Permissions Editor: Adele Hutchinson

Printed in the United States of America

Library of Congress Control Number: 2013934215

This book is printed on acid-free paper.

13 14 15 16 17 10 9 8 7 6 5 4 3 2 1

CONTENTS

Chapter 1

AN OVERVIEW OF THE THEORETICAL INFORMATION NECESSARY IN THE FIELD OF SCHOOL SOCIAL WORK

A BRIEF HISTORY OF SOCIAL WORK IN SCHOOLS

The history of school social work is about 100 years old in the United States. It can be followed along three paths of history: the socioenvironmental, the professional, and the legal histories. It can be chronicled by situations that occur in the environment, educational, or societal as well as the historical and legal decisions that have occurred.

Socioenvironmental

After the inception of compulsory education (that is, when the law mandated that children receive an education) at the beginning of the 20th century, which was created through individual state enactments, social work services began in schools with a focus on attendance and academic achievement. In the years immediately following the Great Depression, the focus shifted to socioeconomic circumstances and primary needs such as food, clothing, and housing. A decade later, during the conservative era following the end of World War II, social workers in schools turned their attention to the intrapsychic and interpersonal issues of their students (Leiby, 1978). By the 1960s and 1970s, school social workers were faced with social and political upheavals, which placed a new emphasis on issues such as racism, drug abuse, child abuse and neglect, and changing social times including protests and violence resulting in a more "humanistic approach to education" (Allen-Meares, 2004, p. 35).

In the 1980s, group work and the inception of legislation for the handicapped became the new focus for school social work resulting in increased responsibilities through special education programs for school social workers. Teamwork and evaluations were now involving social work interventions along with consultation, evaluation, and services for classified students. These responsibilities continue today. Between the 1990s and today, changes in the social environment including gender, single-parent households, the growth of technology, changes in welfare, school-based violence, and community control of schools have become major issues (2004). In addition to the special education responsibilities, advocacy, support for students and families, as well as primary prevention and crisis intervention have become the purview of our present-day school social workers.

Professional

The professional growth of school social workers evolved from the days of the "friendly visitor" in the early 1900s, to the present national standards for practicing school social workers. In the early years, agencies outside of the schools supplied the schools with social workers. In 1913, Rochester, NY, was the first to hire school social workers. By 1919, a nationwide association of visiting teachers was established, which lasted 10 years. After 1929, school social work services were reduced due to the Depression resulting in a shift to social casework during the 1930s and 1940s. This move to casework stemmed from the absence of funds for public school personnel.

During the 1950s, the focus shifted again toward cooperation with other school professionals. In 1955, the National Association of Social Workers (NASW) recognized the specialization of school social work. A more professional title, *school social worker,* was proposed in the 1960s, phasing out the former "visiting teacher" label. Throughout the 1970s and 1980s, a move was made to help handicapped students through evaluation, consultation, and treatment. More recently, in the last two decades, some states have developed requirements for the practice of school social work. Additionally, the creation of the National School Social Work Association and a credential was established by NASW. (The credential information can be found at http://www.socialworkers.org/credentials/default.asp.) This governing body felt the essential need for such services in the schools and therefore provided a special credential. As the needs of special students with disabilities were defined, the federal government provided legislation that was enacted by the individual states. Thus, social workers offer services in the schools through the Individuals with Disabilities Education Act (IDEA) (Allen-Meares, 2004).

Legal History

Between 1900 and today, many legal initiatives have developed influencing the position of social workers in schools. Between 1852 and 1918, all the states instituted compulsory education. The reason for this was a need to prevent illiteracy in children sparked by the influx of immigrant children. The idea of a democratic society was also an influence. Discipline and civic duty bolstered the move for public school education as well as the need to curb child labor (Leiby, 1978). Horace Mann was an educational reformer who saw public school education as an answer to the social dilemmas of the poor and common man created by the influx of immigrants (Leiby, 1978). In 1917, the Smith-Hughes Act included vocational education as a mandate, which led to employment in a vocational field directly out of high school. During the Depression years (1929 to mid-1940s), the Civilian Conservation Corps established educational agendas in the camps. During the following decade (1950s) and through the 1980s, the courts ruled on many cases, which made significant changes to education. In 1954, in *Brown vs. The Board of Education of Topeka* U.S. Supreme Court Chief Justice Earl Warren said, "We conclude, unanimously, that in the field of public education the doctrine of 'separate but equal' has no place" (www.pbs.org). This decision overturned the 1896 court case of *Plessey v. Ferguson*. The original ruling of *Plessey v. Ferguson,* which mandated racial segregation, was in violation of the Equal Protection Clause of the Fourteenth Amendment of the U.S. Constitution.

The Elementary and Secondary Education Act of 1965 provided title programs establishing grants for compensatory educational programs (www.ed.gov). The Civil Rights Act (1964) influenced the advocacy position of school social work for public programs to be desegregated (www.ourdocuments.gov/doc). Section 504, the Rehabilitation Act (1973), established accommodations for students with verified disabilities. Public Law (PL) 94-142 (passed in 1975) ensured that all handicapped children would receive an education (Wright & Wright, 2007). In 1974, the Family Education and Privacy Act gave parents full access to their child's school record and the ability to change information that they found incorrect (Wright & Wright, 2007). In 1990, PL 94-142 was altered and became the Individuals with Disabilities Education Act (IDEA). It was again revised in 1997 and again in 2004 including a functional assessment that can be completed by the school social worker. For a complete understanding refer to Chapter 4. A revision of the Elementary and Secondary Education Act of 1965 was passed in 2002 and renamed the No Child Left Behind Act. The main objective of No Child Left Behind is

". . . to ensure that all children have a fair, equal, and significant opportunity to obtain a high-quality education and reach, at a minimum, proficiency on challenging state academic achievement standards and state academic assessments" (Wright & Wright, 2007, p. 299). It requires testing each year in grades 3 to 8, "highly qualified teachers" in each classroom, "research-based instruction," parental decisions and involvement, selection of schools, and public reporting of student progress (p. 299). (See Chapter 4 for more details.)

TIME LINE

1838–1920

- 1838: Influence of Horace Mann
- 1852–1918: Compulsory education in all U.S. states was accomplished
- 1896: *Plessey v. Ferguson*
- 1913: Social work services begin in schools; attendance and academic achievement were the emphasis; Rochester, NY, hires first school social worker
- 1917: The Smith-Hughes National Vocational Education Act
- 1919: National Association of Visiting Teachers established
- 1920s: School social workers called *friendly visitors*

1929–1950

- 1929: Great Depression
- 1930s: Shift in school social work services: food, clothing, shelter were emphasized as result of the Depression
- 1940s: Reduction in school social work services and a shift to casework
- Civilian Conservation Corps established education in camps
- World War II: School social work focus on intrapsychic and interpersonal issues

1950–1980

- 1950: School social worker begins cooperating with school professionals
- 1954: *Brown v. Board of Education of Topeka*
- 1955: National Association of Social Workers (NASW) recognizes specialty of school social work
- 1960: Name of *visiting teacher* changed to *school social worker*
- 1960–1970: School social worker face issues of racism, drug abuse, child abuse and/or neglect, and "humanistic approach to education" (Allen-Meares, 2004)
- 1965: Elementary and Secondary Education Act

- 1973: The Rehabilitation Act Section 504
- 1974: Family Education and Privacy Act
- 1975: PL 94–142
- 1970s: School social worker focuses on handicapped children

1980–Present

- 1980s: Group work for school social workers
- 1980s: Increased role with special education for school social workers
- 1980s: School social worker focuses on handicapped children, including evaluation, consultation, and treatment
- 1980s: Teamwork for school social workers, including consultation, evaluation, and services for classified students
- 1990: Individuals with Disabilities Education Act (IDEA)
- 1990s–present: School social worker deals with changes in family systems, growth of technology, school violence, community, and control of schools
- 1997: IDEA revised
- 2002: No Child Left Behind Act
- 2004: IDEA revised
- 2000s: Requirements for school social work practice established by states
- 2000s: NASW creates special credential for school social worker

A SYSTEMS APPROACH

At the turn of the 20th century, the term *systems* no longer only referenced military and government interactions but rather included managerial, philosophical, and scientific interrelationships as well. Social work was very much influenced by this theory because it helped understand the *person in the environment* concept.

The social work systems approach has its etiology in the biological theory developed by Ludwig von Bertanlanffy (Allen-Meares, 2004). Both speak of the interrelationships of the organism (person) with its (his or her) environment. Social work focuses on the person in the environment, better known by social work professionals as PIE. We realize that the impact of the environment on the person and that of the person on the environment is reciprocal. Therefore, our need is to have an approach that recognizes this unique philosophy. Putting the responsibility for the problem on the client alone defeats our purpose. We look at the variables that are contributed by the environment in which the client functions. The systems theory emulates the biological theory in that it recognizes and takes into account the mutual relationship between an organism (person) and its (his or her) environment. For example, a young girl became hysterical in her English class one morning. Her teacher could not illicit from her the cause of this reaction. I interviewed the child in a quiet, comfortable, and safe environment. She shared with me that her stepfather had beaten her mother the night before as well as the family dog. He also threatened to kill the dog. She was told by her mother that she had to come to school, but when she arrived, she was overwhelmed with emotion and was unable to verbalize the situation. Learning can only take place under conditions that are supportive and safe. This child felt safe in school and therefore could express her feelings. The school environment, as opposed to her home, was supportive and safe. When the child understood after contact with her mother that everyone at home was going to be cared for, she could then resume her academic work. This case is a clear example of the interrelationship of environments and the need to modify the living environment to allow for the client to function in the school milieu.

Each of us exists within an intricate system of micro and macro environments that affect one another on many levels. The school as an organization needs to be examined from the perspective of how it functions in its interrelationship with the child, parents, and community. It was established for the purpose of educating children. The micro level includes the child and the teacher; the child and the administration; the parent or guardian, the teacher, and administration; and the teacher and the administration. Children are sent to school to learn, and the process can only be successful with the cooperation of the family and the teacher. The teacher becomes the substitute parent (*in loco parentis*), and the child therefore is in the care of the teacher. It is a trusting relationship that permits communication and socialization. The teacher must be interactive with the student and receive information that the child is learning. Without these elements, education could not exist as it does today. Children need to have an alliance with the teacher and the teacher with the student. Parents need to believe that their child is being treated with respect and dignity as well as being given the essential academic components by the teacher. Teachers must also feel that there is respect and open communication with the parent(s) or guardian(s). At times, the relationship of the child to the administration becomes one of discipline. When the child's education is not successful, the administration must intercede to find the proper ingredients for the educational process to succeed. Parents and administrators are often called on to intervene when the academic success of the child is in question. The interaction of these people sometimes becomes the pivotal component for preparing a plan for intervention so that the student's education can be maximized. The teachers and administrators must work together to ensure the education of each child is carried out systematically and with regard for the individual child. For example: A child is disciplined for not having completed an assignment. The grandparent had died the night before but the child could not come to explain his loss. When the child did not give the teacher an adequate answer for not having done the assignment, he was sent to the principal's office. Again, the child said nothing. When the parent was contacted, the explanation was given and the policy consequence was not enforced. The child was then sent to the social worker for a counseling session to deal with his loss. The social worker views this scenario as a positive situation, since the needs of the child and the teacher were considered. In this way, the social worker can feel the PIE is reciprocal, and it fulfills the ideal of the systems approach.

On the macro level, the school is a community organization that provides for the welfare of the minors living in that environment. The school board is made up of representatives of the community who make policy and programs that govern the education of those children. This makes the school a vital component of the community that is entrusted with the human resources: the children. If the school is to function successfully as part of the community, it needs to provide the children with not only an adequate education but also an exceptional experience. The community, in turn, must communicate with the school board and give input to their needs. The credentials of the personnel must be carefully managed, and the school facility must be a safe and secure environment where community members feel confident that the inhabitants are carefully monitored. The school organization must relate to other community organizations, and reciprocity should exist between the resources of all community agencies. The school must remain open and available for use to other agencies in the community and to the community members. The community representatives (the board of education) must have dialog and respond to the community at large. For example, a beloved coach was losing his position because of budget cuts. The students and parents presented the need for this coach and this position to be kept because of the importance this program had to the students, parents, and the community at large. The community members presented their case at an open board of education meeting. After serious consideration, the board decided to reinstate the coach and the program based on the case presented to them. In this case, the social worker was queried by the parents and students as to how to proceed with the handling of the dilemma and gave them a socially acceptable and feasible way of handling the issue. They followed her advice and were successful.

The social worker in a school must be a viable, active player in the interaction of the systems. The school is considered an open system. This openness occurs on a continuum with some systems being more viable and open to the interactions that occur between the system parts—that is, one that is influenced by different systems on both a micro and macro level at various times. To maintain equilibrium, the school can receive and give data as a way of maintaining balance. The school is affected by the social, economic, and political climate that surround it.

For example, *zero tolerance* is a concept that comes about because of the conservative political climate. *Gang influence* is a social phenomenon that very much impacts the dropout rate in school. The economic forces in a society facing recession cause students to have fewer supplies and often cause larger classroom size. Because the relationships between social worker and client are so interconnected with the relationships outside of this micro system, school social workers play a viable, active role in maintaining the equilibrium between both the micro and macro systems of their clients. As stated earlier, the impact of the PIE is paramount in understanding the open system concept.

On the macro level, a school and its community are impacted by the federal, state, and local regulations and laws, which provide a foundation for how a specific district must operate. This macro system surrounds the school system as seen in the following examples. Federal mandates such as the No Child Left Behind Act of 2001 and the Individuals with Disabilities Education Act of 2004 (discussed in Chapter 4) govern much procedural structure for each state, who in turn have varying interpretations of these acts, which affect each state's schools municipality. States are mandated to implement these acts, and variations in interpretation are seen in different states.

Internal influences on school programs and policies are essential. Primary or universal prevention is a first-line defense against a difficult problem and is broad stroked to give exposure to the majority of students. It involves teaching about the problem and how and why one should avoid getting involved. It targets those who are not yet involved. Preventative programs for such elements as school violence, dropout, bullying, and suicide and homicide as well as high-risk behaviors (drugs, drinking, and smoking) are known as *primary or universal prevention* programs, because they target those who are not yet involved in the problem behaviors. These reach a majority of students and thus impact the environment of the community as well. As these variables are enacted in the schools, students then respond to them and often cause changes to them thus creating the reciprocity of the systems approach interacting.

Secondary or selective prevention is aimed at helping those who are experimenting with the problem behavior but have not gotten fully involved in it. In addition to macro programs in the school prevention arena, micro programs exist to help students and their families deal with personal problems such as mental health issues. Many children and adolescents face mental health needs that often are unrecognized or unmanaged by pediatricians and parents, resulting in more children who are likely to go untreated (Committee on School Health, 2004).

Mental health services (secondary or selective prevention) can be either administered in the school setting or supplemented by wrap-around or auxiliary services in the community. These are micro systems where the student and/or his or her family are directly impacted by the inside or outside services available through the school environment. For example, a 12-year-old boy on the brink of academic failure was referred to the school social worker. During the session, the child disclosed that his parents are divorced and he lives with his mother and younger brother and has no contact with his father, who is an active alcoholic. The school social worker needs to assess the therapeutic needs of the student and his mother and brother as well as involvement in supportive agencies in the community to avert the child from emotional distress and school failure. Both the family and the student can be helped by counseling services in the school, a possible recommendation to Al-Anon, involvement with Big Brother, Big Sister, a support group for single parents within the community, et cetera. The first issue to be dealt with is to assess the supportive needs of the student. This would be done through a personal interview with the student. After realizing that the family is in crisis, the parent would be called in for an interview with the social worker. Getting the mother to explain specifically what is going on at home with her son would aid the social worker to add support and explain how important it is for the mother to receive support from the community agencies. A list and the phone numbers of these agencies would be given to the mother for her to pursue. The social worker might suggest counseling sessions with the mother and son with the school social worker as well. This illustrates the interaction between an internal micro system with services available in the external macro system.

As a school social worker, one must be adept in his or her ability to access community resources for students and their families. When problems become serious involving multiple levels of intervention (tertiary or indicated prevention), systems theory becomes essential to reach out to the community and access the services needed by students and their families. Tertiary or indicated prevention is used after a diagnosis has been given. It includes prevention of relapse and/or progression of the impairment. For example, a student returning from a facility for drug addiction may require the services of a local addiction counselor, Narcotics Anonymous, family counseling, Al-Anon for family members, and possibly even probation. Probation for drug addiction sometimes can be a serious deterrent for further drug use.

AN ECOLOGICAL PERSPECTIVE

As a subset of the systems approach, the ecological approach differentiates itself by being more practical and based on the life science model (Bye & Alvarez, 2007). This refers to the relationship of organisms and their living environments.

It includes the concept of homeostasis. That is, a change in one part of the organization causes a reciprocal change in another part (Bye & Alvarez, 2007).

There is a reciprocity of systems that tends to create a homeostatic environment. It is viewed as an adaptive pattern between the systems. The give-and-take of this perspective lends itself to adjust the environment to the student as well as the student to the environment. As both the student and the environment are vibrant and ever-changing systems, the balance between these systems must remain in equilibrium.

This approach is similar to the strengths perspective in social work as the focus is not on changing the student but rather developing a fit between the student and his or her environment. A school social worker needs to assess the environment of the school and find a solution that fits from the outside environment (Ambrosino, Hefferman, Shuttlesworth, & Ambrosino, 2000). In the early years of being a school social worker, I realized that there weren't any Alateen meetings in the local area, despite that at the time many adolescents were abusing alcohol in school. Through extensive networking and outreach, I was able to institute a meeting in a local mental health agency. The local Alcoholics Anonymous chapter cosponsored this intervention and provided transportation for students who wanted to attend meetings.

The situation I faced illustrates an ecological approach in practice. School social workers using this approach effectively will need to maintain a "dual focus" (Dupper, 2003, p. 5). This focus entails helping the students develop ego strengths as well as utilizing the community resources to provide needed services. Additionally, with the continual growth of technology and the Internet, it is essential that school social workers avail themselves of the community resources and interact with all the components in the ecological system.

STRENGTHS PERSPECTIVE

The strengths perspective is one of the most recent practices in social work. Evolving over the past 30 years, this theory moves away from the pathological (traditional) model.

According to Dennis Saleebey, it is a paradigm shift. That is, it is a move away from the traditional individual treatment or medical model. In their research, Sybil and Steven Wolin realized that children who had suffered severe emotional trauma in childhood had grown up to far surpass the expectations of anyone who had treated them (Saleebey, 2001). The history of the strengths perspective dates back to Jane Addams, who looked for the power in people to use as a building tool to their present life (Saleebey, 2008). In the 1980s Rapp and Chamberlain were working with the mentally ill and believed that the traditional approaches did not work. They coined the term *strengths perspective* and used it to work with that population. They believed the support and development of a client's strengths would lead to successful adaptation to their environment. Their efforts proved successful (Saleebey, 2008). The strengths perspective requires a change in attitude and awareness from pathological or deficits to identifying clients' strengths. The basic principles of the strengths perspective are: each of us has "assets, resources and capacities" (Saleebey, 2008, p. 70); everyone knows what is "right for them" (Saleebey, 2008, p. 70); trusting that a person will overcome his or her adversity helps produce the change; and no one can predict a person's maximum capacity for growth (Saleebey, 2008).

Dennis Saleebey explains the following components for use of the strengths perspective: focusing on the resilience of the individual or system being examined, but not ignoring the hardship experienced; avoiding the pathological approach exhibited in the diagnostic manual; and examining (which is not unethical) the strengths and abilities of the client to bring to the surface the awareness that one does possess these abilities and traits (Saleebey, 2001).

Developmental Theories

For a school social worker, understanding developmental theories are essential. What is seen as normal at one time in a child's or adolescent's life may be perceived as regressed or abnormal in other developmental stages. Charles Darwin was the first to study the development of a child through observing and communicating with them. In 1877, he published a book titled *The Expression of the Emotions in Man and Animals*. He wrote this book after the birth of his son. It documented his child's development. He believed that understanding adult life and its development would come from the comprehension of childhood experiences and observations (Austrian, 2002).

There are many developmental theories varying in philosophical origins or beliefs that pertain to children or the understanding of children. I examine the theories of four developmental psychologists in this section. These theorists were chosen because of their great influence on the field of child development and their substantial influence on many others who followed. Sigmund Freud's theories came from treatment of adult patients and were concerned with the pathology that originated in early childhood. The mother-child dyad was his primary concern. Anna Freud's work emanated from her work with children and their parents. The theories that came from her work and that of White and Heinz reflect both innate and maturational concepts in mental development. Both the Freuds and Erikson examined the influence of the environment in child development. The biopsychosocial concept evolved from their work and is very much utilized by social workers (Austrian, 2002). Jean Piaget's work is of particular interest because it deals with cognitive development, which is essential knowledge for those social workers in the educational environment. His work as that of Darwin was done through observation of children in their natural environment.

Sigmund Freud

Freud is recognized as the father of psychoanalysis. He originally worked as a neuropathologist treating people with physical distress. Through his work with hypnosis, he realized that much of the problem behaviors (particularly with hysteria) he witnessed came from a psychological origin. He then began his research into the psychological realm for answers to the pathology of his patients (Robbins, Chatterjee, & Canda, 2006). He developed the theory of mental life being divided into the conscious, the preconscious, and the unconscious. Much of what he found regarding normal and abnormal behavior was linked to the unconscious and early childhood experiences.

He also developed the structural theory of personality consisting of the id, the ego, and the superego (Ryckman, 2004). Defense mechanisms were the constructs described to protect the ego from anxiety in the face of the battle that ensues between the id (instinctual process) and the superego (conscience), which tells us the difference between right and wrong (Ryckman, 2004). Freud is seen as the foundation to much of the psychodynamic theory and therapy that followed.

Although Sigmund Freud worked primarily with adults, his theories were based on child development particularly stemming from childhood traumas or crises. This theory is referred to as the *Theory of Psychosexual Development* and includes five developmental stages, which are defined below.

- *Oral stage*: Occurs between birth and 18 months. Pleasure in this stage is obtained from oral gratification. It is pleasure received from the infant's own body referred to as *autoerotic*.

- *Anal phase*: Occurs between 18 and 36 months. The child is interested in the anal excretions and toilet training. The child at this time is aware of his or her environment. This is the period where the child begins to assert his or her independence.

- *Phallic phase*: Occurs between ages of 3 to 5 years old. It is the precursor to the genital period. At this time, the child experiences pleasure from touching his or her genitals. This is the period when the Oedipal or Electra complex arises. In the Oedipal period, the young boy becomes rivalrous with his father until he realizes that he cannot take his mother from his father and thus identification with the father ensues.

In the Electra complex, the girl realizes she does not have a penis and develops a feeling of rage toward the mother for depriving her of a penis. She would need a penis so that she could experience her mother in the same way as her father does. She then turns toward the father to give her the penis (a baby as a substitute) but then is rejected by the father. It is a more difficult phase for a girl, since she must turn against her primary object (her mother) (Austrian, 2002).

- *Latency stage*: Occurs anywhere from 5 to 12 years old. During this period of development the child is seen as having developed a superego or conscience. Sexual issues are not in the forefront of the child's development, but cognitive and social issues seem to take precedence. Children enjoy school and play as well as being with peers. Resolution of the Oedipal/Electra crisis is seen as the beginning of the latency period, while puberty and sexual awakening is seen as the completion of this period (Austrian, 2002).
- *Genital stage*: Freud was not as interested in this stage as in the first two stages of development. After the Oedipal/Electra crisis was resolved, most adult development would be molded by those early experiences. The genital period is one where the physiological development leads the way for psychosocial development. The person is capable of orgasm and procreation. The goal of this period is to mate with an appropriate sexual partner. Genital life becomes the central theme. The Oedipal issues again resurface but must be overcome before genuine sexual interpersonal relationships can emerge. Sexual fantasies are usually a prelude to the actual sexual encounters (Austrian, 2002).

Anna Freud

Anna Freud expanded on the work of her father by focusing on a more in-depth exploration of the behaviors of children and adolescents. She did this through observation and interview. She was interested more in the ego development in children than her father. Her view of the ego evolved from that of her father's (the ego arises out of the id) to that of the ego psychologist who viewed the ego as a separate innate entity. She also developed the concept of ego defenses (Robbins, 2006). She was also able to link the defenses to the appropriate developmental stages (Turner, 1986). During World War II, she focused on the environmental impact on children and adolescents. This, of course, has a direct influence on the field of social work. Based on her observations, Anna Freud recognized the following stages of development in children and adolescents:

- *Infancy Stage*: In this stage, there is no differentiation between the self and others. The "part object" refers to the infant internalizing the object until his or her needs are fulfilled and then withdraws. With "object constancy," the infant is able to know the object or mother will be there for them. The child knows and maintains the object internally.
- *Anal Stage:* In this phase, the child is controlling and domineering. He or she asserts his or her independence in the environment.
- *Phallic Stage:* This phase is expressed with competitiveness with the same-sex parent and wanting the opposite-sex parent.
- *Latency Stage:* The child's energy is placed into friends, school, and activities.
- *Preadolescent:* In this stage, the child returns to the need-fulfilling relationship and an ambivalent relationship with the object.
- *Adolescence:* In this phase, the child is interested in sexual functioning with relationship outsiders (Austrian, 2002; Freud, 1965).

Erik Erikson

Erik Erikson was born in Germany in 1902. He taught in Anna Freud's Montessori school and was later seen by her for psychoanalysis. He was not trained as a therapist but later on, while at Yale School of Medicine, received a grant that he used to study the child rearing of two Native American tribes. This helped him develop the psychosocial theory that very much influences our field of social work (Austrian, 2002). Erikson was interested in the healthy development of children where the Freuds focused more on pathology. Erikson looked at ego development through societal influences. He examined development in view of changes in society such as the industrialization of this country (Erikson, 1963). The Freuds examined development up to and including adolescence, while Erikson thought that development didn't end until the person's life was over. In the 1940s and 1950s, Erik Erikson's study on the developmental phases not only focused on children and adolescents but also focused on development across the life cycle. His observations initiated his theories of positive development of the individual's interaction with his or her environment. Today, Erikson's theories greatly align with the social work practices in schools. The following are the developmental stages (relevant to school aged children/adolescents) given to us by Erikson:

- *Trust vs. Mistrust:* (Birth to 18 months) At this time, the primary object provides love, care, and consistency, which contribute to an infant's development of basic trust.

- *Autonomy vs. Shame and Doubt*: This normally develops in the infant from 18 months to 4 years. The child needs to be in charge of his or her body functions by developing independent bathroom habits. With the parents' help, the child will develop security and the ability to make decisions.

- *Initiative vs. a Sense of Guilt*: This occurs in the range of ages 4 to 6 years. At this stage, the child is developing competence and the development of superego (conscience). The child should be able to develop his or her own goals and focus on their achievement.

- *Industry vs. Inferiority:* This stage usually occurs between the ages of 6 and 12. The child does good "work" at this stage. This entails both school work and play outside of their family. Their "work" is to develop skills in new tasks.

- *Identity vs. Role Confusion*: This stage should occur between the ages of 13 and 22. Thus, it signals the end of childhood/adolescence. It is a time of role development leading to the final resolution of issues such as peer group, occupation, and sexuality. A sense of loyalty and development of one's own values is paramount during this stage. Involvement in the community and the culture is also part of the rite of passage during this time (Erikson, 1963).

Jean Piaget

As Charles Darwin studied his child's behavior and development from natural observation so did Jean Piaget. He was innovational in the understanding and chronicling of intellectual growth and mental development from infancy to adolescence. His initial observations involved watching his own children in their development. His theory views mental growth as being continuous and influenced by the social and physical environment (Piaget, 1967). His work has a direct effect on that of the school social worker, since knowledge of this type of development is essential in the school environment. As social workers looking at child development, we must know what is age appropriate to the child. It helps us view behaviors and communications as healthy and normal. The following is a synopsis of his developmental phases:

- *Sensory-Motor Stage*: This occurs between birth and age 2. The child only knows what he or she has directly experienced. Toward the end of this stage, the child realizes that when an object is hidden it still exists.

- *Preoperational Stage*: This occurs between the ages of 2 and 7 years old. At this stage, the child believes that all things can be explained. He or she makes up stories to support the reasons that he believes things happen. He or she animates objects and doesn't realize that natural phenomena are not man-made.

- *Concrete Operations*: This stage occurs during ages 7 through 11. During this time, the child is able to perceive actions in his or her mind. For example, he or she can add or subtract in his or her head with no need for seeing the concrete objects. Reversibility is recognized by the child. It is called concrete, because the child only deals with objects that are physically there. Conservation is a concept acquired during this period. That is, the child is able to see that a quantity remains the same even if its physical appearance is altered.

- *Formal Operations*: This stage is seen during ages 11 to 16. During this stage, the child can think abstract thoughts, understand hypotheses, and draw conclusions. He or she is able to understand the difference between the present and the future. He or she develops values and morals. This is the last developmental stage proposed by Piaget, although the depth and understanding of knowledge does increase throughout adulthood (Singer & Reverson, 1978).

Evidence-Based Practice Modalities

The concept of *evidence-based practice* is defined as "conscious, explicit, and judicious use of current best evidence in making decisions about the care of individual patients" (Sackett et al., 1996). It involves therapeutic interventions based on substantiated research. It also is important for the school social worker to add to the body of evidence-based knowledge by evaluating his or her practice and circulating this knowledge to the professional community (Raines, 2008). There are many evidence-based modalities, but they all have the same basic structure, which involves assessment of the problem, intervention using valid and consistent research methods, intervention that applies the research, evaluation of the intervention using valid and reliable methods, and sharing documentation of the results (Raines, 2008). In the subsequent section, I chose two forms of evidence-based therapy to share with you. These were chosen for their viability in the school milieu. They are both structured and short-term in duration. Both can be used with individuals, groups, and families.

According to Raines (2007), the concept of *evidence-based* refers to research that has withstood "rigorous, systematic, and objective procedures" arriving at knowledge. Evidence-based practice is based on actual observation and experimentation. It is concerned with statistical analysis to test the question being presented. It also is involved with continually replicating this method and obtaining the same results. It should be an experimental design with control study participants as well. This theory does appear in peer-reviewed journals that are objective, governed by the experts in the field, and scrutinized scientifically (Raines & Alvarado, 2007).

Cognitive-Behavioral Theory

The modality of cognitive behavioral therapy is evidence-based and a major practice theory in social work. According to Corcoran (2006), it is "a broad class of present-focused interventions with a shared focus on changing cognition (thoughts, beliefs, and assumptions about the world), changing behavior, and building clients' coping skills" (p. vii).

It is a present-focused therapeutic intervention therapy. It focuses on changing cognition, which includes thoughts, beliefs, and assumptions that one holds about his or her environment and developing coping abilities in the client (Corcoran, 2006). According to Braswell and Bloomquist (1991), there are six stages of this intervention for children: (1) assessment, (2) treatment-connected assessment, (3) the treatment plan, (4) school consultation, (5) termination, and (6) follow-up. The assessment includes a diagnosis, treatment, and development of a plan for the student. The next step (treatment plan) is preparing for change and subsequently involves skills training, which include the micro-systems of the child. Consultation with the teacher and counselor in an effort to find out the specifics of the child's progress is an essential component of this plan. Termination is the process where the child reviews the progress made and prepares for his or her independence with newly learned skills. Follow-up, after a given period of time, is important to assess whether the gains made are still applicable and to review the structure of the implemented plan. The type of skills focused on depend on the needs found in the assessment process. Skills might include learning how to study for a test, communicating with peers or a teacher, resolving a disagreement with a friend, and/or getting along with parents.

Example: A student came to me because she failed a test. She was anxious and said that she was stupid. As part of the treatment assessment, I asked what grades she had received before this test in that class. They were all average or above grades. We then reviewed the study plan before a test and built on the already established study skills. I consulted with her teacher to ascertain if there were any changes in the student's behavior or academic performance. The answer was negative. I reviewed the information with the student and terminated the intervention but asked her to return after the next test in that class to see if the intervention had helped. It had.

The advantages of cognitive-behavioral therapy, in schools, are derived from the fact that it is a present-focused treatment that is sequential and has structure. It is short-term in nature and can be used in a variety of treatments. Individuals, groups, and families can benefit from this intervention. It is cognitively based and therefore easier to administer in a school setting. It is also problem focused so that when the problem is solved the therapy is complete. The aforementioned reasons make this modality ideal to be used in the school environment.

Dupper points out the effectiveness of cognitive behavioral therapy as a two-point sequence involving (1) assessment, which includes the process of behavioral interactions and cognitive distortions that constitute the aberrant behavior, and (2) development of skill-coping mechanisms and empathy (Dupper, 2003).

Cognitive-behavioral therapy is explored in more detail in Chapter 9.

Solution-Focused Therapy

Solution-focused therapy is another evidence-based practice modality. It is based on a positive strengths model and avoids labeling issues as pathology. It also relies on the client's motivation to change. Discussion of the problem and its definition are avoided, but what the client would like the situation to be is emphasized. It is based on a "constructionist epistemology" (Gingerich & Wabeke, 2001, p. 34). That is, meaning is built on how the client sees himself or herself and the major players in his or her life. The theory revolves around what a person thinks is conceivable in his or her situation. Language becomes the vehicle for the conversation between the therapist and client(s). They work together to develop meaning that leads to change (Gingerich & Wabeke, 2001). Problems are not solved but the method of getting to an imagined goal is the focus of treatment. The miracle question and scaling are two unique components of this therapy. The miracle question asks a client the question: "What would it be like if you awakened tomorrow and your problem was solved?" You then ask them to describe the ideal. That becomes the goal of treatment. Scaling is the process of asking "on a scale of 1 to 10, how do you see the problem?" This question gives a frame of reference for comparison, and the client can see when the problem area is getting better. This modality is used well with individuals, groups, and/or families.

Attachment Theory

John Bowlby did his empirical research with orphans during World War II, which gave rise to the attachment theory. Bowlby proposed that healthy psychological development is based on the development of emotional "affectional bonds or attachments" (Raphael, 1983, p. 68). Bowlby (1977) defines attachment theory as ". . . a way of conceptualizing the propensity of human beings to make strong affectional bonds to particular others and of explaining the many forms of emotional distress and personality disturbance, including anxiety, anger, depression, and emotional detachment, to which unwilling separation and loss give rise" (p. 201). Additionally, he explains attachment behavior as ". . . any form of behavior that results in a person attaining or maintaining proximity to some other clearly identified individual who is conceived as better able to cope with the world" (Bowlby, 1988, pp. 26-27).

Bowlby made a radical departure from the traditional thought that attachment was based on drives, that is, sex and food. A child, according to Bowlby, will develop "internal working models" (Ornstein & Moses, 2002, p. 4). These models are based on the interactions with significant caregivers. Thus, the child is a product of what his or her parents have given as their perception of him or her. These perceptions are carried throughout the individual's life. A secure base is another concept brought to the attachment theory by Bowlby. A secure base is developed by having a primary caregiver who provides safety and security (Ornstein & Moses, 2002).

Intrapsychic Humanism Theory

This intervention modality is based on the theory of providing a mechanism for helping the child develop a base for self-regulating his or her behavior, which can generalize across environments. It affords a child who has not developed an inner identity, because of the absence of nurturance, the ability to develop a sense of positive well-being (Pieper & Pieper, 1990). It also helps the child develop positive relationships and enhance academic learning by addressing the different motives that children have while in an academic milieu and helping teachers regulate negative behaviors in a positive, compassionate way (Tyson, 2000). The theory renders an intervention whose goal is to provide children with a conflict-free, positive image of himself or herself, even if the environment is ridden with conflict, pain, and loss (Pieper & Pieper, 1990). It empowers the child to believe that he or she has caused their significant others to provide love and also provides the child with a sense of well-being (Pieper & Pieper, 1990).

Play Therapy

One of the most widely used interventions with children is play therapy. It is a natural way of observing children in an environment that is comfortable and safe. Children are able to uncover their inner conflict areas through fantasy, which makes it easier for them to deal with. They can express their feelings in an indirect way without hurting those whom they love. There are different modalities of play therapy based on various theories. The ones selected for school purposes are: object-relations play therapy, experiential play therapy, dynamic play therapy, and narrative play therapy.

- *Object-relations play therapy* is used with young children who exhibit emotional and behavioral difficulties. It is founded on the attachment theory of John Bowlby, Margaret Mahler, and Donald Winnicott. It is used by having the therapist and child engage in play to further the interpersonal relationship between them (Schafer & Kaduson, 2006). The relationship between the child and therapist is the catalyst for growth and resolution of the child's difficulty.

- *Experiential play therapy*: Dr. Carol Norton (2007) explains that in this intervention the child arrives at his or her emotions through his or her experiences. This process is not cognitive, but through the experiences a cognitive understanding of the world is formed. The child doesn't think about his or her experiences but uses his or her senses to incorporate information. This in turn produces an emotional response. Experiences with the environment, according to this school of thought, enable a child to move through developmental stages. Experiences help a child progress developmentally. The experiential approach to play therapy helps a child be empowered over his or her emotional life (Schafer & Kaduson, 2006).

- *Dynamic play therapy* is a developmental approach elucidated by Steve Harvey, PhD to help a child and his or her family work toward communication and understanding. "Movement, dramatic storytelling and artistic expression" (Schafer & Kaduson, 2006) are used to confront the issues of the child and his or her family (Schafer & Kaduson, 2006).

- *Narrative play therapy*, according to Ann Cattanach, helps a child express his or her life experiences and thus helps him or her understand, contemplate, connect to, and alter. Through this process, the child can view himself or herself and make the necessary changes with the help of the therapist. The child and therapist also develop a space and story for the child to create his or her own identity (Schafer & Kaduson, 2006).

Crisis Theory

Over the last 50 years, crisis theory has developed from the theories of Eric Lindemann, Gerald Caplan, Howard Parad, Peter Sifneos, and Naomi Golan. It is used with individuals, families, groups, and communities. It is an eclectic approach that embraces the following concepts: each individual or group is subject to environmental and intrapsychic stressors that can cause a disruption in their personal or collective equilibrium. It could be a single event such as the September 11th tragedy or a compilation of events in one's life, which results in altered and/or anxious or panic-stricken behavior. There are several stages in this process. First, the person tries to use his or her own defenses to cope with the stress. If this effort is unsuccessful then emergency status develops, and stressors continue to create pressure. If the stressor continues, a "precipitating factor" may initiate a state of crisis. Additionally, a threat might be perceived either to oneself or a group, bringing forth more intense anxiety. Often, the intensity of the situation produces new energy and may result in problem solving activity. Usually, crises are time-limited and do resolve in 4 to 6 weeks. There is often an increase in ego strengths resulting from overcoming the dilemma. This development of ego strengths or coping skills usually gives rise to better adaptive mechanisms for dealing with these issues or other problems that arise in the future (Golan, in Turner, 1986). If you can overcome adversity once, you know that you gain the confidence that you can do it in the future.

SUMMARY

The purpose of this chapter is to present an overview of the history of social work in the schools. The history is divided into the areas of socioenvironmental, professional, and legal. The intention is also to explain and summarize the theoretical perspectives used in the school system. Because the ecological and systems approaches are those relied on heavily by the school social worker, these were explained in detail and examples of their use in school were given. The theories and modalities that are very useful in schools were examined. These included developmental theories (S. Freud, A. Freud, E. Erikson, J. Piaget), cognitive-behavioral, solution-focused, attachment-based, intrapsychic humanism, play therapy, crisis intervention, and strengths and resilience perspective. These are elucidated in depth in later chapters.

ACTIVITIES

Activity 1: Develop an intervention plan for a student looking at the systems/ecological approach. Apply one of the interventions described for that individual case in terms of individual, group, or family intervention.

Activity 2: Discuss a case that you may have had in your practicum, and explain the theoretical underpinnings of the technique you used in that case.

SELF-REFLECTION QUESTIONS

1. Compare the use of evidence-based practice interventions as opposed to those that are not research substantiated.
2. Discuss the importance of understanding and applying developmental theory to the practice of school social work.

CLASS DISCUSSION QUESTIONS

1. What significance did the *Brown v. The Board of Education of Topeka* do for the field of school social work?
2. How do the developmental theories play a role in the function of a school social worker?

Chapter 2

A Typical Day?

INTRODUCTION

A typical day in the life of a school social worker is less than typical. This chapter is more of an overview of many responsibilities that school social workers experience. I am not suggesting that all these are expected in one job description but may vary idiosyncratically depending on the state and individual position. For the most part, a social worker can schedule appointments in advance and follow a systematic plan. The school is a microcosm of life and thus vulnerable to the crises which evolve. Included in these crises are suicide ideation and attempts, runaways, adolescent pranks, sudden deaths, bomb scares, fires, false alarms, fist fights, gang violence, and many more events that I have experienced in over 20+ years as a school social worker. Aside from these extraordinary events, the day is filled with individual and group counseling sessions, joint staffing meetings, supervision, schedule planning for special education students, disciplinary meetings, parental meetings, preevaluation conferences, writing individual education programs, attending conferences, planning and giving workshops, and developing and presenting programs to students, faculty, and parents. Emphasis and variations occur depending on the school level of practice. There are differences between the elementary, middle, and high schools.

With the local school district adopting different ways of dividing these three levels, this example of a typical day will be generic. Usually the school year begins around Labor Day (some places in the United States start in August and others in September). In other places, the school year is not interrupted with a summer vacation but have two-week vacations every few weeks. For the most part, school social workers have the same recesses that all school faculties enjoy. If special education workups need to be completed in the summer, the social worker should be available. The school year may commence with a faculty meeting where the chief school administrator begins with faculty achievements of the preceding recess period, goals and objectives for the school year, and the social worker holding on to the hope that the students will have a successful school year academically, emotionally, and socially. Many departments share a lunch break together, and sometimes the social worker is not a social member of any school group, since he or she is the only professional from this discipline in the school system. The hope is that he or she has a cadre of associates with whom he or she can spend some social time. In some school districts, the social worker is a member of the special services department, which includes the special education teachers, the learning consultant, and the school psychologist. The afternoon of the first day is usually filled with department meetings and for the social worker catching up on many of the messages that arrived during the summer.

THE START OF THE SCHOOL YEAR

At times, the first weeks of school are filled with parental and student meetings of classified students who need changes to their schedules, which involve changes to their Individual Education Program (explained further in this chapter). This aspect leads the social worker, in his or her capacity of case manager, to days filled with meeting students and/or parents, teachers, and guidance counselors and thus making the necessary alterations to the schedule and the educational program. Both the schedule and the education program need to correspond and therefore must be changed to comply with the educational statutes.

The next step in the process of school year commencement is that of meeting with all the students with whom the social worker has responsibilities. This is called *case management*. According to Franklin, case management resembles "old fashioned" social casework. Case management and casework share the common goal of providing services to students so that they can take advantage of their educational milieu (cited in Allen-Meares, 1999). Social work case management links students to their educational services such as monitoring their education and therapeutic interventions when necessary (Franklin, Harris, & Allen-Meares, 2006). Overall case management in schools include coordinating efforts between the parents and the school, giving advice to parents and students about students' rights regarding special education, making referrals to needed services, and reviewing the students' records (Green & Twill, 2006). If the family is bilingual and English is not the first language, all written material needs to be given in the native language. If counseling services are needed, the social worker should be prepared to find culturally competent resources in the community and share those with families.

Some students may report being unhappy in their present placement, and the case manager must assess the situation and may need to intervene as an advocate for the student. It is always preferable for the student to try to advocate for himself or herself first. Role playing with the student often eases the anxiety and the rehearsal better prepares the student for the intervention.

Example: Dan came to the case manager with issues of being intimidated by his teacher. The teacher had made the remark that Dan would end up in jail like his father. This statement was corroborated by the teacher's aide, and therefore an intervention needed to be initiated. The teacher was asked to attend a meeting with the case manager and the child. The school social worker prepared Dan by having him practice talking to the teacher in a nonconfrontational way. This was achieved, and the student was able to handle himself in the meeting and learn advocacy principles that he would be able to use in other situations. The teacher was apologetic, and the situation was resolved.

Sometimes the beginning of the school year would be the time when parents would ask for additional services than those that were listed in the child's Individual Educational Program (IEP). These services have to be evaluated by the child's case manager or supervisor of special education regarding the student's needs, and if necessary, another IEP meeting would ensue. IEP meetings could be requested at the discretion of either the parent or guardian or the educational staff. As is discussed in Chapter 4, an IEP is mandated every year for special education students but can be initiated if deemed necessary by the child's constituents or the school team.

Example: Jake's parents requested that teachers fax assignments to them on a daily basis so that they could monitor his homework progress. Teachers were reluctant to accommodate this request since it was an imposition for them. The need for this accommodation was rationalized since Jake had organizational difficulties and often lost his assignments. This accommodation was added to his IEP.

Example: A case that came to mind at the beginning of the school year was that of Tommy. He was a 16-year-old sophomore who had been a classified student and placed on home instruction because he was under the court jurisdiction for molesting a 5-year-old boy. The school administrators did not want Tommy to return to school, but the court was the ultimate decision maker in this case. The judge decided that the boy should return to school, and therefore he needed a schedule to accommodate his special needs. He also needed an updated IEP since he was a special education student. It was always difficult to contact Tommy's mother (a single parent who suffered with lung cancer and worked at a local diner as a waitress). She was contacted, and in fact, the social worker had to meet her at work so that we could discuss and get her input on his education program.

Classroom observations are sometimes needed during the first weeks of school. Permission from the teacher is essential in this case. Observing a student in his or her natural environment is an excellent tool for witnessing interpersonal dynamics. Nonverbal expressions are also important to notice in this natural setting. A student who is being evaluated for special educational services needs to be observed in his or her natural environment as part of the educational work-up. Each evaluative team member should avail himself or herself of this observation because it is mandated as part of the evaluation.

Teachers are also in need of reviewing educational plans of their students during the first week of school. A child's case manager (this could be the social worker) may need to be available to the teachers for specific instructions or clarifications.

VERY SPECIAL NEEDS STUDENTS

Sometimes the case manager is placed in charge of multiply handicapped students. Such students' needs are extremely unique and need to be supervised very closely.

Example: John was a 16-year-old student with spina bifida and confined to a wheelchair. His mainstream teachers (those teachers of regular education classes) had to meet to understand his needs and capabilities before he started in their classes. His motoric abilities were quite slow, and therefore he had to have assignments modified (in length) to prevent him from laboring over assignments for hours. He could not be given a timed test, so his IEP read untimed as a modification to testing situations.

Example: Joe was a normally bright child with cerebral palsy. Before he was permitted to be in any teacher's class, according to his IEP, the teachers had to have special training in the Heimlich maneuver. This training was given by his private physical therapist. A list of foods that he was not permitted to eat during the school day was also included in this lesson. Joe had to have his own aide, a special individual learning environment (physical place) and a laptop computer. He could not write, and all his reading had to be taped. His classes were all college preparatory.

Example: Sam was also a normally intelligent child who suffered from debilitating muscular dystrophy. He attended all college preparatory classes and was capable of doing what other students in the class could do. He could not write but used a laptop computer and printer in class.

The social worker could see the unique individual involved in these horrendously physically challenging situations and view the child for who he or she was not the disability with which he or was burdened. The social worker in these cases had to advocate for the students to ensure that each of them received the best education possible. The child's needs were the priority, and the school had to accommodate them.

Example: Sometimes, the social worker is faced with a student from a different cultural background. There was a young man, a senior at the high school, who was born in Portugal. He had difficulty with the English language and writing exercises. His teacher did not understand the impact of this difference and when the parent was contacted, she was guarded and fearful of hearing that her son wouldn't graduate. The social worker set up a meeting among the parent, student, and teacher. When each understood where the other was coming from, it was decided that the young man would go to the ESL teacher for help and guidance on his writing assignments. It worked but the other issues of the family in the community were also a concern. The social worker found resources in the community for the parents and helped them get family counseling in their native language.

GROUPS

Each school year, the social worker in the school identifies the needs of the student population. Often, this is done through a needs assessment instrument or through interviewing key members of the faculty and/or student body. Without question, group intervention is a method of reaching the largest number of students in the junior and senior high school environment. Peers play a major role in the lives of these students; therefore, group intervention is essential.

The social worker is the ideal school professional who can form and watch the group process unfold. The selection of group members is the first step in developing a group. Soliciting group member candidates from the faculty and especially the guidance counselors (or in some cases the social worker acts in the capacity of guidance counselor) is a good starting point. Children of divorce, underachievement, overachievement, and bereavement groups, are just a few of the many topic-specific groups a social worker can initiate. Groups can also evolve out of a crisis situation. Often, the social worker may enlist the services of another counseling professional as coleader. This aspect of the group can lead to interdepartmental cooperation as well as having someone else to process the group events after each group session.

Interviewing the candidates for a group is a very important aspect of group membership. IEP-mandated groups have goals that have been outlined in the IEP, which may include socialization skills, coping skills, anger management skills, and so on. Therefore, these groups are already established, and sometimes depending on the mandates and the number of students mandated, social workers may not have a choice as to which students are in their groups so as not to violate the IEP mandate.

Above all, establishing group purpose and goals is essential to the successful accomplishment of groups. The social worker has to be confident that the members are compatible. Important issues such as the rules of the group, the length of time needed, and the time limits of the group must be discussed before a candidate can become a member. The social worker must decide whether or not the group will be closed or open. That is, in a closed group members will begin and end together as opposed to an open group where members can be added or eliminated as the group continues. Confidentiality must be established and discussed before the initial phases of the group can unfold. More about group intervention specifics are discussed in Chapter 10.

INDIVIDUAL COUNSELING

Some of the many activities in which social workers engage in the school involve working individually with students. In a large number of school districts, the social worker in the school spends approximately half of his or her time counseling students. School linked social workers spend the majority of their time counseling students. Children are referred for counseling through a referral process usually unique to each school system. Many times a child is referred through his or her guidance counselor, teacher, school administrator, parent, peer, or himself or herself.

Issues of counseling usually involve interpersonal conflict or intrapersonal difficulties. In schools, issues of attendance, grades, and tardiness are usually signals of student distress. The rules of counseling should be set down in the first session. These involve mainly the concept of confidentiality. Further exploration of this area is discussed in Chapter 6.

Short-term and successful practice interventions work well in the school setting. The question arises as to how to best engage children in the process of therapeutic intervention. These include but are not limited to solution-based therapy, cognitive behavioral therapy, intrapsychic humanism, secure-based therapy, and crisis intervention. Assessment tools such as the Behavioral and Emotional Rating Scale (BERS) (Epstein & Sharma, 1998), Behavioral Self-Concept Scale, Children's Beliefs About Parental Divorce, Depression Rating Scale (for children), Reason for Living Inventory for Adolescents, Self-Concept Rating Scale for Children, and Self-Control Rating Scale (for children) (Corcoran & Fischer, 2000) can be used not only to assess the child but also as a first step in building an alliance. A school social worker must check with a supervisor to be certain whether or not parental consent is needed before administering an instrument to a student. This issue is governed by individual school districts. The assessment is often the first treatment session as well. It becomes very cathartic for a client to speak about the issues that they are dealing with, their worries, and concerns. Further discussion about these intervention skills is presented in Chapter 9.

PREEVALUATION INTERVENTIONS

Before a child is evaluated for special education, the administrative code mandates that preevaluation interventions are tried (Turnbull, 2005). These might include but are not limited to changes in class schedule, counseling, family counseling, medical examination, audiological evaluation, vision testing, and tutorial help. These interventions must be documented and shown to have been used as interventions before an evaluation can take place. *Prereferral interventions*: Interventions delivered in the student's regular classroom that attempt to improve learning prior to a referral for formal special education evaluation (National Center for Learning Disabilities, 1999–2006).

Response to Intervention (RtI) is a preliminary step in documenting the appropriate interventions the school has employed prior to the referral process for special education. Since the Individuals with Disabilities Education Act (IDEA) was reissued in 2004, the RtI method of early assessment and intervention with an evidence-based therapeutic intervention was initiated by many states and school districts for students with behavioral and/or emotional problems.

A SOCIAL DEVELOPMENTAL HISTORY

In Chapter 4, the components and examples of a social developmental history are given. A school social worker uses this tool as part of the Child Study Team Evaluation process, when a student is referred for an evaluation because of learning needs or deficits the student is assessed by the team. A home visit is the ideal way to complete a social developmental history. Meeting a parent (or parents) in his or her home helps the social worker see firsthand an essential part of that child's environment when he or she is not in school. A simple notepad and pencils can help the social worker take notes in the areas of discussion that need exploration. Any more formal tools might cause intimidation on the part of the parent and impede the therapeutic process. An important aspect of this evaluation is to find out firsthand from the child's parent what he or she thinks the presenting problem is. A parent's perception is very helpful to the social worker and empowers the parent in a situation which is extremely difficult for him or her. Other components of a social history include (a) identifying information, (b) family members (go back to grandparents' information) and dynamics, (c) developmental milestones, (d) parental observation of the child's interaction with family and friends, (e) the child's school history, (f) rules and directions that the child is given at home and how he or she follows these, (g) the child's medical history, and (h) a genogram or ecomap (see Chapter 4 for a full description).

A social developmental history also includes an interview with the child and his or her perception of what the problem is. A classroom observation is also required. This process should take approximately one-half day depending on the intricacy of the child's life.

AN INDIVIDUAL EDUCATION PROGRAM

This procedure usually takes place after the first marking period, since students' problems seem to surface at that point. An Individual Education Program occurs after a student is found eligible for special education services. It defines a child's program and plans his or her education by presenting the present levels of performance and the goals and objectives to provide the student with a successful school experience. The Individual Education Program is a team-based process, and IDEA legislation clearly dictates that it is a team-based process, where parents are considered integral members of the team. The components of an IEP and an example are discussed in Chapter 4. An IEP can take up to one-half day or even more. Research must be done beforehand so that teacher, administrator, child, and/or parental input can be given. The school social worker does encourage meaningful parental involvement in the process. The goals and objectives in an educational plan should be developed during the meeting as an outgrowth of the current levels of performance. Decision on state testing exemptions or requirements need to be discussed and evaluated at the IEP meeting. A transition plan is also essential at the junior and senior high school level, because this determines what the future holds for the student and what type of program the student is planning on completing. Realistic assessment of strengths and weaknesses must go into this determination.

STAFFINGS/PREREFERRALS

Staffings (sometimes called *prereferrals*) are interdisciplinary meetings to discuss referrals, progress of certain students in jeopardy of failure, and plans for programs or policy changes. The professional personnel included in staffings are social workers, psychologists, learning specialists, administrators, substance abuse counselors, medical staff (nurses), and guidance counselors. These usually take place on a bimonthly basis, and the length is determined by the number of students and the issues to be addressed. They usually involve several hours of the day.

The importance of staffings is to gather information on students from various sources and to give the case manager all the information necessary to fully help the student achieve personal and academic goals. The difficulty involved in such dissemination of information is that of confidentiality. Unfortunately, confidential information may be given to staff members who do not abide by the ethics of confidentiality. More is discussed in Chapter 6 about the issues of confidentiality and student rights.

PEER MEDIATION AND CONFLICT RESOLUTION

Peer mediation programs are usually successful in high school environments, although they have also been known to be more successful when initiated on the elementary school level. They help the social worker reach a larger base of students who are in need of intervention (Vazsonyi, Belliston, & Flannery, 2004). Such programs involve training students in the basics of crisis intervention. Mediation is under the umbrella of conflict resolution. *Mediation* can be defined as "... a communication process in which the individuals with a problem work together, assisted by a neutral third party, to solve the problem" (Schrumpf, Crawford & Bodine, 1997). It fosters problem solving without authority figures. Peers are used as the neutral third party in a dispute. Preparation as a peer mediator can be implemented through a 2-day workshop for student candidates dealing with the tenets of crisis intervention and the role playing of specific cases. Details are examined in Chapter 12. Peer mediation can also be done as a "cadre approach" or a "total school approach" (Gerler, 2006). The former is a means of training a small group of students to become mediators for the entire school population. The latter is a way of training the entire school population to deal with issues as they arise (Gerler, 2006). (A helpful website for peer mediation is http://www.acrnet.org/ [Gerler, 2006].) Issues that often come to the attention of peer mediators are (a) interpersonal issues, (b) eating disorders, (c) suicidal ideation/attempts, and (d) depressive symptoms. Those who act out behaviors such as fighting, stealing, drug use, and other forms of violence are brought to peer mediation as well. Acting out behavior is the better choice.

The mediators need to be fully aware of their boundaries and their responsibilities to report to the peer mediation advisor any dangerous or serious situations that go beyond their realm of a student's ability. The following are the steps used in peer mediation:

- Open the discussion among those in question
- Gather information given by all sides
- Find and focus on common ground
- Create the opportunity for discussing options
- Evaluate these and choose one
- Write a formal agreement among those disputants, have each sign, and give each a copy (Peer Mediation Training Manual, 1998)

Once the formal agreement is established, the peer mediator's work is complete. A follow-up should be by the social worker (or other faculty advisor) to ascertain that there is compliance with the established agreement (Angaran & Beckwith, 1999).

The social worker is sometimes called on to resolve conflicts between students and students, students and teachers, and students and family members. Conflict resolution is identifying and implementing solutions to the problems in conflict situations. The best way to achieve this goal in a nonviolent way is to satisfactorily meet the needs of the disputants and even improve the relationship of those disputants in question (*Peer Mediation Training Manual*, 1998).

The basic techniques involved in conflict resolution are the following:

- Define the problem nonjudgmentally
- Examine ways of resolving the problem
- Evaluate your options and decide on a solution (1998)

DISCIPLINARY MEETINGS

The school social worker is often involved when special education students are being disciplined. Schools are permitted to suspend a classified student for up to 10 days. The removal of a student for more than 10 days, either consecutive or cumulative, can be considered a change of placement. This would trigger the possibility of a manifestation determination review, functional behavioral assessment, behavioral intervention plan, and review of the IEP and recent testing results. The discipline that is imposed may not be given if it is the result of the child's disability as per administrative code. For example, if a child with Attention Deficit Hyperactivity Disorder is asked to be still for an extended period of time he or she will not be able to comply. This noncompliance should not result in disciplinary action. Therefore, the social worker must be astute in his or her knowledge of the student and his or her IEP and/or functional behavioral assessment and intervention plan (see Chapter 4). It is often the social worker's concern to see that a child is not punished beyond the extent of his or her ability to understand or to gain better functioning as a result of it. Ideal punishments and consequences should be short in duration and constructive and positive in dimensions.

Example: A punishment of a ninth-grade boy who was accused of throwing a firecracker into a garbage receptacle outside of the school building and never admitted to the infraction was suspended through his final exams. The school administrator decided that the child should be given his final exams in the fall since his suspension ended after the last day of school. The social worker, astute to the child's disability, explained that the child had a short-term memory problem as documented in his IEP and therefore would be penalized in the area of his disability. The administrator had to rescind that punishment and allowed the child to take the exams under the auspices of the social worker.

CRISES IN THE SCHOOL ENVIRONMENT

The types and number of crises in a school environment vary greatly because of the student body and faculty members, the events that are going on in the students' homes or community, and the crises in the country or world.

Some of the most difficult situations are those involving student and faculty death and the type of death experienced.

Suicide and Death

The events of a completed suicide are devastating to the school community, especially when the suicide is that of a member of the student body. The experience is crushing and the social worker must work as a member of the crisis team to help the students and faculty grow through such an event. This is not an easy feat to accomplish, but if a plan is in place beforehand, it will be less stressful. A plan for response to suicide in the school is discussed further in Chapter12, but some of the components of such a plan are as follows:

- Inform faculty separately from students, preferably prior to the students' awareness
- Assemble the crisis team

- Have the team work in the areas that they are assigned such as the cafeteria, library, students' lounge, and so on.
- Have a list of victim's closest friends and associates and reach out to them
- Have teachers report any child who is showing signs of grief and assign the student to his or her counselor
- Inform all parents of the tragedy (best done through e-mail)
- Contact the local mental health center for back-up help
- Contact local clergy
- Crisis team needs to reach out to the victim's family

Example: In the 27-year period that I was in the position as a school social worker, I experienced one completed suicide of a student. The young man was unknown to me and gave no traditional warning signals of suicide. The aforementioned plan was developed as a result of this experience.

Example: The death of a faculty member is a very difficult situation to deal with in a school situation. One experience that stands out as an extremely difficult one was the death of a faculty member on a class trip to a physics competition at a college campus 1 hour away from the high school. The teacher had a heart attack and died while sitting in a chair in the lobby of the building where the competition was held. A student found him and thought he was sleeping and reported back to the other faculty member on the trip. The faculty member called 911 and left for the hospital with the deceased man while the students were left in a classroom in that building. They did not know the teacher had died but were told that he had suffered a heart attack. The steps taken were as follows:

- The social worker was sent to the site to accompany the students home.
- The students were in shock, and when they returned to school, a group crisis meeting took place with the social worker leading the group.
- When the social worker finally ascertained that the teacher had died, she contacted the parents of the students who were on the trip and then worked with the students in what became a grief/bereavement group.
- Those children and their parents were contacted the following day, and further counseling services were offered to the children.
- The social worker attended all the deceased teacher's classes the following day, processed the feelings of the students, and fielded the questions that ensued.
- A memorial service was held at the school a few weeks later.

Runaways

Rarely do students run away from home, but some do and others just run away from school. If a student runs away from home, it becomes the purview of the parent or guardian, child welfare agency, and the police. The parent must report the runaway to the police and follow the policy that the police department puts forth on this issue.

Example: This occurred several years ago when three students planned a runaway and executed it. They took their money out of their individual savings accounts and pooled it. They bought bus tickets that got them as far as South Carolina from New Jersey. After getting off the bus, they went to an open meadow and ate the food they had taken from home. One of the three decided to call her mother and return home. The other two followed soon after. The mother of the first girl who called home had alerted the local police department and the school authorities.

Before the first girl called home, the administrators questioned their friends but got no leads. The social worker was also involved as a liaison for the runaway children and their parents and conducted family sessions when the girls returned. One must keep in mind that the ability of law enforcement to locate a runaway depends on the interest and/or willingness to search for a missing child, level of cooperation among various agencies, and the size of the geographic catchment area of the authorities.

In the event of a runaway from school, the social worker is usually contacted to see what leads he or she might have as to the state of mind of the absent student. The police and the parents of the child would be contacted immediately. In this case, it usually takes minutes for the police to locate and pick the child up. The social worker would conduct a follow-up crisis intervention session with the student as well as a family session.

Adolescent Pranks

Adolescents are full of fantasies and imagination. Many pranks come to mind, which would be very serious. One is setting a fire or pulling the fire alarm. School policy should govern the consequences of this behavior when there is endangerment to students and/or faculty. Firearms or other weapons would be another very serious offense. With the metal detectors now available in the school, the administration and law enforcement have these in check. There should also be school policy that governs such an act. The social worker should check into these policies early into his or her tenure in a school. If they do not exist, he or she should discuss the prospects of developing plans with his or her supervisor.

Less serious pranks come to mind like making announcements over the public announcement system (PA system) without permission.

Example: One prank that deals with this was that of high school seniors who, through the PA system, gave the code for a group of students to release mice and golf balls in the hallways. Pandemonium resulted, and those students were suspended. The principal had a mild heart attack at this time and had to be hospitalized. The social worker worked with these students to have them understand the consequences of their actions. She also worked with the vulnerable students (who reacted to the confusion) to allay their anxiety.

ACTS OF VIOLENCE

There are many acts of violence that are seen in the school environment. Prevention is the first key to curtailing violence. A focus on academic achievement, structured after-school activities, mutual respect for students and teachers, and parental involvement are very important in preventing these problems. Having students aware of school policies and giving a safe place for discussion of feelings is also very helpful. It is essential that students know the warning signs of violence. This knowledge helps children report behaviors that seem aberrant. Threatening or explosive behavior, threats of violence, drug and alcohol use or abuse, withdrawal, lack of motivation for academic endeavors, previous violent behavior, and animal cruelty are just some of the warning signs of impending danger. Acts of violence in my school were treated swiftly and accurately. The procedure was that the students would be isolated and the school social worker would be called in to help calm the student. The parent(s) or guardian(s) would be summoned, and the situation would be explained to them. The consequence would be school suspension and depending on the severity of the act possible referral to the Child Study Team for consultation and/or evaluation. Most acts of violence did not result in expulsion.

Fires and Fire Alarms

In my experience, a few fires occurred in the school. They were mainly started accidently by someone smoking in the bathroom. Fire alarms, on the other hand, were often pulled by a student who wanted to shorten the day or just have some excitement. Unfortunately, it is a very disturbing event.

Example: I remember once there was a rash of smoke (stink) bombs ignited at school. The culprits in all these cases were found and suspended. My worry, as

I found myself in the street after the alarm went off, was that the perpetrator was one of my students (either case managees or counselees).

Bomb Scares

Another very serious problem is calling in bomb scares. Students sometimes do this to get attention or to lessen class time. It is a very frightening situation that leads to fire department involvement and class disruption. In one school, the consequence of such an act was to lengthen the school day for as long as it took to find out it was a false alarm. Social workers might counsel these children, but often the callers are never identified. Several times in my career as a school social worker I was faced with bomb scares. Most times, the perpetrator was not found, but if they were found, the consequences would have been severe. Most likely the result would have been suspension or expulsion.

Fistfights

This type of violence is seen more often in high school and results from the inability to resolve conflicts through peaceful means. If the event is known in advance, peer mediation or conflict resolution can resolve the problem. A social worker who may get this information in advance most likely could see the students individually then prepare them for conflict resolution. School districts should have policies in place for these behaviors as well. If the fistfight occurred before mediation could take place, the students would be suspended and on their return would be asked to resolve the dispute with a mediator.

Gang Violence

A *gang* is defined as any identifiable group or club that exists without the sponsorship or authorization of the school and that engages in antisocial or criminal behavior or activity that is disruptive of the school environment (http://www.kusd.edu/media/pdf/policy/5000/5438.pdf).

This phenomenon has seen an increase in the suburban areas as the family structure breaks down. Gangs must be weakened through individual and family intervention. A school social worker could involve juvenile officers in his or her particular district to do prevention programs or colead groups with the social worker. Family involvement is essential, if it is possible, and can also be done through social work intervention. School policy must also address this issue by placing it in the student handbook. In my school we had one altercation between rival groups who wore certain colors. This crisis was resolved by imposing the aforementioned plan. It occurred during a school break, and on the return to school the colors had disappeared. I attribute the positive results to the intervention of the parent(s) or guardian(s), the local juvenile officer, and the social worker.

A typical school policy for dealing with gangs can be found here http://www.kusd.edu/media/pdf/policy/5000/5438.pdf

PROCEDURES FOR DEALING WITH GANGS AND GANG-RELATED ACTIVITIES

1. All school district employees have a responsibility to report to their immediate supervisor any suspected gang-related activities.

2. Any student known to be a member of a gang or participate in gang activities will be barred from representing the school as a member of an athletic team or as a participant in cocurricular activities. Resumption of participation in school activities will be determined by the school principal.

3. Student work containing gang symbols will not be accepted for grading purposes when a gang symbol has been placed on the assignment by the originator of the assignment.

4. Gang-related graffiti or damage to school property will result in appropriate administrative and police action. The parent or guardian will be notified, and a conference with the parent or guardian, student, and principal may be held. Restitution will be sought from those responsible for related damages.

5. When a serious gang-related incident occurs on school premises, at school-related activities, or on sites normally considered to be under school control, a letter will be sent to all parents of students in the school informing them *in general terms* about the incident and emphasizing the district's concern for safety and outlining the action taken at the school level regarding the incident.

6. Wannabees are to be dealt with, as appropriate, under the terms of this policy/rule. For purposes of clarification, *wannabees* are groups of youth not affiliated with recognized gangs but who engage in gang-like activities and/or mimic gang behavior (retrieved from http://www.kusd.edu/media/pdf/policy/5000/5438.pdf).

Things to Sometimes Ignore

Sometimes it is best *not* to deal with inconsequential behaviors. Students who talk about magic or other forms of occult behavior may be best ignored.

Example: The instance that comes to mind is that of finding chicken feet outside of a student's locker. The social worker was contacted about this event. When dealing with adolescents, making an issue of this kind of activity can cause a copycat effect or more pranks. Without knowing who perpetrated the act, an investigation would only bring more attention to aberrant behaviors. The social worker in this situation suggested that the administrator throw the chicken feet in the garbage and if no other events occurred to just let it go. The advice was followed and there were no more occurrences of this nature.

CONFERENCES

Social workers in schools are often in charge of conferences that are training events for faculty and staff. Conferences such as drug and alcohol education, anger management, and child abuse are just a few that a social worker might be able to offer the school faculty. The more help that the social worker provides and lets the faculty know his or her strengths and abilities the better the rapport with the school professionals will ensue. Usually, the impact of having an outside specialist was very helpful. In my school, we used the local police department for drug and alcohol education, and a Division of Youth and Family Services (now known as the Division of Child Protection and Permanency) worker for child abuse intervention techniques. DCPP (in NJ) is the state's agency that oversees and investigates child abuse and neglect. Examples of some of these programs are offered in Chapter 12.

Many of these same programs were offered during assembly time for students and were mandatory sessions. Classes were taken to the assembly by the teacher. Often these programs would also be offered in the evening for parents and guardians.

MIDDLE OF THE SCHOOL YEAR

In the middle of the school year social workers are often faced with students being referred for academic deficiencies as well as emotional difficulties. This is also the period of time when the Annual Planning Meeting of special education students would take place. They should take place on anniversary dates. It is a hectic time that is faced by social workers who have to be involved in multitasking. Unpredictable and sudden interruptions often occur and priorities have to be made.

CONCLUSION OF THE SCHOOL YEAR

Often in the last marking period, the social worker must be involved in visiting and conducting annual reviews for out-of-district students. This activity sometimes involves travel to different states or parts of one's own state, and may constitute overnight stays. It is important to know and be aware of students' placements out of district. All social workers in schools are responsible for the education and welfare of their case management students.

There may be times when a student must be removed from a placement because of institutional abuse.

Example: A developmentally disabled child at the age of 13 was placed in a residential school. At the annual meeting, when his father brought him to the men's room, the boy described what one of the counselors did to him in the bathroom. When these allegations were investigated by the child welfare organization of that state they were validated. The child was immediately removed from that placement and sent home with his parents pending the investigation. This matter is most serious and must be immediately acted on for all concerned.

SUMMARY

This chapter is presented as an example of what a typical day for a school social worker could be. It is not all inclusive and was more subjective than objective, since it was based on my own personal experience. One can hope to schedule appointments in advance and try to follow a specific plan, but since the school is a microcosm of life the events that occur are often unpredictable. Crises such as suicide, runaway, pranks, sudden death, bomb scares, fires and false alarms, fistfights, and other forms of violence can occur. Ordinary events during the day can encompass counseling sessions, staff meetings, supervision, meetings of various types, as well as preevaluation conferences, writing individual education programs, attending conferences, planning and giving workshops, and developing and presenting programs to students, faculty, and parents.

ACTIVITIES

Activity 1: Levels 1 & 2: Ask your field supervisor in your practicum to describe a case in the school that stands out as unique to his or her practice of school social work.

Activity 2: Level 1: Develop a preintervention evaluation plan for a student.

Level 2: Choose one area that was discussed in this chapter such as the preevaluation and evaluation process and create a plan for a student from a practice example.

SELF-REFLECTION QUESTIONS

1. What professional and personal characteristics are needed by a person to function effectively in a school setting?
2. Please explain the roles that a school social worker has regarding those played in generalist practice. These include enabler, mediator, integrator, general manager, educator, evaluator, broker, facilitator, initiator, negotiator, mobilizer, advocate, and outreach worker.

CLASS DISCUSSION QUESTIONS

1. Describe in detail a student observation that you have experienced in the school setting.
2. Describe a unique situation with a student that you have encountered in the school and explain what the advocacy needs are for that child.
3. Considering the last case cited, describe the appropriate steps for a social worker to take in such a situation.

Chapter 3

INTRODUCTION AND DEFINITIONS: DISCUSSION OF THE SKILLS, TECHNIQUES, AND ESSENTIAL PRACTICES

INTRODUCTION

The school social worker is in a very unique situation. He or she is trained differently than anyone else on the faculty, administration, and staff of that institution. The mission of the agency is also distinct. Its purpose is to educate children in the academic areas and prepare them for secondary, higher education, or vocational training. Practical aspects of school social work are examined in this chapter as well as the unique and operational definitions that are used in this field of practice. Some social workers function as members of the child evaluation team while others provide counseling and other services specifically.

BACKGROUND OF SOCIAL WORK IN THE SCHOOL SETTING

As we know from Chapter 1, the position of the social worker in the school was derived from the need to monitor academics and attendance. This phenomenon occurred in the United States 100 years ago as a response to child labor in the factories and the influx of immigrants. The schools did not feel adequate to handle the upheavals and changes such as the large number of immigrants as well as their cultural and language diversity. One of the ways the schools chose to deal with these problems and their ramifications was to hire school social workers, known then as visiting teachers. Social workers were considered advocates to the new influx of students as well as liaisons to the families who were foreign to this system and sometimes found themselves in adversarial positions with the school's personnel. Jane Addams, as we know, was a social work innovator who brought the settlement house movement to the United States. At Hull House, the first settlement house, she tried to integrate the immigrants into the community by providing education for children and parents alike. She realized that these new-found citizens needed to be connected to the community through an educational vehicle. At Hull House, immigrants were taught first the English language so that they could get work or begin to get an education. Hull House also developed a plan where bricklayers would work one week and attend classes at a local school the next so as to develop the skills of the newly arrived immigrants (Addams, 1910). Hull House provided a kindergarten as well as classes in music, art, and drama (Raatma, 2004).

THE PARTNERSHIP

Since we are functioning in an educational setting as opposed to a mental health setting, we consider the school a *secondary setting*. The primary purpose of schools is education but the social worker functions to assist not only helping students attain optimal academic performance but also social and emotional well-being. The school social workers are referred to by Bronstein and Abramson (2003) as *resident guests* (p. 328). As such, they are perceived as supportive personnel for the faculty and administration.

Social workers' partnership with educators continued through the years and evolved into a permanent role. This endeavor included not only the original reasons for our involvement in school but also extended to our role in the educational acts and policies that developed in the following years (e.g., PL 94-142, passed in 1975, Individuals with Disabilities Education Act, Rehabilitation Act 1973, No Child Left Behind 2002, and various other policies and legislation throughout the years including the most recent update of IDEA in 2004). We became participants in the evaluation and classification of students and the developers of educational planning that ensued. We eventually became behavioral specialists in the school and guardians/providers of a plan to help students achieve appropriate behaviors to better access their education. This was, indeed, a unique position for a social worker in the milieu of the educator. Therefore, it is important to define the terms that are used by the social worker in that environment.

Let us begin with a working definition of *school social work*. According to the National Association of Social Workers (NASW) standards it is ". . . Services provided in the setting of an educational agency by credentialed school social workers. This specialty in social work is oriented toward helping students make satisfactory adjustments and coordinating and influencing the efforts of the school, the family, and the community to achieve this goal" (2002, p. 3).

A licensed or credentialed school social worker is expected to meet state requirements that are issued by state boards of education or other state agencies that license educational personnel or professional social workers (NASW Standards for School Social Worker Services, 2002). Each state should have a website for the Division of Professional and Occupational licensing board. These agencies develop and establish standards for licensure for their state. An example of such requirements can be obtained from each state's board of education. The following are the requirements of a particular state: Iowa.

"The individual applying for this endorsement must have:

A Master's degree in social work from an accredited school of social work, including a minimum of twenty hours of course work related to assessment, intervention, resource coordination, and education and a practicum in a school setting.

The study must include:

- Courses in general education issues such as school law, foundation of education, and psycho-educational measurement
- Courses in special education such as exceptional children and special educational regulations.

A practicum experience in a school setting under the supervision of an experienced school social work practitioner. The practicum must include experiences in assessment, direct services, consultation, community liaison and documentation. If the individual has served as a school social worker for two years the practicum experience can be waived;

- Completion of an approved human relations component (Individuals completing the approved school social work program at the University of Iowa are exempted from the human relations course because the content is included in the regular master's degree curriculum)
- Preparation that contributes to the education of the handicapped and the gifted and talented" (Iowa State Education Department).

PURPOSE OF SOCIAL WORK IN THE EDUCATIONAL SETTING

The purpose of social work in schools is to contribute to the school success of students. *School success* can be considered the social, emotional, and academic competence of each child. The social worker's task is to provide a setting for both teaching and learning where children can have the optimal environment to develop their educational skills and to build knowledge. Children also need to learn how to solve problems and make decisions as well as adapt to the environment in which they live and learn. Sometimes with social work intervention, students are expected to take charge of their own learning needs and be able to advocate for themselves. The concept of self-advocacy has students addressing these issues (Astramovich & Harris, 2007). According to Van Reusen, "*Self-advocacy* has been deemed as the ability to assertively communicate or negotiate one's interests, desires, needs, and rights" (cited in Astramovich & Harris, 2007, p. 271). All these skills need to be developed by children as well as having them deal with their own social, emotional, and physical development and the environment in which they live.

The social worker is hired either through a school board of education or through a related services program. The related services organization works with the schools and often provides therapy and free services to school children and their families (services that are mandated by the Individualized Education Plan and counseling are two of the services that can be provided). These are sometimes referred to as *wraparound services*. The therapy can take place on or off the school campus. The services provided by these school social workers entail therapeutic interventions and counseling. Sometimes referrals are given by school personnel, other times self-referrals occur; parental, guardian, and family referrals are also possible. The clients in these cases can receive individual, group, or family counseling or therapy administered through a variety of interventions. These social workers deal only with students in this capacity and are not members of the school-based child study team, nor do they perform school social work duties such as developing Individual Education Programs. Although they provide short-term and crisis intervention, they usually do provide more intensive services than those social workers who are mandated members of the Child Study Team.

Prevention services are also in the purview of the school social worker. Prevention programs in the schools are usually a trifold effort. They include presentations to faculty and staff, students and parents, and the community. Prevention services are useful in giving structure and policy for an issue before it takes place. Prevention programs such as violence prevention, substance abuse prevention, and child abuse prevention have shown positive results in the schools. School connectedness and/or attachment has been associated with the prevention of problems including academic achievement and improved mental and physical health (Jonson-Reid, 2009). The following website might be helpful in developing prevention programs in schools: http://www2.ed.gov/admins/lead/safety/edpicks.jhtml.

A social worker in the school is often a member of a *Child Study Team* also known as the *Committee on Special Education* or *Student Study Teams*—that is, one of the professionals mandated by law to participate in the referral and evaluation process of special education or as it is sometimes now referred to as *Exceptional Children's Services*. Members of that professional team include a school psychologist, a learning specialist, a physician(s), a teacher, a parent or guardian, and sometimes a nurse. Other professionals who may also be added to the evaluating team are an occupational, speech, or physical therapist, and in some schools, the extended team includes a guidance counselor and/or school administrator.

The school social worker, hired through the board of education and responsible for carrying out the mandates of IDEA 2004 for social work, is considered school-based. The local school agency is responsible for educational programs. The social worker in the school is a provider of special education and many times works as part of the mandated CST (exceptional children's services). Social workers could be involved in counseling that is mandated through a child's educational plan. They also may work with students who are unclassified using interventions with individuals, families, and groups in a counseling capacity. Some of the work of school social workers involves special education, although they do provide services to students within the general education population. Many of the children who go undiagnosed and suffer with mental illness are not classified. These students may be referred to the school social worker for assistance and this help is an important contribution that social workers make in the educational setting. School social workers are involved with classified students providing "direct instructional activities or special learning experiences designed primarily for students identified as having certain disabling exceptionalities in one or more aspects of the cognitive process or as being underachievers in relation to general level or model of their overall abilities" (Utah Office of Education, 2006). Special education is provided through the legal process of evaluation and classification. This process is discussed in detail in Chapter 4.

DEFINITION SECTION: TERMS DEFINED THAT ARE USED IN THE SCHOOL SYSTEM

Early intervention services are provided to children under the age of 3 years. Their purpose is to help children with developmental lags to catch up to their peers before kindergarten.

Mandated preevaluation interventions are strategies used to accommodate a student's educational needs prior to initiating a formal referral for evaluation. They sometimes can prevent a child from being classified with a disability and are less restrictive (Wright & Wright, 2007). Response to Intervention is the current process and is discussed below.

Prereferral interventions are delivered in the student's regular classroom and attempt to improve learning prior to a referral for formal special education evaluation (National Center for Learning Disabilities, 1999–2006). *Response to Intervention* (RtI) is a preliminary step in documenting the appropriate interventions the school has employed prior to the referral process for special education. Since IDEA was reissued in 2004, the RtI method of early assessment and intervention with an evidence-based therapeutic intervention was initiated by many states and school districts for students with behavioral and/or emotional problems. The RtI method is proactive and establishes the identification of students at risk rather than students who are already showing deficit areas.

The RtI method has been used successfully for students with learning difficulties. "The RtI model requires implementation of sound educational interventions prior to a discussion of special education placement" (Chaney, Flower & Templeton, 2008, p. 110). In a recent study, this intervention was used, and the level of response to the intervention was observed. The results showed that the majority of the students with emotional and/or behavioral difficulties did not need special education evaluation after this intervention (Chaney, Flower & Templeton, 2008).

In order for a student to be evaluated for special education, a referral must be submitted. A *referral* is a written or formal statement of specific academic performance or behavior that does not meet the criteria of what is expected of that student at that cognitive, emotional, or social stage of development. A formal referral in writing is necessary for the evaluation process to begin. As suggested before, since the inception of IDEA 2004, evidence of previously used interventions needs to be submitted to document that other efforts have thus far failed at helping the student succeed.

An *eligibility conference* is necessary before an *Individual Educational Plan* (IEP) meeting can take place. This conference consists of the evaluating team and the parent(s) or guardian(s) ascertaining whether or not the child is deemed in need of special education and classification. This can only occur based on the evidence presented by the examining professional team member.

Informed Parental Consent must be obtained before an initial evaluation can take place. This means that the parent(s) must understand, in his or her native language, the entire process of evaluation and the possibility of eligibility for special education. All the implications need to be explained to the parent before consent is given.

If a child is deemed eligible for special education by the Child Study Team, an IEP must be developed. Eligibility for an IEP requires that the child is classifiable under IDEA as one of the classifications developed by the federal guidelines for special education. An eligibility conference and statement must precede an IEP. The parent(s) or guardian(s) must agree to the classification before an IEP can be put in place. The following are the classifications permitted under IDEA 2004 and allow a child to receive services as deemed necessary by his or her defined disability.

- Specific Learning Disability
- Speech or Language Impairment
- Visual Impairment (including blindness)
- Traumatic Brain Injury
- Intellectually Disabled
- Serious Emotional Disturbance
- Hearing Impairment (including deafness)
- Orthopedic Impairment
- Autistic
- Other Health Impairments

A child with attention deficit hyperactivity disorder (ADHD) and pervasive developmental disorder (PDD) may qualify for special education services because he or she meets the definition of a child with disability, possibly under the category of Other Health Impaired or another one that better defines his or her needs (Special Education in the United States, 2006).

The IEP outlines the student's present levels of performance, goals and objectives, modifications to the curriculum, transition statement, any ancillary services required for that student's success in school, and a statement of least restrictive environment. A sample of an educational plan is included in Chapter 4.

Least Restrictive Environment (LRE) is a milieu where children with disabilities can have an education with regular education students to the extent that the disabled student is able (Wright & Wright, 2007). It requires a school district to provide an education for a disabled child "to the maximum extent appropriate" with nondisabled students (Wright & Wright, 2007, p. 23). This means that a child with a learning disability needs to be placed in a regular classroom with supplementary services and aids (if necessary). If these accommodations still do not provide enough help for the student's success then a more restrictive environment may be sought. The LRE must be tried first. It is a stepwise procedure to finally place a child in a self-contained educational setting.

Free and Appropriate Public Education (FAPE) is meant to provide all children with access to public school no matter how severe his or her disability may be. This includes preschool, elementary, and high school education. A child in special education receives this education until the age of 21, at which point the student is given a high school diploma, and the school district is no longer responsible to educate that student.

Local Educational Agency (LEA) is the local agency administered by the board of education to provide an education for public and secondary schools under its jurisdiction. In special education, the term is used when referring to the responsible school district for the development and financial responsibility for a special education student who is placed out of the school district.

Presently, the school social worker may perform the duties of a *case manager*. The tasks involved are: "organizing, coordinating and sustaining activities and services designed to optimize the functioning of students and/or families" (NASW Standards for School Social Worker Services, 2002, p.7).

Prevention is very much in the purview of the school social worker. Universal prevention would include efforts made to prevent problems from occurring. Once the problem occurs, the social worker would take steps to limit its effects (selective prevention). Indicated prevention would involve helping the affected students and employing interventions to limit the return of the problem. Prevention is a key element in the maximization of a child's education. The school social worker's job description includes individual, group and family counseling, as well as policy and program development to deal with prevention as presented above. The special education component of the profession lends itself to secondary and tertiary prevention.

INTEGRATED SCHOOL SOCIAL WORK SERVICES

The school social worker functions in many roles in the schools in addition to having to fulfill the responsibilities outlined in the special education laws. These include *advocating* for at-risk students. *Consultation* with school personnel, parents, and students is yet another responsibility. *Empowering* parents and students to advocate for themselves is essential as well as having open communication between home and school. *Collaboration* with families, teachers, and community to assist student success is another role played. *Referrals* to community agencies and follow-up are an important role to help students connect and follow through on referrals. Sometimes the social worker needs to *mediate* problems that are occurring between students and teachers, students and parents, students and students, and teachers and parents. Of course, the role of *educator* is also within the purview of the school social worker.

The school social worker, hired through the board of education and responsible for carrying out the mandates of IDEA 2004 for social work, is considered school based. The local school agency is responsible for educational programs. The social worker in the school is a provider of special education and many times works as part of the mandated CST (exceptional children's services). A school social worker could be involved in counseling that is mandated through a child's educational plan or can work with individuals, families and groups in a counseling capacity. Some of the work of school social workers involves special education although they do provide services to students within the general education population. Many of the children who go undiagnosed and suffer with mental illness are not classified. These students may be referred to the school social worker for assistance and this help is an important contribution that social workers make in the educational setting. School social workers work with classified students giving "direct instructional activities or special learning experiences designed primarily for students identified as having certain disabling exceptionalities in one or more aspects of the cognitive process or as being underachievers in relation to general level or model of their overall abilities" (Utah Office of Education, 2006). Special education is provided through the legal process of evaluation and classification. This process is discussed in detail in Chapter 4.

A *student* in school is any person who is required by the state to attend a school and participate in an educational program (NASW Standards for School Social Workers, 2002). In the area of special education, a student can be a person of preschool age through the age of 21.

As mentioned above, the *Individuals with Disabilities Education Act* (IDEA) is a federal law implemented to ensure "a free appropriate public education" for the disabled student tailored to his or her individual needs provided in the least restrictive environment and is the primary federal program that authorizes state and local aid for special education and related services for children with disabilities. On December 3, 2004, President Bush signed the Individuals with Disabilities Education Improvement Act, a major reauthorization and revision of IDEA. The new law regulates services to students with disabilities and not only preserves the basic structure and civil rights guarantees of IDEA but also makes significant changes in the law. Most provisions of Public Law (PL) 108–446 went into effect on July 1, 2005. The requirements regarding "highly qualified" special education teachers became effective immediately on signature (http://www.cde.ca.gov/sp/se/lr/ideareathztn.asp#regu). This act requires schools to provide learning aids, testing modifications, and other educational accommodations to children with disabilities. It also provides opportunity for due process (http://www.cde.ca.gov/sp/se/lr/ideareathztn.asp#regu).

A *Manifestation Determination Review* is administered to a disabled student when a rule has been broken. Its purpose is to determine whether or not the child's disability has caused the infraction or if the IEP has failed to properly support the child's behavior (Wright & Wright, 2007).

A *Functional Behavior Assessment* is ". . . a process of assessing the purpose or function of a student's behavior in relation to its context (i.e., surrounding environment) so that appropriate interventions can be designed to meet his or her unique needs" (Scott, Nelson, & Zabala, 2003, p. 216). It is developed in response to a child's difficulty with behaving appropriately in the school setting. When a special education student's behavior is being considered for discipline, an interdisciplinary team is convened to perform this assessment. It, if deemed appropriate, will result in a *behavioral intervention plan.* The plan comprises the steps to be taken in the event that a behavior occurs.

The assessment has the following components:

- a description of the behavior in question;
- specifics of that behavior such as intensity, severity, and so on;
- includes other variables that may be causing the behavior;
- scrutiny of the function and intent of the behavior;
- environmental changes to alter the behavior; and
- plan for appropriate behaviors as alternatives (Constable, Massat, McDonald, & Flynn, 2006).

Positive Behavior Support involves a program of reactive and proactive response. Reactive responses result after a situation has taken place and there is a need to discipline. This usually involves the administrative office of discipline. Proactive response involves interviewing, observing, focus group input, historical data, a screening system for behavior disorder, and disciplinary reports. It is implemented through a group or task force process, and its purpose is to provide help to students before a problem occurs (Marchant, Anderson, Caldarelli, Young, & Young, 2009).

Independent Educational Evaluation (IEE) is conducted by a qualified professional not employed by the school agency, but this evaluation is paid for by the school district (Wright & Wright, 2007). This intervention is usually requested by the parent(s) because of lack of confidence in the school district or in response to not accepting the results of the original evaluation.

Mainstreaming is placing special education students in regular classes when they are believed competent enough to be integrated into that environment (possibly with modifications to the curriculum). This process helps these students share an academic and a social environment with their nonclassified peers. It is also part of what is considered a "least restrictive" environment—that is, an environment that is part of general education (Wright & Wright, 2007).

A *Self-Contained Program* is a class in the public school or an out-of-district program devised to give a student the most supportive environment for his or her disability. The *least-restrictive program* must be tried before a self-contained program is deemed appropriate or in the child's best interest.

Out-of-District Special Education Placement can occur if a student is not having success in the most restrictive comprehensive public school; placement may be sought in either a public or private facility. These are schools that only have special education students, and most often the teachers in these facilities are certified in special education.

Ancillary Services can include modifications to the curriculum or classroom, extended time to complete tasks, assistive technology devices, an aide or notetaker, and other accommodation to allow regular classroom participation (http://www.hoagiesgifted.org/eric/faq/services.html).

Related Services is the term used for those services a child with a disability needs to benefit from special education. These are often specific services provided directly to the child, such as speech therapy, occupational therapy, orientation and mobility services, transportation services, or counseling (http://www.hoagiesgifted.org/eric/faq/services.html).

School-linked versus school-based social work are provisions for out-of-school treatment or counseling but are paid for by either the school board or the community. At times, the school social worker needs to refer a student to services in the community. Community mental health or family counseling services are often offered as school-linked services with agencies in near proximity to the school location.

504 Accommodations of the Rehabilitation Act are given if a student is not in need of special education but requires accommodations in the classroom. This may be necessary because of a disability, and therefore he or she is entitled to accommodations under Section 504. Its purpose is to protect a student or employee from discrimination based on his or her disability (Wright & Wright, 2007). If there is a complaint to be made regarding a 504 accommodation, the Office of Civil Rights holds the authority for settling that complaint.

A Due Process Hearing is an intervention used to resolve disputes between the school district and the parent.

SOCIAL WORKER'S VERSUS EDUCATOR'S BACKGROUND

A social worker is trained to examine the circumstances in which the child is involved. The child's environmental milieu is considered. It is based on the ecological and/or systems approach and includes the micro, mezzo, and macro systems that impact on the child's life. Not only is the education of the child the focus of the social worker but also important are the emotional, physical, spiritual, and social aspects. A school social worker does not need to hold an educational degree.

The teacher or educator is trained with the child's best interest in mind but must focus on the educational success of that student. This is the essence of the child's purpose in school and is the main focus of the educator. The educator is concerned with content, and the social worker is concerned with context.

Example: Let's follow an actual student through the process of an educational difficulty from inception to the conclusion of his high school career. John was a ninth-grade student in a comprehensive high school. He was of average intelligence and in a college preparatory program. During the course of his first semester in high school, he was not handing in his homework and was behaving like the class clown. His antics included blurting out wise cracks and sexual innuendos and sometimes cutting classes. Several of his teachers had sent him to the vice-principal's office for discipline. He was an athlete, and during a football game (in which he participated) he was blurting out ethnic and racial slurs toward one of the opposing team members. He again was sent to the vice-principal for discipline. The vice principal in turn referred him to his guidance counselor. She surveyed his teachers and came up with a profile of a student who was failing courses and was disruptive. A referral to the CST was made, but the evaluation process was not started. A preliminary intervention was made with the school social worker who began a cognitive-behavioral intervention and also met with his teachers in an effort to employ the use of RtI before an intervention of a full-team evaluation was done. The teachers were given strategies to help the behaviors in the classroom. John did not respond, so a CST evaluation was initiated. The parents were contacted and asked to come to school and discuss the possibility of an *evaluation for special education*. They were told that they would receive a formal letter regarding the evaluation and their consent to this process was needed before the work-up could begin. Informed parental consent was essential before the initial evaluation. The parents consented, and thus the CST had 60 days to complete the process. A psychiatric evaluation was requested as part of this assessment, since the presenting problem was behavioral. After the testing, social history, and psychiatric evaluations were completed and an eligibility conference was held, under IDEA 2004 John received the classification of *severe emotional disturbance***.** The next part of the process was to develop an IEP. This could only occur if the parents agreed to the initial classification. They did, and an IEP conference ensued. John was deemed a special education student and entitled to a FAPE. A least restrictive program had to be the placement since that was the current procedure. Because the problem was emotional and behavioral in nature a functional behavior assessment needed to be developed. A behavioral intervention plan was the outgrowth of that assessment. John was given a supportive class (resource room) but was mainstreamed for most of his classes. He was also given related services, which included counseling once a week with the school social worker for a half hour. His family was advised that *wraparound services* would be provided for the family at a local mental health center. These would be considered school-linked services and would be financed by the school. They would receive five sessions, and then the progress would be evaluated collaboratively. As John's education evolved, his father died suddenly in an automobile accident. John's world was shattered, and despite enormous support and emotional intervention, he did not succeed academically. He was given a new IEP conference and placed in a more restrictive environment. It was a self-contained program for students with emotional difficulties.

The plan was put in place, and John responded, began to raise his grades, and behave more appropriately in class. He eventually graduated from that program.

SUMMARY

Chapter 3 was developed to explain the unique and esoteric terms that are specific to school social work. The origins of social work in schools were discussed as well as the roles and responsibilities of a social worker in the school setting. The social worker is, in fact, the only one in his or her position in the school with a different focus than the other professionals in the school environment. The main objective of the school is education. Teachers' and administrators' main function is to educate those in their care. Social workers are concerned with the psychosocial, emotional, and spiritual aspects of the child in the educational milieu as well as the child's educational success. A case was presented and followed through the process of initial problem to placement and eventually high school graduation.

ACTIVITIES

Activity 1: Levels 1 & 2: Examine the functions of a school social worker regarding the specific areas of expertise needed in this field as opposed to general practice.

Activity 2: Levels 1 & 2: Find the qualifications for credentialing a school social worker in your state.

SELF-REFLECTION QUESTIONS

1. What is meant by the social worker's place in a "secondary setting"?
2. What are the duties of a school social worker on the child evaluation team?

CLASS DISCUSSION QUESTIONS

1. After reviewing the case example, what alternative interventions might have been attempted other than the one stated?
2. What are the possible implications of being the only social worker in a school setting?
3. What are the advantages of a school social worker housed in the school environment as opposed to being in a nearby facility?

Chapter 4

SPECIAL EDUCATION COMPONENT AND SCHOOL SOCIAL WORK

INTRODUCTION

In chapter 2 the definition of special education is given, and in this chapter the mandate of the Individuals with Disabilities Education Act (IDEA) (PL108–446) and the No Child Left Behind (PL107–110) legislation is discussed. How these new acts impact school social workers is examined. See Appendix A for an excerpt from IDEA. The responsibilities of the social worker in his or her capacity on a child study team (CST) is to participate in the evaluation team for deciding whether or not a child is classifiable and entitled to special education services. Also in this process, a social worker fulfills the role of advocate for the student and the family.

As in all examples in this book, the names of the participants and places have been changed to protect confidentiality. A social developmental history of the child would be completed by the social worker. An example of one is given with the necessary components to ensure that it is comprehensive. An example of a genogram and ecomap are also given in this chapter. Services would be indicated through an Individual Education Program (IEP) and counseling services are sometimes included in this document. Counseling services would be provided by the social worker as defined by related services. Positive Behavioral Interventions and Supports are mandated by IDEA. Social workers as well as teachers are to define, teach, and support positive behavioral models making these a part of schoolwide education programs (Constable, Massat, McDonald, & Flynn, 2006). An activity sheet is included for development of an IEP and classification summary.

Issues of discipline for special education students such as manifestation determination, the functional assessment plan, and the subsequent behavioral intervention plan are presented. If the child's behavior is a manifestation of his or her disability a functional behavioral assessment and behavior intervention plan must be provided (Wright & Wright, 2007).

The Individual Family Service Plan (sec. 632[4][C] of the IDEA) is derived for early intervention programs. It is more comprehensive than the IEP, is developmentally oriented, and is focused on family strengths and needs (Constable, Massat, McDonald, & Flynn, 2006).

The Family Educational Rights and Privacy Act (FERPA) is a federal law that protects the privacy of student education records. The law applies to all schools that receive funds under an applicable program of the federal Department of Education (http://www.ed.gov/policy/gen/guid/fpco/ferpa/index.html). Issues concerning confidentiality are discussed, as well as what teachers and school personnel should be told and what should be kept confidential.

INDIVIDUALS WITH DISABILITIES EDUCATION ACT

The Individuals with Disabilities Education Act has conceptualized the way an educational system is to provide a free and appropriate education for each and every child. "Since IDEA service delivery programs are associated with a child's educational progress, school personnel must show the linkage of planned interventions with educational outcomes and provide evidence of direct and indirect benefit" (Franklin et al., 2006, p. 893). The responsibilities of the social worker in his or her capacity are to participate in the team of experts. The social worker is included among school personnel who provide services and interventions to special education students. A social developmental history is the major contribution of the social worker to the evaluation process but is not mandated directly by IDEA to perform that task (Wright & Wright, 2007). Some states do mandate social workers to perform social developmental histories as part of an evaluation.

NO CHILD LEFT BEHIND AND ITS IMPACT ON SPECIAL EDUCATION

The main objective of the No Child Left Behind Act is ". . . to ensure that all children have a fair, equal, and significant opportunity to obtain a high-quality education and reach, at a minimum, proficiency on challenging State academic achievement standards and state academic assessments" (Wright & Wright, 2007, p. 299). It requires testing each year in grades 3 to 8, "highly qualified teachers" in each classroom, "research-based instruction," parental decisions and involvement, selection of schools, and public reporting of student progress (p. 299). Its goal is to have all children attend "high quality schools" and is intended to raise the academic standards for students across the country (Simpson, LaCava, & Graner, 2004). If schools do not reach the stated level of proficiency, the federal government can impose monetary sanctions as well as "corrective action" for both the state and the school district (2004).

The No Child Left Behind legislation gives individual states more power over school districts and allows them to administer the educational process more closely. It proposes that all students including those in special education will achieve a "proficiency" level as based on assessment exams. Parents have been given more power over their child's involvement with the school and are permitted to examine much of what the child creates in the classroom as well as surveys and instruments that deal with the child's physical or mental well-being. If parents are not satisfied with the school's achievement, they have the right to transfer the child to another school in the district with a better record. Accountability is the key, and standards set must be achieved by the 2013–2014 school year (Simpson, LaCava, & Graner, 2004). This legislation has impacted on special education in some ways. Each classified child must participate in the state testing programs regardless of his or her academic ability. Although students can have modifications for the administration of these tests, it is often difficult for students to participate in such a program since they do not have the skills. There needs to be more allowance for evaluation and accommodation for children with learning difficulties (2004).

Each teacher must be *highly qualified* not only in special education but also in an academic subject area. This statement means that each must have state certification in both. This concept will probably allow for more teacher expertise, but if many choose a subject area that is already popular, it will be difficult for these teachers to get a position and also difficult for the schools to hire teachers in less popular areas. Special education teachers need to be eligible as highly qualified both in special education and one other subject area.

In 2010, President Obama introduced proposed reform to the No Child Left Behind Act. Although accountability is still the essence of the "blueprint for reform," the difference is that the focus would be on individual schools' and students' growth and achievement relative to where they were previously. Poorer schools would also get more intensive help to raise the bar. Overall, the attempt to have more students graduate from high school and pursue a career or profession would be the goal. Instead of punishing failing schools and states, the hope would be to reward success for those places that have made some improvement (Barnett, 2010).

FAMILY EDUCATIONAL AND PRIVACY ACT

The Family Educational and Privacy Act (FERPA) deals with privacy, parental rights and at age 18 students' rights to their records and an explanation of those records. It protects confidentiality of records of all schools involved in funding through the Department of Education (Seiber, 2007). This may apply to private as well as public schools. The educational records included in FERPA are (a) student's date and place of birth, (b) parental information, (c) grades and courses taken, (d) special education records if they exist, (e) disciplinary reports, (f) medical and attendance records as well as degrees attained, (g) social security number, and (h) pictures (Toglia, 2007). School officials with educational interests, other schools to which the student may go, financial aid officials, accrediting agencies, officials in cases of emergencies of health and safety, and judicial orders can receive the records without parental and/or student consent (2007). The Patriot Act of 2001 allows federal officers with a court mandate to view these records without consent (2007). The No Child Left Behind Act allows for military personnel to receive directory information, which includes name, address and/or e-mail, enrollment status, place of birth and date, and physically identifying information (2007). Schools must maintain records for 5 years after the student has left. Law enforcement authorities can have access to these records, and in emergencies of safety, these records can be released without consent (Wright & Wright, 2007).

THE INDIVIDUALIZED FAMILY SERVICE PLAN

The Individualized Family Service Plan (20 U.S.C., 1436) is used in place of an IEP since it fulfills the IDEA requirements for infants and toddlers (Wright & Wright, 2007). It is a written document that helps families and professionals describe what needs to be accomplished to help a child develop his or her full potential. It is a collaborative effort that outlines the strengths that are to be developed, and provides a statement of the services that are available to fulfill the child's needs (Cash, Garland, & Osborne, 1991).

It includes a "multidisciplinary assessment," "family directed assessment," and "written individualized family service plan" (Wright & Wright, 2007, p. 141). The first assessment includes identification of strengths and weaknesses and what can be provided to meet those needs. The second area focuses on the resources and concerns of the family and the supports that can be put in place to help them. The third section outlines the steps to be taken for transition of the child. It further describes the child's current level of development; strengths of the family; and expectations of the interventions specifically stated with frequency, length, and intensity of the interventions. Review must take place once a year (Wright & Wright, 2007). Parents are included as part of the multidisciplinary team. It provides a case manager responsible for its execution and the procedure to be followed to support the child to the next level (Cash, Garland, & Osborne, 1991). Its focus is developmental and best assessed by a school social worker (Constable, Massat, McDonald, & Flynn, 2006).

The following is an outline of the plan:

1. Present levels of development: physical, cognitive, communication, adaptive, and social emotional (as judged objectively)
2. Statement of family's concerns, resources, and priorities
3. Statement of goals and when and how much will be achieved
4. Specific early intervention procedures based on evidence-based practice
5. Services to be provided in the natural milieu
6. Onset, length, duration, and frequency of services
7. The person in charge of this plan
8. Steps in the transition to preschool plan (Wright & Wright, 2007).

RESPONSE TO INTERVENTION

As described in Chapter 3, Response to Intervention (RtI) is a preliminary step in documenting the appropriate interventions the school has employed prior to the referral process for special education. Since the Individuals with Disabilities Education Act (IDEA) was reissued in 2004, the RtI method of early assessment and intervention with an evidence-based therapeutic intervention was initiated by many states and school districts for students with behavioral and/or emotional problems. The RtI method is proactive and establishes the identification of students at risk rather than students who are already showing deficit areas.

Although RtI is not specifically named in IDEA, the concept of preintervention strategies is noted. The main idea of RtI is to prescreen all children to evaluate through evidence-based procedures the needs of students and then to match those needs with academically researched interventions. It therefore provides appropriate education for all children and identifies those students who may be in need of special education.

The major components of an effective RtI program are "high quality classroom instruction; research-based instruction; classroom performance [designing assessments internally]; continuous progress monitoring; research-based interventions; progress monitoring during intervention; fidelity measures [an evaluation of teacher behaviors observed and developed by other teachers]" (National Research Center on Learning Disabilities, 2005).

The three-tier model is structured for a range of 8 to 12 weeks for each. Tier 1 is research-based instruction provided by a regular teacher. Students' progress is assessed through curriculum testing. It reveals which students are at risk for not keeping up and who will need more support. Tier 2 is for those students who are not keeping up with the others and require more intense instruction to become proficient on their grade level. It provides small group instruction, but the students are not classified. Tier 3 may be special education, depending on the school. It involves intensive supplementary teaching. The instruction is usually given by a teaching expert (a special education teacher in some cases). It is more likely than Tier 2 to be individualized for a particular student. Monitoring on this tier is continuous (National Research Center on Learning Disabilities, 2005). The three-tier model is presented in the chart below.

Social Developmental History

A social developmental history of the child would be completed by the social worker. An example of one is given with the necessary components to ensure that it is comprehensive. An example of a genogram and/or ecomap is also included in this social worker's work-up. A genogram or ecomap is not an essential part of

Step	Tier	Responsibility
1. General screening of all students	1	Shared by General Education and Special Education
2. Implementing general Education and Monitoring Responsiveness to General Education	1	General Education
3. Implementing a Supplementary Diagnostic Instructional Trial and Monitoring Responsiveness	2	Shared by General Education and Special Education
4. Designation of Disability, Classification of Disability, and Special Intensive Instruction Placement and Monitoring Responsiveness to Special Intensive Instruction Placement	3	Special Education

(National Research Center on Learning Disabilities, 2005)

a social history but can be useful in engaging the family in the process of the developmental and family histories. It is a helpful visual image of the family's medical and psychiatric histories and the relationship among family members, and is the shorthand for the narrative of the social developmental history. It also helps the social worker recall information when writing the narrative.

A genogram is extremely useful in developing the psychosocial history of a student and his or her family. It is a pictorial depiction of usually three generations of a family. It displays the intergenerational and generational relationships among family members as well as their health and psychosocial standing. It helps the family visually see the interpersonal and emotional issues that are unique to them. The family members are an integral part of this project's development and can identify themselves and their feelings by viewing this document.

An example of a genogram:

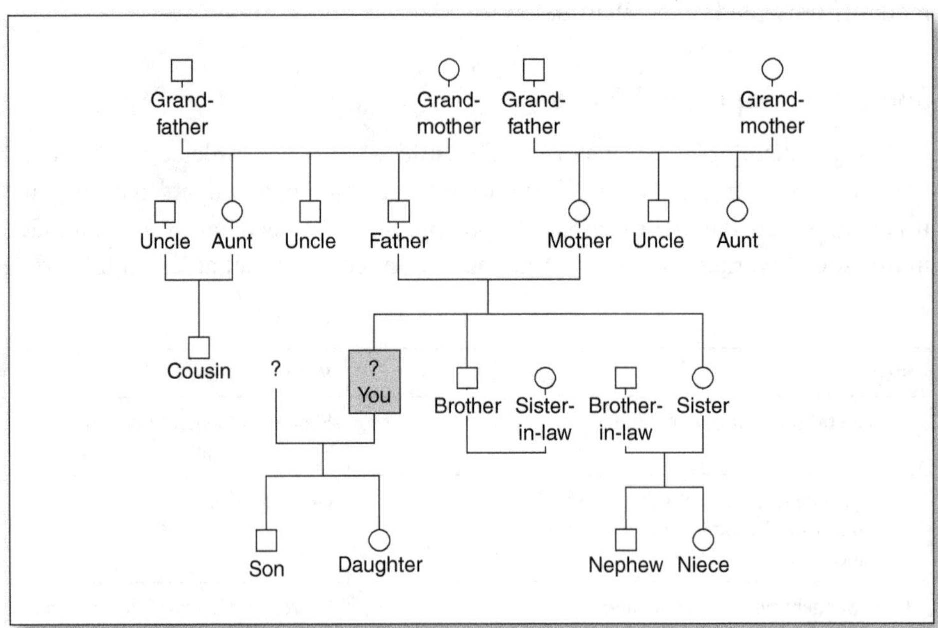

Retrieved from http://www.genopro.com/genogram/templates/

An ecomap is another visual representation of a family and the environment in which it exists. Individuals can see themselves and their families in relationship to the external systems around them. Such systems as schools, health care facilities, work, spiritual communities, and so on are depicted on an ecomap. It becomes an extension of a genogram as the individual and his or her family are impacted by the environment that surrounds them. It can be very helpful in assessing, planning, and intervening on behalf of the client and the client system.

An example of an ecomap:

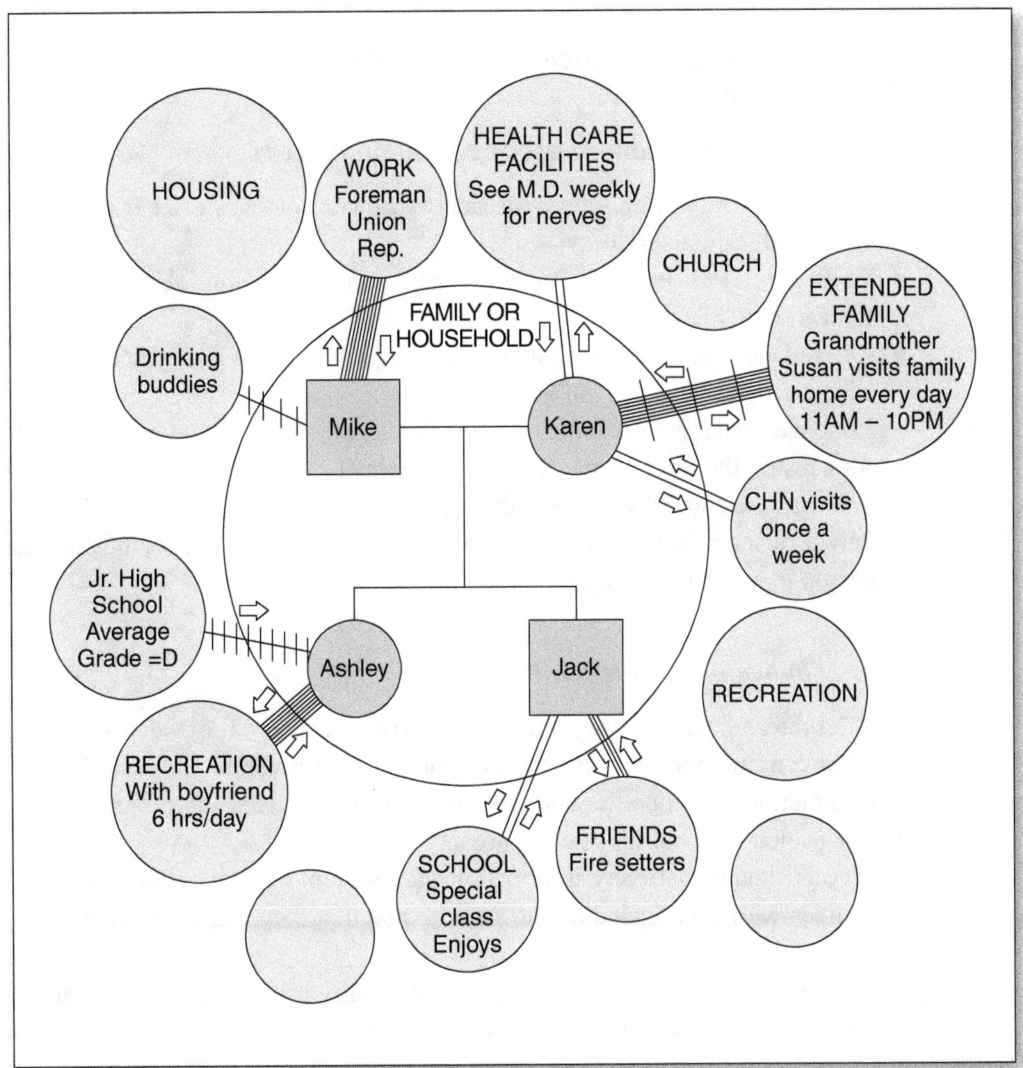

Retrieved from http://www.uic.edu/nursing/genetics/Lecture/Family/ecomap.htm

Services are defined through an IEP, and counseling services are sometimes included in this document. Counseling services would be provided by the social worker as presented in related services.

THE INDIVIDUAL EDUCATION PROGRAM

The Individual Education Program better known as the IEP has several steps. These steps are mandated by federal administrative code. The steps in this process are outlined as follows:

Steps in the Evaluation Process from Referral to Classification

Step 1: Initial Referral for Special Education Process

- Written referral asking school district to evaluate student (to see if they need special education services)
- Written referral initiated by the chairperson of Committee of Special Education (CSE)
- Referral can result in request that student be tested to see if they need special education services
- Principal meets with parents to see if they agree child should be evaluated
- As a result, the referral may even be withdrawn
- Who has the authority to make the referral?
- Parent, teacher, school professional, doctor, judicial officer, or designated person in a public agency

Step 2: Individual Evaluation Process

- After referral, parents are asked to give written consent for evaluation
- After consent, outline of procedural safeguards is given to parents
- Completion of evaluation will determine needs (services and programs)
- The evaluation is of no cost to parents
- Parents should share any information they may have about child's skills & abilities with CST including the parent(s) so that they can consider it when making decisions
- The evaluation must include: physical exam, psychological evaluation, social history, observations of child in current educational setting, other tests and assessments that are appropriate, and vocational assessments
- Results are given to parents with copy of report
- Parents are invited to attend a meeting with committee where all scoring and assessments are explained
- If parents feel evaluation was inappropriate, then they can request an Independent Educational Evaluation (IEE)

Step 3: Eligibility for Special Education

"A student with a disability means a child as defined by Educational Law; who does not turn 21 before September 1st; who is entitled to attend public school; who because of mental, physical, or emotional reasons, has been identified as having a disability, may have autism, deafness, deaf-blindness, emotional disturbance, hearing impairment, learning disability, intellectual disability, multiple disabilities, orthopedic impairment, other health impairment, speech or language impairment, traumatic brain injury or visual impairment (blindness)" (http://fcpe.adelphi.edu/Social_site/committee_special_ed.htm). These terms are defined in section 200.1 (zz) of the Regulations of the Commissioner of Education. To receive special education services, his or her disability must impact a student's academic functioning to the degree that a specially designed education plan is needed. According to Wright and Wright (2007), a child with a disability, ". . . means a child–

(i) with intellectual disability, hearing impairments (including deafness), speech or language impairments, visual impairments (including blindness), serious emotional disturbance (referred to in this title as 'emotional disturbance'), orthopedic impairments, autism, traumatic brain injury, other health impairments, or specific learning disabilities; and

(ii) who, by reason thereof needs special education and related services" (pp. 57–58).

- CST must identify one disability category that best describes disability
- Committee then creates and implements an IEP
- Parents are given written notice of committee decision
- If parents disagree with decision, they may request a mediation or impartial hearing

Services that May Be Implemented

- Specially designed instruction, supplementary services provided in class, consultant teacher services, related services, resource room, special classes, home and hospital instruction, placement in an in-state or out-of-state approved private school and/or 12-month special services program

Step 4: Individual Education Plan (IEP)

- After eligibility is established IEP is created.
- The IEP is developed at a meeting with all the members of the CST including the parent(s), and a copy must be presented to the parent at the end of this meeting. It does not denote compliance, and there is a waiting period for the parent to accept the IEP and placement.

- Development must consider: the child's strengths, parental concerns, results of individual evaluation, results of any state or districtwide assessment and exams, and any unique needs related to the disability of the child.
- IEP is then created from a discussion that is held by CST on child's level of functioning.
- CST agrees on goals that child should work toward and discusses supports, services, and modifications that child will need in order to reach the goals set out by Committee. Goals are derived from the present level of functioning.
- The Committee decides the location where the services should be provided which should be the LEAST RESTRICTIVE ENVIRONMENT.
- A copy of the IEP is given at the meeting and a final draft sent to child's parents or guardian, teachers, and other service providers who will be working with the child.

Step 5: Annual Review and/or Reevaluation

- Child's IEP is reviewed by the Committee once a year to determine if it needs modifications or revisions.
- Child will have a reevaluation at least once every 3 years to review need for the special education programs and services.
- A reevaluation may also occur when conditions warrant or when requested by a teacher or parent.
- Time lines are in place so that delays are avoided (prepared by C. Pfaff, student, 2005).

An IEP consists of several parts as mandated by federal legislation. These include but are not limited to the following: (a) student data; (b) present levels of performance; (c) special circumstances such as limited English proficiency, visual or hearing impairment; (d) annual goals and objectives; (e) evaluation criteria, procedures and schedule; (f) recommended program; (g) explanation of participation in regular and special education program; (h) related special education services such as speech therapy, occupational therapy, physical therapy, counseling, assistive technology, transportation or other; (i) necessity and/or rationale for an extended school year; (j) curricula modifications or instruction strategies necessary for participation in regular or special education; (k) supplementary aids or services; (l) rationale for why student participates in regular or special education (least restrictive environment); (m) graduation requirements (for high school students); (n) whether or not the student will participate in state mandated proficiency tests (exempt or nonexempt status); (o) transition services and strategies to achieve those outcomes; (p) assent for those under 18 years of age and consent by parents or legal guardian.

AN EXAMPLE OF A SOCIAL DEVELOPMENTAL HISTORY

Pleasant Regional High School District

Social History

I. General Information

Date of Interview: November 11, 1998

Name: Daniel Smith

Address: 33 Corona Drive

Ridgeway, New Jersey

Phone Number: 622-0333

Interviewed: Mr. & Mrs. Smith in their home

II. Identifying Information

Daniel is a tall, slender, normally-developed African-American male in the 10th grade at Pleasant High School. He is a quiet and charming young man. He appears uninterested and disconnected in both his academic and extracurricular environments. He seems more relatable and comfortable with peers; although in these interactions, he is guarded on a personal level.

III. Presenting Problem and Referral

His English teacher referred him for lack of class preparation, failure on tests, and lack of participation in class. Upon gathering information from his other teachers, he does have failing grades in three other classes because of lack of participation in homework, class work, and test achievement. His pattern is consistent.

He is presently a 10th grader at Pleasant High School and has had a history of school failure dating back to the fifth grade. As a high school student, his freshman year ended with two failures, and he did not attend summer school.

IV. Family Members

Daniel is the younger of two boys in an intact family setting. His family is of African-American heritage.

(Continued)

(Continued)

Family Constellation:

Charles Smith—father	He was born and raised in New York City. He came from a large family, where most of the children are college graduates. He has a master's degree in reading and an advanced degree in Adm. and supervision in schools. He teaches elementary school in New York City. His birth date is 5/8/50.
Jane Hay—mother	She was born and raised in rural North Carolina. She attended 1 year of college and works as an administrative assistant in New York City. She has some very successful music recording entrepreneurs in her family.
Mac—brother	He is a high school graduate who graduated from Pleasant High in 1994. He did not go on to school or work but became involved in a relationship, which resulted in a child. He is a very personable young man but has not pursued a career since completion of high school.
Marianne Rann—Mac's girlfriend	She is a high school graduate who lives with the family, significant other, and her daughter. Mac and she often have conflicts that result in her leaving the home and also leaving her child.
Andrea Mae Rann—baby	She is the daughter of Mac born on 6/26/97.
Daniel-—identified student	He is a quiet, withdrawn but charming young man. He has had visual tracking training, has mixed dominance, and poor vision.

Extended family includes two elderly grandmothers who are seen often and would be considered viable members of an extended family. His maternal uncles have their entertainment business in New York City.

V. Developmental History

Daniel was a full-term baby weighing 8 lbs. 10 ozs. at birth. He was slightly jaundiced. He was colicky for the first 3 months of life. He walked at 9 months and spoke words at 8 months. He was fully potty trained at 2 years old. He enjoyed being read to and liked to play basketball. (His father is a baseball coach at school.)

VI. Medical

Daniel is a healthy young man. He has not suffered any childhood illnesses and does not contract colds and flu easily. No operations or hospitalizations were experienced. He is tall and slender. He is normal in his age-appropriate physical development (i.e., broad shoulder, facial hair, and muscular development). His last physical took place before he began high school and was normal.

VII. Educational History

Daniel is consistently a quiet and reserved person. He went to private school in New York City (before moving to the suburbs) and did not have many friends. He played sports early on but did not get involved in school sports. He left school in New York City during first grade. He presently feels alienated from the school and even with extreme prodding (such as personal encouragement from coaches and students) does not participate.

VIII. Social Relationships

Daniel idealizes his brother and seems to have a distant relationship with both parents. He is not particularly attached to his grandparents, aunts, or uncles.

His relationship with peers is also distant. He does not have any close friends.

He does not partake in drugs and alcohol according to his parents. His parents have a great deal of trouble with consistent discipline. They spend a great deal of time during the week with commuting and doing the household chores.

Daniel started school in Ridgewood during first grade at Samson School in Ridgewood. In fifth grade, he had a change of attitude, and his academic achievement went down. No particular event occurred to precipitate this change according to his parents. Since then he has been a marginal student.

Interview with Student:

Daniel is a quiet, rather guarded young man. He shows a great deal of bravado about not needing help in school. He did respond and develop a relationship with the social worker easily. He feels mistreated in school by his teachers who he feels pick on him because of his brother and racial prejudice. Daniel needs to let people see him as an individual with many fine characteristics.

IX. Home Environment

The home is a warm and mostly predictable environment for Daniel. Outside of Mac's inconsistencies, the family remains stable and comfortable.

Both parents work extremely hard to have a lovely, comfortable home in the suburbs.

(Continued)

(Continued)

X. Summary

Daniel is a young man from an intact family setting of African-American background. The family's adjustment to Ridgewood was difficult because of racial discrimination. Daniel has some minor learning problems dating back to elementary school. Vision is impaired as well as difficulty with visual tracking problems. He also exhibits mixed dominance or cross dominance, which is the inability of an individual to use one part of the body mainly over the other. In normal dominance "... an individual can use both sides reasonably well, one hemisphere generally overrides the other with respect to preferential use and skill" (Gabbard & Hart, 1996, p. 290).

He would profit from a small, structured environment at school for one period a day to help him with structure and organizational difficulties. He would also need an advocate in the school environment to help him receive the services and accommodations that he needs.

____________________ ____________

Joan Jones, PhD L.C.S.W. Date

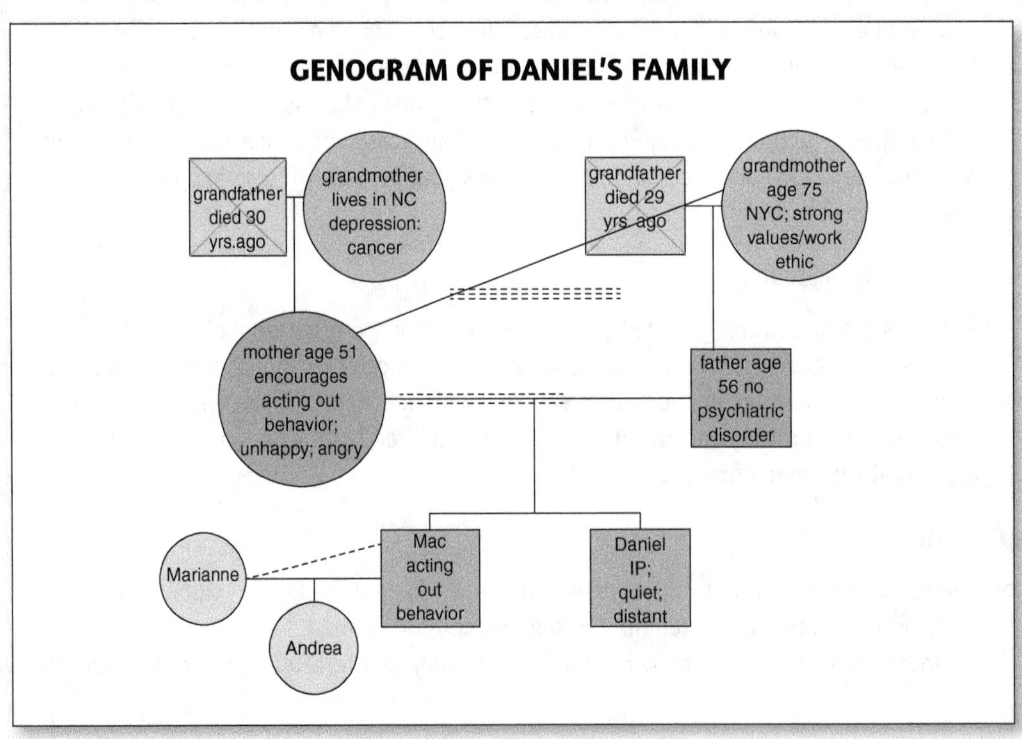

Practice Sample

With the above information construct an ecomap of Daniel and his world:

Practice Sample

Based on the following information develop a social developmental history:

George's parents have been separated since 1997. Mr. Moore took a position as the CEO of a company in upstate New York and at that time told his wife that he was leaving her. At present, Mr. Moore has been hired by a large corporation as the chief operating officer, and although he has moved to Chicago, he still maintains an apartment in northern New Jersey but plans to move closer to his children when he is in the area. He does live with a significant other at the present time. George's mother became very upset and depressed about her divorce and the full responsibility for caring for her children on a daily basis. She did rise to the occasion and seems to be doing better. George seems to have identified with his mother's pain and as the oldest child of three (a younger sister age 12 and a younger brother age 10) has experienced the most severe emotional reaction to the loss of his father. His grades in school fell. He became very argumentative with certain teachers, which culminated in his being asked to leave St. Vincent's High School. The Moores recognized his emotional distress, and George began psychotherapy in the spring.

As per parental request, the CST was required to complete an evaluation on George. The reason for this request is that George's case is presently being reviewed for expulsion by the Pleasant Board of Education. He was apprehended with an ounce of marijuana behind the school by two police officers. He is an eleventh grader at Pleasant High School.

(Continued)

(Continued)

Practice Sample

With the following template, construct a genogram of George and his family:

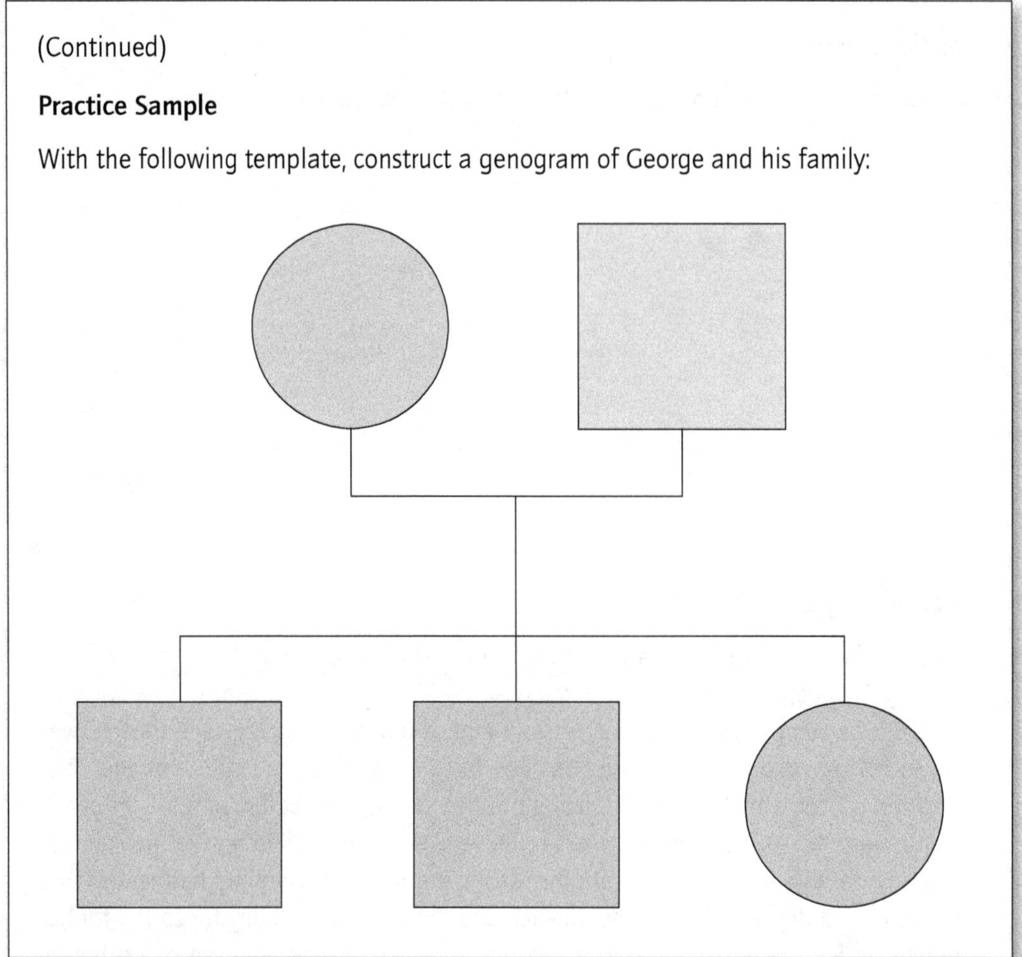

Manifest Determination

As of July 1, 1997, schools have been mandated to make a determination as to whether or not a school policy violation by a special education student is related to his or her disability– the "manifestation determination" (Meloy, 1999, p. 8). According to IDEA 2004, the law requires that all members of the team including the parents review the file to decide if the negative behavior was a result of the disability, was related to the disability, or was a result of the school not implementing the IEP (Wright & Wright, 2007).

An interpretation of the IDEA 2004, Part B, Section 1415: Procedural Safeguards (see Appendix A) mandate for Manifestation Determination is as follows: An IEP team including the parent(s), not just an administrator in charge of discipline, review the data on a particular special education student to decide if there is a relationship between a current instance of misconduct and the student's disability, in order to make decisions about the consequence for the misconduct as well as the student's continuing educational and behavioral needs. This review must be conducted if a student with a disability is removed from school for more than 10 days either consecutive or cumulative (Wright & Wright, 2007). The specific tasks of the IEP team are to answer these questions:

1. Is the IEP appropriate, including a behavior management plan?
2. Is the IEP being implemented as written, including appropriate behavior management procedures?
3. Did the disability prevent the student from understanding the impact and consequences of the behavior in question?
4. Did the disability prevent the student from controlling the behavior in question?
5. Did the school fail to properly implement the IEP?

Example: George did need a manifestation determination after he was classified, since he was considered for expulsion. The following was the manifestation determination used for him. He was also given a behavioral intervention plan.

CST Manifestation Determination 11/21/05

George Moore: Grade 11

Since there was no prior contact with the student, it is reasonable to assume on the information received through the evaluative process that:

1. The judgment of the student was impaired, and the student was unable to assess the impact and consequences of the behavior.
2. The student's disability did impair his ability to control the behavior (Jarolmen, 2005).

A Functional Behavioral Assessment

In George's case, a functional behavior assessment plan would be devised by an interdisciplinary team. The outline of the components would be as follows:

a. A description of the behavior in question
b. Review of the records

c. Checklist data/student-assisted interview

d. Team meeting

e. Develop hypothesis

f. Direct observation

g. Statement of antecedents, target behavior, consequences

h. Functional assessment observation form

i. Reinforcers for intervention

j. Examine behavior in the environmental context

k. Statement that hypotheses have been tested through experimentation (Weber & Killu, 2005).

Behavioral Intervention Plan

If a functional behavior assessment finds a need, then a behavioral intervention plan is developed by the team. This plan becomes necessary when discipline is in question. It focuses on specific behaviors that are being evaluated. It should contain measurable goals and outcomes. Methods for developing positive behaviors and discipline employed to curtail negative behaviors should be explained. Parental input is important in this plan as well as the child's agreement to the particulars of the plan (Constable, Massat, McDonald, & Flynn, 2006).

"These are some important things . . . to consider when the intervention plan is created:

- The plan should be created with input from all people that the child works with, so that they can agree on expectations as well as rewards or consequences.
- A plan should specifically define behaviors and consequences, but should still be adaptable to different places: the classroom, the playground, music class, daycare, etc. Consistency will help the child learn what is expected of them.
- The plan should focus on positive supports, such as rewards before resorting to consequences or punishments, and should focus on using positive skills that a child already has to help them shape alternative behaviors.
- It might be necessary to make changes in the child's academic program, or they may need some support that will help them learn a different behavior.
- A plan might need to include some kind of change in the physical setting, such as where the child sits and does work.
- A plan's effectiveness can be affected by student absences due to illness, suspension, or expulsion.

- A Behavior Intervention Plan [BIP] should be evaluated to make sure that it is being followed, and to make sure that it is working effectively. A BIP should be reviewed at least annually, but can be reviewed whenever any member [of the team] feels that a review is necessary. A BIP might be reviewed when:
  - A student has reached his or her goals and objectives and new goals and objectives need to be decided on
  - The child's situation has changed, and the BIP doesn't address the child's most current needs
  - There is a change in placement; or
  - It is clear that the original BIP is not producing positive changes in the child's behavior" (http://www.mpf.org/SPIN/FAQ%20Sheets/BehInterPlans.html).

Positive Behavior Intervention and Support is an area mandated by IDEA. Its purpose is to have social workers and teachers reach both the special and general education students. The function of this procedure is to define, teach, and support positive models of student behavior. It is used as a preventative measure to avoid disciplinary problems and to be proactive in the development of appropriate models of behavior. Both social workers and teachers are mentioned as professionals in IDEA to carry out this function (Constable, Massat, McDonald, & Flynn, 2006).

The Individual Educational Program

The following is an example (these vary by state and local schools) of components and necessary questions to be examined in an Individual Education Program.

ANNOTATED INDIVIDUALIZED EDUCATION PROGRAM (IEP) FORMAT

Charter Format

IEP Team Meeting Date: ________________________

IEP Implementation Date (Projected Date when Services and Programs Will Begin): ____/____/____ Mo Day Yr

Anticipated Duration of Services and Programs: ____/____/____ Mo Day Yr

Annotation: Dates

IEP Implementation Date (Projected Date when Services and Programs Will Begin)
The IEP shall be implemented as soon as possible after its completion.

Anticipated Duration of Services and Programs:
Indicate the last day that the student will receive services and programs of this IEP. This date must not be more than 1 year. If the IEP implementation date is 12/14/03, the anticipated duration date must be no later than 12/13/04.

Student Name: ______________________________ DOB: ______________
Age: ____
Grade: ____________ Anticipated Year of Graduation: ______________
Charter School: ____
Parent Name: ____
Address: ____
Phone: (H) ____
(W) ____
District of Residence: ______________________________ Other Information:
County of Residence: ____

Annotation: Demographic Information

Complete the items included above. Additional information that the school has found to be useful may also be included. For example, if a language other than English is spoken in the home, it could be included under **Other Information**. If there is nothing to include in this space write "none."

IEP TEAM/SIGNATURES*

The Individualized Education Program (IEP) Team makes the decisions about the student's program and placement. The student's parent(s), the student's regular teacher and a representative from the local education agency are required members of this team. A regular education teacher must also be included if the student participates, or may be participating in regular education. Signature on this IEP documents attendance, not agreement.

NAME (typed or printed) **POSITION** (typed or printed) **SIGNATURE**

Parent

Parent

Student*

Regular Education Teacher

Special Education Teacher

Charter Representative (Chair)

Community Agency Rep.**

Vocational Teacher (if appropriate)

Individualize

* The IEP team must invite the student if transition services are being planned or if the parents choose to have the student participate.
** As determined by the school as needed for transition services.

Annotation: IEP Team/Signatures

The section is used to document the attendance of the IEP members who are present at the IEP meeting.

The IEP team meets, discusses options, and makes decisions concerning what will constitute an educationally appropriate individual education program for the student, and develops an IEP. This section should be completed at the beginning of the meeting.

Annotation: Members of the IEP Team

The composition of the IEP team is key in determining the appropriateness of the IEP. The additional requirements added by the Individuals with Disabilities Education Act (IDEA '97) reflect the shift in focus of these amendments to the regular education curriculum.

Consistent with previous requirements, a single member of the IEP team may meet two or more of the qualifications, but the IEP team may not consist of fewer than two people in addition to the parent(s).

Each IEP team shall include individuals who meet the following qualifications:

- One or both of the student's parents.
- The student, if the purpose of the meeting is to consider transition service needs, or if the parent chooses to have the student participate.
- At least one special education teacher for the child.
- At least one regular education teacher if the student does or may participate in the regular education environment.

(Continued)

(Continued)

- A charter representative other than the student's teacher who:
  - is qualified to provide or supervise special education,
  - is knowledgeable about the general curriculum, and
  - is knowledgeable about the availability of the resources of the charter school.
- For a secondary level transition age student, other public agencies who are likely to be responsible for providing or paying for transition services, including representatives of career technical programs, shall be invited.
  - An individual who can interpret the instructional implications of the evaluation results.
  - Other individuals at the discretion of the parent or agency who have an interest in the student and have knowledge or special expertise regarding the student.

PROCEDURAL SAFEGUARDS NOTICE

I have received a copy of the Procedural Safeguards Notice. The school has informed me whom I may contact if I need more information.
Signature: ______________________________ Date Received: _________________

Annotation: Procedural Safeguards Notice

Prior to the IEP meeting, parents receive the *Procedural Safeguards Notice* with *Permission to Evaluate, Permission to Reevaluate* and the *Invitation to IEP Meeting*. This section is included to provide documentation that the parent has been provided with the necessary notice required by law. The parent(s) must sign and indicate the date acknowledging receipt and knowing whom to contact.

I. SPECIAL CONSIDERATIONS THE IEP TEAM MUST CONSIDER BEFORE DEVELOPING THE IEP. ANY FACTORS CHECKED MUST BE ADDRESSED IN THE IEP.

Is the Student Blind or Visually Impaired?

_____ No

_____ Yes—Team must provide for instruction in Braille and the use of Braille unless the IEP Team determines, after an evaluation of the child's reading and writing skills, needs, and appropriate reading and writing media (including an evaluation of the child's future needs for instruction in Braille or the use of Braille), that instruction in Braille or the use of Braille is not appropriate.

Annotation: Is the Student Blind or Visually Impaired?

The IEP team must provide Braille and Braille instruction to any student who is identified as having visual impairment unless the team determines that Braille is not appropriate for the student. This provision was new to IDEA '97 in that it required the IEP team to provide information on why Braille should not be taught to a student with visual impairment.

A learning media assessment is one way to come to this decision. The IEP team could then incorporate the results of the learning media assessment into the IEP, documenting the student's present need for Braille and the likelihood of future need.

The learning media assessment is part of the functional vision assessment and uses a variety of indicators in assisting the team to determine which methods of reading and writing will be appropriate for the student with visual impairments both now and in the future. The learning media assessment includes (a) clinical information, which documents medical information about the student's medical condition and visual prognosis; (b) a functional vision assessment, which assesses the student's use of vision; (c) assessments of the student's ability to read, write, and compute; and (d) indicates the student's use of sensory channels to acquire information.

The IEP team should adopt a systematic method of documenting this information for all students with visual impairments, including children with multiple disabilities, when visual impairment is present.

QUESTIONS IEP TEAM MIGHT ASK:

- Is there a pattern of reliance on vision, touch, or other senses to gather information?
- Is the student able to read his or her own handwriting?
- Does the student have a portable method of reading and writing?
- Is the student's academic progress impeded by the current method of reading?
- Is there a prognosis for continued vision loss or is the vision stable?

Is the Student Deaf or Hearing Impaired?

_____ No

_____ Yes—Team must consider the child's language and communication needs, opportunities for direct communications with peers and professional personnel in the child's language and communication mode, academic level, and full range of needs, including opportunities for direct instruction in the child's language and communication mode in the development of the IEP.

(Continued)

(Continued)

Annotation: Is the Student Deaf or Hearing Impaired?

For students who are deaf or hard of hearing, considerations must be made considering the communication and language needs of the student and the student's opportunities for direct interaction with peers and educational personnel in the student's own language and communication mode. Opportunities for direct interaction (without the need for an interpreter) in the student's own language and communication mode must also be considered. All students who use manual communication (American Sign Language, Manually Coded English, or Total Communication) as their primary method of communication should be given consideration for placement into a classroom or program in which the teacher, other students, and the ancillary support services providers understand and use the appropriate form of nonverbal communication.

QUESTIONS IEP TEAM MIGHT ASK:

- What is the student's typical mode of communication?
- Is an interpreter or transliterator needed for the student to participate in and benefit from classroom instruction and/or social interaction?
- What opportunities exist to foster communication with the general population?
- What opportunities exist for direct instruction (without interpreter support) in the student's language and communication mode?
- Does the student require assistive devices to assist in the development and use of meaningful language used in direct instruction?
- What other considerations (e.g., mode of communication used at home) should be addressed?

____ COMMUNICATION NEEDS

Annotation: Does the Student Have Communication Needs?

The team must give special consideration to the communication and language needs of the student. This is determined by observations of daily interactions with a variety of communication partners (professionals and peers) in a variety of settings. Consideration should also be given to the mode(s) of communication used by the student to receive information and/or provide information (communicate) to others. Family input is critical to comprehensive communication considerations.

QUESTIONS IEP TEAM MIGHT ASK:

- What is the student's typical mode of communication?
- What opportunities exist to foster communication with the general population?

- Does the student's communication skills impact on learning?
- Does the student require assistive devices to assist in the development and use of meaningful language used in direct instruction?
- What other considerations (e.g., mode of communication used at home) should be addressed?

____ ASSISTIVE TECHNOLOGY, Devices and/or Services

Annotation: Does the Student Require Assistive Technology Devices and/or Services?

Assistive technology device means any item, piece of equipment, or product system whether acquired commercially off the shelf, modified, or customized that is used to increase, maintain, or improve the functional capabilities of a child with a disability. *Assistive technology service* means any service that directly assists a child with a disability in the selection, acquisition, or use of a device. This includes any special equipment or technology that students may need to help them participate in school including state- and schoolwide assessment and the services required for assessment and implementation of these devices.

QUESTIONS IEP TEAM MIGHT ASK:

- Does the student need assistive technology
  - to be in the least restrictive environment?
  - to access the general curriculum?
  - to participate in activities?
  - to access educational and print materials?
  - to access auditory information?
  - for written communication and computer access?
  - for augmentative communication?
  - to participate in state- and schoolwide assessments?

____ LIMITED ENGLISH PROFICENCY

Annotation: Does the Student Have Limited English Proficiency?

Consideration of the language needs of all special education students with limited English proficiency (LEP) must be given "as such needs relate to the student's IEP."

QUESTIONS IEP TEAM MIGHT ASK:

- Has the student been assessed in the native language?
- Is the disability present in the native language?
- What was the first language the student learned to speak?
- What language does the student speak most often at home? With friends? With neighbors?

(Continued)

(Continued)

- What language(s) is spoken most often in the home?
- Was the ESL/Bilingual/Migrant teacher a member of the IEP team?
- How will the team determine how to assess the progress in the general education curriculum?
- How will services be coordinated (i.e., special education and ESL)?
- What accommodations for LEP are necessary for instruction and participation in the PSSA/PASA (Pennsylvania System of School Assessments and Pennsylvania Alternative System of Assessments)?
- What language or mode of communication will be used to address parents or family members?

____ BEHAVIORS THAT IMPEDE HIS OR HER LEARNING OR THAT OF OTHERS

Annotation: Does the Student Exhibit Behaviors that Impede His or Her Learning or That of Others?

For a student whose behavior impedes his or her learning or that of others, the IEP team shall consider strategies and supports, including positive behavior interventions, to address that behavior.

QUESTIONS IEP TEAM MIGHT ASK:

- Does the student's challenging behavior persist despite implementation of informal behavior change strategies?
- Do assessment results indicate that deficits in communication and/or academic skills contribute to challenging behaviors?
- Has the student lost access to instructional time because of in-school disciplinary referrals and/or suspension from school?
- Has the student's behavior contributed to consideration for a more restrictive placement?

____ TRANSITION SERVICES

Annotation: Transition Services

Beginning at age 14 (or younger if deemed appropriate by the IEP team), a statement of the transition service needs of the student must be written as part of the IEP. This means that the IEP team must address the student's course of study (such as participation in advanced-placement courses or a vocational education program). Beginning at age 16 (or younger if deemed appropriate by the IEP team), a statement of needed transition services for the student including, if appropriate, a statement of the interagency responsibilities or any needed linkages must be developed. This is the part of the IEP labeled Transition Planning (see section VII).

It is recommended that the postschool outcomes be developed prior to determining course of study and developing goals and objectives.

____ OTHER

(Specify)____

Annotation: Other

The IEP team should address whether there are any other considerations to take into account when developing an IEP for a student with a disability. For example, for students who turn 18 during the term of this IEP, the team could address voter registration as required as part of the IEP process.

II. PRESENT LEVELS OF EDUCATIONAL PERFORMANCE

HOW THE STUDENT'S DISABILITY AFFECTS INVOLVEMENT AND PROGRESS IN GENERAL EDUCATION CURRICULUM (Include the child's strengths and needs that will affect the student's involvement and progress in the general curriculum.):

Annotation: II. Present Levels of Educational Performance

This section includes a statement of the student's present levels of educational performance, the student's strengths and needs, and how the student's disability affects the student's involvement and progress in the general curriculum. This information should come directly from assessment results.

Student's Present Levels of Educational Performance

This section should provide a snapshot of the student's performance in his or her current educational program and indicate the student's instructional level. The information should be stated in clear, objective, concrete terminology. The method for determining the instructional level should relate to the day-to-day instruction and include a description of the student in all relevant areas and subjects. If the student is currently in special education, information about the student's progress on his or her IEP should be included. If the student has limited English proficiency, a statement of native language performance and of English proficiency level should be included here. All information contained in this section should support the rest of the IEP. The information should be related to recommendations from the Evaluation Report and/or assessment results. If the student is 14 years old or older, this section must be related to the student's postschool outcomes.

How the Student's Disability Affects Involvement and Progress in the General Education Curriculum (including strengths and needs)

This section also includes statements as to how the student is doing regarding his progress in the general education curriculum, and how he interacts with the curriculum in many locations throughout the school. The information should be clear enough to support the continuation, elimination or need for services included in the student's IEP. The IEP team must determine how the student will be involved in and make progress in the regular education curriculum. This determination should be based on assessments that have been made directly in the general education curriculum and programs, and is then reflected in the IEP statement of the student's present levels of educational performance.

This determination will drive the development of the remainder of the IEP.

Also included in this section is a description or listing of what the student does relatively well. This area should address skills and knowledge that the student demonstrates in relevant areas and subjects. Include information about procedures and instructional practices found to be successful in educating the student. For a student who is transition age, include information about the student's interests and preferences.

Individualized Education Program

Include information about the needs the student is experiencing. The needs that are identified must be addressed in the rest of the IEP. This information should support any services included in the IEP.

III. GOALS AND OBJECTIVES: (*Use as many copies of this page as needed to plan appropriately.*)

MEASURABLE EVAL GOAL:

Annotation: III. Goals and Objectives: (Use as many copies of this page as needed to plan appropriately for the student.)

MEASURABLE ANNUAL GOAL(S)

Annual goals are statements in measurable terms that describe what reasonable expectations can be accomplished within a 12-month period. In order for a goal to be measurable, the team must be able to answer the following two questions: What do you want the student to do? How well? There must be a direct relationship between the annual goals and the present levels of performance. The team should not include annual goals that relate to areas of the general curriculum in which the student's disability does not affect the ability to be involved in and progress in the general curriculum.

SHORT-TERM OBJECTIVE/BENCHMARK

EXPECTED LEVEL OF ACHIEVEMENT

METHOD OF EVALUATION

Annotation: Short-Term Instructional Objectives/Benchmarks

Once the IEP team has developed measurable annual goals, the team must develop short-term objectives/benchmarks which serve as a plan for reaching annual goals and a means for measuring progress toward meeting the annual goals. They provide a mechanism for determining whether the student is progressing during the year, to ensure that the IEP is consistent with the student's instructional needs, and if appropriate, to revise the IEP. The team must indicate the expected level of achievement. This may be indicated by a percentage score, number of correct responses, and so on. The method of evaluation must also be indicated on the IEP. List the specific ways in which achievement will be measured and documented.

Note: Specially designed instruction may be listed with each goal/objective and/or listed in Section IV.

REPORT OF PROGRESS ON ANNUAL GOALS

How goals will be measured: ____

How progress will be reported: ______________________________________

1ST

2ND

3RD

4TH

OTHER, IF APPLICABLE

Annotation: Report of Progress on Annual Goals (Include schedule and method of reporting to parents.)

Under the reauthorization of the IDEA, a regular, periodic reporting process at least equal in frequency to traditional report cards issued to regular education students must be described.

(Continued)

(Continued)

How Goals Will Be Measured

The IEP team must decide how the Annual goals will be measured. Progress can be measured by looking at the individual short-term objectives or through some other independent measure. This measurement can be done through formal or informal assessment tools such as rubrics, teacher observation, student self-monitoring, teacher-made tests, chapter tests from textbooks, checklists, inventories, and teacher probes. This will be determined by the IEP team. Progress monitoring is linked to the day-to-day instructional and assessment process. Progress monitoring means that both special and regular education teachers of students with disabilities should assess students as often as students without IEPs.

How Progress Will Be Reported

Next, the IEP team must decide how the progress on those annual goals will be reported to parents. As stated above, this reporting must be done as often as progress for students who are not disabled. Progress can be reported through (a) report cards, (b) addenda to report cards, (c) special progress reporting instruments, (d) by duplicating the goals and objectives page of the IEP to send home to parents, (e) through documented phone conferences with parents, or (f) other means the IEP team decides.

Using the IEP Grid to Report Progress

The IEP grid is to be completed as a progress monitoring device. It is not to be completed when the IEP is being developed. It may be helpful to write the date for when progress will be reported. When using the grid above to report progress, information (via grades, comments, rubrics, etc.) may be written into boxes on this grid each marking period. Then this page, containing the IEP goals and objectives, can be duplicated and sent home to the parents as the progress reporting instrument. If the team has determined that the progress reporting will be done via scheduled phone conferences with the parent(s), the grid provides a place for that documentation.

Note: Specially designed instruction may be listed with each goal and objective and/or listed in Section IV.

IV. SPECIAL EDUCATION AND RELATED SERVICES:

Annotation: IV Special Education and Related Services

The IEP must include a statement of the special education and related services and supplementary aids and services to be provided to the student or on behalf of the student. In addition, a statement of program modifications or supports for school personnel will be provided to the student to:

- ☐ advance appropriately toward attaining the annual goals;
- ☐ be involved and progress in the general education curriculum and Individualized Education Program (*Revised December 18, 2003 Page 9 of 19*)
- ☐ be educated and participate with other children with disabilities and nondisabled children in the activities described in the previous sections.

A. PROGRAM MODIFICATIONS AND SPECIALLY DESIGNED INSTRUCTION: (*Specially designed instruction may be listed with each goal and objective.*)

Annotation: A. Program Modifications and Specially Designed Instruction

Special education means specially designed instruction, at no cost to the parents, to meet the unique needs of a child with a disability. *Specially designed instruction* means adapting, as appropriate, the content, methodology, or delivery of instruction to address the unique needs of the child that result from the child's disability and to ensure access of the child to the general education curriculum so that he or she can meet the educational standards. For each program modification and/or specially designed instruction (SDI), the team must indicate the location and the frequency of the service to be provided. *Location* refers to where the student will be receiving the service. *Frequency* refers to how often the student will be receiving the program modification and/or specially designed instruction. The projected beginning date and the anticipated duration of the service must be listed if they are different from the beginning and duration dates on page 1 of this IEP. *Duration* refers to the anticipated ending date for service. It is important that the IEP team develop specially designed instruction from the assessment information for a particular student in consideration of the student's specific needs and the Pennsylvania academic standards.

Example:

Modifications & SDI Location Projected

Beginning Date

Frequency Anticipated

Duration

Self-monitoring checklist Regular class All reg. Classes

(*Continued*)

(Continued)

Adapted science materials Regular class 1-10-04 5 times per week

Direct instruction reading program Special class 10 periods per week

Digitized communications device across all environments

throughout the school day

B. RELATED SERVICES: List the services that the student needs in order to benefit from or access his or her special education program:

Projected Anticipated**

Service Location Beginning Date Frequency Duration

**Include only if differs from IEP beginning and/or duration dates.*

Annotation: B. Related Services (including supplementary aids and services)

Related services (including supplementary aids and services) refer to transportation and any developmental, corrective or other supportive service needed to assist a student with a disability to benefit from special education.

Examples of related services include (a) medical services for diagnosis or evaluation purposes, (b) early identification and assessment of disabilities in children, (c) speech/language pathology, (d) physical and occupational therapy, (e) audiological services, (f) social work services in schools, (g) psychological services and orientation, (h) job coaching, (i) mobility services, (j) school health services, (k) parent counseling and training, (l) recreation, (m) counseling services, (n) and rehabilitation counseling services. There could never be a complete listing of possible related services, since related services must be developed on an individual student basis.

If the IEP team determines that a student has an educational need for a service in order to benefit from education, then it must be provided. For each service, the team must list the location and the frequency of the service to be provided. *Location* refers to where the student will be receiving the service. *Frequency* refers to how often the student will be receiving the related service.

The projected beginning date and the anticipated duration of the service must be listed if they are different from the beginning and duration dates on page 1 of this IEP. *Duration* refers to the anticipated ending date for service.

Example:

Projected Anticipated**

Service Location Beginning Date Frequency Duration

Speech and Language Therapy Classroom 11/1/03 1 hour per week 4/1/04

(Programming synthesized 30-minute individual communication device)

C. SUPPORTS FOR THE CHILD PROVIDED FOR SCHOOL PERSONNEL:

____

____

____

____

Annotation: C. Supports for the Child Provided for School Personnel

If school personnel who provide support to a student with a disability, such as regular educators, need supports to implement the IEP, they must be described in this section. This section provides an opportunity for the team to discuss and articulate what specific supports or training are necessary for school personnel to provide FAPE. This could include any aids, resource materials, training or equipment. For each support, the team must list the location and the frequency of the support to be provided. *Location* refers to where the student will be receiving the support. *Frequency* refers to how often the student will be receiving the support.

The projected beginning date and the anticipated duration of the support must be listed if they are different from the beginning and duration dates on page 1 of this IEP. Duration refers to the anticipated ending date for support.

Example:

Projected Anticipated**

Support Location Beginning Date Frequency Duration

Teacher of students with classrooms weekly visual impairment and/or orientation and mobility specialist will consult with regular education teacher regarding

(Continued)

(Continued)

instructional ______________________________

and environmental adaptations ______________________________

and accommodations ______________________________

EXTENDED SCHOOL YEAR: The IEP Team has considered and discussed ESY services and determined that:

____

____

Annotation: D. Extended School Year

The IEP Team has considered and discussed ESY services and determined that (a) the ESY MUST be considered for all students with disabilities; (b) the IEP team shall determine eligibility for ESY services; and (c) if there is a need for such services, the team must determine the services to be provided.

The IEP team must indicate whether the student is eligible or is not eligible for ESY and the basis for the determination. This determination must be made even if the child's parents have not specifically requested that their child be evaluated for ESY programming.

In considering whether a student is eligible for ESY services, the IEP team shall consider the following factors, however, no single factor will be considered determinative:

- ☐ Regression—whether the student reverts to a lower level of functioning as evidenced by a measurable decrease in skills or behaviors that occur as a result of an interruption in educational programming.
- ☐ Recoupment—whether the student has the capacity to recover the skills or behavior patterns in which regression occurred to a level demonstrated prior to the interruption of educational programming.
- ☐ Whether the student's difficulties with regression and recoupment make it unlikely that the student will maintain the skills and behaviors relevant to the IEP goals and objectives.
- ☐ The extent to which the student has mastered and consolidated an important skill or behavior at the point when educational programming would be interrupted.
- ☐ The extent to which a skill or behavior is particularly crucial for the student to meet the IEP goals of self-sufficiency and independence from caretakers.

- ☐ The extent to which successive interruptions in educational programming result in a student's withdrawal from the learning process.
- ☐ Whether the student's disability is severe, such as autism or pervasive developmental disorder, serious emotional disturbance, severe intellectual disability, degenerative impairments with mental involvement, and severe multiple disabilities.

The determination of eligibility must be based on the above factors, as well as reliable sources of information regarding a student's educational needs, propensity to progress, recoupment potential, and year-to-year progress may include the following:

- ☐ Progress on goals in consecutive IEPs.
- ☐ Progress reports maintained by educators, therapists, and others having direct contact with the student before and after interruptions in the education program.
- ☐ Reports by parents of negative changes in adaptive behaviors or in other skill areas.
- ☐ Medical or other agency reports indicating degenerative-type difficulties, which become exacerbated during breaks in educational services.
- ☐ Observations and opinions by educators, parents, and others.
- ☐ Results of tests including criterion-referenced tests, curriculum-based assessments, ecological life skills assessments, and other equivalent measures.

The need for ESY services will not be based on any of the following:

- ☐ The desire or need for day care or respite care services.
- ☐ The desire or need for a summer recreation program.
- ☐ The desire or need for other programs or services which, while they may provide educational benefit, are not required to ensure the provision of a free appropriate public education.

ESY should not be confused with meeting all goals. Some personnel and parents think that if all goals are not met during the year, ESY is provided to meet the objectives listed. This is incorrect. The annual goals are predictions of where the child will be based on current performance. With appropriate data collection and progress monitoring, parents will be

(Continued)

(Continued)

aware of student's performance. If the prediction was incorrect, the data collection procedures will provide the information necessary to review and revise the IEP.

When ESY services are offered, the IEP must contain a description of the type and amount of ESY service, the projected beginning dates, anticipated duration of service, and the frequency and location of the service. *Location* refers to where the student will be receiving the service. *Frequency* refers to how often the student will be receiving the service.

Example:

The IEP team has determined that the student is eligible for ESY services. This determination was based on progress reports by the occupational therapist indicating that following extended breaks in service, the student's manipulation skills deteriorated significantly.

Projected Anticipated**

Support Location Beginning Date Frequency Duration

Special Education teacher Home 7-5-04 Daily 8/26/04

30-minute session ________________

V. PARTICIPATION IN STATE- AND SCHOOLWIDE ASSESSMENTS

STUDENT PARTICIPATION—STATE ASSESSMENTS

This section applies to student's age and/or grade eligible for the PSSA/PASA

(Reading, Math—grades 5, 8, 11; Writing—grades 6, 9, 11)

_____ Student will participate in the PSSA without accommodations.

OR

_____ Student will participate in the PSSA with the following accommodations:

PSSA Reading (grades 5, 8, 11) ____

PSSA Math (grades 5, 8, 11) ____

PSSA Writing (grades 6, 9, 11) ____

OR

_____ Student will participate in the Pennsylvania Alternate System of Assessment (PASA).

(Effective beginning the 2000-01 school year; the alternate assessment in Pennsylvania is PASA).

If the IEP team has determined that it is not appropriate for the student to participate in the PSSA, the team must explain why the PSSA is not appropriate:

____

____

Choose how the student's performance on the PASA will be documented:

_____Videotape (which is kept confidential as all other school records)

_____Written Narrative (which is kept confidential as all other school records)

STUDENT PARTICIPATION—SCHOOLWIDE ASSESSMENTS

Individualized Education Program

_____ Student will participate in the school assessments without accommodations.

OR

_____ Student will participate in the school assessments with the following accommodations:

____

____

____

OR

_____ If the IEP team has determined that it is not appropriate for the student to participate in the schoolwide assessment, they must explain why the assessment is not appropriate for the student and how the student will be assessed.

____

____

Annotation: V. Participation in State- and Schoolwide Assessments

It is required that all students participate in state- and schoolwide assessments. The IEP team must make several decisions about the student's participation in state- and schoolwide assessments. The team must first determine if the student can participate

(Continued)

(Continued)

with no accommodations needed in the assessment. If the answer to this question is "yes," then the student will participate in the assessment without accommodations.

The team may decide that the assessment is appropriate for the student to take but that certain accommodations that are used in the classroom during instruction and/or assessment are needed. These accommodations must be listed on the IEP. These accommodations must be allowable for the assessment and should not be something that would give the student an unfair advantage.

The third choice that the team may make is that the student is unable to take the assessment even with accommodations. If this is the decision made, then the reason for this decision must be indicated on the IEP. In addition, an alternate assessment must be indicated—for the statewide assessment, the PSSA; the alternate must be the state alternate assessment, PASA. For a schoolwide assessment, the team must indicate how the student will be assessed.

VI. LEAST RESTRICTIVE ENVIRONMENT

EDUCATIONAL PLACEMENT

Annotation: Educational Placement

IDEA regulations require that the Local Education Agency (LEA) ensure that a continuum of alternative placements is available to meet the needs of children with disabilities for special education and related services. The continuum must include instruction in regular classes, special classes, special schools, home instruction, and instruction in hospitals and institutions. In addition, the continuum must make provisions for supplementary services (such as resource room or itinerant instruction) to be provided in conjunction with regular class placement. The number of hours per week that the student receives special education services must be specified.

Examples:

Part-time Emotional Support 15 hours per week

Resource Learning Support 5 hours per week

Itinerant Speech & Language Support three-quarter hours per week

Explanation of the extent, if any, the student *will not participate* with nondisabled children in the regular class and in the general education curriculum:

Annotation: Explanation of the Extent, If Any, the Student Will Not Participate With Nondisabled Children in the Regular Class and in the General Education Curriculum

The IEP must include an explanation and a description of those activities, if any, where the student will not participate with nondisabled children within the regular education class and school activities.

These required IEP statements should be based on current assessments and evaluations that have been performed with full consideration of the least restrictive environment (LRE) intent, including the provision of the full range of supplemental aids and services within the regular education curriculum. It is the responsibility of each public agency to ensure that to the maximum extent appropriate students with disabilities, including those in public or private institutions or other care facilities, are educated with children who are not disabled. Special classes, separate schooling, or other removal of children with disabilities from the regular educational environment occurs only when the nature or severity of the disability is such that education in regular classes, even with the use of supplementary aids and services, cannot be achieved satisfactorily.

Percentage of time the student receives special education outside of the regular education classroom:

_____ Less than 21% outside of the regular education classroom

_____ 21–60% outside of the regular education classroom

_____ 61% or more outside of the regular education classroom

Annotation: Percentages of time the student receives special education outside the regular education classroom

This section applies to students with disabilities receiving special education outside their regular education classroom in regular schools with nondisabled students.

Indicate which of the three categories best represents the percentage of time the student receives special education outside the regular classroom.

Location of Program: ____

Annotation: Location of Program

The information on location of program as well the percentage of time the student receives special education outside of the regular education classroom should be listed on Penn Data.

(Continued)

(Continued)

If the student is receiving special education in a regular building with nondisabled peers (a) indicate the amount of time in the previous section, and (b) write the name of the school here.

If the student is receiving special education in one of the following locations: (a) Write "N/A" in the previous section (percentages), and (b) indicate the name of the "facility" or "hospital," or write "instruction conducted in the student's home."

- Public Separate Facility (NonrResidential), e.g., Special education center
- Private Separate Facility (Nonresidential), e.g., Day student in an APS
- Public Residential Facility, e.g., State operated residential facility
- Private Residential Facility, e.g., Residential student in an APS
- Hospital, e.g., Long-term admissions
- Correctional Facility, e.g., Students receiving services while incarcerated
- Out-of-State Facility
- Instruction in the Home, e.g., IEP Team placements

VII. TRANSITION PLANNING

Annotation: VII. Transition Planning

Transition services means a coordinated set of activities for a student with a disability that are designed within an outcome-oriented process that promotes movement from school to postschool activities, including postsecondary education, vocational training, integrated employment (including supported employment), continuing and adult education, adult services, independent living, or community participation. Services must be based on the individual student's needs, taking into account the student's preferences and interests.

1. Will the student be 14 years of age or older during the term of this IEP?

   _____ No (Not necessary to complete this section)

   _____ Yes—Team must address the student's courses of study and how the course of study applies to components of the IEP.

Student's courses of study:

____

____

Annotation: Will the student be 14 years of age or older during the term of this IEP?

The IEP must include a statement of the transition service needs focusing on the student's courses of study (such as participation in academic or advanced-placement courses, a vocational education program, daily living skills, or preparation for employment).

2. Will the student be 16 years of age or older during the term of this IEP or is the student younger and in need of transition services as determined by the IEP team?

   _______ No (Not necessary to complete this Section)

   _______Yes—Team must address and complete this Section

Annotation: Will the student be 16 years of age or older within the duration of this IEP or is the student younger and in need of transition services as determined by the IEP team?

For each student beginning at age 16 (or younger, if determined appropriate by the IEP team), a statement of needed transition services, and if appropriate, a statement of the interagency responsibilities or any needed linkages must be included.

DESIRED POSTSCHOOL OUTCOMES: Define and project the desired postschool outcomes as identified by the student, parent, and IEP team in the following areas. State how the services will be provided and person(s) responsible for coordinating these services.

SERVICE HOW SERVICE IS PROVIDED

PERSON RESPONSIBLE

Post-secondary Education/Training

Employment

Community Living

a) Residential

b) Participation

c) Recreation/Leisure

(Continued)

(Continued)

Annotation: DESIRED POSTSCHOOL OUTCOMES

Transition should be an outcome oriented process. Desired postschool outcomes are a required part of the IEP. These outcomes should guide the IEP process and the student's educational program. As the IEP team determines the needed services to meet the outcomes, it must indicate where those services will be provided. Also, the term must specify the frequency and duration of the services if they differ from those listed on page 1 of this IEP.

1. In the first column labeled "Service," the IEP team must address the outcome areas and indicate the services needed by the student based on his or her needs, interests, and preferences. The IEP team must list activities and services for the coming year to support the outcome. These services and activities may include instruction and related services, community experiences, acquisition of daily living skills, functional vocational evaluation, or adult living. If the student plans to attend community college after graduation, possible responses for this column may include visiting campuses, orientation to the campuses, applying to the colleges, and so on. The following questions may help guide services.

QUESTIONS IEP TEAM MIGHT ASK:

Postsecondary Education/Training

- ☐ Does the student want or need postsecondary or training programs?
- ☐ What subject major is the student interested in studying to prepare for future employment?
- ☐ Can the student express his or her need for support services and accommodations if needed?
- ☐ What type of accommodations will the student need in a postsecondary setting?
- ☐ Does the student need assistance in selecting an institution and/or filing applications and financial aid forms?
- ☐ Does the student need assistance from an adult agency to attend a postsecondary institution?

Employment

- ☐ Does the student have a realistic career and/or employment goal?

- ☐ What does the student like to do?
- ☐ What types of employment options are feasible for the student?
- ☐ What types of accommodations will the student need on employment sites?
- ☐ Does the student relate skills or interests to jobs?
- ☐ What types of skills does the student need to acquire or learn to meet the career goal?
- ☐ What types of job benefits does the student need to become an independent member of society?
- ☐ Does the student have job-seeking skills?
- ☐ Does the student need assistance from an adult service provider to find and maintain a job?

Community Living

- ☐ Can the student prepare a grocery list and shop for groceries?
- ☐ Is the student able to prepare meals?
- ☐ Can the student prepare a monthly budget?
- ☐ Does the student know how to pay bills?
- ☐ What public transportation is the student able to use in the community?
- ☐ Does the student have a driver's license?
- ☐ Does the student need special travel arrangements made on an ongoing basis?
- ☐ What recreation or leisure activities does the student enjoy?
- ☐ What accommodations does the student need to participate in leisure activities?
- ☐ Does the student know how to find recreation/leisure services in the community?
- ☐ Can the student locate and use community services such as stores, banks, and medical facilities?
- ☐ Does the student participate in the political process?
- ☐ Is the student knowledgeable about the law? Does the student observe the law?

(Continued)

(Continued)

2. In the second column, labeled "How Service is Provided," the IEP Team will determine the frequency and location of the services to be provided. Possible responses include helping the student arrange visits to selected colleges and completing applications. The team must also indicate the projected beginning date and anticipated duration if they differ from the dates on page 1 of this IEP.

3. In the third column, the IEP team must decide who will be responsible for overseeing the services and activities that have been listed. This person should be designated by job title or position rather than by name. This column might list the guidance counselor as the person responsible.

After completing the grid, the IEP team should review the present levels of performance and develop goals and objectives to work toward attaining the outcomes.

STATEMENT OF COORDINATED TRANSITIONAL SERVICES AND ACTIVITIES NEEDED TO SUPPORT DESIRED POSTSCHOOL OUTCOMES: (Instructional areas should support the desired postschool outcomes for the student. Examples such as Instruction and Related Services, Community Experiences, Acquisition of Daily Living Skills, Functional Vocational Evaluation, and Adult Living may appear as annual goals, short-term instructional objectives/benchmarks, and/or specially designed instruction, based on the student's needs.)

____

____

____

Annotation: Statement of Coordinated Transitional Services and Activities Needed to Support Desired Postschool Outcomes

The statement of *long-term*, integrated activities and services that are needed to help the student progress to reach his or her postschool outcomes. This section is for looking ahead at future services or needs of the student. An example may be: Activities for selecting a college and program will be reviewed with the student prior to senior year. The student will visit campuses and contact college personnel to find out about student supports that are available.

LINKAGES

List the agencies that may provide services and/or support (before the student leaves the school setting):

Agency Name Phone Number

Responsibilities/Linkages

Annotation: Linkages

Collaboration and linkages with community agencies are important when the student and his or her IEP team is planning for and implementing postsecondary transition. IEP teams must: (a) identify the appropriate and necessary community agencies, (b) invite their participation as active members of the transition IEP team, and (c) monitor the fulfillment of community agency commitments made as a part of the transition IEP planning process.

The intent is to:

- ☐ Identify any and all community agencies that can assist in ensuring the successful transition of an eligible student based on the selected outcome(s).
- ☐ Provide students and families with information regarding available community agency resources and how to access them as a part of postsecondary transition.
- ☐ Utilize the services of community agencies to enhance transition programs, services, supports, and assessments that are or will be provided by the school.

It is important that the linkages are clearly specified in the IEP and that these linkages are stated in a collaborative process. It is important for the IEP team to understand that the school is responsible to provide items specified in the IEP (Individual Education Program: Annotated Individual Education Program (IEP) Format: Charter Format, 2003).

Example: An Actual IEP from the State of New Jersey

INDIVIDUALIZED EDUCATION PROGRAM

Pleasant High School District
PVHS 236 Pleasant Avenue - Ridgeway, NJ 07642
Secretary / (201)358-7081

Student Data

Student Ban, Ann	D.O.B./C.A. 3/3/89/ 16Yrs. / 1 Mo.
Classification (would be specific learning disability in new classifications) NI	Conference Date ___6/12/98_______
Case Manager Joan Jones	Classification Date 06-12-98
Guidance Counselor Bob Josephson	IEP Implementation Date
Gender Female	_9/1/98________
Parent/Guardian Liz and Bill Ban	ID Number MAHE02
Address 732 Wane Court	Type of Meeting Annual Review Native Language English
City/State/Zip Ridgewood, NJ 07675-	Lang. of Instruction English Admin. Code: Given___x_______ Date__6/12/98__
Phone (home) (201)622-0898	Prise: Given___x_______
Phone (work) ______________	Date___6/12/98________
Phone (other) ______________ School Pleasant High	Grade/Teacher 10/ Roncold Program Modified Mainstream

PARTICIPANTS

("Participants" does not signify approval of IEP)

Title	Name (printed)	Signature
LDT-C		
Psychologist		

Social Worker ______________________________

Speech/Language ______________________________

Medical ______________________________

Teacher ______________________________

Parent/Guardian ______________________________

Student ______________________________

Administrator ______________________________

Guidance Counselor ______________________________

Other ______________________________

Other ______________________________

____

CURRENT EDUCATIONAL STATUS

Ann had made a good adjustment to the high school environment. She is doing inconsistent work in the elements of biology. She is not doing well and is not following through on assignments. She needs to make up assigned labs. Her I.Q. is in the above average range. In English, Ann has strong reading skills. Her work and study habits are inconsistent. She did well on her autobiography. She is inconsistent in language and frequently comes to class without her textbook. In math, she is doing average work and participates in class, but notes and homework are poor. In history, she is failing because of poor work and study habits.

She seems to be having some social interaction. She needs to be able to accept help as she needs it. Her physical health is good.

STATEMENT OF ELIGIBILITY

The Child Study Team and other required persons met jointly with the parent(s) to develop this IEP and reconfirmed that Ann continues to be eligible for special education services and remains classified as NI.

GOALS AND OBJECTIVES

(Goals and objectives are estimates of proposed achievement. Progress will be monitored and changes recommended to ensure that the student continues to be challenged.)

Goals and Objectives for Ann Ban

Instructional Area: ORGANIZATIONAL SKILLS Level: 7–12

Goal: The student will organize self to complete homework T (15)

Progress:

1 2 Objectives: Student

- __ __ - will utilize a daily assignment pad to write down all assignments
- __ __ - will prioritize work for timely completion
- __ __ - will create schedule for work completion and revise as necessary with teacher assistance
- __ __ - will create schedule for work completion and revise as necessary without teacher assistance
- __ __ - will return completed daily homework assignments

Goals and Objectives for Ann Ban

Instructional Area: ORGANIZATIONAL SKILLS Level: 7–12

Goal: The student will resolve difficulties related to successful classroom performance (25)

Progress:

1 2 Objectives: Student

- __ __ - will attempt to solve problems independently
- __ __ - will ask teacher for help at an appropriate time

Goals and Objectives for Ann Ban

Instructional Area: AFFECTIVE Level: 7–12

Goal: The student will accept authority. T (10)

Progress:

1 2 Objectives: Student

__ __ - will follow directions provided by an authority figure
__ __ - will accept supervision from all teachers (classroom, art, music, etc.)
__ __ - will follow rules and regulations of school

Goals and Objectives for Ann Ban

Instructional Area: AFFECTIVE Level: 7–12

Goal: The student will develop a positive self-image. T (40)

Progress:

1 2 Objectives: Student

__ __ - will express knowledge of strengths and weaknesses
__ __ - will identify and express positive thoughts regarding self
__ __ - will express knowledge of one's own unique personal characteristics

(Objectives, see KEY below.)[1]

[1]KEY: A = Achieved P = Partially Achieved (% Achieved) I = Introduced, Not Achieved N = Not Introduced (1. inconsistently, 2. ongoing, 3. with prompting, 4. requires assistance, 5. with reminders, 6. emerging)

EVALUATION CRITERIA, PROCEDURES AND SCHEDULE

Completed Homework

Completed Class work

Progress Reports

Report Cards

RECOMMENDED PROGRAM

Modified mainstream

Participation in Regular and Special Education Programs

Subject	Regular	Special	Subject	Regular	Special
Language Arts			English	CPEng3	
Reading			Math	basic geom.	
Social Studies			History	US Hist 2	
Science			Foreign Lang.	Int. Span 2	
Study Skills		Study skills	Computers		
Library (Media)			Health		
Music			Art		
Physical Ed.	PE11/ Health		Related Arts		
Electives	Drawing		Electives		
Homeroom			Lunch		
half-time Vocation			Workstudy		

ANNUAL GOALS AND OBJECTIVES: The goals and objectives for regular education courses (mainstream) are contained in the Board of Education approved curriculum, which is available in the board office and local school building.

LANGUAGE TO BE USED FOR INSTRUCTION: English

LENGTH OF SCHOOL DAY/SCHOOL YEAR (Rationale for exception if appropriate):

Length of School Day:

The program for Eva will be 5 days per week for the full school year of at least 180 days.

EXTENDED ACADEMIC SCHOOL YEAR:

N/A

EXPLANATION OF WHY THE PROGRAM AND PLACEMENT IS THE LEAST RESTRICTIVE ENVIRONMENT

Ann is a youngster who is classified as neurologically impaired. She is in mainstream academic classes with organizational support from the resource center teacher in study skills. This is the least restrictive program and places Ann in a school she would attend closest to home if not disabled.

Related Special Education Services

SERVICE : Begin // End // Frequency // Duration
n/a

CURRICULAR OR INSTRUCTIONAL STRATEGIES NECESSARY FOR PARTICIPATION IN REGULAR OR SPECIAL EDUCATION

Extra time for tests and long-term assignments

Use of calculator

Spelling not counted

SPECIALIZED EQUIPMENT

Calculator

TECHNIQUES AND STRATEGIES FOR SOCIAL AND PERSONAL DEVELOPMENT

- ☐ 11 Coordinate home and school involvement with a behavior management plan
- ☐ 12 Create situations where mutual cooperation is needed to obtain a reward
- ☐ 13 Discuss and model examples of desired behavior
- ☐ 15 Discuss problems privately
- ☐ 19 Encourage and provide opportunities for interactions with peers

☐ 22 Encourage on-going counselor contact

☐ 23 Encourage participation in extracurricular activities

☐ 39 Help the student identify and focus on strengths

☐ 47 Maintain communication with parent(s)

(The above numbers were selected from a list of goals.)

RATIONALE FOR THE TYPE OF EDUCATIONAL PROGRAM AND PLACEMENT

Based on current evaluations and classification decisions as delineated in the eligibility report, Ann's current educational status, and the consideration of all educational options, this IEP represents an appropriate educational program and placement affording the least restrictive environment appropriate to Ann's educational needs. In selecting the least restrictive environment, consideration has been given to participation in the regular classroom program to the maximum extent appropriate, making use of necessary supplemental aids and services. The proximity of the placement to Ann's home, the ability of the program to implement the IEP, any potentially harmful or beneficial effects for Ann or other students as well as Ann's communication, self-esteem, and socialization needs have been considered.

EXEMPTION FROM REGULAR SCHOOL REQUIREMENTS

Exemption

Include Rationale, if exempt.	Yes	No	Test modification
Participation in local testing programs (K–12)		No	
Districtwide testing		No	

Early warning test - Reading		No	
Early warning test - Math		No	
Early warning test - Writing		No	
Core course proficiencies			
Other PSAT/SAT	x		extra time /reader

EXEMPTION FROM LOCAL DISCIPLINARY POLICIES & PROCEDURES - DISCIPLINE

Ann shall adhere to all rules of conduct, which are stated in the Board of Education Policies and Student Handbook.

ROLES OF SPECIFIC SCHOOL PERSONNEL

- ☐ School Administrator shall be responsible for implementation of the IEP and for ensuring that relevant school personnel are informed of its contents.
- ☐ The Case Manager and Teacher shall conduct an annual review of the student's educational program.
- ☐ The Case Manager shall be responsible for transition planning. The Case Manager shall be responsible for implementation of the IEP and for ensuring that relevant school personnel are informed of its contents.
- ☐ The Guidance/Vocational Counselor shall serve as a liaison to postsecondary resources and make referrals to the resources as appropriate.
- ☐ Role of Parent: To monitor attendance, meet with teachers and team members as needed, and participate in recommended programs and annual reviews.

HIGH SCHOOL GRADUATION REQUIREMENTS

Alternate Requirements

Exemption Rationale for State Endorsed

Yes No N/A Exemption Diploma

Attendance					
Credit Hour Requirements	--	--	--	-------------------	-------------------------
English		X			
Social Studies/U.S. History		X			
Mathematics		X			
Physical Science/Natural Science		X			
Practical/Performing/Fine Arts		X			
Physical Education/Health & Safety		X			
Career Education		X			
Local Requirements		X			
Curriculum Proficiencies	--	--	--	-------------------	-------------------------
English		X			
Social Studies/U.S. History		X			
Mathematics		X			
Physical Science/Natural Science		X			
Practical/Performing/Fine Arts		X			
Physical Education/Health & Safety		XX			
Career Education		X			
Local Requirements		X			

HIGH SCHOOL PROFICIENCY TEST

H.S.P.T. - READING

Exemption:	No
Test Modifications: ☐ Extended time ☐ Give assistance with directions ☐ Test in small group setting	**Rationale for Exemptions:**

H.S.P.T. - MATHEMATICS

Exemption:	No
Test Modifications: ☐ Extended time ☐ Give assistance with directions ☐ Test in small group setting	**Rationale for Exemptions:**

H.S.P.T. - WRITING

Exemption:	No
Test Modifications: ☐ Extended time ☐ Give assistance with directions ☐ Test in small group setting	**Rationale for Exemptions:**

TRANSITION

TRANSITION (AGE 14+)

PUPIL PREFERENCES AND INTERESTS: Ann would like to attend college. As a transition plan it is suggested that she begin at a junior college where study skills can be developed.

POST SECONDARY OUTCOMES (underscore appropriate areas):

Postsecondary Education, Vocational Training, Integrated Employment, Continuing and Adult Education, Adult Services, Independent Living, Community Participation

---

TRANSITION SERVICES:

Instruction:

Community Experience:

Employment/Postschool Adult Living:

Daily Living Skills/Functional Vocational Evaluation:
(If appropriate)

Rationale if transition services are not needed:

__________ Ann **________ is in the __** 10th**___grade and is following a program designed and approved by the ___________** PVHS **___________ Board of Education, which is in compliance with the State of New Jersey requirements. As such, _____**Ann **__________________ is being prepared for postsecondary areas of educational programs, work settings and independent living in the same way as any of the fellow students who are not classified.**

Note: Annual goals and objectives may be coded to correlate to postsecondary outcomes.

CONSENT

STUDENT ______________________________

1. I have received a draft of my child's IEP. I give my consent to have this IEP implemented. This copy serves as notice of action.

____

Signature

____

Date

2. I give consent to have my child's program implemented at the earliest possible date. Therefore, I waive the 15-day waiting period.

____

Signature

____

Date

Please be advised that you have the right to appeal any decision regarding your child's classification, program or placement (N.J.A.C. 6:28 and Due Process Rules Regarding Hearings 1:6A-1 et seq.).

Practice Exercise:

Please use a template to develop your own IEP for George:

Please use a template to develop your own IEP for Daniel:

SUMMARY

This chapter focused on Special Education and how the school social worker functions in his/her capacity. An overview of IDEA and the implications for the practice of school social work since this law was adopted were discussed. There was a discussion of the mandate of IDEA- Individuals with Disabilities Education Act (P.L.108-446). Also presented was student and family participation in the evaluation process. The school social worker's participation in the evaluation and classification process was also explained. A social developmental history was presented and an example was given. The ecomap and genogram were shown as an enhancement to the social history. Examples of each were given. The IEP was discussed in detail and the role of social worker as advocate with students and families in the evaluation/classification process was explained. An IEP template was given as well as an example. Specific parts of the IEP were also elucidated. The "No Child Left Behind" legislation was also explained.

SELF-REFLECTION QUESTIONS

1. Since the implementation of IDEA 2004 what notable changes have been made in the areas of school social work?
2. Student and family participation in the evaluation process have ensued. What effects have these had on the position of the school social worker?

CLASS DISCUSSION QUESTIONS

1. After the class has completed the ecomap of Daniel's family, have two student volunteers put them on the board, and the class can discuss the diagrams.
2. After the class has done a social developmental history on George, have two students share their sample and get class input.
3. Have the class develop a functional behavioral assessment for George. Discuss the components in class.

Chapter 5

Collaboration and Consultation With Parents, Faculty, Staff, and Administration

INTRODUCTION

Working in collaboration with parents across educational and socioeconomic barriers is essential for maximizing the student's potential in the school environment. The social worker's role as "advocate" is strongly emphasized in this chapter along with case examples. Working with educational advocates on behalf of the student is also discussed.

Presently, the social worker in the school is even more essential than in the past. Help for the economically marginalized through government intervention is diminishing, and more than ever, the gap between economic classes has widened. This phenomenon leads to increased numbers of children in schools in precarious economic situations. The high divorce rate, single parenting, and precarious living situations also contribute to the need for a mental health professional in schools.

Observation in the classroom can help the social worker give better input to teachers working with children who are having difficulties. Collaboration of educators and social workers in the schools can lead to maximizing the success of the students as well as create an atmosphere of rapport between the professionals. Although both professions have a similar goal—the welfare of children—the social worker works with the ecological perspective and focuses on the strengths of the student. Teachers focus on the individual and what is lacking in the student (Bronstein & Abramson, 2003). Although this difference is apparent, it can be remedied through compromise and collaboration. This chapter explores methods of collaborating as well as specific services that social workers can provide to teachers and administrators in an effort to help students. Programs such as in-service workshops on bullying, child abuse, and student behavior including ADHD are discussed. Specific examples of teamwork between teachers and social workers are also addressed.

One of the most important functions of a school social worker is to assist school administrators and teachers to deal effectively with parents and guardians. This area is a social worker's strength, and facilitation of the communication and positive partnership is essential in helping a child in the school setting.

Infusing mental health into the school curriculum as a way of helping teachers help students is another area of interest. Such classroom activities as writing a letter of support to a friend who has a problem, learning skills in conflict resolution, and so on are some of the activities that teachers can develop to help children with feelings (Dubuque, n.d.).

Because of the unique position that a school social worker has, the area of safety, and safety measures and policies are addressed in this chapter.

PARENTAL INVOLVEMENT

Children whose parents are involved in the educational process show significant success as opposed to those whose parents are not involved or are disinterested. We can have parents who are interested in their child's education but are unable to get involved because of external factors. Sometimes a parent's overburdened lifestyle and social economic status (SES) may impede on his or her ability to be involved. It can also occur if parents are unable to engage with the school because of language barriers (i.e., the inability to speak English). They are sometimes embarrassed or self-conscious. Keeping parents involved for the long term seems the most effective way to help children. Basically, two areas stand out as important in enhancing a child's academic performance and motivation. These are home-school communication and learning at home. Some of the issues involved in communication are parent teacher conferences, talking to the teacher at school, checking the school's website for homework, and being informed about events and school news. Regarding home learning, the following specifics are cited: checking homework, setting goals with the child, helping them study, and talking to the child about their school day (Brock & Edmonds, 2010). In a study cited by McAllister Swap (1993), most parents are willing to become involved in their children's education. The highest level of achievement is seen when parents behave in the capacity of home tutors. It should begin early in the child's education and proceed through the elementary school years. Programs have been developed to help involve parents in the educational system.

An Elementary School Program

A parent follow-through program was developed to help engage parents in the education of their children that included the following components:

- Parents were employed spending half of their time as classroom aides and the other half making home visits.
- Encouraging parents to participate in one of several roles: tutoring their own child, paid aides, helping with decision making in the schools, adult learning, being the audience, and volunteering in the classroom.
- Giving families help in receiving social, psychological, and physical services (Swap, 1993).

High School Intervention

In a high school program, counselors met individually with parents before their children began in school. Both attendance and academic standing of those students whose parents met with counselors were higher than those whose parents did not. Overall it appears that when parents and teachers work cooperatively it is a win-win situation. Teachers become more enthusiastic, and parents are more positive when they see teachers as "people" willing to solve problems together (Swap, 1993).

Four Models of Parental Involvement in Schools

1. The *Protective Model*: This model proposes that the roles of parents and educators be kept separate. Parents hand over the responsibility of educating their children to the schools and thereby hold the school establishment responsible for the outcome.

2. The *School-to-Home Transmission Model*: The parents are asked to help support the school in its mission. Children know that their achievement is guided by the cooperation of their home and school. Teachers and administrators should let parents know what they should do outside of school to foster their children's development. Parents have a reciprocal response to foster the values and conditions that the school environment endorses. This model does

not propose a two-way interaction. Parents are asked to endorse and support the school with their children.

3. The *Curriculum Enrichment Model*: This incorporates the parents into the school curriculum. It is predicated on the idea that families have much to offer the school. In the case of minorities and immigrant families, their contribution is essential to the success of their children in school. When family values and culture are included in the curriculum, all children benefit from the enriched environment (Swap, 1993).

4. In the last model, the ideal is presented. This is called *New Vision: The Partnership Model*. Its purpose is to enhance the curriculum and the cooperation by having teachers and parents work together in the community to enrich the learning environment. The characteristics of this model include cooperative communication between parents and educators, supporting education at home, teacher and parent mutual support (teachers providing workshops for parents and parents volunteering to help in the school milieu), and parents and teachers participating in working together on committees and community councils to help each other in their common goal: success of the students (Swap, 1993).

It is apparent that parental involvement in their child's academic difficulties leads students to getting help. Parents need to support their children in these situations. If the parent is aware that the child needs extra help that the teacher is willing to provide, they usually will facilitate the arrangement. In essence, all parents, students, and teachers seek the success of the student as the most important priority.

Some of the characteristics for developing working relationships with parents come from Allen-Meares. These include awareness of the family's individual situation, putting a positive spin on the parent/child dyad, knowing the needs of the family, and not inflicting one's value system on the family (Allen-Meares, 2004). A partnership with the family is seen as the best way to support a child and foster his or her success.

A home-school notebook is suggested by Bye and Alvarez. Daily or weekly communication can take place through such a system. School social workers are important conduits for having such a system in place. They can translate educational terms so that parents can understand them and support the students and teachers in their goals (Bye & Alvarez, 2007).

Social workers can train parents in an effort to help them get connected to the school personnel. The social worker is in a unique position to coordinate efforts for parental involvement. It is said that parents have the ability to support the school and regulate their child's behavior (Ouellette & Wilderson, 2008). It is incumbent on us to get parents involved to provide these assets. Parent management training is most helpful when done for 6 to 8 weeks with a trainer as the leader. It seems to help reduce the acting out and anti-social behavior of students when their parents have been involved in these sessions. Parent retention is a significant problem to this process. It was found that phone calls in between sessions, child care provisions, and home visits all lend to the successful participation in such a program. Web-based technology for parents has been used successfully. Videoconferencing, web homework, and grade books are successfully being used to create the partnership of parents and schools. This new communication eliminates the need for parents getting to a location at a certain time and the need for childcare. Interactive chat is also helpful in this process and proving successful, as is the possibility of using Skype (or some form of interactive computer technology). For parents who don't have a computer, the school district should provide the laptop, training, and software (Ouellette & Wilderson, 2008).

In an evidence-based study, it was found that parent tutoring and encouragement were the variables that contributed to the successful elimination of one school-based problem (Fishel &Ramirez, 2005). Parent involvement included not only helping children at home but also being involved in the school community, volunteering in school activities, and partnering with the school personnel in decision making for their student (Fishel & Ramirez, 2005).

Example: At one point in my career, the principal called me to help with a group of boys who were acting out. They were out of control both in school and out. I conducted a 6-week group evening session for these parents. In the community, the boys had set up a shack (behind the house of one of the parents involved) and were hanging out there at night, and cutting school and staying in this compound. The parent whose property it was located on was being intimidated by her son and told if she attempted to stop him, he would run away from home. With the encouragement and support of the other parents, this family was able to take the shack down one weekend and eliminate at least one source of acting out behavior. The boy did not run away.

WORKING IN COLLABORATION WITH EDUCATIONAL ADVOCATES

Educational advocates coming into the school on behalf of students and parents are somewhat intimidating. The position of the school social worker is such that he or she should philosophically be working collaboratively with these advocates on behalf of the student. If one views the advocate as a specialist in their own field, the school personnel should look at the collaboration as an enhancement to their efforts to provide the best education possible for the student.

Advocacy can be defined as defending or promoting a child in the academic environment (McAloon, 1994). It has many facets. A child can be his or her own advocate. A teacher may advocate on a child's behalf to a parent or school official. A counselor may advocate on the child's behalf when a parent or teacher does not see the situation clearly. Ultimately, it is in the purview of the school social worker to advocate for the child.

It is sometimes best when an outside advocate becomes part of the educational process. They can shed new light on the child's difficulties or make appropriate recommendations that the school did not envision. The goal is that all involved work collaboratively for the benefit of the child (student). This is the overriding goal of the educational process. If an advocate or third party gets involved in advocacy as an adversary, the process gets bogged down and can lead to costly legal situations and loss of precious school time for the student involved. It behooves the school social worker to address these issues and to work at overcoming adversarial positions. It is also our position to help provide the best education possible for our students. We should not cave in or shy away from the advocate's position in an effort to defend the school district from financial involvement.

Example: In a unilateral placement by a parent, our district was mandated to pay for an outward bound program in the Pacific Northwest. After a CST evaluation, the members of the team opted to pay for this placement to avoid further financial expense for the school district. I was the dissenting vote fearing that there might be danger for the student in such a placement as well as ignoring the "least restrictive environment clause" of special education mandate. It was not an approved program (investigated by the state). A group of the child study members visited the program to determine the adequacy of the program, and it was then decided that the district would support the placement. The strengths perspective is an especially good place to start. When we identify what the student is able to accomplish, we can then put our efforts on building the appropriate educational plan to maximize the student's abilities.

DEVELOPING RAPPORT WITH FACULTY AND STAFF

Very little is said in the literature about the relationship between the faculty and school social worker, yet it is a very significant part of the social worker's responsibility. If the social worker does not have credibility with the faculty and staff then it will be difficult at best to help students in their academic endeavors. It is a key component to the successful resolution of academic difficulties in the classroom. It is incumbent on the school administration especially the principal to help this partnership to develop. The principal is the point person in explaining to the faculty and staff the services that are offered and to frame the social worker's role in a positive way (Molyneaux, 1950). Many times, this explanation does not work. It then becomes the responsibility of the social worker to develop a rapport with the teachers and staff. Being present and available is the very first and positive thing a social worker can do. Faculty becomes distrustful of someone who is not seen as a member of their group and as a peer. Being available in times of crises is another component of the social worker's development of rapport. We must keep in mind that the teachers often become frustrated with a child's seeming inability to learn or when the child is exhibiting behavior that is aberrant. Guidance and support for that teacher is essential and often is the icebreaker that begins to foster trust.

Visibility is evident when a social worker is giving a workshop that faculty find useful. Practical advice and examples are always helpful to teachers. The "how to deal with" workshop is especially accepted by the teachers. Giving them theory or jargon is likely to alienate them. One wants to be a vital part of the system, and gaining the trust and cooperation of teachers is paramount. Workshops dealing with problem behaviors, working with an influx of a new ethnic minority, and guiding them on dealing with aberrant behaviors are all workshops that can serve a practical use, as well as current issues such as bullying, child abuse, and behaviors that are disruptive including those of a student with a diagnosis of ADHD.

Example: As the liaison of the child protective agency, I offered workshops to teachers for the identification and reporting of child abuse and neglect. These workshops were given in practical terms with a step-by-step guide for dealing with these situations. Support by the social worker was always a part of these interventions. Another place where guidance was given was in the event of a death on campus. The social worker would again be addressing the faculty to guide them in the interaction with students. Many times the teachers themselves had recently suffered a loss, and their personal feelings would play a part in the social worker's support. At times, teachers would come for personal advice and referrals. The social worker should always try to accommodate their needs and reassure them that any information would be kept confidential. It is essential for the respect of the faculty to behave in a most professional manner.

I also developed bullying awareness programs as the school social worker. Many times teachers do not know a method of dealing with bullying. In these cases, they sometimes ignore the problem, which exacerbates the situation. Understanding the mechanisms and the environment in which bullying thrives as well as clear-cut ways of dealing with the problem helps teachers and their students. Using a program such as *The Steps to Respect*, where the central core is taught by the teacher, uses him or her as a coach, and has valid, researched evidence to support its success is a good first step (*Steps to Respect Overview*, n.d.). In some states (New Jersey as an example), new bullying laws have been passed, and faculty must learn how to implement the outlined procedures. The social worker is an ideal person to define the program and help the school district implement these policies and procedures. Social workers in the schools can research such programs and teach the faculty and administration the best ways to use such a program. The social worker can also become a consultant to the teacher when showing him or her how to implement the program.

ADHD: Attention Deficit Hyperactivity Disorder is a very popular diagnosis in the schools today. It is sometimes a catchall diagnosis for all acting-out behaviors. The school social worker, in cooperation with the school psychologist and the learning disability specialist, can offer teachers a workshop on identification and skills to use when dealing with a child having this disorder. Teachers should be taught the difference between organic (brain wiring or biologically based) and emotional (caused by functional problem such as anxiety disorder) ADHD. There are many skills to help teachers support their students who are labeled with this problem. Proper seating, redirection, and positive reinforcement are just some of the preliminary ways a teacher can help a child cope. If these interventions don't work then further evaluation and interventions need to be examined. Some of the tools used to diagnose ADHD are (a) the Child Behavior Checklist, (b) Conners Parent and Teacher Rating Scale, (c) ADHD Rating Scale-IV, (d) Brown Attention Deficit Disorder Scale, and (e) the Conners/Wells Adolescent Self-Report of Symptoms (Greydanus, Pratt, & Patel, 2007). This list is not exhaustive. Aside from medication, some of the more specific interventions being used for this condition are psychotherapy, cognitive behavior therapy, support groups, parent training, educator and teacher training, biofeedback, meditation, and social skills training. There is no convincing research that one works better than another (Greydanus et al., 2007).

Consultation and Observation

A teacher will often seek help from the social worker involving a situation with a student. If at all possible, direct observation of these students is preferable. Permission must be procured beforehand from the teacher. A social worker knows that the domain of the classroom belongs to the teacher and that they are in charge and hold the primary responsibility for what occurs in that classroom. Always respect that position and rapport will be built. *Consultation* is defined as the professional service of a specialist to a person in direct involvement with a student. It is a collaborative, problem-solving process (Allen-Meares, 2004). The model of consultation should be combined with the strengths perspective used as the theoretical underpinnings. Teachers are encouraged to brainstorm with the social worker and come up with solutions that he or she feels confident in. It then becomes the decision of the teacher as to the most appropriate method to use and therefore will be compatible with their role in the classroom.

Berzin et al. (2011) have researched the role of the school social worker and consultation. They describe three levels: (1) home-school-community liaison, (2) consultant, and (3) system-level specialist. School professionals can consider a great variety of ways to have the social worker support the objectives of the school. Social workers have used the first level most aptly, but they need to tap into the consultation and school level activities such as helping on school committees, professional development, and participating in the everyday activities of the faculty and students. One must keep in mind that teachers are first responders who need to receive the support of the mental health professionals such as the school social worker. The consultant role is that which is most familiar to social workers. It is working on a one-to-one basis with the classroom teacher. The system-level specialist supports the ecological perspective, because it sees the social worker looking at all systems related to the child in the classroom and the issues of the teacher. This relationship only comes after rapport is developed (Berzin et al., 2011).

According to Bye and Alvarez, a model for consultation is suggested, which consists of a contract (either verbal or written) and outlines the ". . . purpose, objectives, ground rules, expectations, resources and time lines for the consultation" (Bye & Alvarez, 2007, p. 182). They also suggest a model for consultation which includes the following components:

- A building of the relationship
- Contracting for what is to be accomplished
- Defining the problem
- Brainstorming for alternatives
- Developing a plan
- Evaluating the action taken (Bye & Alvarez, 2007).

Again, when working with teachers in consultation, the strengths perspective is most effective. A behavioral intervention plan is most effective in the IEP process. Many students need behavioral intervention plans to supplant maladaptive behaviors with adaptive ones. A behavioral intervention plan is described in Chapter 4.

Dupper outlines the steps to facilitate the consultation process with teachers. The following is a step-by-step description of the process:

- "Listen attentively to teacher frustrations with classroom problems.
- Provide a 'sounding board' for teacher ideas.
- Compliment teacher actions when successful.
- Offer encouragement when teacher efforts are less than successful.
- Instruct teachers in how to assess classroom problems in a sympathetic manner.
- Help identify and, whenever possible, take an active role in recruiting additional resources or seeking alternative solutions that may be available elsewhere in the school.
- Help teachers help themselves, as in peer coaching.
- Make school-based consultation available to a greater number of consultees.
- Inform teachers of the best available treatment technologies.
- Guide teachers through the problem solving process of consultation.
- Assist teachers in treatment implementation and evaluation.
- Help teachers make assessment information relevant for intervention" (Dupper, 2003, p. 174).

ASSIST ADMINISTRATORS AND TEACHERS TO WORK POSITIVELY WITH PARENTS

It is said that if social workers and educators learn more about the preparation of the other discipline better collaboration and productivity will be seen. It is important that we see that teachers focus on education (cognition) and social workers focus on the psycho-emotional-social aspects of the child. The mission that is shared is that of helping children. Based on the commonality, the two professions need to cooperate with each other. Supporting the other discipline will help fulfill their common mission. For teacher training, the focus is on developing excellence in content areas. Social workers are dedicated to ethics, values, class, race, and gender issues. The clients' right to self-determination and confidentiality is essential to the social worker but not as high a priority with the educator. Because of this, the two professions sometimes differ on the source of the student's problems (Bronstein & Abramson, 2003).

The social worker has the unique role as the liaison between the school professionals and the family. Many teachers and administrators need our help in learning how best to deal with parents. Our training, ethics, and value system are such that we have developed the ability to deal with people of various backgrounds. We also use the ecological approach to examining a situation and thus see the need for changes in various systems not just the child and family. Teachers may even accompany social workers on home visits. This procedure helps teachers see the child and parent(s) in their natural environment and may even change the teacher's perception of the child. Having administrators involved with providing computer communication for parent(s) is another way of facilitating the contact (Bye & Alvarez, 2007). There are two models of familial involvement: the deficit model and the leadership model. The deficit model sees the school environment as the norm, and the children and parents have to conform to its values and policies. In the leadership model, the parent(s) actively engage in development of school policy and programs. The families then assume a strengths perspective role and are enabled to become an integral part of the school community (Bye & Alvarez, 2007).

Bowen (1999) sees that home conditions that support learning include family involvement and home learning activities. The family and school should have knowledge and educational philosophy in common. The parents should understand what is going on with their child academically and know the teaching methods being used. The school social worker is the ideal professional to facilitate this communication.

Example: In my capacity as school social worker, I participated on Middle States Evaluations. On those committees (which met in the evening), parents, teachers, and board of education members met collaboratively and carried the same weight in the decision-making process. We worked on issues that involved cultural competence, which is essential for teachers and administrators. The school social worker should be at the forefront of explaining cultural differences and modeling respect for the differences. (Refer to Chapter 7 on development of cultural diversity.)

LIAISON WITH FAMILY AND SCHOOL

Bronfenbrenner believed that parental involvement in schools was essential to a worthwhile education (Bronfenbrenner, cited in Comer & Haynes, 1991). Parents can be involved in many levels with their children's schools. They can support programs, be involved in everyday activities and in developing and planning. For this parental involvement to occur, the social worker may be the conduit for participation, and many times must convince the administration that parental involvement can enhance the school environment.

Comer and Haynes (1991) outline a model (the School Development Program) for enhancing the involvement of parents in the school. It contains three mechanisms: a school planning and management team, a mental health team, and the parent program.

1. The school planning and management team involves all adults involved with the children including parents, administrators, faculty, and staff. It has three purposes: focusing on school climate and academics, staff development and evaluation, and changing of school program as needed.
2. The mental health team focuses on child development and appropriate behaviors exhibited at different stages of development. Members share knowledge and skills in dealing with children of differing age groups. It enhances relationships between faculty, parents, and students.
3. The parent program focuses on social development and includes motivating students to achieve in the academic environment (Comer & Haynes, 1991).

These teams were involving parental participation on three levels:

- Level 3 included general participation of all parents.
- Level 2 included more direct involvement such as helping in the classroom.
- Level 1 included parents who were elected by their peers to participate in the School Planning and Management team (Comer & Haynes, 1991).

Each of these levels was designed to have parents participate with different responsibility and to accommodate different comfort levels. It is felt that when parents are involved in the school community it enhances the child's education and creates linkages that are necessary for maximum communication. The school social worker will play an integral part in implementing such a program.

In our current schools, the issues of diversity and the lack of teacher knowledge of the diverse cultural backgrounds of their students tend to inhibit the parental involvement. It is no longer a question of the need and success of parental involvement for their children in schools; the new dilemma that remains unsolved is how to bridge the gap of cultural diversity (LaRocque, Kleiman, & Darling, 2011).

Example: One of my fondest memories of working with parents was on the Middle States Evaluation Team. One assignment was to evaluate the programs in the school including guidance and special services. I was the chair, and we evaluated the programs with an overview collected from the faculty, students, and parents. It was tedious work, but the comradery that our participation forged set the stage for many more parent-faculty encounters. I was asked to do presentations at the Parent-Faculty Association meeting on various subjects of interest to the parents. It was a wonderful experience.

SAFETY ISSUES

In all that has been said in this chapter regarding social workers needing to be involved directly and integrally in the community and with parents and other significant adults in the lives of the children, we must now consider the safety issues for the school social worker. Many reports cite the fact that social workers are at risk particularly when working with children and child protection. An NASW study reports that 51.3% of social workers feel unsafe in their jobs (Trainin Blank, 2005). Many of us are verbally assaulted; some are even physically harmed or killed. It is often unreported in our field. We are often in denial about the potential violence that we may experience. Safety issues should include common sense. Always let the agency know where you are going and whom you are visiting. Keep a cell phone with you. Sometimes, the agencies do provide these for their workers. Know the school's policy on home visits. Here are some tips from the article *Safety First: Paying Heed to and Preventing Professional Risks* by Barbara Trainin Blank:

BEFORE A HOME VISIT

- Have a safety plan in place. This should include precautions to avoid danger as well as strategies to help you manage a confrontation if one occurs.
- Start with a safety assessment: learn all you can about the family's history—have they had violent encounters with the police, schools, or social services? Is there a history of mental illness in the family? Some of these details will be noted in agency records. For others, you may have to consult informal sources, such as your supervisor, co-workers, or colleagues from other agencies.
- Home visits should be made with the full knowledge of your agency supervisor—time of departure, time of return, other activities while on the trip, and so on. Do not conduct a home visit when you feel uncomfortable or threatened, and return to the agency and report your experience.
- Give serious consideration to the street, neighborhood, or area where the family lives. You might want to exercise extra caution.
- Identify potential safety risks while in the home. Remain alert and observant. Listen outside the door for any disturbances, such as screaming or fighting. When knocking on the door, stand to the side, not in front of it.
- Note if the people you're speaking with are intoxicated. Scan the environment for any weapons and note any drug paraphernalia.

WHAT CAN AGENCIES DO?

- Acknowledge client violence toward human services workers as a real and legitimate practice concern.
- Implement specific safety precautions in the office and field.
- Establish a worker safety manual that explains policies and procedures, and establish cooperative safety protocols with other organizations you work with.
- Affirm to all staff it is okay to ask for help.
- Establish a worker safety committee.
- Develop a team approach or buddy system in cases in which a client has a history of violent behavior.
- Give a clear consistent message to clients that using violence to solve problems is not acceptable, and help clients learn nonviolent strategies to resolve their problems.
- Establish a firm protocol regarding possible filing of criminal charges against violent clients.

SOME TIPS ON DE-ESCALATION TECHNIQUES

- Appear calm, centered, and self-assured even if you don't feel it.
- Use a modulated, low, monotonous tone of voice.
- Do not be defensive. Even if the comments or insults are directed against you, they aren't about you.
- Be respectful, even when setting limits firmly or calling for help.
- Never turn your back for any reason. Always be at the same eye level, but do not maintain constant eye contact. Allow extra physical space between you. Keep your hands out of your pockets.
- Do not get loud or try to yell over a screaming person. Wait until he or she takes a breath; then talk.
- Empathize with feelings, but not with the behavior. Do not interpret the client's feelings in an analytic way; do not argue or try to convince.
- Trust your instincts. If you feel the de-escalation isn't working, STOP! Tell the person to leave, call for help, or leave yourself (Trainin Blank, 2005).

Example: After thinking about this area of safety, I realized there were several times in my career when I was at risk. A very depressed young man of 16 had just lost his father, and his mother asked me to come to the home and speak to the boy, because he had stopped coming to school. He was in his room, and I went in with his mother. He got up and grabbed his samurai swords and began flailing them in the air. I thought for sure that he was going to turn them on me, but all my support and finally my silence did not prevent him from turning them on himself. He pierced his skin superficially but did not harm himself. He was seen in an emergency room that afternoon and entered a psychiatric hospital where he stayed for 6 months.

INFUSION OF MENTAL HEALTH INTO THE CURRICULUM

Mental health issues are often neglected in the school curriculum. As with all neglected areas, they become taboo and often misunderstood. We teach children about health issues as they relate to physical issues, but unfortunately mental health is not addressed. Many children, when faced with aberrant behaviors, will make fun of those exhibiting them. We hear words like "weirdo," "retard," and "mental," just to name a few of the derogatory terms used to describe people exhibiting mental illness. Education of students about mental illness would be a preventative measure to avert such problems. In a small Canadian community, a curriculum in mental health for elementary school children was begun. A prescale evaluated the attitudes of these children toward mental illness. The results were negative. After the curriculum was administered, their attitudes improved. Depression, anxiety, and ADHD were discussed. The presenter was the regular classroom teacher. Besides improving the children's attitudes toward mental health, it was hoped that those children who would experience symptoms would seek help early on to alleviate further complications and distress (Lauria-Horner, Butcher, & Brooks 2004). Knowledge is power. Each child will be exposed to mental illness somewhere in his or her life. It is important to include this issue in the curriculum. Writing a support letter to a friend who has a problem and learning skills in conflict resolution are some of the classroom activities that teachers can develop to help children with feelings (Dubuque, n.d.). Teaching children how to deal with death is another area of mental health that is neglected and may be included in the curriculum. Writing a sympathy note, learning about the death of a pet, and reading books (on the students' level) dealing with death awareness should help children with knowledge of this area, which is very much a taboo in our society.

Parents may also be given seminars by the school mental health professionals in an effort to make them aware of the issues they or their children may face. It is another venue for including parents in the school environment.

Teachers also need to be aware of mental health issues and how they apply to the students in their classrooms. A model is presented in the Masset, Constable, McDonald, and Flynn text. It calls for (a) the need for teachers to know about various mental illnesses and their symptoms, (b) the need to apply appropriate skills to the problem using problem-solving interventions, (c) self-confidence to be able to apply the needed skills to the situation with confidence and security, and (d) the need to remain objective in the situation (Massat et al., 2009). The school social worker is an integral part of this model. He or she can assist the teacher in the identification of the problem(s) and the appropriate intervention(s) to be used in the classroom with the student(s). It behooves the social worker to work in a collegial approach. Working out problems by brainstorming and communication lends itself to the strengths perspective and to a more permanent solution to the problem at hand.

RECOGNIZING THE NEEDS OF THE MARGINALIZED

The social worker in the school is even more essential presently than in the past. Help for the economically marginalized through government intervention is diminishing, and more than ever the gap between economic classes has widened. Many of the former students who felt school was a negative experience become those who are marginalized. The schools are developed with middle class values in mind, and consideration for other cultural, social, or ethnic groups is often left on the margins of the school environment. Looking at families and their values and experiences should be considered when developing policies in school.

Parental involvement and education is difficult to achieve for those living on the margins. When educating this population, the social worker needs to consider the basic necessities such as nutrition, keeping food from becoming toxic, budgeting of money, and keeping one's home in good repair to maintain the safety and health of the children. Providing guidance becomes secondary to these needs. Advocacy skills are also important and empowering to marginalized parents. Building a community support system also helps parents get help from the resources in their community. Social workers need to be respectful of the differences in these families and through professional skills build a trusting relationship that will incorporate these parents into the school community. Experiential learning is much more effective than lectures and reading materials and will help these parents understand what the needs of their children are and give them the skills to access them (The Rural and Appalachian Youth and Family Consortium, 1996).

Ditrano and Silverstein (2006) cite two important factors necessary for inclusion of parents into the school milieu. These are "social capital (access to important social networks) and cultural capital (knowledge of how the system works)" (p. 366). Parents become a support system for each other with the help of the professionals who give them guidance and information. These are empowering constructs.

SUMMARY

In this chapter, the focus was on the collaboration with school personnel, parents, and students. The role of the social worker as liaison was the thread that connected the different areas of concern. Cultural competence is an important facet of our work and facilitates the collaboration across SES barriers. The social worker's role as liaison was emphasized as a very important aspect of this consultation and collaboration. Working with outside professionals was also discussed. Developing rapport with faculty and staff is the key to this communication. Observation in the classroom creates a bond that enables teachers and social workers to brainstorm together to develop good solutions. Safety is a very important but neglected issue, and social workers need to be aware of the pitfalls. Infusion of mental health into the curriculum provides information and helps develop compassion for those who are afflicted. Working with a marginalized population is a challenge that must be met, and social workers can help facilitate the communication.

ACTIVITIES

Activity 1: Level 1: Observe an interview of your supervisor with a parent.

Level 2: Go to your teachers' cafeteria or lounge and introduce yourself to someone whom you have not yet met. What issues would you address in that conversation?

Activity 2: Level 1: Plan a lesson for infusing a mental health concept into the classroom.

Level 2: Describe how you would approach a teacher with the idea of infusing mental health into his or her tenth-grade English class.

SELF-REFLECTION QUESTIONS

1. What methods would you use to help the faculty understand your position as a new social worker in the school? Please explain.
2. What do you need to know before you see a student referred to you by a teacher? Should you interview the teacher first?

CLASS DISCUSSION QUESTIONS

1. You are at a home visit. The parent begins to threaten you with violence. The parent tells you that if she doesn't like what you say she will turn her dogs out on you. She has two large, ferocious dogs. What steps would you take to protect and/or remove yourself from the situation?
2. From the perspective of cultural competence, what do teachers need to know to effectively include parents from diverse cultures in the school environment? If you have a student from Iraq who you suspect has learning difficulties, how would you engage the parents of that student?

Chapter 6

ETHICAL DILEMMAS

INTRODUCTION

In the school setting, ethical dilemmas arise from several areas. The *need to know* is an educational concept that often has to be considered by the social worker regarding his or her involvement with teachers, counselors, and administrators. The fact that most public school–aged children are under the age of 18 presents another variable for consideration by the social worker. Social workers must look at the deontological ethics (absolutist approach) and teleological-relativist ethics (where the ends justify the means). The Code of Ethics as established by the National Association of Social Workers (NASW) is discussed in relation to the school as the agency and the children as clients. The stages of ethical decision making are presented and include (a) gathering information and case details, (b) differentiating between practice and ethics, (c) knowing the conflict involved, (d) consulting the ethics code and talking to colleagues and supervisors, (e) identifying alternatives, (f) looking at the advantages and disadvantages to various people involved, (g) knowing your own personal values, (h) deciding which will be your priority, and (i) documenting your decision (Franklin et al., 2006). Cases are included and students are taught the application of ethical decision-making models and given examples of ethical dilemmas to solve. Whether or not teachers should be privy to information that does not impact on a student's education is also examined.

WHAT IS ETHICS?

According to Guttmann (2006), "Ethics, or moral philosophy, is a branch of philosophy that deals with the study of what is good and bad, right and wrong, and includes values, principles and theories" (p. 2). Ethics can be looked on as a structured consideration of moral decisions. Issues such as the client's right to self-determination should always be considered by the professional social worker.

Example: This concept might be explained in the case of a 14-year-old girl planning to have sex. What is the school social worker's ethical conduct in such a situation? Should he or she try to dissuade the adolescent from participation, or should he or she be offering the client ways to protect herself from harm? Does he or she keep it confidential or share it with the parent? (Some school districts prohibit the discussion of sex [e.g., New York City Department of Education].)

Ethics are reasons for our making moral decisions in specific cases. It gives us a foundation on which to base our decisions in a theoretical and systematic way. According to Levy (1976), social workers are described as "professional altruists" (p. 13). As such, the well-being of others takes precedent over oneself. This idea is the foundation of social work ethics and an ethic to which we all must subscribe. The various fields of practice in which social workers participate make ethics even more complex. Levy describes the working relationship of social worker to client as "affective neutrality" (p. 134). That is, he or she must maintain a balance of objectivity between his or her ability to see the facts clearly and his or her ability to maintain a caring relationship. This conduct of the professional is intricate and needs guidelines in order to maximize the social work services.

Ethics for School Social Workers

The issue of ethics arises in the schools for the social worker. The difficulties involve working with minors and also working in a host environment. Issues of sexual involvement of minors, drugs and alcohol use, threats made by students, eating disorders, and various other situations are problematic when it comes to confidentiality and ethical concerns. One must be self-reflective and understand one's own values and ethics on a personal and professional level. Example: How would you evaluate a student who jokingly says he is going to kill an adversary?

Ninety percent of social workers in the field have attested to having read the Code of Ethics. In a study done by Nikki Nelson-DiFranks (2008), results reveal that most social workers believe in the code and follow the code in their behavior. Also discussed was behavior being concordant with the code. It was found that when behavior was consistent with the code there was less disjuncture ("dilemma-induced distress") (p. 168). Infusion of ethics into the curriculum seems to be the preferred transmission of the code. The curriculum seems unable to assume another course; although through the research, one does not see a separate course as enhancing the adherence to the code (2008).

There are six core values that the social work code of ethics ascribes to for all social workers across every area of practice. These are (1) service, (2) social justice, (3) dignity and worth of the person, (4) importance of human relationships, (5) integrity, and (6) competence (Social Work Code of Ethics, 2008). These values must be understood by the individual and applied with wisdom in the area of engaged practice. For those social workers in the school, it is the school environment and the constituents that comprise this milieu. These include the students, parents, faculty, staff, administrators, board of education, and the community at large. Example: When faced with a student who smells of alcohol, what is the course of action a social worker should take? If the social worker has given ground rules to the student for their work together and one of those rules is that confidentiality cannot be kept when drugs or alcohol is involved, then the answer is clear. Setting ground rules with adolescents helps keep boundaries clear and avoids breeches of trust. Also, clarifying areas where confidentiality cannot be kept must be given during the first session.

MODELS IN ETHICAL DECISION MAKING: DEONTOLOGICAL, TELEOLOGICAL, AND SOCIAL CONSTRUCTIVISM MODELS OF ETHICAL DECISIONS AS EXAMPLES

The major schools of thought in ethical philosophy are deontological and teleological.

- *Deontological* is an absolutist philosophy. One needs to follow common rules in order to make decisions. Example: A social worker must always tell the truth no matter what the circumstances (Raines, 2004).
- *Teleological* is a relativist position. That is, one believes that the "end justifies the means" (Reamer, 2006). This model ascribes to the "utilitarian" ideal. That is, one must evaluate the situation and make a decision based on the pros and cons and the client's needs. The answers would vary based on the individual situation being evaluated (Raines, 2004). Example: Perhaps, one would stretch the rules slightly to give needy children access to the free lunch program.

These decisions must be reflected on before one comes to the situation at hand. One must keep in mind that these issues involve self-reflection, which is a standard of the profession. *Ethics* are principles that are neither black nor white, and therefore careful consideration by the professional must be taken before decisions are made. Supervision and discussion with other professionals often clarify the issues at hand. Remember that other professionals who are not closely involved in the situation can be more objective. Other school professionals (principal and/or administrator) may have a different perspective, which may conflict with the social work Code of Ethics. Each situation needs to be evaluated on its own merit with its own particular set of circumstances.

- A social constructivism model of ethical decision making involves an interactive process. In this model explained by Ginter, "what is real evolves through interpersonal interaction and agreement as to what is 'fact'" (cited in Cottone, 2001, p. 39). That is, decisions are never made by one individual but by a consensus of parties, and that become the reality. Reality becomes "a truth" not "the truth" (Cottone, 2001).

The steps in social constructivism in ethical decision making include (a) gathering information from the parties involved, (b) determining the essence of the relationships involved, (c) consulting professionals, (d) negotiating with those involved in the conflict, and (e) responding in a way that establishes the decision that most agree on (Cottone, 2001).

Example: A 13-year-old boy is brought in for counseling by his grandmother who signs the consent form. The boy tells the counselor that the mother is his legal guardian (assessment shows this to be true) and so the consent is fraudulent. The counselor then consults the supervisor and director of the organization (consulting other professionals). They decide that the mother must be consulted and give the counselor permission to contact the mother (consulting others involved). The mother does not respond, so the grandmother is consulted and asked to help. She tries to get permission from her daughter, who refuses. Then the grandmother seeks and is awarded custody of the child. Now the counseling can resume since the grandmother is the legal guardian (2001). All parties are satisfied with the resolution.

The Need to Know in School Social Work

"Information should be shared with other school personnel only on a need-to-know basis and only for compelling professional reasons. Prior to sharing confidential information, school social workers should evaluate the responsibility to and the welfare of the student. The responsibility to maintain confidentiality also must be weighed against the responsibility to the family and the school community. However, the focus should always be on what is best for the student" (www.sswaa.org, 2001).

According to the School Social Work Association (2001), school social workers should know the laws governing their practice. There are state, local, and school board policies which govern confidentiality in the school setting. A wise mantra is as follows: "Telling is about keeping people safe: tattling is about getting people in trouble" (Raines, 2004, p. 64).

Safety is the first and foremost issue in school social work. In a school setting, keeping the student body safe and the individual student client safe overrides any other outcome. Remember, social work is not a popularity contest, and sometimes for the greater good, one has to divulge information.

Example: A case example would be a student who tells you that a party will be held on a particular weekend in the Smith residence. He also tells you that alcohol and drugs will be available at this gathering. What is your ethical responsibility in this situation, and how would you handle it with the student informant?

Historically, social work services for children and adolescents were viewed as an area where interagency collaboration and sharing of information was important to the welfare of the clients since these agencies worked together for the good of the children and adolescents. In recent years, there became divisions and independence of these agencies who then demanded regulations for the sharing of information. In assessing child welfare cases, the school social worker is mandated by law to share any information about neglect and/or abuse of minors. If this information is not divulged, the social worker may be subject to prosecution. In the 1974 Family Educational Rights and Privacy Act (FERPA), parents and legal guardians were given access to school records and the ability to share that information with whomever they wished. This issue can definitely become a conflict when the school social worker is trying to protect the rights and confidentiality of his or her client, the student. Again, setting the ground rules for services is essential. In cases of abuse or neglect, it is important to let the adolescent know from the onset that confidentiality is not permitted. You must clearly let students know that it is your legal obligation to report such issues to the child protective services of your state.

Example: In 1976, *Tarasoff v. University of California Regents*, the therapist was charged with breaking confidentiality if the threat of harm was an issue. This decision arose through a Supreme Court mandate. As a result of this case, the victim as well as the enforcement agency must be informed if harm is intended by the patient or client. This was extended to juvenile justice in cases where the offender would be a danger to himself or herself or others.

Example: In a particular school, there was once a case where a student in a psychotic state threatened to kill the president of the United States. The professional psychiatrist who examined the child felt that he was serious, and the FBI had to be called in for an investigation.

The above mentioned situations are areas of interagency collaboration where harm is present. As a professional, if a social worker determines that harm may come to the student (client) or the student or school population at large, it is the responsibility and duty of that social worker to ensure the safety of all the individuals involved by breaking confidentiality (Jonson-Reid, 2000). The statement of confidentiality with exceptions should always be given to students at the beginning of the initial session.

CONFIDENTIALITY IN SCHOOL SOCIAL WORK

One of the most important and difficult issues in school social work ethics is confidentiality. Raines outlines a seven-step process in dealing with this issue.

1. "Know Yourself"—Each of us has a professional and personal self. For example: One might believe in pro-choice but does not accept that concept for herself. All social workers must abide by the NASW Code of Ethics. Those who are not members of the organization are subject to the code as well. Raines suggests that the social worker make a conscious effort or a written list to examine personal and professional values. Examine the similarities and differences and come to terms with how he or she would like to handle these conflicts in situations related to practice (2004).

2. "Analyze the Dilemma"—One must examine who tends to gain or lose in the situation. In the school setting, the client system is the first consideration. Next are your coworkers or peers: social workers, members of the evaluation team, and/or teachers. Administrators are on the next rung. Last are the family members of the client. Regarding confidentiality, these groups have a right to know about behaviors that may cause harm. The continuum of responses to not telling includes being an outcast, getting fired, and having legal charges filed against you, depending on the group in question. The next issue is which values of the social worker are conflictual. The social worker has the responsibility of protecting the client and the school community at the same time (2004). According to Raines, the two rules to live by are as follows:

   a. "Everyone is safe
   b. Everything is confidential"

Letter "a" supersedes letter "b." The next issue is whether self-determination trumps paternalism. Since our clients are minors, assent is all we can achieve. Assent is not a legal commitment but allows for some self-determination.

Example: In a recent study I conducted, I asked for assent from student participants, but parental consent was essential before the student could participate.

3. "Identify the Courses of Action"—The social worker has three alternatives.

   a. Keep everything confidential
   b. Share the information to protect all involved
   c. Let the student know your concerns, and try and have him or her share the information with the necessary parties (Raines, 2004).

4. "Seek Consultation"—Look for outside experts who know the area that you are having difficulty with and ask them for advice. There is no need to give names or breech confidentiality while doing this. We all need to seek assistance from other professionals, since often we are too close to the situation to see it clearly. Each of us should carry malpractice insurance in addition to any insurance provided by the school district. The case of *Tarasoff v. Regents of the University of California* was a case that involved warning a woman that her boyfriend discussed killing her in therapy. As was stated in the court disposition, "The protective privilege ends where the public peril begins" (cited in Raines, 1976, p. 347). Besides informing the police of the danger, as social workers we can contact the potential victim or have a doctor admit the student to a hospital for observation and clarification.

5. "Manage the Clinical Concerns"—We should never underestimate the harm potential of the student. We need to assess the client's potential for possible violence. This assessment includes: the frequency and duration of the ideation; the specificity of the plan; and if action has not yet been taken, implementing the plan.

6. "Enact the Decision"—It is now time to act on the decision you have made using the process mentioned above. Are you acting impartially and not based on personal experience? Can you generalize this decision based on past case histories or your own experience? Is your decision justifiable to the client and others? There are often stakeholders who feel that the decision is not satisfactory. Many want to do things punitively or according to their own value system. It is imperative that you use the process so that you are professionally able to rationalize your position.

7. "Reflect on the Process"—Review the process after it has been resolved and use your self-reflective mode to evaluate your decisions. Part of our professional experience is based on the review process of our decision making. One should ask himself or herself if the decision came about with enough consultation and having considered all the possible variables in the situation. One should also evaluate how much of one's personal values affected this decision. Overall we must ask ourselves if it was the correct decision under the circumstances (Raines, 2004). Debriefing with other professionals, redefining weaknesses in policy, and avoiding pitfalls is always very helpful.

When Confidentiality Ends

The following is a list of situations that warrant breaking confidentiality:

- When the client plans to hurt himself or herself or another person
- When child abuse or neglect is suspected
- When the court mandates the information
- When the social worker makes an assessment for the court
- When hospitalization is essential for client safety
- When there is litigation against the social worker for malpractice
- When the client is threatening to hurt the social worker
- When the social worker enlists the court to collect fees for services rendered (Loewenberg et al, 2000).

ETHICAL DECISION MAKING

The basic responsibility of the social worker, as stated previously, is to the client. Ethical decision making includes first and foremost the *ethical principles screen.* These include:

- Protection of life—this concept is extremely important and not to be taken lightly.
- Equal treatment—each of us should treat people in similar circumstances in a consistent manner.
- Autonomy/freedom—The client should be respected in the decisions that he or she makes.
- Least harm—The social worker should attempt to choose the least harmful of all alternatives.
- Quality of life—The social worker should attempt to provide the best quality of life under the particular circumstances assessed.
- Privacy and confidentiality—This principle should be kept unless harm or unsafe conditions will result.
- Truthfulness and full disclosure—At the onset, the practitioner should lay out the ground rules and let the client know the boundaries and abilities that his or her services provide (Loewenberg et al, 2000).

The next step in ethical decision making involves *boundaries and dual relationships.* Included in this step are the following:

- Identify the issues involving boundaries and dual relationships (if any).
- Identify the client system these issues are probably going to impact.
- Look at options and evaluate the positive and negative possibilities.

- Consider the ethical theories, codes of ethics, and legal implications; also consider the values being evoked and if and how they conflict with your own.
- Get supervision and legal advice, if necessary.
- Make your decision and document the process you used to arrive at that conclusion.
- Observe, evaluate, and support your evidence (Reamer, 2001).

As Zur (2007) states, "Therapists are not judged by the outcome of their actions, as there is no guarantee that there will be no harm. They are judged by the integrity of their methodologies and decision-making processes."

Example: It would be hard for a school social worker to take on club advisement, class teaching, or duty obligations, since these duties might interfere with the relationship and cause dual relationship issues. If you were told by an administrator in the school that you would have to teach a class as part of your contractual responsibilities, how would you respond?

Stages in Ethical Decision Making

It is important to think issues through before making decisions when faced with ethical dilemmas. These steps should be documented so that if any questions about the decision arise, the social worker will have a record of "good faith" measures taken (DuMez & Reamer, 2003). The Code of Ethics also suggests code consultation, collegial collaboration, cultural sensitivity, and professional judgment be taken into consideration in each dilemma faced (2003). The stages in ethical decision making include the following steps:

- Gather information and assess the issues in question—Who are the stakeholders and what are they going to win or lose by your decision?
- Separate practice issues from the ethics of the case in question—Conflicting values present an ethical dilemma, but if there is no clouding of the issue, then use best practices standards rather than ethical decision making.
- Identify the conflicting values—One then must prioritize which values are more pressing.
- Get help—consult other professionals, the Code of Ethics, and supervisors. Following the Code of Ethics will help if issues of ethical behavior arise.
- Identify alternatives—Look at the possible ways of handling the situation and the ethical efficacy of each.
- Evaluate the costs and benefits to the stakeholders—One must examine what the consequences will be to each of the stakeholders depending on the decision that is made.

- Clarify and examine your own values—Doing this will help prevent bias in the decision-making process. Look at your own decision-making style and bring that to the decision-making agenda.
- Decide which priority to make first and be able to rationally support your choice—One must use professional standards and ethical principles and practice wisdom to make this decision.
- Record the decision in your case notes—In this step, one should document the actions taken and the method of arriving at one's decision (Franklin et al., 2006).

SOCIAL WORK CODE OF ETHICS

The social work code of ethics was originally adopted in 1960. A new code was established in 1979 then revised in 1990 and 1993. The current code of ethics was adopted in 1996, and cultural competency standards were added in 2001.

The code provides direction for professional behavior and practice, tries to educate professionals in solid ethical conduct, and provides for professional accountability. It is an impetus for helping us with and improving our professional practice. The code talks about conflicts of values, principles, and standards but does not tell us what takes precedence. These are considered ethical dilemmas.

Some of the highlighted areas are the ethical responsibilities to the client, to colleagues, in practice settings, as professionals, to the profession, and to society. These are as follows:

1. Responsibilities to clients:
    - Commitment to clients—promote well-being of clients.
    - Self-determination—help clients to identify and clarify their goals.
    - Informed consent or assent—provide services only in a professional context
    - Competence—only provide services within the limits of their education, training, and licensure.
    - Cultural competence—understand culture and its function in behavior and have the knowledge base of their clients' cultural background. One must be sensitive to the cultural nuances of the different people and cultural groups.
    - Conflict of interest—avoid interference with professional judgment. Social workers must inform the clients of this conflict and do all they can to protect the client. The practitioner should not take advantage or exploit the client.
    - Privacy and confidentiality—the social workers can disclose information with proper consent. They should protect the confidentiality except in the areas that have been previously stated. If possible, they should inform the client before the disclosure is made. Disclosure to third-party payers should only be done with the clients' consent. They should protect clients'

confidentiality in legal proceedings to the limit of the law. Care should be taken to secure written records. Disclosure should occur only after every possible protection is exhausted.

- Access to records—social workers should provide access to records for clients. If it is felt that these can do harm, then the social worker should take care to interpret and support the client through this process.
- Sexual relationships—under no circumstances should the social worker engage in sexual contact with the client or with the client's close relatives. They should not provide services to former sexual partners.
- Physical contact—this should be avoided. This contact would include cradling or caressing clients.
- Sexual harassment—this includes sexual advances, requests, and either verbal or physical conduct referring to sex.
- Derogatory language—respectful language should be used in any and all communications about the client. Remember your professional role.
- Payment of services—these should be fair and reasonable for the clients. Consideration should be given to the clients' ability to pay. Avoid bartering with clients.
- Clients who lack decision-making ability—the interest and rights of the client should be protected.
- Interruption of services—social workers should make alternative plans for clients in cases of interrupted services. If you no longer can provide services because of illness or a move, an alternative should be set up, and a smooth transition should be facilitated.
- Termination of services should be made when the client no longer needs the services. Always avoid abandoning the client, since this may have a detrimental effect on the client. Termination is a process and should be done gradually to protect the client from harm.

2. Ethical responsibilities to colleagues:

   - Respect for colleagues is essential. Avoid negative criticism.
   - Confidentiality should be respected.
   - Interdisciplinary collaboration should be clearly defined.
   - Disputes involving colleagues should be kept on a professional level without involving clients and/or employers. Exploitation of such disputes must be avoided.
   - Consultation with colleagues should be initiated when needed, keeping in mind to always protect the interest of the clients when disclosing their information.
   - Referral for services—referrals to specialist should be made when the difficulties go beyond the social worker's expertise.

- Sexual relationships with students, supervisees, or educators should not be engaged in.
- Sexual harassment is prohibited.
- Impairment of a colleague should be confronted and support and aid should be sought.
- Incompetence should be dealt with, and remedial measures should be taken.
- Unethical behavior must be dealt with.

3. Social workers' ethical responsibilities in practice settings:

   - Supervision and consultation are important.
   - Education and training are essential.
   - Performance evaluation needs to be done with clearly stated criteria.
   - Client record should be accurate and reflect what has transpired.
   - Billing should be fair and in-line with services rendered.
   - Client transfer should be done in a clear and professional manner.

4. Social workers' ethical responsibilities as professionals:

   - Competence is essential.
   - Discrimination is not acceptable practice.
   - Dishonesty, fraud, and deception should not be participated in.
   - Impairment should not interfere with one's professional responsibility to clients.

5. Social workers' ethical responsibility to the profession:

   - Work toward the maintenance of high standards.
   - Evaluation and research—social workers should promote research to add to the knowledge base of the profession.

6. Social workers' ethical responsibilities to the broader society:

   - Promote social welfare.
   - Engage in social and political action to help those downtrodden to have equal access to resources.
   - Provide professional services in times of professional emergencies (NASW, 1999).

Conflict of interest may interfere with the functioning of sound practice. When this occurs, the social worker should tell the client of the situation and take responsible steps to alleviate the situation, which may include termination of treatment. If treatment is terminated, the social worker practitioner must take the proper steps to refer the client to a competent professional. Sometimes the nature of school social work may challenge the Code of Ethics. Here are some specific instances:

- IEP meetings ending counseling,
- Institutional racism may occur in our schools, and how to deal with that when you have a disproportionate amount of children of color in special education classes receiving services.
- English language learners (ELL) and children receiving limited services or no services at all.

CONFIDENTIALITY CHECKLIST

_ I have clarified my own personal and professional values.

_ I have identified the primary stakeholders in ethical issues.

_ I have identified the primary competing values.

_ I regularly provide an ethical orientation to new clients.

_ I obtain informed consent (and informed assent) to treatment.

_ I have identified several courses of action.

_ I obtain clinical consultation about difficult issues.

_ I obtain legal advice about difficult issues.

_ I am familiar with the laws regarding the treatment and rights of minors.

_ I carefully consider the clinical implications.

_ I make sure the decision is impartial, generalizable, and justifiable.

_ I review and document my decision-making process.

_ I always keep my personal written notes in a locked file cabinet.

_ I always use a computer password to protect private electronic files.

_ I always write public documents in clear, inoffensive language (Raines, 2004, p. 76).

ISSUES INVOLVED IN E-THERAPY

Ethical issues are now becoming an issue with the onset of e-therapy. Many therapists are resorting to this form of therapy, since clients are hard pressed for time and it is also time and/or financially efficient for the therapists. Some disorders for which e-therapy is being used include depression, eating disorders, alcohol and other substance abuse treatment, and stress-related problems. Jacobs cites significant changes in those receiving computer-based therapy in 76% of cases, whereas those receiving face-to-face treatment showed significant improvement in 91% of cases in this research study (cited in Santhiveeran, 2009).

Some ethical concerns include practice with clients in states other than the ones in which the therapist is licensed, confidentiality, treatment of minors, and responding to emergencies. In the Santhiveeran study, the findings suggest that many areas of ethical concern were not being addressed. The "duty to inform" the clients of the risks and benefits of treatment, how to use safeguards on the computer (e.g., encrypting information and communication), and alternatives to this form of therapy were not always discussed by the therapist (Santhiveeran, 2009, p. 8). The therapists in many cases did not state the limits of their e-practice or the states in which they were licensed. Issues of confidentiality were also not shown on the websites. Limits of confidentiality including maintenance of records and the methods used to protect confidentiality were not expressed. The procedures for emergencies were sometimes listed, but often the backup plans were sorely lacking (2008).

It is paramount that the National Association of Social Workers (NASW) revise the Code of Ethics to include these newfound methods of therapeutic intervention. As with other areas of media communication, guidelines and procedures need to be in place to better serve the clients involved. The use of Facebook, Twitter, e-mail, and other social media needs guidelines and parameters as well.

SUMMARY

In this chapter the ethical considerations for a school social worker were presented. The "need to know" concept and the issues of confidentiality with underage students were explained. Models of ethical decision making were given as well as case examples. The Code of Ethics as established by NASW was discussed in relation to the school as the agency and the children as clients. The stages of ethical decision making were given. A discussion of what teachers should be ethically privy to was made. Issues of e-therapy were also considered.

ACTIVITIES

Activity 1: Level 1: Discuss the appropriateness for an intern or school social worker to have a sexual relationship with the parent of a student client.

Level 2: Discuss the ethical issues of school social worker's romantic involvement with a single parent of a public school student after that student has left or graduated from the program and there are no other students from that family who would be attending your school.

Activity 2: Level 1: In your capacity as a school social worker, discuss your ideas about agreeing to an educational placement for a student because the other team members believe it is appropriate.

Level 2: As a school social worker you are asked to consent to a wilderness placement that is unknown to you or other members of the child study team. The reason for this consent is based on parental pressure and the school's need to avoid legal fees. All the other team members have agreed because it appears to be an "appropriate" placement based on the testing and interviewing of the student and family. None of the team members have seen the placement since it is in Idaho. In some outward-bound (wilderness) programs, you have heard of both physical and emotional abuse. Describe the steps you would take to resolve this issue.

SELF-REFLECTION QUESTIONS

1. If another professional is not behaving in an ethical manner in the school you are working in, what is your responsibility for reporting the infraction? To whom do you report it?
2. What is the best way to deal with boundary issues of families with whom you are working?

CLASS DISCUSSION QUESTIONS

1. A school social worker was asked by a principal to become a class advisor. It was more of a command than a request. As such, the social worker took on this responsibility but soon found it was a conflict of interest since several of her case responsibilities were members of that homeroom in which she had charge. As a result, she was compelled to resign, which caused conflict between her and the administrator. What do you see as her options?
2. You receive an anonymous phone call saying that one of your case responsibilities is being abused by a parent or boyfriend. After requesting that the person give his or her name, they hang up on you. What are your responsibilities to report this case to the child welfare authorities?

Chapter 7

Proficiency in Working With Cultural Competence

INTRODUCTION

One of the more significant challenges in working as a school social worker is developing cultural competency. There are competency assessments included in this chapter. *Cultural competence* as defined by Derald Wing Sue (2006) in his book, *Multicultural: Social Work Practice*, is as follows: "Cultural competence is the ability to engage in actions or create conditions that maximize the optimal development of client and client systems. Cultural competence social work practice is defined as the service provider's acquisition of awareness, knowledge, and skills needed to function effectively in a pluralistic democratic society (ability to communicate, interact, negotiate, and intervene on behalf of clients from diverse backgrounds), and on an organizational/societal level, advocating effectively to develop new theories, practices, policies, and organizational structures that are more responsive to all groups" (p. 29). Cultural competence in the educational domain is viewed as the ability to teach children from diverse backgrounds. According to Constable, Masset, McDonald, and Flynn in their book *School Social Work* (2006), "Culturally competent school social workers recognize, affirm, and value the worth of individuals, families, and communities and protect and preserve their dignity" (p. 301). The authors view cultural competence as the ability of students to successfully learn in an environment which is sensitive to their diverse background. Cultural competence includes self-knowledge and awareness. Viewing children's strengths as an important part of their culture is essential. Knowing and understanding one's own diversity is also important (Franklin et al., 2006). Some of the principles for developing a culturally competent practice would include the following:

1. "there is no single American culture;
2. members of each cultural group are diverse;
3. acculturation is a dynamic process;
4. diversity is to be acknowledged and valued" (Freeman, Franklin, Fong, Shaffer, & Timberlake, 1998, p. 121).

It is important to remember that the generic qualities of counseling are culture bound and reflect the majority culture's beliefs and attitudes. We must be aware of our value system and avoid stereotyping, according to Wing Sue (2006), who also believes that the natural environment plays a part in the treatment of many multicultural groups. Always be ready to provide multilingual services to clients because this may be essential, especially in the school environment. It is also important to acknowledge institutional racism and oppression that exists in communities, systems, and to specific marginalized groups.

The first challenge to cultural competence is assessing the needs of families and their children from diverse backgrounds and uncovering the barriers that obstruct the help needed. IDEA states that if a student is to be evaluated, the parents must be provided with rules and regulations regarding the evaluative process in their native language. It is often difficult to find a native speaking translator since some languages are obscure in our culture. Sometimes accessing the interpreter will postpone the evaluation process and cause the student an unnecessary delay in receiving services. A school social worker must make every effort to find these services. It is illegal for an evaluation meeting to be conducted in a language that parents are unable to understand. The other side of this dilemma is to ascertain whether or not the child is having difficulties academically, socially, and/or emotionally and that the problem being experienced is not the result of cultural or language differences. Unfortunately, English Language Learners and children of color are disproportionately represented in special education in the United States.

Example: A young girl who was a recent immigrant from Portugal came to our school. Her teachers felt that she had a perceptual difficulty not being able to process the material given. After deciding that an evaluation was deemed necessary, the first step was to get the letter and the rules and regulations translated into her native language so that the parents could understand the process. A referral for an evaluation was initiated, and the decision (made by the parents and the team) was to go ahead with the evaluation, but we needed to get evaluators (psychologist, social worker, and learning consultant) who would be able to test her in her native language. It was the responsibility of the social worker to find these professionals, and the student was tested in her native language. The results ascertained the deficiency she had, and she was given the help she needed for an auditory processing problem.

The next difficulty that emerged was in finding competent providers of services who are culturally and/or racially diverse and more specifically culturally competent. It is suggested by Spencer and Clarke (2006) that "lay providers" who come from the community be enlisted to help with the issues schools and professionals face in dealing with culturally and/or racially diverse students. It is better to use an independent interpreter and not the child or sibling of the child who is the subject of the discussion. As we know, increased parental involvement in the educational process leads to more academically, emotionally, and socially successful students. It is therefore deemed essential that parental involvement be sought, even if it is difficult to find an interpreter in their native language.

CULTURAL COMPETENCE ASSESSMENT TOOLS

Self-Awareness and Personal Knowledge

Each of us must be aware of our own personal identity; our identity in a social, economic and political milieu; our own cultural biases; and our self-reflection. We each must recognize our values and attitudes and be sure not to impose these lenses on the clients in our practice. It is easy to say that we need to recognize and assess our own values and attitudes but difficult to be self-aware of these. According to Sisneros, Stakeman, Joyner, and Schmitz (2008), it is imperative that you take a self-awareness survey and then administer it to a family member who is a generation younger or older than you. The following is a scale developed to assess our knowledge of these attitudes and values:

1. "What is your ethnic or racial background? What has it meant to belong to this group?
2. Where did you grow up and what other racial/ethnic groups resided there?
3. What was your first experience with feeling different?
4. Did your family see itself as similar to or different from other ethnic groups?
5. What are the values of your racial/ethnic group?
6. What is your earliest memory of race or color?
7. What emotion did you experience?
8. With whom did you discuss this experience?
9. What are your feelings about being white or a person of color?
10. For people who are white: How do you think people of color feel about their color identity?

11. For people of color: How do you think people who are white feel about their color identity?

12. How have you experienced a sense of power or lack of power in relation to your racial/ethnic identity, family, class identity, gender, sexual orientation, and professional identity?" (2008, pp. 21–22).

After examining the results, you need to think about how your own personal experience of multiculturalism and how this experience influenced the way in which you see people who are different from you. Has the person you interviewed shared the same views as you? Did they have any effect on your values? Has this survey raised issues for you as to whether or not you'll be able to work with those who are different from you (Sisneros et al., 2008)? If you find that the results of your survey and of your relatives leave you with discrepancies between the social work values and your own, you must decide what actions or interventions you might take to resolve this inequity. It can be overcome, but dealing with the reality is the first step in this process.

THE MULTICULTURAL AWARENESS, KNOWLEDGE, AND SKILLS SURVEY (MAKSS)

Multicultural Awareness

1. One of the potential negative consequences about gaining information concerning specific cultures is that students might stereotype members of those cultural groups according to the information they have gained.

   Strongly disagree Disagree Agree Strongly agree

2. At this time in your life, how would you rate yourself in terms of understanding how your cultural background has influenced the way you think and act?

   Very limited Limited Fairly aware Very aware

3. At this point in your life, how would you rate your understanding of the impact of the way you think and act when interacting with persons of different cultural backgrounds?

   Very limited Limited Fairly aware Very aware

4. The human service professions, especially counseling and clinical psychology, have failed to meet the mental health need of ethnic minorities.

   Strongly disagree Disagree Agree Strongly agree

5. At the present time, how would you generally rate yourself in terms of being able to accurately compare your own cultural perspective with that of a person from another culture?

   Very limited **Limited** **Good** **Very good**

6. The criteria of self-awareness, self-fulfillment, and self-discovery are important measures in most counseling sessions.

   Strongly disagree **Disagree** **Agree** **Strongly agree**

7. Promoting a client's sense of psychological independence is usually a safe goal to strive for in most counseling situations.

   Strongly disagree **Disagree** **Agree** **Strongly agree**

8. How would you react to the following statement? In general, counseling services should be directed toward assisting clients to adjust to stressful environmental situations.

   Strongly disagree **Disagree** **Agree** **Strongly agree**

9. Psychological problems vary with the culture of the client.

   Strongly disagree **Disagree** **Agree** **Strongly agree**

10. There are some basic counseling skills that are applicable to create successful outcomes regardless of the client's cultural background.

    Strongly disagree **Disagree** **Agree** **Strongly agree**

Multicultural Knowledge

At the present time, how would you rate your own understanding of the following terms:

11. Culture

    Very limited **Limited** **Good** **Very good**

12. Ethnicity

    Very limited **Limited** **Good** **Very good**

13. Racism

    Very limited **Limited** **Good** **Very good**

(Continued)

(Continued)

14. Prejudice

    Very limited **Limited** **Good** **Very good**

15. Multicultural Counseling

    Very limited **Limited** **Good** **Very good**

16. Ethnocentrism

    Very limited **Limited** **Good** **Very good**

17. Cultural Encapsulation

    Very limited **Limited** **Good** **Very good**

18. In counseling, clients from different ethnic/cultural backgrounds should be given the same treatment that White mainstream clients receive.

    Strongly disagree **Disagree** **Agree** **Strongly agree**

19. The difficulty with the concept of "integration" is its implicit bias in favor of the dominant culture.

    Strongly disagree **Disagree** **Agree** **Strongly agree**

20. Racial and ethnic persons are underrepresented in clinical and counseling psychology.

    Strongly disagree **Disagree** **Agree** **Strongly agree**

Multicultural Skills

21. How would you rate your ability to conduct an effective counseling interview with a person from a cultural background significantly different from your own?

    Very limited **Limited** **Good** **Very good**

22. How would you rate your ability to effectively assess the mental health needs of a person from cultural background significantly different from your own?

    Very limited **Limited** **Good** **Very good**

23. In general, how would you rate yourself in terms of being able to effectively deal with biases, discrimination, and prejudices directed at you by a client in a counseling setting?

    Very limited **Limited** **Good** **Very good**

24. How well would you rate your ability to accurately identify culturally biased assumptions as they relate to your professional training?

    Very limited **Limited** **Good** **Very good**

25. In general, how would you rate your skill level in terms of being able to provide appropriate counseling services to culturally different clients?

    Very limited **Limited** **Good** **Very good**

26. How would you rate your ability to effectively secure information and resources to better serve culturally different clients?

    Very limited **Limited** **Good** **Very good**

27. How would you rate your ability to accurately assess the mental health needs of women?

    Very limited **Limited** **Good** **Very good**

28. How would you rate your ability to accurately assess the mental health needs of men?

    Very limited **Limited** **Good** **Very good**

29. How well would you rate your ability to accurately assess the mental health needs of other adults?

    Very limited **Limited** **Good** **Very good**

30. How well would you rate your ability to accurately assess the mental health needs of persons who come from very poor socioeconomic backgrounds?

    Very limited **Limited** **Good** **Very good**

Utilizing This Self-Assessment Inventory As a Pretest and Posttest

Once you have completed the self-assessment inventory, look at the specific items you rated as 'very limited' and use them to identify areas that need strengthening. The aim of this survey is to assess where you are now with respect to multicultural awareness, knowledge, and skills. Do you notice any specific strengths or weaknesses among these three areas? In which areas do you have the most strengths? Which areas need the most improvement? Do you have any ideas of how you can increase your multicultural competence in the areas of awareness, knowledge, and skills? Reading in the area of multicultural counseling is one way to begin increasing your ability to work in multicultural situations.

Source: (Corey & Corey, 2002, pp. 20–23)

If we can become aware of ourselves and our clients then we are less likely to expect our clients, students, and their families to behave in ways that are within our own comfort zone.

ISSUES OF CULTURAL COMPETENCE WITH THE GROWING IMMIGRANT POPULATIONS

The 2000 census shows that the Latino population in the United States has increased 61% since 1990. The 2004 American Community Survey reports that the Latino population is presently 14.2% of the overall U.S. population (Velazquez, Earner, Lincroft, 2007). Since the year 2000, the Latino population has increased 43% according to the Population Reference Bureau in 2010 (www.prb.org). It is estimated that the Latino/Hispanic population will triple in the future and by the year 2050 will account for about 30% of the U.S. population (www.chadwickcenter.org). These statistics have a huge impact on the public school system. What complicates the situation is the fact that these individuals are part of various cultural groups that are distinct. The Hispanic population in the United States is highly diverse and includes people from both Central and Latin America (www.chadwickcenter.org). As such, the language as well as the customs and behavioral patterns are diverse. The complexity of this situation puts the school social worker in a unique position to advocate for students and their families within the school and the greater community. English Language Learners require additional services and very particular needs when they encounter standardized testing and cultural differences as well as other cultural nuances in the school environment. Many of the parents have great difficulty with the English language, and their educational backgrounds vary; some are highly educated while others do not share that resource. Schools may lack the resources necessary to provide adequate information and resources to these families and children. They are sometimes underdocumented and are fearful of the school and the authority or power it presents. Some immigrants fear that if they are involved in the school community they will be subject to having their children taken away. The Latino cultures highly regard school authorities and this aspect may impair a family's ability to appropriately advocate for their children. Some of these children are living in the poverty range and are not able to access Temporary Assistance for Needy Families (TANF) or other public welfare support. Many times. the status of families is varied. Parents might be underdocumented, while their children who have been born here are citizens. There are special policies on the state and federal level that regulate these various statuses of families. Some states such as Alabama and Texas prohibit public schools from registering children who are undocumented.

Example: A father was arrested as an underdocumented immigrant. Since his wife covered up his whereabouts, she was given a prison sentence, and when he was discovered he was deported to his native country. The minor children ages 12, 10, and 8 years old were put into foster care, while their mother served her prison term.

The above scenario is one in which the school social worker could prove helpful. Trying to keep consistency in the school environment for the children would be one possibility as well as helping the foster parents with the children's academic concerns. Helping the children communicate with their natural parents would also be a supportive effort.

There are many immigrant groups represented in the public school systems, and some are better able to navigate the system than others. The No Child Left Behind Act impacts on these children particularly, because it requires them to take tests even if they don't understand the language of the examination. Children are being retained and are getting older in the earlier grades, which contributes to the social and emotional needs of this population. Assessing the acculturation levels of these children is essential, and the social worker needs to be involved in this process as well as engaging the parents and the communities and helping the families increase their social networks.

SEXUAL ORIENTATION (LGBTQ) ISSUES IN SCHOOLS

The harm reduction model as described by van Wormer (2003) explains that people who engage in risky behaviors need to be supported. She concludes that LGBTQ behavior in high school is one of those behaviors and that students do not have role models or support systems to guide them through the pitfalls. Schools, unfortunately, do not deal with the issues of same-sex relations as they do with heterosexual interactions. Therefore, preventative health-related measures are not explained, and if discussed, same-sex relationships are sometimes presented in a negative fashion. Many young LGBTQ children and adolescents in schools are bullied and made fun of. Some of these children resort to maladaptive coping mechanisms such as suicide attempts. Rejection very often causes self-loathing and results in suicidal ideation followed by attempts. Homophobia is strong in the school environment. Those faculty and staff who may be gay must keep silent and cannot help students for fear that they will lose their jobs. Harm reduction has been helped by groups such as Parents, Families and Friends of Lesbian and Gays Safe

Schools Program. In the United States, 150 chapters of these alliances have been formed to educate the students, parents, faculty, and staff and to support the young people who are in this situation (van Wormer, 2003). Respect for diversity and monitoring behaviors that are oppressive are essential for harm reduction. The school social worker can be a leader in bringing these programs to the school, providing preventative programs, and also in reaching out to students who have been victimized. Providing individual counseling and information about the Parents, Families, and Friends of Lesbians and Gays (PFLAG) with appropriate poster displays (contact information) will help in allaying the problems that arise from lack of knowledge and prevention. Inviting speakers and leading discussion groups can also be helpful in preventing oppression (van Wormer, 2003).

Schools seem to be a breeding ground for harassment of LGBTQ children. By starting conversations within our classrooms about anti-gay discrimination and by discussing LGBTQ people in our studies, some of the stigma and taboo would be lessened. It is easy to relate these themes into curricula about family diversity, respect for differences, the civil rights movement, the gay rights movement, discrimination of ethnic and racial origin, and other areas of study (Hanlon, 2009).

Example: When I was as a school social worker, a young man who had been making suicidal threats came to my attention. When interviewed, he revealed that he was gay and had been rejected by another young man who he thought shared his sexual orientation. The gay student was sent to our district by his parents in the hopes that living with relatives in another area would dissuade him from his sexual orientation. With individual counseling, he was finally able to "out" himself, and although he was still depressed, he was able to gain the support of the relative with whom he lived.

Example: Tyler Clementi, a Rutgers University (New Jersey) student, committed suicide after being spied on by his roommate who exposed Tyler's sexual orientation and taunted him. This case resulted in the Anti-Bullying Law that was passed in the state of New Jersey in 2010 and whose policy must be followed in the public schools in that state.

RACIAL AND ETHNIC DIVERSITY

The National Center for Education Statistics gives the dropout rate for Whites, Blacks, and Hispanics. For the year 2009, the dropout rate for Whites was 5.2, 9.3 for Blacks, and 17.6 for Hispanics. A significant dropout rate decrease is noted between 2000 and 2009 (from 11% to 8%). The Hispanic dropout rate has been higher since 1972, although it is declining.

Status dropout rates of 16- through 24-year-olds in the civilian, noninstitutionalized population, by race/ethnicity: Selected years, 1980–2009

Year	Total[1]	Race/ethnicity				
		White	**Black**	**Hispanic**	**Asian/Pacific Islander**	**American Indian/ Alaska Native**
1980	14.1	11.4	19.1	35.2	—	—
1985	12.6	10.4	15.2	27.6	—	—
1990	12.1	9.0	13.2	32.4	4.9	16.4
1995	12.0	8.6	12.1	30.0	3.9	13.4
1998	11.8	7.7	13.8	29.5	4.1	11.8
1999	11.2	7.3	12.6	28.6	4.3	—
2000	10.9	6.9	13.1	27.8	3.8	14.0
2001	10.7	7.3	10.9	27.0	3.6	13.1
2002	10.5	6.5	11.3	25.7	3.9	16.8
2003	9.9	6.3	10.9	23.5	3.9	15.0
2004	10.3	6.8	11.8	23.8	3.6	17.0
2005	9.4	6.0	10.4	22.4	2.9	14.0
2006	9.3	5.8	10.7	22.1	3.6	14.7
2007	8.7	5.3	8.4	21.4	6.1	19.3
2008	8.0	4.8	9.9	18.3	4.4	14.6
2009	8.1	5.2	9.3	17.6	3.4	13.2

(U.S. Department of Education, 2011).

According to Dupper, the school social worker should assume the leadership role in the area of educating both faculty and students to the issues of racial and ethnic interactions. Dupper cites studies where multicultural understanding is linked to improved academics and decreased rate of dropout. When students feel that they belong, they are more likely to continue their education and also graduate from high school. He also suggests that the school social worker acquaint faculty and staff with the neighborhoods that students are living in. The school environment is another area where the social worker can help with displays showing all racial and ethnic backgrounds. The social worker must be cognizant of the fact that some parents and students will need information in their native language (Dupper, 2003).

Dupper gives a procedure for changing racist behavior in the schools. The following bulleted outline can be most helpful:

How to Change Racist Behavior in Schools

- Articulate a clear statement of expectations regarding racism.
- Establish and enforce a series of consequences for violations of those expectations.
- Respond to racial incidents quickly and fairly by gathering adequate evidence. Corrections should be remedial.
- Discourage students from congregating on the school grounds according to race.
- Design seating assignments with a priority on integration.
- Rely on peer counseling whenever possible.
- Seek advice and support from parent and student advisory boards.
- Enlist the help and advice of key minority leaders in the community for teacher workshops, assemblies, and arbitration of racial incidents when appropriate.
- Reward those who strive to reduce racism in their schools and classrooms.
- Hire and assign an appropriate balance of minority faculty and staff to act as role models and provide an adequate base of authority for policies and discipline. (Dupper, 2003, p. 163)

RELIGION

The first amendment to the U.S. Constitution prohibits the government from involvement in religion. That is, the government ideally should be neutral. As the conservative, Christian influence infiltrated the schools in the 1990s, prayer and the mention of God were seen as less a violation of the Constitution than in the past. The moral values of the religious right also infiltrated the schools, and we saw more condemnation of issues about condom distribution and sex education arise with controversy. In 2012, the issue of organizations including birth control in their health care plan also became a national issue. The voucher system was and still is in political contention. Some states (Ohio in particular) allowed assistance to parents for their children in private or parochial schools. The Supreme Court upheld this decision (Allen-Meares, 2004). The question now is: Do we allow government money to be given to parents who choose to send their children to parochial schools? If this is the case, what will the fate of the public school system be? Will it be undermined?

These issues came to the fore at a time when the federal government was favoring the conservative, religious right. Because the political climate in Washington varies, it is unclear what the position of schools will be regarding religious involvement and moral teachings in public schools. Some of the legal interpretations involving religion and schools are as follows:

- Public schools can teach about religion but can't teach religion.
- Students have the right to their religious observations as long as they are not disruptive.
- School facilities can be used by noncurriculum-related groups as long as they are accessible to all student groups.
- Religious holidays cannot be celebrated in schools, but the nonreligious facets of the holiday can be observed.
- Students are not required to say the Pledge of Allegiance if it is against their religious beliefs to do so.
- All nonrelated school literature distribution can be regulated by school authorities. (Whittaker, Salend, & Elhoweris, 2009)

When our path is clearly set on a conservative religious agenda, the rights and freedoms of those minority religions are questioned. Children in school are sometimes discriminated against as not fitting into mainstream practices. These children are often bullied and oppressed by those of the majority. The fundamentalist sects of many religious groups are populations that do come to the attention of the school social worker. It is important that we deal with these groups from a social work ethical perspective. Nonjudgmental practice and respecting the beliefs of others, even those beliefs that are different from our own, are essential and a challenge to many social workers.

We are faced more and more with the fundamentalist religious sects. In some cases, these groups have a political connotation such as the terrorist groups that are in existence. They seem to use fundamentalist religious philosophy to rationalize behaviors that are sometimes harmful. We must employ "practice wisdom" so as not to invade our clients' private and personal religious beliefs. It is not in the purview of the school social worker or any public employee to delve into the religious background of our constituents. Our position should be to understand religion and its concomitants only in the context of how it impacts our students. We must protect our students' rights to freedom of religious practice under the First Amendment to the U.S. Constitution (Franklin et al., 2006).

SOCIOECONOMIC STATUS

Studies have found that working class children have more difficulty with being successful in an academic environment. They are sometimes deprived of the exposure to educational pursuits to which middle class children have access. (The communities where these children live tend to have schools that are underresourced and underserviced. Classes tend to be overcrowded, and social and emotional supports are in high demand. These schools also have more classified children in need of receiving special education services.) This imbalance in exposure leads to a gap between the classes and puts the children of working class families at a disadvantage regarding academic grades and college entrance. Many of the standardized tests are said to be culture bound, which furthers the culture divide. Even when they get to college, the divide still exists. The way classes are structured (with discourse and self-disclosure) would leave a student of a working class family with feelings of inadequacy and alienation (Casey, 2005).

Other issues that create the divide are lack of medical insurance and lack of appropriate clothing, which may increase the amount of absenteeism among the working class families' children. Working class families' children are more likely not to receive medical treatment when they get sick, which can cause longer absences. These situations also correlate with poorer academic achievement.

It appears that dreams and hopes of a successful life do not vary across the socioeconomic status (SES) lines. All children begin with these but circumstances often interfere, leaving children of the working class depressed, and often their reality distorts their perception leaving them willing to accept a life with less success. It is within the purview of the school social worker to help these students focus on the here and now in an effort to get them to strive for a better outcome (Franklin et al., 2006). Institutional racism and oppression are often factors that interfere with the academic success of some children. While some schools do an excellent job of bridging the academic gap by providing extra services to children and families, others lack the motivation and/or resources, and their failure is seen in increased dropout rates. Families impacted by severe trauma and/or poverty have difficulty accessing basic needs, and as a result children suffer in school. Mental health issues and lack of supports in the school and community impact children's academic progress. Groups can sometimes be helpful in having students look at what they would like to achieve and the ways of projecting a positive self-image to achieve these goals. Time lines can be helpful in connecting current behavior to activities for the near future to an adult image that one is trying to achieve (Franklin et al., 2006). Focusing on the strengths of the student helps him or her achieve these goals. It is essential that our students coming from low income or working class families be guided and given the support necessary to succeed. Our statistics show that more than half of adolescent children from the working class families do not complete high school within the allotted 4 years (Franklin et al., 2006). It is our goal as social workers to give students access to their dreams.

SUMMARY

In this chapter, the focus was on the development of self-awareness of cultural competence. Practical assessment tools were presented in order to understand our own biases and cultural discriminatory practices. Racial, ethnic and religious diversity were explored. A special emphasis was placed on immigrant populations who are in need of special attention particularly with the influx of underdocumented workers as well as immigrant populations that come to the US legally and fully documented. Issues of sexual orientation and LGBTQ issues were also examined. Religious issues in the school were also discussed. The impact of socio-economic status on education was explained.

ACTIVITIES

Activity 1: When referred a student from a different ethnicity, what issues would you discuss regarding ethnic and/or racial differences? When would you address these?

Activity 2: Describe a counseling intervention with someone that would focus on ethnicity whether the same or different. How would you deal with ethnocultural transference and countertransference?

SELF-REFLECTION QUESTIONS

1. Is cultural competency essential for all school social workers no matter what school district they work in?
2. What is the best way for a school social worker to be an effective culturally competent social worker?

CLASS DISCUSSION QUESTIONS

1. Discuss ways of intervening with multicultural groups in an effort to "level the playing field."
2. What are the areas of multicultural self-awareness that you need to work on?
3. What will be the fate of public education if the voucher system is adopted in various states?

Chapter 8

Current Societal Issues Affecting Children in Schools

INTRODUCTION

A current overview of issues facing children in schools seems overwhelming. These issues do not only affect children but society in general. We need to face these issues and plan what we can do to alleviate the causes and help children to succeed in school. With the worldwide net becoming a reality for all socio-economic groups, issues of bullying such as cyber bullying and gender bullying are important to our school-age children. Suicide has even become a concomitant of this phenomenon. Homelessness and the inability of children to receive any form of a compulsory education leaves a segment of our children in danger of illiteracy and the loss of a basic right of all children to a free and public school education. Poverty has become a substantial problem in our stressed economy. In 2008, 20.7% of children between the ages of 0 and 17 were living below the poverty threshold (which was $21,756 for a family of four in 2009) (U.S. Census Bureau). This situation has significant implications for the school community. Are our schools providing for immigrant, underdocumented, and refugee children who have come here with families in need of a safe life where they can live in freedom? What policies do we have in place for this powerless contingent in our schools? If children are traumatized by the loss of their parent(s) to placement in prison, the effects of foster placement as well as loss will also affect these children's ability to function to their potential. Abused children or those under the auspices of the Department of Human Services are dramatically affected educationally. School violence, which has become a less than shocking occurrence in the recent past, is an issue that must be faced. Policies need to be instituted as well as counseling for those who have suffered the effects of these events. In our present society, the LGBTQ adults have formed a newer-family constellation. The children in these families will need support (as will their parents) to overcome any issues of discrimination they might face. Children of a veteran(s) or a parent(s) serving in the armed forces in war zones face many unique issues. Some children suffer the loss of a parent in these situations twice: The first time when their parent(s) goes away and sometimes, the next when their parent(s) is tragically killed. These are but a few of the recent issues facing our school children. As time evolves, new and pressing demands of society will become issues in need of attention in our school environment.

HOMELESS CHILDREN AND EDUCATION

Of all homeless people, 25% to 39% are children. There are over one million homeless children in the United States. Contributing to this dilemma are the problems of unemployment and significant reduction of social welfare services. The homeless numbers are on the rise, which leads to many families being turned away from shelters because of lack of space. They end up on the streets or sleeping in their cars or trucks. Homeless children are less the object of concern than their poverty-stricken parents. We tend to focus on them, since they are unemployed and responsible for the children. Many homeless children exhibit developmental delays and issues of social and emotional concerns. One-third of these children exhibit the symptoms of clinical depression. Many homeless children witness domestic violence, and 27% exhibit serious behavioral problems (Hicks-Coolick, Burnside-Eaton, & Peters, 2003).

Many homeless children do not receive an education (43% according to Hicks-Coolick, Burnside-Eaton, & Peters, 2003) and are not registered in school, and 50% of them are held back at least one grade. Many are in need of an extended school day and/or summer programs, remediation of academics, and therapeutic interventions. Tutoring, support with attendance, and cultural competence are needs to be addressed by those dealing with homeless children.

The McKinney-Vento Act was passed in 1987. It was restated in the No Child Left Behind Act in 2001. It requires that states provide students experiencing homelessness with public education and provide help for their success in schools.

Key provisions of the act include:

- Students who are homeless can remain in one school, even if their temporary living situation is located in another school district or attendance area, if that is in their best interest. Schools must provide transportation.

- Children and youth who are homeless can enroll in school and begin attending immediately, even if they cannot produce normally required documents, such as birth certificates, proof of guardianship, immunization records, or proof of residency.
- Every school district must designate a homeless liaison to ensure the McKinney-Vento Act is implemented in the district. Homeless liaisons have many critical responsibilities, including identification, enrollment, and collaboration with community agencies.
- Every state must designate a state coordinator to ensure the McKinney-Vento Act is implemented in the state.
- Both state coordinators and homeless liaisons must collaborate with other agencies serving homeless children, youth, and families to enhance educational attendance and success.
- State departments of education and school districts must review and revise their policies and practices to eliminate barriers to the enrollment and retention in school of homeless children and youth (http://naehcy.org; Wright & Wright, 2007).

The good news is that even though not all children are enrolled in schools more have been enrolled since this legislation was enacted.

AN UPDATE ON BULLYING

With the worldwide web becoming a reality for all socioeconomic groups, issues of bullying such as cyber bullying and gender bullying are important to our school-age children. Suicide has even become a concomitant of this phenomenon. We have seen the recent suicide of young people who have been bullied on the Internet. It becomes imperative that we define bullying and bring it to the consciousness of parents, educators, and children alike. Many states have now passed stringent laws on bullying, and these laws must be implemented in schools. (Bullying is also discussed in Chapter 12.)

The nature of bullying is fundamental, whether it takes place on the playground, in the classroom, or on the Internet. The definition of *bullying* includes the following components:

1. "Bullying is aggressive behavior that involves unwanted, negative actions.
2. Bullying involves a pattern of behavior repeated over time.
3. Bullying involves an imbalance of power or strength" (http://www.olweus.org/public/bullying.page).

Bullying takes many forms. It can be verbal with calling of bad names, insults, or false rumors. It can be physical including hitting, kicking, and spitting. It can be nonverbal and nonphysical such as isolation or exclusion of one person, stealing, threatening gestures, or forcing one to do an act that is against his or her will. It can also take the form of racial, sexual, gender, or cyber bullying (Yerger & Gehret, 2011).

The causes of bullying vary. Many feel that it comes from environmental issues such as having authoritarian parents who use physical control and are inconsistent in their disciplinary measures. The influence of peers seems to play a more important role in recent times than in the past. Modeling peers' behavior and identification with the aggressor are a few of the reasons for bullying behavior (Yerger & Gehret, 2011).

The American Medical Association has deemed bullying a "public health concern" (Yerger & Gehret, 2011, p. 318). Victims often exhibit somatic symptoms, but the long-term effects of the problem often leave them with mental health issues, particularly depression or suicidal ideations and the worst case scenario, suicide (Yerger & Gehret, 2011).

Part of the No Child Left Behind Act is the Elementary and Secondary Education Act, which includes assistance for states to prevent violence and drug use. By 2011, 49 states have laws against bullying. The schools need to train educators and students in issues involving bullying. Schools need to create an environment that (a) helps the victims; (b) gives clear and precise consequences for bullying; (c) allows closer observation of students, especially during free time; (d) teaches students how to deal with bullying, including empowering the victims; and (e) includes a committee to deal with policy and practices related to bullying (Yerger & Gehret, 2011). Refer to Chapter 12 and the Olweus Prevention Program. Other programs include the Bully-Proofing Your School, PATHS Curriculum, Second Step and Steps to Respect, and Safe School Ambassador (SSA) program, which trains student leaders in various social groups to intervene in bullying situations (Yerger & Gehret, 2011).

Gender-based bullying includes sexual harassment both within and across the sexes. Gender-based bullying can occur if a male is seen by other males as not displaying the traditional characteristics of the gender. Females who are seen as not as feminine as the stereotype are also targets of bullying. The intersexual bullying, usually involving male perpetrators, is experienced in date violence as well as glances and comments that are hurtful. In our society heterosexual men are seen as more powerful than women or gay men. They therefore are labeled bullies when they engage in the aggressive acts against the less powerful. It is probably a very common form of bullying but is not always recognized as a pernicious act (Anagnostopoulos, Buchanan, Pereira, Lichty, 2009).

An Update on Suicide Among Children and Adolescents

Suicide among children and adolescents has always been a serious problem since the beginning of the 20th century. With the increase of cell phone and cyber bullying, we witness more deaths from suicide associated with these forms of communication. We find it appalling that such cruelty exists among young people. Although this is occurring, the Center for Disease Control noted that suicide in these age groups has decreased 25% since 1992 (Anonymous, 2004). The method of suicide has also changed. Violent suicides from gunshot wounds have decreased and suffocation (i.e., hanging) has increased.

Youth suicide climbed from the 1960s to the 1990s and peaked in the mid-1990s. Since that time, suicide has declined. The suicide rate in the United States has come to its lowest point in 30 years. The carbon monoxide suicides have decreased because of the changes in car exhaust regulations, and overall suicides from other methods have also declined. An issue of controversy is whether the use of antidepressant drugs specifically the SSRIs (selective serotonin reuptake inhibitors) caused the drop in the number of suicides in this age group. It was found that since the warnings about prescribing these drugs for children and adolescents has surged the rate of suicide in the United States has gone up by 14% (Bursztein & Apter, 2009). Prudent use of medication is seen as the best way to deal with these problems.

IMMIGRANT CHILDREN, UNDOCUMENTED CHILDREN, AND REFUGEE CHILDREN

It is of primary importance to define the difference between immigrants, refugees, and undocumented (or underdocumented, as I like to say) persons before proceeding. An *immigrant* is one who comes to a country because of a personal decision that is usually based on economic betterment or to join family members who have left their native country. A *refugee* is one who immigrates to another country because of fear of documented persecution. They are usually welcomed and given help through government and private agencies. *Undocumented* (*underdocumented*) immigrants are those who come to a country through illegal means and do not have the proper visa or other legal document permitting them to enter the new country (Bricker & Rosen, 2010).

Immigrant Children

The statistics show that immigrant children are the fastest increasing area of population growth. In 2008, 25% of those 17 and under were living with immigrant parents (Tienda & Haskins, 2011). Educational access will be the determinant of whether or not these children will achieve social integration and economic independence. Five million of these young people now live with a parent(s) who is not of legal status in this country. This fact may prevent them from accessing the needed services and benefits to a successful education because of the complexity of our government agencies (2011). Additionally, 21% of these children live in households that are not English speaking. Essentially, this becomes a problem when they compete with native students in math and reading scores on standardized tests. Poverty and low earnings of parents usually lead to poor school entry preparedness. In high schools, the immigrant children seem to fare better, especially African and Asian children. Junior colleges seem to attract this immigrant population, since they are local and lack entrance requirements. Texas and California are giving in-state tuition to undocumented students to help them attain an education. Legislation needs to be instituted to help these children gain access to higher education.

In our society where the aging population needs the support of younger workers, it would behoove us to improve the early education and help non-English speaking children to access education as an asset to our productive society and to help the burgeoning senior population in this country (Tienda & Haskins, 2008).

Igoa (1999) explains in her paper "The Inner World of the Immigrant Child" that it is necessary to examine four areas to understand the needs of the immigrant child. These are: (1) supplying them with a place to feel safe and comfortable in school, (2) language arts books that reflect their needs and equal those of the native students, (3) early intervention programs for immigrant children, and (4) art as a method of connecting and communicating. These children are brought here without their approval and are immersed in a culture that is foreign to them in all aspects. By providing the aforementioned elements, they may have an opportunity to succeed.

Undocumented Children

Undocumented children in our country are permitted to attend school K–12 in most places. They are prohibited from voting, holding a job, or getting financial aid to attend postsecondary schools including junior and 4-year colleges. In the last 10 years or so, the rights of undocumented children have become more restrictive. Since changes in the welfare laws (1996), children who come here undocumented are not allowed to have services such as Medicaid, TANF, SSI, and the state children's health insurance unless they have been in residence for 5 years or more. There are now approximately 12 million undocumented people living in the United States, many of whom are families. The number of undocumented children who live below the poverty line is 40% (Gonzales, 2009). This is an extremely vulnerable population. The Development Relief and Education for Alien Minors Act (referred to as the Dream Act) has failed to pass in Congress. The purpose of this act is to give legal status to people who are under 30 years old, were brought to this country before the age of 16, and who are going into the military or enrolling in college. Some states have passed this act, but the number of those states allowing undocumented students to pay in-state tuition has leveled off, and many states have instituted prohibitions for students who are undocumented to attend college (Miranda, 2011).

Refugee Children

Refugee children are different from other immigrant children in that they are fleeing usually unsafe or dangerous conditions and have often experienced horrors of war and oppression. Many will suffer from Post Traumatic Stress Disorder having witnessed murder, rape, desecration of religious places, and starvation to mention only a few horrors of their experience. They usually arrive with just the clothes on their body, unable to bring any of their belongings. As such, they are vulnerable to the ills of a culture where they do not know the language, customs, or lifestyle of those with whom they share a classroom (not even the teachers). They often remain in refugee camps for an undetermined time before being thrust into a country they know nothing about. There are six million refugee children worldwide (as of 2006) (Strekalova & Hoot, 2008).

Some of the issues faced by their teachers are language, parental values, identity of the children, socioeconomics, and discrimination. It is difficult to relate or try to learn new languages, because some teachers are faced with children speaking multiple languages in one classroom. Parents of these children are often reluctant to share the experiences of their children and resist teachers asking questions about the children's past. Because children come with a different identity and often lose their original identity when in the process of immigration, it is difficult for them to adapt to the identity that is thrust on them in school. Discrimination and xenophobia can damage the self-image, motivation, and academic progress of these children. Teachers, with the help of social workers, can present the differences through drama or creating a multiethnic environment in the classroom. Social workers can seek out community resources especially for those from low socioeconomic backgrounds (which comprise a majority of these immigrants) (Strekalova & Hoot, 2008).

These children are often experiencing behavioral problems. They are sometimes withdrawn or acting out explosively. With their traumatic history, concentration and academic performance are at risk. Lack of trust in adult figures is another possibility that needs to be recognized and addressed by teachers (Strekalova & Hoot, 2008). Overall, social workers are essential in bringing this knowledge to the teachers and administrators and helping them cope with the myriad issues that arise with a refugee population.

CHILDREN OF INCARCERATED PARENTS

With the burgeoning number of adults being incarcerated, the "silent victims" (their children) have been severely impacted. There are approximately two million children in the United States with imprisoned parents. This number has doubled since 1991. One and one-half million of these children have parents incarcerated in federal and state prisons (Dallaire, Ciccione, & Wilson, 2010). About 10 million more children have parents who have been previously incarcerated. Parent-child separation is seen as an indicator of problems in school and in the community (Miller, 2006). Attachment issues and depression are but a few of the problems experienced by these children. Acting-out behaviors and delinquency are also seen with these children. Of all the children with incarcerated mothers, 50% are placed with a grandparent as opposed to 15% of children with incarcerated fathers. This fact leads to a greater deal of disruption among those children whose mothers are incarcerated. The rate of female incarceration has increased 400% since 1986 (Miller, 2006). Keeping parental contact through communication and visitation is important, yet half of incarcerated parents do not receive visits from their children. Dishonesty about the parent's incarceration can lead to mistrust and withdrawal of these children. Two sample programs show promise in helping children of the incarcerated. Girl Scouts Beyond Bars was created through the state of Maryland to help form attachments between children and their incarcerated mothers. Living Interactive Family Education in Missouri works on the relationships between male inmates and their children (Miller, 2006).

Many of these children suffer academically, socially, and emotionally in the school environment. Often these children feel stigmatized and are aware of what others are thinking about them. Elementary school children seem more vulnerable than high school children. Many of the assignments in elementary school seem to emphasize the home conditions and the absence of a parent. For example, some assignments around the holidays such as Mother's Day and Father's Day involve making cards for parents or at other times the children are asked to draw pictures of their families (Dallaire et al., 2010). According to the teachers in the first study, which was qualitative, children of incarcerated parents were tardy more often, cried more than the other children in class, received unstable caregiving, and the teachers had lower expectation of these children. In the second study, which was quantitative, the teachers saw these children as more vulnerable and had lower expectations of the girls than the boys. In both studies, it was found that elementary school children suffered more than older children (Dallaire et al., 2010).

CHILDREN INVOLVED WITH THE DEPARTMENT OF HUMAN SERVICES AND EFFECTS ON EDUCATION

About 3.5 million children in the United States are referred to the Department of Human Services, particularly Child Welfare Services, each year. (This figure does not reflect those children who have been abused where the abuse was not reported.) Twenty-five percent of these children are identified as victims of child abuse and/or neglect. As opposed to the 12% in the general population, 61% of them are displaying deficits in their behavior and development (Stahmer et al., 2009). In a study conducted by Stahmer et al., it was found that toddlers who show difficulties in cognitive functioning in preschool years can show improvement with support and training of foster care parents and/or parents who receive help through the child welfare system (2009). Maltreatment contributes to the interruption of developmental progress and may even impact the future development throughout the life cycle (Cicchetti & Toth, 2005). Affective regulation is an area seen as impacted by maltreatment in children. Those children physically abused in the first 5 years show difficulties with information processing in school, were hypervigilant to cues involving hostility, and aggressively expressed hostility when even mildly provoked. Insecure attachment was evidenced in maltreated children of pre- and early school-age. Abused children were more likely to exhibit academic risk, problems with peer relationships, ego deficits, and depression (2005). They also showed a lack of empathy toward their peers.

Another area of child involvement with human services is parental use of welfare. In Ku and Plotnick's 2003 study, the children of welfare recipients (independent of income) were found to be associated with poorer educational achievement. Although children whose mothers are on welfare theoretically share more time with their parent, their self-esteem is usually impacted by the dynamic of labeling them as welfare children. The negative role model of a nonproductive parent may also impact the children's need to strive for higher academic achievement. These effects were more prevalent in middle and adolescent years. During these stages, children striving for autonomy may well be stymied by a parent's dependence. These older children would also be affected by the stigma attached to welfare recipiency (2003). Social workers might run groups for these children or help classroom teachers develop relationships with the students to better serve their academic growth.

POVERTY

Poverty can be defined economically based on the income of a family. It can also be defined in a broader sense and include ". . . not only material assets and health capacities but also capabilities, such as social belonging, cultural identity, respect and dignity, and information and education" (Engle & Black, 2008, p. 244). The earlier onset of childhood poverty leads to more lasting and long-term effects in the educational setting. Early educational lags only lead to wider discrepancies throughout the educational process. The results of these discrepancies are seen in test scores, retention, need for special services, and eventually dropout. Truancy, delinquency, and premature exiting from school are some of the major consequences of these problems (2008). Family environment is the first learning experience where values and culture are transmitted. The stimulation, exposure to cultural events, and even a higher level of vocabulary tend to limit the early experiences of poor children. An essential aspect in readiness for preschool is availability of books and the oral reading experience. These aspects of readiness are often missing in the homes of the poor or the homeless. The need to invest in early educational projects for poor children can be seen in some projects such as the Child-Parent Program in Chicago where children involved in this program were more likely to be high school graduates, find jobs, and even go to college (2008). One must be cautioned that many of the early gains made in these programs do not extend to middle and high school grades. Empowerment of the poor is a necessary ingredient for helping children and families rise from poverty.

The poor or underclass can be divided among minority groups, working class, and those below the working class (welfare or undocumented). The underclass may be residents of the inner city, which is plagued by unemployment, single mothers, violence, and drugs. There are also poverty-stricken families in rural areas. Even though these people suffer with different issues, they are not served well by educational institutions (Connell, 1994). Poverty is often looked at as a deficit in the individual student and not in the cultural and value-ridden society in which we live. Educators must recognize the power differential and help the children of poverty to have the power to succeed and make a more productive life for themselves. The poorest children have suffered more in recent years since welfare reform in 1996. Those from minority backgrounds, welfare, single parent homes, and noncitizen parents are receiving less help than before (Joo, 2011).

VIOLENCE AND WEAPONS IN SCHOOLS

Violence in Schools

When we think of the violence in schools that has been perpetrated in recent times, we all but wonder what is going on in our society. Is this wave of violence isolated incidents or can it be attributed to other factors? We live in a culture of violence. Children are exposed to death and destruction on a daily basis as an integral part of the society in which we live. Our schools are microcosms of our culture and can contribute to a positive or negative environment. Characteristics of schools that contribute to a positive environment are "collaborative leadership, teacher collaboration, professional development, and learning partnerships" (Finley, 2004, p. 68). When school violence occurs, a more authoritarian atmosphere arises with punishments and more stringent restraints and rules imposed. These become part and parcel of everyday life in schools and become accepted as the best way to deal with the problems. Simple solutions are given for very intricate problems. Supportive interventions by teachers, achievement of students, and positive school and classroom environments are elements that help prevent school violence (2004). There are always the exceptions to the rules, but overall, creating an atmosphere of positive feelings and help when needed seem more reasonable and at least provide a plan that would limit violence in school. A partnership model where teachers and students have input seems more likely to be a violence deterrent than the dominator model where few make rules and do not listen to the ideas and issues of both the teachers and students (2004).

Some of the characteristics and behaviors seen in those students who commit violent acts are as follows: aggressive and impulsive behaviors, isolation from school activities and peers, academic failure and or struggles, deficit parenting, domestic violence, and child abuse (Perry, 2001). These signs do not ascertain violent behavior but may be indicators with the proper set of circumstances. Inclusion of isolated students needs to be encouraged, and education about coping with issues of disrespect and especially bullying needs to be included in the curriculum.

Weapons in Schools

The incidence of weapon carrying to school has been investigated through the years. The Center for Disease Control reported that in 2004 17% of students in the 9th through 12th grade had carried a weapon once or more within a 30-day period (cited in Finkenbine & Dwyer, 2006). Early studies of junior and high school students found that those students who carried weapons to school did not do so for protection. It was seen as a rather common practice by those who carried weapons to school and a peer-related behavior. As listed above, the characteristics of those weapon carrying students include drug and alcohol use, not living with biological parents, not feeling closely bonded with parents, fighting and other aggressive acts in school, and defacing school property (Bailey, Flewelling, & Rosenbaum, 1997). In the Finkenbine and Dwyer study, those who carried weapons were usually cited for other aggressive behaviors and were poor students by their own admission (2006). Mental health services, lower intelligence, substance abuse, and poor judgment were also significant variables among study participants who carried weapons to school. Of those students in the Bailey study, 15% admitted to carrying a weapon to school. Other variables that resulted were that the students (carrying weapons) were male, non-Whites, and from urban and suburban areas. Heavy use of alcohol was another significant variable (1999). Although this study is dated, the characteristics remain constant except for the racial aspect of this study.

The research substantiates the fact that supportive environments where teachers, administrators, and staff partner with students help alleviate the problem of students carrying weapons to school. Providing adults and students in schools with the tools necessary to prevent weapon carrying is essential. Training and a supportive environment help people feel safe in a school milieu. The metal detectors and police presence in school can damage the positive environment and reduce the atmosphere of safety in the schools (Gastic, 2010).

PARENTS, FAMILIES, AND FRIENDS OF LESBIANS AND GAYS, AND CHILDREN OF GAYS OR LESBIANS

PFLAG National is a nonprofit organization dedicated to providing support, education, and advocacy for those dealing with and understanding issues surrounding lesbian, gay, bisexual, and transgender (LGBT) people. Their core goals are as follows:

> "**One.** Build the capacity of our organization at every level so that we may have all the resources, in the form of information, people and funding, necessary to move forward in our work with the greatest possible effect.
>
> **Two.** Create a world in which our young people may grow up and be educated with freedom from fear of violence, bullying and other forms of discrimination, regardless of their real or perceived gender identity or sexual orientation or that of their families.
>
> **Three.** Make our vision and our message accessible to the broadest range of ethnic and cultural communities, ending the isolation of families with lesbian, gay, bisexual and transgender family members within those communities.

Four. Work toward full inclusion of lesbian, gay, bisexual and transgender persons within their chosen communities of faith.

Five. Create a society in which all LGBT persons may openly and safely pursue the career path of their choice, and may be valued and encouraged to grow to their full potential in the workplace.

Six. Create a society in which all lesbian, gay, bisexual and transgender persons may enjoy, in every aspect of their lives, full civil and legal equality and may participate fully in all the rights, privileges and obligations of full citizenship in this country" (http://community.pflag.org).

As counselors, we need to be able to understand the issues of the gay and lesbian headed families and the goals of this in an effort to support the families who need our assistance in schools.

In the United States, the number of lesbian mothers is approximately one to five million and one to three million for gay fathers. The total number of children from this cohort is about four to 14 million (Lambert, 2005). If children come from families in which the stress and conflict of divorce and separation occurred, there are more issues of adjustment as to whether or not the families are heterosexual, lesbian, or gay. In another report by Dr. Shiller (2007) from Yale University, it is stated that children from gay or lesbian homes, when compared to those from heterosexual homes, show no differences in mental health or social adjustment issues.

The question always posed resounds with the issue of whether or not children of gay or lesbian families are as psychologically healthy as those from heterosexually headed homes. Children from gay or lesbian homes do not develop sexual orientation or gender role behavior based on their parent's sexual orientation (Lambert, 2005). Psychological development (including psychiatric involvement), self-concept, and moral development have not been shown to be significantly different between children of gay or lesbian and heterosexual families. Another area of concern was that of peer relationships. Research indicates that there doesn't appear to be a difference between those of gay or lesbian families and heterosexual families (2005).

It is hoped that as school social workers we might develop family diversity workshops for both teachers and students implementing ideas of acceptance and openness about these issues. Integrated in these workshops would be self-knowledge, inclusive learning, and problem-solving activities. Understanding our own biases is part of the process of self-knowledge and acceptance of diversity. Regarding inclusive learning, each student needs to be identified as an individual not a child of a parent with a different sexual orientation. In a workshop, one can include activities for problem solving that would enhance the diverse classroom situation. We need to keep in mind that brainstorming together is much more enriching than trying to solve problems by yourself (Koerner & Hulsebosch, 1996). Teachers and students through workshop activities become consciously aware of language that is used and learn how to deal with egregious statements. Having lessons that help children deal with diverse family situations or having a bulletin board depicting diverse family styles may help awareness and at least educate the school community (1996).

CHILDREN OF SOLDIERS AND/OR VETERANS

Military deployment involves various situations, such as training, keeping peace, and participation in warfare. Currently in the United States, the period of deployment ranges from 6 to 18 months (Sheppard, Malatras, & Israel, 2010). Of those presently in the military service, 42% have children and 14% are women (some of who are mothers) (2010). Some of the negative concomitants of deployment are child maltreatment, mental health issues of children, and lack of family stability both physically and emotionally. According to Sheppard, Malatras, & Israel, the Army Central Registry reported 1771 families with deployed parents had recorded incidents of child maltreatment, particularly neglect (2010). Since the Iraq and Afghanistan conflicts, two studies showed lower grades in all academic areas for children of deployed soldiers.

Regarding mental health issues, research has shown that deployment of parents has a negative effect on children. Aggressive and angry behaviors as well as passive behaviors such as sadness, depression, and anxiety have been shown to be significantly increased in children of deployed parents as opposed to those children in the control groups (Sheppard, Malatras, & Israel, 2010). Physical stress level, heartbeat, and increased blood pressure have been shown to be present in the children of deployed military personnel (2010). The greater the length of parental military deployment, the more problematic the child's adjustment becomes as referenced in Sheppard et al.

Overall, awareness and understanding of these issues by school personnel may help allay the problems that the children of deployed military experience in the school environment. It behooves school social workers to assess the issues that these children may face and work cooperatively with families and teachers to provide the needed support for these children. This can be done individually or on a schoolwide basis.

SUMMARY

The purpose of this chapter is to review the current issues that children face in our society at the beginning of the 21st century. As times change, we as school social workers must keep abreast of current societal trends and problems that arise for our school students. Keeping up to date on the issues will help us to deal more intelligently and professionally with them.

This chapter included some of the overriding issues of our times: homeless children, problems of bullying in our schools, suicide among young people, immigrant children including undocumented and refugee children, children of incarcerated parents, human services participants, victims of poverty, school violence, children of diverse family configurations, and children of military personnel. Although these challenges are diverse in nature, we as school social workers must strive to address and remedy them as our children face them regularly.

ACTIVITIES

Activity 1: Level 1: Choose an area of concern from this chapter and outline an intervention that you might use.

Level 2: Choose one of these areas of concern and one that has occurred in your school. Using the evidence-based perspective, how would you treat the problem area?

Activity 2: Level 1: What are the areas of policies needed in your state that would be most essential? Why?

Level 2: Investigate policies in your school placement that deal with three of the above current issues.

SELF-REFLECTION QUESTIONS

1. In view of the changing landscape of our country regarding incoming groups, what provisions do you think should be made to accommodate these populations?
2. What part should a school social worker play in the development of school policies for one of the areas of need found in this chapter?

CLASS DISCUSSION QUESTIONS

1. What experience have you had with each of the issues presented in this chapter?
2. Do you think that you can proficiently deal with the problems involved with children from diverse background either coming from the United States or from another country? Are you self-aware on each aspect presented in this chapter?

Chapter 9

Engagement, Assessment, and Intervention Skills in the School for Individuals Using Evidence-Based Practice Modalities and Other Practice Methods

SECTION I

INTRODUCTION

In the first section of this chapter the idea of referral—self, teacher, counselor, administrator, or family—is discussed. Depending on the age and developmental maturity of the child, engagement is considered. Before effective assessment can take place, engagement is essential. Assessment can take place informally through the interview process or more formally through assessment scales or inventories. Such tools as adaptive behavioral rating scales and self-concept scales are specifically presented with the idea of effective use in the school practice. Different scales are proposed for different developmental age groups. A definition of Evidence-based Practice (EBP) is presented as well as its components. Intervention skills are explained.

More specifically some evidence-based practice modalities such as Cognitive-Behavioral Therapy and Solution-Focused Treatment are discussed. These are presented since they are easily adaptable to the school environment. Specific issues seen more commonly are presented with intervention skills that are useful. The place of school-linked services in the referral of students is explained as well as examples given of when these services should be recommended.

REFERRAL

Students are referred to the school social worker in several different ways. These are: self-referral, school personnel (guidance counselor, teacher, administrator, etc.), parents, community agencies, and other students. Rarely are referrals discussed in the literature. The method of referral is varied and does not follow a specific structure.

Example: Some school districts have formal referral forms that are filled out by the person making the referral. (Example retrieved from http://admin.loudoncounty.org)

SCHOOL SOCIAL WORK REFERRAL FORM

Date: ___/___/___

Student Name: ____________________ (M / F) Grade level:

Classroom Teacher: ______________________________

Referred by: ______________________________

Parental Notification: Y / N

Academic Status: ______________________________

Disciplinary History (if any): ______________________________

____

Has this student previously been referred by you? Y/N

If so, when and for what reason: ______________________________

____

Reason for present referral:____

____

____

____

These are often developed for faculty, staff, and administrators to use. Informal referral usually takes place by parents, peers, and self-referrals. Other schools are less formal, and oral communication is the method of referral. The reasons for referral to the school social worker are varied. These range but are not limited to dangers involving suicidal threats, eating disorders, peer or gang involved crises, absenteeism or truancy, pregnancy or unsafe sexual activity, school failure, and behavioral disruptions.

Often, these referrals are appropriate, but at other times they are not. It behooves the school social worker to evaluate whether or not the referral is appropriate. Depending on the extent of seriousness of the problem, the social worker may choose to refer the students to other services or outside agencies.

In terms of evaluations for children with special needs, the social worker can develop an outreach referral plan to community agencies, which include hospitals, doctors, and social service organizations, to ensure that all children in need of school services are given the opportunity to attend school. Of course, evaluations are essential for these children as they must be given the appropriate education that enables them to maximize their potential. A school screening process needs to be put in place to ensure that children are identified. Prereferral services include giving services to children before evaluation takes place (RtI is an example of this concept). If all supports that are put in place don't help the child attain success in school, then a formal referral to the Child Study Team would be the next step in the process. Before kindergarten, many school districts screen incoming students for issues that may impede their learning. A member of the team and a classroom teacher are sometimes the professionals who do this work.

ENGAGEMENT

Before one can attempt to assess a client successfully, engagement is essential. A school social worker needs to listen to the client and show empathic understanding of him or her prior to assessment. As Constable, McDonald, and Flynn suggest, understanding them personally and talking about everyday life is important in engaging the client(s) (2002). Empathic listening with attention and interest in what the client is saying helps in the engagement process. Using words of encouragement and urging the client to continue expressing his or her thoughts leads to a more well-developed relationship. This process gives entree into the assessment phase of therapy. Showing positive regard and acceptance of the client(s) essentially creates a sense of trust and willingness to cooperate with the social worker (2002). Nonverbal communication also gives the client(s) the feeling that he or she is being cared for. Relationship building can help facilitate the assessment and evaluation of the student in the school setting. Many times in schools children are spoken of as though they were not present. The best way to engage children in the school milieu is to ask their opinion or have them participate in the conversation about themselves. This attempt is usually received with great relief and helps build the self-esteem of the students participating. It also allows the students to realize that the social worker is sincerely interested in them, and their thoughts and feelings. Thus engagement begins.

Example: As a seasoned school social worker, observing a student social worker is important. In a junior high school, I had the opportunity to sit in on a session. The child (student) was referred for not doing her homework. The social work student began by asking her why? The child didn't know the answer and became silent and withdrawn. I received permission to speak and asked the girl what she liked to do after school. She began by telling us that she loved to dance. This was the icebreaker that helped the student social worker proceed with assisting the student with her problem.

Engagement can occur as early as kindergarten. Most of the time, engaging a child in a game, a snack, or group activity can help in the engagement process. The key is developing that personal connection that will allow trust to develop.

In the upper elementary grades, reassuring the child of confidentiality and letting them know the parameters of it will give the social worker a chance to develop this most needed element.

High school–aged children are more difficult to engage, unless they are personally seeking the help. Even then, they can be suspicious of the contact. Discussing apprehensions and letting them know something about yourself and what you do in your capacity can help in this process. An honest approach to this age group is most effective. Keep in mind that by this stage in their educational experience attitudes and opinions have been formed. Many have been tainted by poor academic performance and negative responses to behaviors. Let them know how they were referred and for what reason. This will help in rapport building.

ASSESSMENT

"Assessment is a comprehensive process of deriving meaning from data, achieving a broad but detailed description and understanding of individuals, behaviors, and environments, and the reciprocal interactions among each of these elements. Properly carried out, assessment is a dynamic synthesis and evaluation of multiple sources of data believed to be relevant to the status of the individuals, behaviors and environments being examined" (Reynolds, 1984 cited in Kayser & Lyon, 2000, p. 197). It is not one aspect of a person or group but as we know it in social work a confluence of person in environment (PIE).

Informal Assessment

The informal assessments that social workers do are unique to the profession. Since our training encompasses multilevel assessment processes, we do become extremely adept at the informal type of assessment. Having a background in child development is essential to this process. We gather information about social-emotional status, academic functioning, familial and other venues of support, and medical or health background. These areas and the synthesis of this information enable us to assess the student well (Harrison & Harrison, 2009). Informal observation and examination of school and guidance records also adds to our fund of knowledge (Pryor, 1996).

Social workers assess whether or not the interviewee is exhibiting age appropriate behavior. A course in child development is imperative for a school social worker to experience. Knowing "normal" developmental tasks of each stage or grade level helps assess the child's comfort level in his or her environment.

Body language is another area for a social worker to examine. One can look at eye contact, posture, and signs of anxiety such as fidgeting, foot shaking, and so on. Visual signs such as tears welling up in the student's eyes, frowning, grimacing, clenching of the jaw, or stamping of the feet are all signs of emotional expression. Watching children at play is also very revealing. The social worker might observe aggressive behavior, passive-aggressive signs, or possibly passive behavior. How a child handles stress or crisis can also be observed in watching children's play or other forms of interaction with peers and adults. In most cases with younger children, play behavior is a valuable informal assessment tool.

Some of our training skills also enhance our assessment. Active listening, reflection, partializing, reframing, and redirecting are some of the skills that are taught in graduate education (Harrison & Harrison, 2009). These techniques give us advantages over other school counseling faculty who have not been trained in the same way. Needless to say, empathy that social workers exhibit helps comfort and relieve clients when discussing sensitive and difficult areas of concern. A concern such as suicide potential is an area where social workers seem to be well prepared to evaluate. In the Singer and Slovak study (2011), 90% of the school social workers interviewed reported that their graduate studies had prepared them for assessing suicidal risk and providing important interventions.

More Formal Assessment Tools

Testing is a method of obtaining information but only one aspect of the full picture. The following are those assessment tools that are used along with observation and interview methods:

Standardized Assessment Tools: (The examples that will be given are by no means complete but rather a sample of what is available).

- *The Young Children's Empathy Measure* is used to assess the cognitive and affective perception of a preschool child's empathy (Poresky, 1990).
- *Depression Rating Scale* is an instrument to measure the degree and intensity of depression in children from ages 7 to 13 years (Birleson, cited in Corcoran & Fischer, 2000).
- *Behavioral and Emotional Rating Scale* is an instrument that has separate scales for youth, teachers, and parents. It helps measure the personal strengths of children ages 5 through 18. It measures five areas of a child's strength: (1) interpersonal strength, (2) family involvement, (3) intrapersonal strength, (4) school functioning, and (5) affective strength. This assessment is helpful as a prereferral tool and for placing children for specialized aid. It can be given in schools, mental health arenas, and child welfare agencies. There is a second version developed for the Hispanic culture (Epstein & Sharma, 1998).
- *Children's Cognitive Assessment Questionnaire* is a scale that measures test anxiety for school-aged children. It measures self-defeating versus self-enhancing thoughts. It was normed on fifth- and sixth-grade children (Zatz & Chassin, cited in Corcoran & Fischer, 2000).
- *Children's Perceived Self-Control Scale* is an 11-item scale including "problem recognition, commitment, self-regulation and habit reorganization" (Corcoran & Fischer, 2000, p. 519). It was normed on fourth and fifth graders (Humphrey, cited in Corcoran & Fischer, 2000).
- *Child Report of Posttraumatic Symptoms and Parent Report of Posttraumatic Symptoms* is designed to be both a self-scale and a parental report. It was

normed on middle elementary school students in both urban and rural schools (Greenwald & Rubin, cited in Corcoran & Fischer, 2000).

- *Adolescent Concerns Evaluation* was derived to assess runaway potential for adolescents. It doesn't answer the question "why" but can be a valid indicator (Springer, cited in Corcoran & Fischer, 2000).
- *Assertiveness Scale for Adolescents* provides scenarios for adolescents to choose how they would respond. It can be used on students in grades 6 through 12 (Lee, Hallberg, Slemon, & Haase, cited in Corcoran & Fischer, 2000).
- *Behavioral Self-Concept Scale* is an instrument used to measure school-related self-concept. The authors feel that children's self-concept can be influenced by the school milieu. It was normed on fourth and fifth graders (Williams & Workman, cited in Corcoran & Fischer, 2000).
- *Behavior Rating Index for Children (BRIC)* is used by people who observe children. It measures the degree of behavioral difficulties. It can be used for children of all ages (Stiffman, Orme, et al., cited in Corcoran & Fischer, 2000).
- *Childhood Personality Scale* was developed to measure personality and competence in children. It is a parental reporting scale examining children's behaviors both positive and negative (Dibble & Cohen, cited in Corcoran & Fischer, 2000).
- *Children's Cognitive Assessment Questionnaire* is used to measure enhancing and defeating cognitions related to test anxiety. It was normed on middle elementary school children. Self-defeating cognitions hinder test performance, while enhancing thoughts help in test performance. This scale would be especially useful in a school setting (Zatz & Chassin, cited in Corcoran & Fischer, 2000).
- *Eyberg Behavior Inventory* was designed to measure behavioral conduct of children and adolescents ages 2 through 17. It measures "aggression, noncompliance, temper tantrums, disruptive and annoying behaviors, stealing, lying . . ." (Eyberg, cited in Corcoran & Fischer, 2000, p. 540). It is a parental rating scale that is used often (Eyberg, cited in Corcoran & Fischer, 2000).
- *Family, Friends, and Self Form* is a scale which assesses adolescents regarding family and peer relationships, personal reflections, and psychological adaptation. It is used to assess adolescents at risk of acting-out behavior (Simpson & McBride, cited in Corcoran & Fischer, 2000).
- *Hare Self-Esteem Scale* is used to assess self-esteem in children 10 and older. It was normed on fifth- and eighth-grade children. It measures self-esteem

in the child's environment including family, school, and peers (Hare, cited in Corcoran & Fischer, 2000).

- *Homework Problem Checklist* is an instrument given to parents to assess the problems that children are encountering with homework. Frequency and intensity of the problem is assessed (Anesko, Scholock, Ramirez, & Levine, cited in Corcoran & Fischer, 2000).
- *Index of Peer Relations* assesses the degree, gravity, and quality of peer relationships. It is a self-reporting instrument (Hudson, cited in Corcoran & Fischer, 2000).
- *Multi-Attitude Suicide Tendency Scale* is used to measure suicidal capability in adolescents. It assesses attitudes toward life and death. It was normed on children ages 15 through 18 years old. It is an important scale for those dealing with troubled adolescents (Obach, et al., cited in Corcoran & Fischer, 2000).
- *Concern Over Weight and Dieting Scale* assess tendencies in adolescents toward eating disorders. It can be used when there is a suspicion of anorexia or bulimia (Kagan & Squires, cited in Corcoran & Fischer, 2000).
- *Conners' Teacher Rating Scale* is an assessment tool for teachers to assess "hyperactivity, conduct problems, emotional indulgent, anxious passive, asocial, daydream-attention problems, and hyperactivity index . . ." (Dupper, 2003, p. 212).
- *The Young Children's Empathy Measure* assesses preschool children's empathy. This is considered a measure of social development and evaluates the child's ability to feel the emotions of others (Poresky, 1990).
- *Brown Attention Deficit Disorder Scales for Children and Adolescents* assesses deficiencies in executive functioning which is considered the basis of ADHD. There are different scales for 3 to 7 year olds, 8 to 12 year olds, and 12 to 18 year olds (Brown, cited in Corcoran and Walsh, 2006).

EVIDENCE-BASED PRACTICE IN SCHOOL SOCIAL WORK

According to the National Association of Social Workers (NASW) website, "evidence-based practice is a process in which the practitioner combines well-researched interventions with clinical experience and ethics, and client preferences and culture to guide and inform the delivery of treatment services" (http://www.socialworkpolicy.org).

Evidence-based (EB) *practice* in schools can be defined as practices using ". . . guidelines, standards for care, empirically supported treatment manuals and protocols, and expert consensus reviews on the best way to treat a client population" (Vandiver, cited in Franklin, 2001). The philosophy for using evidence-based practice is to use the best practice that is empirically based for the specific problem the child or adolescent is experiencing. It is the mandate of our profession to use the most appropriate and effective intervention that we know. School social workers have been advocating for such practices for many years. The Interdisciplinary Council on Developmental and Learning Disorders (http://www.icdl.com/) is an organization that develops practice guidelines for professionals working with children, adolescents and families of special education students (Franklin, 2001). Its journal, *Journal of Developmental Processes*, is available online and is free. It provides a developmental model for helping professionals deal most effectively with children with learning challenges.

There are four phases of evidence-based social work practice:

1. Questioning—This involves choosing a target or social problem that you wish to explore. It may be the exploration of a particular aspect or the effectiveness of the intervention that you plan to apply. An example of this would be: Does the group process work for children of divorce in the schools?

2. Searching—This entails being guided by the EB question and finding or looking for appropriate resources to answer your question. A record of the information should be kept systematically.

3. Analyzing—This effort involves evaluating, identifying the parts, and synthesizing the information to arrive at evidence that supports your findings and inferences.

4. Applying and Evaluating—Once the process is complete, the social worker then shares with the client the needs and what he or she believes will best alleviate the distress. The client must be an informed consumer so it is essential to include him or her in the selection process of the treatment plan.

Substantiating and sharing the information with professionals in the system is essential for EB information. It is developed to be shared.

The NASW has put forth two standards for research-based school social work practice. These are:

1. "School social workers shall use research to inform practice and understand social policies related to schools" (Standard 17);

2. "School social workers shall be able to evaluate their practice and disseminate the findings to consumers, the local education agency, the community, and the profession" (Standard 23) (Raines, 2008).

COGNITIVE-BEHAVIORAL THERAPY

One of the most well-known modalities that supports evidence-based practice intervention is cognitive-behavioral therapy. Cognitive-behavioral therapy (CBT) is a collaborative effort between the therapist and the client. The child or adolescent takes an active role in identifying the goals, developing targets, practicing the new behavior, and evaluating his or her performance. The therapist both supports and provides structure for this process. It is a modality that deals with the present and focuses on a problem that the child or adolescent is experiencing. It does not look for the etiology of the problem but more directly the solution to the present situation. It is time-limited, usually lasting up to about 16 sessions (one session per week). It basically relates the thoughts, feelings, and behaviors together for a total understanding of the problem, and therefore the solution becomes apparent. The following is an outline of the process:

- *Cognitive process* includes the therapist teaching the child or adolescent the link between thoughts, feelings, and behaviors. It provides the understanding to how people think, act, and feel.
- *Thought monitoring* involves focusing on core beliefs, negative automatic thoughts, or incorrect assumptions. Becoming aware of these thoughts helps the person understand his or her way of thinking. This process helps the person evaluate his or her thoughts and encourages balanced thinking and cognitive restructuring. New cognitive skills are then addressed such as positive self-talk, self-instructional training, thinking of consequences, and learning to problem solve.
- *Affective process* helps the young person identify his or her feelings. Such feelings as anger, frustration, and sadness are addressed, and the concomitant bodily sensations are associated with these emotions. Associations with thoughts, time, places, or activities that evoke negative and positive feelings are explored. These emotions are rated on a scale and help evaluate changes. Relaxation training, guided imagery, and/or breathing exercises help manage these emotions.
- *Behavioral process* is the third part of this process. When thoughts and beliefs are challenged, new behaviors that conform to the changes in cognitive functioning that follow must be tried. Through imagining or in vivo experiments, the new behaviors are tested. In the process of coping with difficult experiences, exposure on a gradual basis is designed to allow the student to become accustomed to the uncomfortable situation. Role playing, modeling and rehearsal for difficult situations are among the behaviors that are used in CBT.

- *Positive reinforcement* is among the very important components of CBT. In schools, charts and stars as well as other types of feedback that promote positive reinforcement of behaviors are given. Some schools use token economies where children are given a number of tokens for each positive accomplishment. Tokens are then accumulated and rewards are purchased with them (Stallard, 2002).

Example: In the class that I supervised for emotionally disturbed upper classmen in the high school, we gave fake dollar bills (changing the size so we didn't break the law) as rewards. At the end of the week, those who had received a certain number (which each student knew at the onset) were permitted to go on an outing that was prepared for them. Those who didn't would stay behind and complete unfinished work. This motivational technique, although very simplistic, had a good track record of students achieving the set goals for the week.

SOLUTION-FOCUSED BRIEF APPROACH

Another modality that supports evidence-based practice is solution-focused brief approach (SFBT) therapy. SFBT therapy is based on a model of mental health, not pathology. Clients are asked how they would like things to be different rather than being asked about the problem that brought them to therapy. Solutions are found rather than solving of problems. Building solutions is an essential component of this intervention. The question is asked about how the client would like things to be different and how they would go about achieving that goal. Then they are asked how they would proceed in keeping those changes in place. Looking for times and events that are exceptions to the problem is also part of this process (Berg & DeJong, 1996). Talking about the problem is not desirable and only reinforces helplessness. The following are the steps in the interview process for SFBT:

- Asking the *miracle question* is having the student tell the therapist how things would be if the problem were solved (e.g., If you woke up tomorrow morning and your life was ideal, explain how it would be.).
- Asking if change is happening and what the student has done to create that change.
- Figuring out what it would take to have the change continue.
- Monitoring the situation until the client can confidently maintain the change.

One would start with the miracle question. This would be followed up by asking for a specific picture of what would be different, what would others observe in seeing the change, and how will that make the situation different for you and those around you (Gingerich & Wabeke, 2001).

Another important component of this modality is the *scaling question*. This procedure gives the student the opportunity to rate the change and thus quantify for himself or herself what has occurred. Usually a 10-point scale is used.

The next part of this process is the *coping question*. That is, what are the ways that you have used to cope with this problem thus far? What has or hasn't worked for you?

The final phase of the process is the *consultation phase* where the therapist leaves for a few minutes and comes back with a message for the client. The therapist usually begins with a positive statement. It then ends with a homework assignment to keep up the good work or to try what has been suggested in the miracle question (Gingerich & Wabeke, 2001).

In the school environment, this modality is usually used with behavioral disordered children. Some positive results have been seen with children suffering with depression, anxiety, and substance abuse. This process has been tried in school groups as well and has worked effectively. It can also be used with parents and children. Teachers can also be trained to carry out solution-focused interventions in the classroom (Gingerich & Wabeke, 2001).

Example: When counseling a high school special education student, I asked the miracle question. The young man had been involved in a series of impulsive behaviors, which caused him to become classified as emotionally disturbed for educational purposes. He had recently been suspended for having a knife in his pocket and trying to sell marijuana to another student. When I asked him what would his life be like if he could wake up tomorrow and have changes in his life, he responded with a memory of his fifth-grade experience. He told me he was happy then, was doing well in school, and getting along with his parents. He liked his teacher and had good friends. He wasn't in trouble and enjoyed his hobbies of playing basketball and the piano. He became relaxed and wanted to revert to those feelings. We then worked on trying to get him to a place where he would feel as he did then.

ASSESSMENT OF SOME OF THE MOST COMMON PROBLEMS SEEN IN SCHOOL-AGED CHILDREN

Autism

Autism is usually seen in children during the age of 3 years and is now diagnosed by age 4. Autism should be diagnosed by a team of professionals including the social worker. Psychiatrists, pediatricians, and speech, occupational, and physical therapists are the experts who need to collaborate for this assessment.

Early intervention is the key to the highest functioning autistic children. Diagnosis is achieved through assessing behavioral symptoms. Medical information includes the child's social interactions, language development, and motor skill development. Prenatal and neonatal histories are important. These can be assessed by the social worker during the parental interview. Observation of the child at home and school in formal and informal settings is essential. A differential diagnosis would include pervasive developmental disabilities (PDD), fragile X syndrome, and tuberous sclerosis (Corcoran & Walsh, 2006).

Evidence-Based Treatment Approaches to Autism

There is substantial evidence showing that early intervention with autism is essential in achieving the highest level of success. In the evidence-based interventions, findings included better language and communicating skills, significant intellectual growth, and lessening of the overall commonly experienced autistic behaviors. Some studies have found that some of the children given interventions are no longer classified as autistic by the time they begin school. *Some of the important components of the treatment processes are as follows*:

- Targeting undesirable behaviors through functional analysis. This will enable the practitioner to understand the purpose of these behaviors and then replace these with prosocial behaviors.
- Increasing positive communication throughout the day is essential.
- These children should be involved with developmentally appropriate activities in each of their environments.
- Interventions in multiple settings are most advantageous: home, special settings, and inclusive education. Children should be given skills at their present level of development and the reinforcement of those skills should occur throughout the day.
- The children should have interaction with peers who run the gamut of abilities.
- Have children continue those prosocial behaviors in natural settings.
- The family of the affected child should be involved in the intervention including goal and priorities for treatment, involvement in support groups and parental skills training, and helping the child function with the new interventions in all environments (Rogers & Vismara, 2008).

Oppositional Defiant Disorder and Conduct Disorder

Oppositional Defiant Disorder (ODD) usually precedes *Conduct Disorder* (CD). ODD is defined as negative, hostile, and defiant behaviors toward people in authority. CD involves these behaviors being solidified with the addition of impinging on the rights of others and breaking rules. The Eyberg Child Behavior Inventory is one scale used by social workers to assess this disorder. Developmental issues need to be considered before a diagnosis of ODD and CD. ODD is usually seen in children before the age of 8 years and before adolescence. CD is usually assessed in adolescence (Corcoran & Walsh, 2006).

Evidence-Based Treatment Approaches to Oppositional Defiant Disorder and Conduct Disorder

It appears that the most efficacious treatment for ODD and CD is parent-training followed by help with older children. Next would be child-training such as cognitive behavioral approaches for younger children.

Anger Control Training is a cognitive behavioral modality for elementary school children. The meetings take place in groups of six on a weekly basis for 45-minute intervals. Goals are set and they role play or discuss vignettes of social confrontations with peers. They learn how to problem-solve and develop prosocial responses and get positive reinforcement for good responses. They learn awareness of feelings and practice in situations which arouse anger (Eyberg, Nelson, & Boggs, 2008).

Group Assertive Training is a peer and counselor lead modality. It is based on a structured training model that must be adhered to. Both counselor and adolescent receive the same training and both are developed on the verbal response example of assertive training (Eyberg, Nelson, & Boggs, 2008).

Incredible Years Parent and Child Training is designed to help aggressive and disruptive children. There is also a module for teachers as well. For parents, it is a 13-session training program where they watch videos that display social learning and development, which is a springboard for discussion. Parent-child interaction is the focus, and parents learn appropriate discipline and how to help their children problem solve (Eyberg, Nelson, & Boggs, 2008).

Multisystemic Therapy is a procedure developed for antisocial adolescents. It is used with families and is community-based. It is given in the home environment and uses cognitive-behavioral techniques, parent intervention, and evidence-based pharmacology. Therapists are available for contact at any time during the 3 to 5 month treatment duration. It has nine core principles:

1. Evaluates how family's environment lends itself to the problem
2. Positive emphasis

3. Try to supplant irresponsible actions with responsible ones
4. Focus on the present
5. Follow interactions and target those that trigger the problems
6. Develop age-appropriate competencies
7. Give help with problems that arise on a weekly basis
8. Evaluate interventions
9. Teach parents the skills to address problems that are generalizable (Eyberg, Nelson, & Boggs, 2008).

Parent-Child Interaction Therapy

Skill training is for parents of 2- to 7-year-old children who are displaying disruptive behavior. It entails 12 to 16 sessions where parents learn attentive skills to positive behaviors and active ignoring of negative behaviors. It is hoped that these interventions will help develop positive parenting skills and interaction that promotes loving discipline. In the next phase, parents learn to give easily understood directions and follow-up with positive response or time-out, depending on the child's behavior. The therapist behaves like a coach helping parents interact appropriately with their child (Eyberg, Nelson, & Boggs, 2008).

Attention Deficit Hyperactivity Disorder

Attention deficit hyperactivity is a disorder commonly found or more commonly overly diagnosed in elementary school-aged children. It is diagnosed by behaviors observed and family history. There are three types: inattentive, hyperactive, and combined. The term *ADD* was eliminated from the DSM-IV in 1994. In adolescence, the impulsivity and antisocial behaviors are more evident. Acting-out behaviors are prevalent in this age group. Psychological testing can assess the attention of the child as well as the intellectual functioning. Conners's scale previously discussed in this chapter is used as part of the assessment process. It is usually completed by teachers and parents. A physical exam is part of the differential diagnosis to rule out medical illnesses. Medication and behavioral interventions are used to combat this difficulty (Corcoran & Walsh, 2006). Direct observation, achievement tests, functional assessment, and curriculum-based measurement are used in early intervention (preschool) children, and the likelihood of less severe symptoms exists when early intervention is made (Leslie, Lambros, Aarons, Haine, & Hough, 2008).

Evidence-Based Treatment Approaches to Attention Deficit Hyperactivity Disorder

Behavioral parent training (BPT), behavioral classroom management (BCM), and peer-focused behavioral interventions (when implemented in a recreational environment) are the most well-established forms of treatment for children with attention deficit hyperactivity disorder (Pelham & Fabiano, 2008).

In behavioral parent training, the parents are given reading material for 8 to 20 weeks and are seen once a week to learn standard behavioral skills, time-out, contingent attention, and point reward system (Pelham, Wheeler, & Cronis, 1998).

In behavioral classroom management, teachers are taught classroom management techniques, and daily report cards are given to both students and parents. This procedure gives constant up-to-date feedback so that behavior can be altered or changed accordingly (Pelham, Wheeler, & Cronis, 1998).

Posttraumatic Stress Disorder

Posttraumatic stress disorder (PTSD) has become more prevalent (in children as well as adults) since 9/11. Many children in the country, even in areas at a geographical distance from the event, have developed symptoms after viewing the events in the media. The syndrome is characterized by reexperiencing the traumatic event through reoccurring thoughts, nightmares, and the actual event. Those who have PTSD use defenses such as avoidance to prevent these symptoms from occurring. Some of the telltale signs of PTSD include increased startle response, hyper vigilance, and the inability to sleep (Corcoran & Walsh, 2006).

Parental report is most important to this diagnosis in children since they often do not have the same ways of letting people know how they feel as do adults. Play, telling stories, and drawing pictures may all be used as diagnostic tools. One of the most used scales for PTSD in children is the *Children's PTSD-Reaction Index*. It is used for children over 8 years old and through adolescence (Pynoos, cited in Corcoran & Walsh, 2006).

Evidence-Based Treatment Approaches to PTSD

Trauma-focused Cognitive Behavioral Therapy

Trauma-focused cognitive behavioral therapy has been noted as the most efficacious form of treatment for PTSD in children and adolescents. Children in this modality are treated individually with behavioral and cognitive interventions. Children are exposed to the stressors through narratives, artwork, or other interventions found useful for exposure to the stressor(s). Parents are involved in either individual meetings or parent-child meetings and individual sessions with children (Silverman, Ortiz, et al., 2008).

School-based Cognitive-behavioral Therapy

In the school-based therapy, children are seen in groups of 5 to 8 for 10 weeks and focus on psychoeducational treatment with "graded" exposure to the stressors through medium of art, composition, and expressive writing. Cognitive coping skills' training was used and included relaxation and thought preventing techniques. The sessions lasted one class period (Silverman, Ortiz, et al., 2008).

Anxiety Disorders

Anxiety is a normal reaction to stressors. It is considered a psychological or physiological defense against a stressor. Some of the symptoms of anxiety include feelings of tension, physical symptoms such as shortness of breath, quickened heart rate, and stomach distress. When the danger is unfounded it then becomes aberrant behavior. There are several types of anxiety disorders seen in children.

- *Separation anxiety* is experienced by young children when the significant figure is not available. School phobia (misnomer) is a form of separation anxiety where the child is afraid of leaving the parental figure.
- *Panic disorder* is the type of anxiety that occurs randomly without warning. Children who suffer from this malady are sometimes afraid to leave their homes for fear that an attack might be precipitated. It is usually not a childhood occurrence and not diagnosed by those before adolescence.
- *Phobia* is a type of anxiety occurring in response to a particular object or event. Children sometimes exhibit social phobias, which are a fear of criticism or negative response by others.
- *Generalized anxiety disorder* is characterized by concern and fretting behavior. It cannot be defined or specifically described by the victim. It can be observed in children in response to a school assignments, exams, oral reports, and so on.
- *Obsessive-compulsive disorder* is denoted by overly thinking which in turn causes the anxiety and then developing behaviors in response to allay the anxiety. It occurs earlier in boys than in girls (Corcoran & Walsh, 2006).

There seems to be a genetic component to anxiety. Observation of parental behavior can also dispose a child to such reactions. A family history and symptom analysis can be helpful in the diagnosis.

Evidence-Based Treatment Approaches to Anxiety Disorder

Cognitive-behavioral therapy in groups or individually prove to be the most advantageous for anxiety disorders in children. It appears that anxiety disorders are the most common form of emotional pathology found in children. Gradual exposure either in the person's natural environment or through imagining the stressor is used in treatment. Developing a procedure for dealing with the stressor is essential in overcoming this condition. Learning relaxation techniques as well as planning rewards and evaluating one's own success are all part of this process (Silverman, Pina, et al., 2008).

Eating Disorders

Eating disorders are at the forefront of our minds with obesity in children a recurring news item and now considered a national epidemic. Many children in inner city environments are victims of this very unhealthy condition. School lunches have also been cited as a culprit in causing this widespread illness in our children.

Basically, eating disorders are characterized by deviations in eating behaviors as well as a distorted body image. Binge eating, anorexia nervosa, and bulimia nervosa are three types of eating difficulties found in school-aged children. *Binge eating* involves overeating with an inability to stop. Many of these victims seek help from self-help groups, and others diet using different programs. *Anorexia nervosa* involves restricting the intake of food and losing body weight. Such concomitants as extreme exercise, working in food preparation, and a drive to achieve academically are some of the symptoms experienced with this disorder. *Bulimia* usually involves binging and purging (either through induced vomiting, laxatives, or diuretics) (Corcoran & Walsh, 2006). The disorder is more prevalent in females and can be seen in adolescent girls particularly in the high school environment.

Assessment of eating disorders involves a clinical interview, formal survey such as the *Concern Over Weight and Dieting Scale* (noted above), and usually a medical evaluation of the client. In a high school environment, the peers or friends of someone exhibiting eating disturbances are usually the first to seek help for the victim. Much of health education in high schools involves imparting knowledge about mental as well as physical problems. Often the school sponsors seminars dealing with adolescent problems including eating disorders. Developing a trusting relationship with the student at risk or blatantly displaying symptoms is essential in getting successful resolution of the eating disorder. Family involvement is also vital in the successful recovery of the student in need. A school social worker can refer to specialists in the field of eating disorders and can help support the student in school but cannot treat the individual as the primary therapist.

Evidence-based Practice Approaches to Eating Disorders

The Maudsley approach to family therapy seems one of the most efficacious. It follows the systems theory of Minuchin with the family viewed as part of the treatment plan. It involves three therapeutic tasks and three phases. The cooperation of the family is first. The second task is to assess the family communication and interactions around the eating disordered person. The last is to help the family members change and help the eating disordered person eat normally and maintain weight gain or loss. Psychodynamic understanding, behavioral training, and homework are all techniques used in this intervention. Refeeding (parents must be united and develop individual plan), negotiating new patterns of interaction (specifically dealing with the eating disorder), and termination (after a healthy weight is achieved new methods of interactions among family members are developed) are three phases used in this procedure (Keel & Haedt, 2008).

Substance Abuse Disorders

In 2001, 1.1 million children in this country ages 12 to 17 met the criteria for substance abuse (Griswold, Aronoff, & Kernan, 2008). Alcohol, marijuana, and cigarettes seem to be the current drugs of choice among adolescents (Burrow-Sanchez, 2006). Alcohol appears to be the most often used drug. According to a recent article in *Pediatrics,* 25 billion dollars per year are spent on media advertising for tobacco, alcohol, and prescription drugs (Strasburger, 2010). As children watch television, they are inundated with advertisements about the positive effects of drinking and using prescription drugs. Tobacco, alcohol, and prescription drugs are very visible when viewing shows and video games.

Many times, adolescents are referred by parents or teachers as a result of behavioral or personality changes. Outbursts of anger, poor or impaired academic functioning, change in mood, lack of motivation, and lethargy and/or excitability are often symptoms of substance use. Motivational interviewing has been a successful mode of assessment and treatment in substance abuse. "Interviewing domains include assessment and feedback; negotiation and goal setting; behavioral modification techniques; self-help directions; and follow-up and reinforcement" (Griswold, Aronoff, & Kernan, 2008, p. 333). Letting the adolescent know from the beginning of the intervention the parameters of confidentiality in your school and state will help develop open and honest reporting by the student. *The CRAFFT Questionnaire: A Brief Screening Test for Adolescent Substance Abuse* is a short survey to help assess whether or not substances are a problem. Two or more "yes" responses signify a problem. The questions are as follows:

C - Have you ever ridden in a **C**ar driven by someone (including yourself) who was "high" or who had been using alcohol or drugs?

R - Did you ever use alcohol or drugs to **R**elax, feel better about yourself, or fit in?

A - Do you ever use alcohol or drugs while you are **A**lone?

F - Do you ever **F**orget things you did while using alcohol or drugs?

F - Do your family or **F**riends ever tell you that you should cut down on your drinking or drug use?

T - Have you gotten into **T**rouble while you were using alcohol or drugs? (Griswold, Aronoff, & Kernan, 2008, p. 334).

The informal clinical assessment of the social worker should take into consideration the following items:

- When did it begin, frequency of use, and has there been an upward progression of use?
- Any physical symptoms such as tolerance development or withdrawal symptoms?
- Have any major events contributed to the use?
- Concomitant disorders?
- Does patient see the advantages and/or disadvantages of use or abuse?
- Motivation for change?
- What strategies have been used in the past to stop the use or abuse?
- Interference in life functioning?
- Social support available?
- Adaptation skills (Corcoran & Walsh, 2006)?

Evidence-Based Treatment Approaches to Substance Abuse Disorders

For substance abuse, treatment using cognitive-behavioral therapy is valuable. It is thought that substance abuse behavior begins with the interaction of a person and his or her environment. As part of this process, development of positive coping abilities in adolescents to deal with stressful events is most helpful. One of the maladaptive coping skills that develop may be drug and/or alcohol use and/ or abuse. Cognitive behavioral therapy for this maladaptive behavior might be the adoption of better, well-used coping skills. Primarily, the initial part of the treatment process is developing a working alliance. Understanding the depth of the problem is essential, and using a treatment modality that is successful and hopefully evidence-based would be best. Realization and confrontation about the possibility of relapse is also essential (Burrow-Sanchez, 2006).

Using the Nathan and Gorman (2002) criteria for evidence-based interventions, Type 1 and 2 were used to evaluate the treatment modalities for substance abuse intervention with adolescents. Type 1 uses randomized control trials, blind assessments, sufficient samples, and sophisticated statistical design for studies. Type 2 uses comparison groups to evaluate a particular intervention. Single subject design is also included in this type (cited in Silverman, Ortiz, et al., 2008).

The findings were that Functional Family Therapy (FFT), Cognitive-behavioral (CBT) group therapy, and Multidimensional Family Therapy (MDFT) were seen as most effective for adolescent substance abuse (Waldron & Turner, 2008).

FFT is an ecological model using family systems and behavioral techniques with multidimensional attributes. Motivation and bringing the family into an understanding of their connectedness is essential in the successful use of this model. Problem solving and communication as well as the therapist working on mezzo systems are all effective in the treatment process (Waldron & Turner, 2008).

In CBT-group interventions such as irrational thinking patterns and ways of best dealing with drug cravings are essential. Learning to avoid environments that lend themselves to risk of drug use is also used in this modality (Waldron & Turner, 2008).

MDFT is a family technique that employs a developmental-ecological systems modality. It uses comprehensive and multiple, stage-oriented components. Treatment addresses the individual characteristics of the adolescent patient (such as cognitive mediators of the person's awareness of the harmfulness of drugs, self-medicating processes [drug use as coping mechanism]), the parent(s) (e.g., parenting techniques, parental stress and coping mechanisms), and other family history of drug users, as well as the communication patterns (degree of interpersonal connectedness) that are related to the etiology and continuation of drug use and concomitant behaviors (Liddle et al., 2001).

Multiple systems are examined in the assessment process, since it took the involvement of all systems for the adolescent to get involved in the current predicament. The purpose of the first stage of treatment is to bring the adolescent and his or her parents back into a functioning relationship. In the second phase of treatment the problem-solving modality is used, and both individual and family sessions are employed. In the individual sessions, developmental tasks and mastery are the focus. Parental attitudes and behaviors that contribute to the problem are addressed. In the final phase, maintenance and generalizing the new skills of life are emphasized.

USE OF SCHOOL-LINKED SERVICES

For school social workers, it is difficult to assess how far into the treatment process one should venture in the school venue. Depending on your assigned duties, which can limit ones available time, the decision would be made. Another variable would be whether or not the school district's policy would disallow therapeutic interventions. Additional information that would need to be assessed is the extent to which the social worker has been trained in therapeutic interventions.

Generally speaking, if the intervention is assessed as a short-term process, it would be acceptable for the school social worker to intervene. Group process is often the therapy of choice in the school environment since it is usually time-limited and employs such treatment modalities as cognitive-behavioral and solution-focused.

Example: One of the groups I was able to run was a focus group for children of divorced parents. The adolescents in the group were from a variety of ethnicities and grades. The support they gave each other and the understanding that their situation was not unique was very helpful. Some of the underclassmen came back the following year and colead the group with me, since they had experienced the process themselves.

Some cities such as New York have school-linked services where children are given treatment either in the school environment or at the agency which is very close to the school. These services are school funded and students receive the services free of charge.

In the case of suicidal ideation, intention or risk the school social worker should always ask for outside consultation with a medical professional or should follow the school policy. In adolescence when the statistics of successful suicide looms higher than most other groups, it is essential to get the consultant's evaluation. Some school districts have policies for this particular adolescent crisis (review of plan noted in Chapter 2).

ACTIVITIES

Activity 1 for Section I: Level 1: What are some informal assessment techniques that you would use to evaluate a student's needs?

Level 2: Discuss an informal assessment that you have been involved in during your practicum. Was there a written referral? Is the case still in progress? What interventions have you used that have worked? As an intern or novice in the field of school social work describe in detail a case in which you would use one of the aforementioned interventions.

Activity 2 for Section I: Level 1: Discuss the feasibility of applying cognitive-behavioral therapy for an adolescent student.

Level 2: Review the intervention strategies in cognitive behavioral therapy and apply some of them to a case you have in your internship.

SELF-REFLECTION QUESTIONS

1. Discuss the efficacy of using cognitive-behavioral techniques with elementary school children.

2. How would you use solution-focused therapy with a depressed adolescent?

SECTION II

INTRODUCTION

This section will focus on several other valid methods of intervention that have been successfully used in the schools. Crisis Intervention, Intrapsychic Humanism, Attachment-based Therapy, and Play Therapy are all used effectively in the school milieu. The efficacy of these interventions is discussed. This chapter focuses on the explanation and possible uses of these interventions with individuals. Assessment and interventions using these modalities is discussed and examples are given. The appropriateness of school-linked services is also discussed.

CRISIS INTERVENTION

Crisis intervention has been around for about 70 years. The theory was investigated and developed by Eric Lindemann in the 1940s after the Coconut Grove fire in California. Since that time, it has been developed and refined. Roberts defines *crisis* as individual (such as a death of a loved one) or communitywide (such as the Trade Towers tragedy). "A crisis can be defined as a period of psychological disequilibrium, experienced as a result of a hazardous event or situation that constitutes a significant problem that cannot be remedied by using familiar coping strategies" (Roberts, 2000, p. 7). A crisis reaction is the response that occurs soon after the traumatic event takes place. Some of the responses to crisis are (a) a feeling of helplessness, (b) confusion, (c) anxiousness, (d) shock, (e) nonbelief, and (f) frustration or anger (Roberts, 2000).

The condition most important in a crisis is first and foremost a stressful occurrence. The belief that the event will have disruptive consequences is the second condition, and the last is the client's perception that he or she cannot change the circumstances with his or her current set of coping skills. Certain characteristics that are seen in the person experiencing the crisis are (a) the event is perceived as threatening; (b) not able to cope with existing skills; (c) the feelings of fear, stress, and confusion; (d) very uncomfortable feelings; and (e) a state of disequilibrium (Roberts, 2000). The duration of the crisis lasts usually from 4 to 6 weeks.

The purpose of crisis intervention therapy is to help the client make the life adjustment to the situation, gather internal ego strengths and rally his or her support system, lower the stress level, and have the client blend this event into his or her conscious life events.

The intervention treatment model used by Roberts (as follows) is a compilation and synthesis of previously used interventions dating back to Lindemann and Caplan in the 1940s. It is based on a time-limited model that seeks to resolve the conflict and crisis in the shortest possible time. A relationship should be developed as soon as possible as well as having the client meet with the therapist shortly after the event. A person is more apt to make successful and expedient changes when the crisis state is still active.

Roberts's Stages of Crisis Intervention

Step 1: Plan and conduct a crisis assessment to ascertain the danger to life or harm. According to Roberts, the assessment should include the following items:

- Decide whether the student needs immediate medical attention.
- Does the person have a specific plan for suicide or homicide?
- If the person is a victim, ascertain how close the perpetrator is.
- Find out if anyone else is in danger or harm.
- Is the person under the influence of a mind-altering substance?
- Find out how the victim has coped with the problem in the past.
- Are there any lethal weapons in the vicinity of the client?

Step 2: Developing an expeditious relationship helps the client deal with the crisis knowing that they are accepted and supported.

Step 3: Specific explanation of the problem is necessary. Reexplaining the event with the specific cognitive facts in the presence of a supportive accepting therapist helps the client explore the feelings attached to the event.

Step 4: The exploration of emotions about the specific details of the event helps the catharsis of feelings attached to the occurrence. Empathic support is essential for this endeavor. Active listening is required to show empathy and support.

Step 5: Examining past coping mechanisms is in an attempt to refine and define previously used coping attempts for the purpose of expanding these and thus helping the client adapt better coping mechanisms. Previously handled crisis coping skills are investigated exploring the strengths of the client in crisis situations. At this point it is suggested by Roberts's model to use solution-focused therapy and the strengths perspective.

Step 6: Restoring the client's equilibrium through an action plan is the next step. This procedure uses the cognitive therapy approach to elucidate the crisis. Roberts refers to this as *cognitive mastery* and describes three parts of this process (Roberts, 2000, p. 20).

1. Cognitive knowledge of the events that led to the crisis and the factors involved in the crisis.
2. What the meaning of the crisis is to the client. How does it impact his or her life, and what effects does it have on his or her functioning?
3. Replacing irrational thoughts and feelings with rational ones. This is done through the cognitive process of restructuring, models, and homework.

Step 7: Follow-up sessions can be planned on anniversary dates. Leaving the door open for the client to return is also part of this last phase of the process. Letting him or her know that you will be there for him or her is helpful and gives the client hope for support in the future (Roberts, 2000).

The Roberts's version of crisis intervention is the latest model seen as innovative in the crisis intervention therapeutic process. It incorporates evidence-based modalities such as cognitive-behavioral and solution-focused therapy into this current model of treatment.

Example: Crisis intervention is a frequently used treatment modality in all school environments from elementary through high school. When a beloved high school teacher died of a heart attack on a class trip, I was left to handle the crisis of the students who had witnessed the event. I had been sent to the site to bring the students home after the event. These five students were first told of the teacher's death after we returned to school. It was a group crisis session, and many of the students in the group had never experienced the loss of a significant person in their life. The first step was to find out if they had ever lost a significant person in their life. I quickly established a rapport with them by explaining that I was there to help them in any way they needed. Most of them were thirsty and hungry, so the next step was to bring nourishment into the room. We then discussed specifics of the day including the last encounter they had with this teacher as well as what they had witnessed on the day of the actual event. I did so with active listening, showing them I had empathy, and giving them support for their feelings as they expressed them. I then asked what impact this event would have on their lives. Through this process, I tried to restructure their thoughts and helped them see the meaning this death had for them as individuals. We spoke of the future and what they would do when they returned to the classroom with the rest of the students who had not been on this class trip. Two of the students resolved to continue the work they had done with this teacher (which they in fact did when they went on to college). I left the door open for them to come to my office at any time to see me and discuss any issues that arose for them as the result of this traumatic occurrence. The trauma for the care-giver is often difficult and needs to be processed with other professionals who are on staff. One must be aware of his or her own feelings to avoid compassionate fatigue.

INTRAPSYCHIC HUMANISM

This therapeutic intervention is based on a model of consistent caregiving even in the face of poor behavior. It helps children seek out positive, trusting relationships for reinforcement as opposed to detrimental attention-seeking behaviors. The goals of this intervention are to help children develop inner resources and discipline (Tyson, 2000). It is often used with children diagnosed with Attention Deficit Hyperactivity Disorder (the three types). It is used in lieu of medication in controlling the negative behavioral symptoms of these disorders. A positive, compassionate environment supports children in maximizing their learning experience.

The hope of this intervention is to help the child become self-reflective and learn to make good choices. Giving children supportive relationships to rely on is optimal in discovering how to make these choices and to experience a positive learning process. The relationship that offers nonjudgmental, accepting responses can help a traumatized or difficult child to view the learning experience differently and to develop a relationship that he or she might have been protecting himself or herself from based on previous negative experiences. Some adolescents after years of negative feedback, view the teacher as an enemy before the class even begins. The behavioral system of rewards teaches a child that his value conditionally depends on good behavior. The alternative used in intrapsychic humanism is to help the child control negative behaviors without feeling a sense of devaluation and to develop a working alliance with his or her teacher. Forming an alliance involves helping the child view and identify his or her strengths. This is achieved through helping the child gain pleasure in the learning environment. A teacher should look at other areas (nonacademic) of school where the child might excel and focus on these to boost the child's self-concept.

Viewing the child's undesirable behaviors with "compassionate regulation" will give the student a role model and an example to follow. Treating a child with respect strengthens self-confidence. The conjecture is that through this path the child will want to increase his learning capacity and skills. When the child realizes that the teacher will be a consistent, unconditional figure, the unwanted behaviors will subside (Tyson, 2000).

Many children come to expect negative responses to their behaviors. Teachers should understand that strides are made with children sporadically, and often a child will revert back to a former behavior. If the teacher greets this behavior with patience and compassion, it is expected to dissipate. One should not expect a constant positive display of behaviors, but improvement should be viewed relative to the original behavioral composite of that individual student. "Old habits die hard" (Titelman, 1996). According to Tyson (2000), an "aversive reaction to pleasure" is what occurs when a child is accustomed to negative responses and must return to that equilibrium which brings about unhappiness. When these incidents occur, the teacher's approach using intrapsychic humanism will be a role model for the child by soothing him or her and helping the child see that supportive figures are more helpful than reverting to negative unhappy feelings. If the child cannot be soothed over time, a therapeutic intervention is the next course of action. Children who exhibit resistance to self-care can be helped by a supportive mentor. Included in this group might be a school counselor, nurse, coach, and so on. Imitating others' behaviors will help the child develop self-care mechanisms. Feedback for children is essential. Fostering collaboration among students also creates a supportive environment. Creating assignments that are of interest to the child is also very helpful. Children learn better in an environment where they have interest and enjoy the activity. This will develop a sense of agency (self-worth and confidence) in the child (Tyson, 2000).

Intrapsychic humanism has used naturalistic settings to develop the research. The modality is based on the idea that psychological change is brought about by a strong supportive relationship. It is felt that children from the age of 3 years will understand what is necessary to nurture a positive relationship and will do what is necessary to create and maintain such a situation (Banerjee, 1997). For children to develop persistent unhappiness and motives that keep them in an unhappy state, they have experienced a loss of love from primary figures, some traumatic event (either environmental or personal), or social inequality (Pieper & Pieper, 1990).

This process is based on the child feeling intrapsychic pain and the desire to be free from that pain. It is essential that the person wants relief from the pain. He or she must be able to trust the therapist and receive gratification from the caregiving experience (Pieper & Pieper, 1990). According to Pieper and Pieper, loss and pain are misinterpreted as pleasure and need to be replaced before the person can enjoy freedom from pathology (1990). Many times with children, they are unwilling to be successful for fear of losing the therapist's caregiving. The therapist must be astute to the response of the child and be able to help the child see that it is OK to continue with well-being and success when treatment is finished. For children, in particular, the developmental needs are fulfilled through the process of intrapsychic therapy.

Example: A child tells the therapist that he has saved a broken toy from the garbage since the toy was going to be lonely. The therapist then pointed out that he (the therapist) would not be lonely if the child got better and no longer needed treatment.

ATTACHMENT THERAPY

The definition of *attachment* is as follows: ". . . the condition in which an individual is linked emotionally to another person. Attachment theory posits that the propensity to make intimate emotional bonds is a basic component of human nature" (Ornstein & Moses, 2002). Attachment therapy is based primarily on the work of John Bowlby who studied children in orphanages in England during World War II. He describes the theory as the ability of humans to form strong affectional bonds to significant others and gives the breaking of these bonds as the explanation for the development of emotional problems such as anxiety, anger, depression, and emotional withdrawal (Bowlby, 1977). Both physical and emotional problems develop as a result of these bonds being broken (Bowlby, 1980). He proposes that healthy psychological development is based on the development of emotional "affectional bonds or attachments" (Raphael, 1983, p. 68). He also indicates that people draw strength from these attachments that give the person the ability to enjoy life (Bowlby, 1980). He uses the ethological theory of Harlow and

Lorenz to support the premise that attachment occurs outside of the animal drives for food and sex and suggests that the etiology of the development of attachments is the need for "safety" and "security" (Bowlby, 1973, p. 182).

Bowlby's work was supported and expanded by Mary Ainsworth. In the "Strange Situation Study," she found that three patterns of attachment occurred. She studied the response of children when their mothers returned after separation. Securely attached children were content on reunion; ambivalent children who showed anger were less compatible with their mothers at home; and those who withdrew from their mothers were less securely based in their home environment (Ainsworth & Bowlby, 1991). Bowlby thus came up with the term *secure base*.

Having this base enables the child to leave his parent (secure base) and venture forth taking risks or chances in life and understanding that the parent will be there on the child's return (Bowlby, 1988). Observations of children who are experiencing a break or separation from the attachment figure exhibit poor behaviors such as screaming, kicking, crying, and so on. These behaviors are viewed as a punitive measure toward the primary figure to ensure that further separations will be averted (Ornstein & Moses, 2002). These attachments are viewed as extremely durable, and even if abuse occurs, the emotional bonds will persist.

According to Ornstein and Moses (2002), the school is in reality the substitute secure base that can help the child develop security and attachment and thus a secure base or can become a source of the child's detachment and withdrawal. School social workers have the opportunity to help a child become and stay connected even if the home base is not supportive. In the course of my experience, some children used the school, the teachers, secretaries, and administrators as substitutes for the gap of secure base in the home environment. Social workers can be instrumental in helping school professionals understand and nurture the child who is in need of an attachment figure.

Example: Two young brothers entered the high school after their mother's death. Custody was given to their father who lived in another state and had remarried. These boys needed a secure base after suffering a traumatic and significant loss. Through my efforts, the secretaries, teachers, and counselors optimized their school experience by providing the base that the boys needed. They used the special services office as a home base. They left their books there and sometimes ate lunch in the office as well. Each of us, myself in particular, spoke to them each day and inquired as to their health, family activities, and school work. It was like a home away from home. They even exhibited sibling rivalry in getting attention from the adults who they visited in this office. They adjusted to the school and their new home as a result of this substitute base.

Securely based children in the school environment are able, after separation from the primary figure, to flexibly return to peers to pursue play and discovery. They will be able to make the transition to school with minimal anxiety and stress. An avoidant-based child would not be able to show anger and in the school environment would exhibit an aloof persona with little interaction with classmates. Ambivalent-based children would show needy behavior. They would be more likely to get involved in daring behaviors that would bring attention from the teacher. These children would show anger when their needs are frustrated (Ornstein & Moses, 2002).

We see children who we call *school phobic* (a misnomer) stay at home and blame fear of school on their absence, when in fact they are experiencing difficulty separating from the attachment figure.

Attachment theory posits that replacement attachment figures can help a child adjust by showing the student that adults (attachment figures) can behave in a consistent and steadfast manner. When a bond is established with this secure base the child has the ability to alter the aberrant behaviors and function well in the school milieu.

The role of the school social worker in this form of therapeutic intervention is to help and guide the teacher in responding appropriately to the child in order to replace the primary impaired attachment formations with more appropriate ones. The social worker can be instrumental in guiding teachers with targeted children who need to have a secure base provided for them. Predictability in the classroom with rules and consequences help these children develop the base that they need. It is a painstaking process that teachers must be coached and supported through in order to successfully provide the needed emotional support for those children. Attachment therapy is very helpful, especially when children have been the victims of loss such as death, separation, divorce, or a move. These children often experience crises in their lives, and social workers and teachers need to be alert to these occurrences in children's lives.

When the relationship with the teacher fails, the school social worker can then become the therapist. In the therapeutic environment, the social worker must encourage the expression of feelings and show empathic responses. According to Ornstein and Moses, the child needs to be able to express his or her feelings while limiting anger and anxiety (2002). Narratives are often helpful for children in this modality. Art and family history examination are also other modes important in this process. The issue of separation from the therapist for school vacation or summer break can be helped by the student taking home a small object of the therapist's or caring for a plant that the child can bring home when school is out. These will ease the issue of separation with the plan of returning to the relationship after the break is over.

Example: One student was very dependent on me (the school social worker), and as the high school years passed she was weaned from the relationship. In her senior year, the student would stop by in the morning just to "check in" and be satisfied with that contact. The student eventually went to college and kept in touch with me for the first 2 years. She successfully completed college and was able to internalize the relationship and develop a secure base.

The group process is another method of therapeutic intervention. Acceptance by peers and the understanding that they too have experienced trauma and loss is most helpful in a student becoming securely attached. Social skills practiced in a group can be extended to other peers during the school day. School activities and school spirit can also help a child become securely attached to the school environment. Learning how to care for others and share with others should be a mandatory part of all school curriculum from the primary grades through high school. The social worker should be a liaison between the family, school personnel, and the community in an effort to help these vulnerable children overcome trauma and loss. Advocating for the creation of programs to help these vulnerable children adapt to the milieu is essential. Sometimes special education evaluation and placement are necessary for maximizing the child's education.

Example: In my school district, we created a homeroom class for these vulnerable individuals, which gave them a positive start to the school day. It was a base from which they could get the essential attachment needs fulfilled and where they could return during the course of the day for reassurance. Outside agencies and wrap-around services could also be instrumental in achieving the secure attachment needed for a successful life.

PLAY THERAPY

Therapy begins at the time of assessment since the child is experiencing his or her feelings during the assessment evaluation. Before the sessions begin, it is important to take a developmental history and possibly create a genogram for indications of familial difficulties. Questions to include in the assessment process are: Are there any drug or alcohol problems in the family? Is there any history of sexual abuse, neglect, or other forms of abuse? Are there any members of the family diagnosed with physical or mental impairment? Has anyone in the family had school difficulties (including a diagnosis of ADHD) (Kadusen, 2006)? It's also important to get an evaluation of the child's school history, social involvement, gross and small motor development, and eating and sleeping habits (Kadusen, 2006). In the initial intake with the child, the therapist may want to explore what toys the child likes best. The next part of the evaluation or therapy session includes drawing a person, tree, and house. I also like to include asking the child to draw a picture of his or her family. Questions are asked about the drawings including asking what the person is doing, and what are his or her favorite and least favorite activities. Through these simple questions, the therapist gets insight into the strengths and difficulties that the child is experiencing.

Example: I sometimes engage the child and parent in the "Thinking, Feeling, and Doing Game" created by Richard Gardner. Its goal is for the child to answer questions that deal with everyday happenings in a child's life. It's important to observe how a child interacts with his or her parent and also to see how he or she responds to winning and losing a game. Other activities include puppet play where the therapist allows the child to choose a puppet and then gets involved with the child in the fantasy game of puppets. Puppets can be used with a theme or story in mind or just through questions and answers.

Play is to children what verbal expression is to adults (Kadusen, 2006). Often children do not express themselves verbally, and this lack of expression leads people to believe that they are not connected to the event. Through play therapy, children can find expression for their feelings concerning an event or worry. Play helps children develop the ability to cope with their feelings in a safe modality (Mader cited in Franklin et al., 2006). Play therapy occurs on both a conscious and an unconscious level. It allows the child to act out through fantasy (small figures, puppets, etc.) what is being communicated from his or her unconscious to conscious mind. It permits children to communicate without words what is also in their conscious world. Traumatic events or experiences are expressed in play. One is able to assess a child's need for help through the medium of play.

Example: In a family who had lost their father, the children created a unique game. When the children came home from the funeral, they began playing a game they called *funeral*. It was a reenactment of the day's events put into a play activity. They were 10 and 7 years old at the time.

Sand Tray Therapy

One of my most important finds was sand tray therapy. It was developed by Dr. Lowenfeld in London in 1926. The process included figures that the child could use to express himself or herself in whatever way he or she wanted. The therapist does not intrude in this process, and the child makes his or her feelings and thinking through this play process (Van Dyk, 1995). The child is allowed to express whatever he or she feels in this process. The child can develop his or her gestalt through this process. The parts of his or her life that may be hidden would be exposed through this process. Often painful memories are revealed, and the therapist must be ready to accept whatever the child chooses to express. Lowenfeld believed that the process used in sand tray therapy was preverbal. That is, the child brings forth pictures in his or her mind rather than thoughts and cognitions. It allows the child to bring different ends to painful scenarios thus making them palatable. It is considered right brain thinking rather than using the rational part of one's brain. The multisensory technique includes the senses of touch, sight, and sound (Kadusen, 2006). It exposes inner conflicts and helps a child deal with them on an external level. As Kadusen explains, it is a holistic method that allows the child to bring forth unconscious feelings, and thus the healing process begins (2006).

Example: A 9-year-old boy in therapy for depression expressed in trichotillomania had recently lost his dog. The boy did not want to discuss it in therapy because he said it didn't matter and outright refused to discuss it. With the use of sand tray therapy he told the story about the dog's death and wept with considerable sadness as a result.

Kadusen speaks of abreaction regarding play therapy. It is the reliving of painful events and the emotions attached to them. It is done piecemeal, and so the emotions expressed do not flood the child's psyche, which helps them deal more appropriately with those feelings (2006). *Abreaction* is a term coined by Freud and used by people who have had traumatic events. It enables them to resolve the feelings attached to the event (Kadusen, 2006).

In the school setting, play therapy can help the school social worker develop a plan by which the teacher, counselor, and administrators can use to alter behavior that is inappropriate (Franklin et al., 2006). Parents also can be involved by showing them how the child's thoughts and feelings unfold through the power of play. As a therapeutic modality, a school social worker can adapt this form of treatment to the differing age groups seen in the school environment.

SCHOOL-BASED AND SCHOOL-LINKED SERVICES

School-linked and school-based services such as community child and adolescent mental health services, home health services, public health services, social services, and child welfare are all resources that can be supportive of the child and family. The services provided by these interventions only differ in the venue of the delivery. In several studies, it was documented that these additional services to students and their families enhance the services provided by school social workers, psychologists, and nurses (Allison, Roeger, & Abbott, 2008). The National Assembly on School-based Health Care's mission is to ensure that all children from kindergarten through high school have immunizations, physicals, mental health counselors, and dentists to oversee the basic health needs of children and adolescents (http://www.nasbhc.org). In many urban centers and less affluent suburbs and rural areas, health services and public health initiatives are inadequate. The addition of school-based and school-linked services potentially provide universal, selective, and indicated preventive services that address the biological, social, and economic needs of students (Clayton, Chin, Blackburn, & Echeverria, 2010).

If school-based and/or school-linked services are available, they should be accessed to help provide students with needed services. Medical services can be used effectively for obesity prevention; monitoring health conditions such as diabetes, epilepsy, and other physical chronic illnesses; as well as providing mental health interventions that require intensive treatment. Children are available during the school day, and the convenience of having these services during times when school is not in session, as well as relieving the financial burden of families, make these services ideal.

CASE STUDY TO BE EVALUATED BY STUDENTS

Joe first came to the attention of the criminal justice system at age 14, when he was arrested for stealing a car. The third child in a minority family of six children, Joe grew up with his mother and siblings in a poverty-stricken area of a large eastern city. He was abused physically by his mother during his childhood and received little positive attention from her. From first grade on, Joe had difficulty in school. He had a short attention span, regularly disrupted the classroom, and rarely completed his schoolwork.

At the time of his first arrest, Joe was in the seventh grade for the second time. He was placed on probation, and his family was referred for counseling. However, because his mother worked long hours, she was never able to arrange the counseling sessions. Joe became more of a problem in school as well as in the neighborhood in which he lived. He began skipping school, experimenting with drugs, and committing a series of burglaries. His mother could not handle his frequent bursts of anger or get Joe to respond to limits she set for him.

When Joe was 16, he spent 3 months in a juvenile detention facility, where he responded well to the structure provided by the program. He was assigned a probation officer and returned to live with his family. The conditions of his probation stipulated that he attend school on a regular basis, maintain a strict curfew, and report to his probation officer monthly. Joe followed these conditions for several months; however, he continued to experience difficulty in school and dropped out 4 months after he returned home.

Case Analysis: As a school social worker, how would you help Joe? Please include: What interventions would you use to enhance his self-esteem and social skills? How would you get his mother involved in the process? What would be the appropriate school supports that you would use for Joe? How would you advocate for him while working in the host institution (the school)? Do you encounter ethical issues?

Explain in detail how you would use *one* of the following techniques to help Joe: CBT, attachment theory, solution-focused therapy, or intrapsychic humanism.

SUMMARY

The purpose of this chapter is to review modalities of intervention: Evidence-based and other modalities effectively used in schools. The definition and explanation of evidence-based practice are elucidated. Engagement, assessment, and intervention skills are explained in the first section of this chapter as well as the use of evidence-based practice. Specific problems, which are more commonly seen in school situations, are described, and evidence-based practice solutions are provided. In the second section, modalities used effectively in the schools are described with examples, and the explanation and use of school-based and school-linked services are examined.

A school social worker must keep in mind the racial, cultural, socioeconomic status, religion, and ethnic diversity of children, families, and teachers as they prepare to handle a situation and decide what interventions will be most appropriate. The resources available in the school and in the community are also considerations when getting involved with students and their issues.

ACTIVITIES

Activity 1 for Section II: Level 1: Choose an intervention from this section and describe how you would use it to intervene with a student.

Level 2: Using a case that involves one of the aforementioned nonevidence-based interventions, describe the assessment, intervention, and the present status of that case.

Is the case still in progress? What interventions of the aforementioned have you used that have worked successfully?

Activity 2 for Section II: Level 1: When would you use play therapy? At what age or stage of development?

Level 2: As an intern or novice in the field of school social work, describe in detail a case with which you would use one of the nonevidence-based interventions.

SELF-REFLECTION QUESTIONS

1. What situations do you think you might encounter that would foster use of one of the above mentioned modalities as opposed to evidence-based (if any)?
2. Do you believe a novice in the field of school social work should engage in nonevidence-based modalities? Why?

CLASS DISCUSSION QUESTIONS

1. Take Joe's case through the steps of evidence-based practice.
2. Give examples of the use of one of the above models from your field placement.

Chapter 10

Engagement, Assessment, and Intervention Skills in the School for Groups Using a Variety of Practice Methods

INTRODUCTION

Group work in the schools can be situational or topic-oriented. Group selection, statement of goals and purpose, and issues of confidentiality are essential for a successful group process to take place. A topic-oriented group may be one that involves children of divorce; children who have experienced loss, under- or over-achievement; and a variety of other subjects. A situational group would be one that occurs as a result of an experience of certain students. For example, I ran a single-session group for students who were classmates of a student who died of cancer and were returning to school for the first time since his funeral. Evidence-based interventions such as solution-focused and cognitive-behavioral can be used in a group.

The various types of groups—support, task facilitation, psychoeducational, counseling, affective, and educational—are presented, and examples of each are given. How members are chosen for a group and the dynamics (i.e., planning, informing educators of absences in class to attend groups, protecting confidentiality) of working with groups in schools is discussed in this chapter. One helpful hint would be to use a class period rotating around lunch or rotating throughout the day. This would be more acceptable to teachers so that students won't miss a significant amount of class time. Case examples are given and students are asked to develop their own interventions on a printout sheet.

WHY GROUPS?

The school is a microcosm of a social milieu that is a fertile training ground for development of psychosocial skills. In the school setting, groups are a conduit for both social and emotional growth and well-being. Group work can be used in the elementary, junior high, and high school years. With the dearth of time and the work assigned to school social workers, group work is efficient as well as beneficial. Age appropriate interventions are discussed later in this chapter. Not only are peer groups of students effective but also working in groups with the parents of students who are engaged in group enhances the effectiveness of the student group process.

One in seven adolescents in school in the United States is not covered by health insurance for mental health issues. More than 52 million children attend public school, and school mental health professionals are in a strategic position to offer assistance to this population. Approximately eight million children are identified as needing mental health intervention. It is estimated that 75% of children with emotional difficulties do not receive services. Issues such as sexual and physical abuse, hyperactivity, family disruption, and violence are the most common issues plaguing our children (Crespi, 2009).

DEFINITION

The definition of *group counseling* according to Gazda, Duncan, and Meadows is ". . . a dynamic interpersonal process focusing on conscious thought and behavior and involving the therapy functions of permissiveness, orientation to reality, catharsis, and mutual trust, caring understanding, acceptance and support" (cited in Gazda, 1984, p. 7). It is designed to share concerns and personal feelings with one's peers and a counselor. The participants are individuals not suffering from severe pathology or needing extensive changes to personality or behaviors. The person gets feedback and learns about himself or herself through the exchanges in the group setting (Gazda, 1984). So as not to single out a student as needing this intervention, it might be offered to every student who would like to participate. Groups in elementary and junior high should not exceed 4 to 6 members and in high school 8 to 12 members.

The definition of a *structured group* is as follows: "A structured group is a delimited learning situation with a predetermined goal, and a plan designed to enable each group member to reach this identified goal with minimum frustration and maximum ability to transfer the new learning to a wide range of life events" (Drum & Knott, cited in Gazda, 1984, p. 10).

A *situational group* is one that forms as a result of a situation that each of the students have experienced. A death of a fellow classmate, teacher, and/or parent(s) (such as the World Trade Center tragedy) might be developed for purposes of dealing with the loss. Homelessness is a stressful situation for children and often leaves them ashamed and isolated. The suicide of someone known to them may need to be processed through the group setting. Possibly coming as an immigrant from another country may give students a sense of alienation, which can be ameliorated by the group process. The basic common denominator is the shared experience of the student group.

GROUP SELECTION

Members are often selected based on the issues to be examined. Some groups are homogeneous (similar members). They may be, based on their age, common problem, or life circumstances. Heterogeneous (dissimilar) group members can be helpful where personal growth is an issue. Experiences and advice from others is supportive and encouraging. These groups are a microcosm of the social environment and help people get legitimate feedback from varying sources (Corey, 2004).

Assessment of Group Members

Group members could be voluntary or involuntary (Ivey, Pedersen, & Ivey, 2001). For the most part, participation in school groups is voluntary. When students are identified through the administration, counselor, teacher, or staff member, the social worker should begin by gathering data about the person. Talking to the person and assessing what the specific needs are by interviewing him or her in a face-to-face context is quite essential. Nonverbal communication can sometimes be more helpful than verbal. The social worker can see whether or not the person has the ego strengths to function successfully in a group setting. Eye contact as well as interpersonal social skills can be evaluated through the interview process. Supplementary information can be gathered from school personnel and family members. As the social worker develops a profile of the student, the worker decides whether or not the proposed group fits the needs of the person in question. Motivation of potential members is also important in the assessment process. The group does not benefit from a person who is motivated to be a member of a group just for the purpose of missing class time or dodging academic responsibilities. Some of the essential ground rules in the school setting are that teachers must be willing to allow a student to leave a particular class and that the student is not missing a test or some other essential academic event when they leave to attend group.

Toseland and Rivas (2005) outline factors that are important in choosing appropriateness of member participation. They include problems in scheduling participants, personal qualities and attributes which may impede participation such as level of social skills and age differences, and whether or not the student's needs are corresponding to group goals and expectations (2005). The potential member should have the ability to communicate appropriately with other students, be motivated to work on the issues at hand, and exhibit suitable behavior (2005).

GROUP PURPOSE

Each group is faced with the idea of planning the purpose and establishing the goals of the group. Included in this planning stage is the determination of the length and frequency of the group meetings. Meetings usually occur on a weekly basis. In the school environment, it is recommended that the meeting time rotates to prevent a student from missing class in a specific subject more than once. If at all possible, meetings should be arranged during a lunch or study hall period. This not only prevents missing valuable class time but also eliminates student participants whose motives involve class absences. Teachers in turn will not look askance on the group process in the school environment if students are not missing their classes regularly. Educating teachers regarding the purpose, content, and expected outcomes of the group is very important in the successful establishment of groups in the school milieu.

Group Goals

Some of the common goals for groups are seen as follows:

- Become aware of one's interpersonal style
- Increase awareness of what prevents intimacy
- Learn how to trust oneself and others
- Become aware of how one's culture affects personal decisions
- Increase self-awareness and thereby increase the possibilities for choice and action
- Challenge and explore certain early decisions that may no longer be functional
- Recognize that others have similar problems and feelings
- Clarify values and decide whether and how to modify them
- Become both independent and interdependent
- Find better ways to resolve problems

- Become more open and honest with selected others
- Learn a balance between support and challenge
- Learn how to ask others for what one wants
- Become sensitive to the needs and feelings of others
- Provide others with helpful feedback (Corey & Corey, 2006, p. 146)

CONFIDENTIALITY IN GROUPS

According to the American Counseling Association, there are standards of ethics for group confidentiality. They suggest it is the purview of the group counselor to emphasize the importance of keeping information that is communicated in the group in confidence. Group boundaries must be discussed as well as the fact that confidentiality cannot be assured (Corey & Corey, 2006). It is important that the group leader be very serious in discussing this issue because he or she sets the tone for the group respecting this value. Some leaders go so far as to have the group members sign a pledge of confidentiality, and others set up sanctions for those who break the trust. The high school is especially vulnerable to breeches of confidentiality. Depending on the state, the law regarding minors' participation in therapeutic group differs. Also, school board policies should be consulted before a group is formed. Many schools prefer that parents are informed that their child will participate in the group process and even are asked to sign a consent form. This process does not ensure that the confidentiality of the child will be breeched. Parents can learn of the group's focus and receive feedback about their child but not the specifics mentioned in the group sessions (Corey & Corey, 2006). When issues of health and safety are in jeopardy, confidentiality must be breeched. This, of course, needs to be explained clearly as part of the ground rules of group participation.

PRACTICAL CONSIDERATIONS

Practical considerations of scheduling a group are important issues. If groups can be scheduled during a study period, lunch period, or before or after school, these would be most beneficial. Besides avoiding students missing classes, having students give up some of their free time might ensure more substantive motivation for group participation.

If this type of scheduling is not possible, then the possibility of rotating the group meeting time shows some advantage. This process ensures that students are not removed from the same class session each time the group meets. As stated before, teachers are more inclined to have a positive response to groups when students are not constantly absent from their classes.

Group meetings should take place in a quiet, secure environment where anonymity can be assured. A room without windows in the door would be best. Also, the meetings should take place in an area that is not in the mainstream of the school. This would help with the privacy issue.

TYPES OF GROUPS USED BY SOCIAL WORKERS

A topic-oriented group may be one that involves children of divorce, children who have experienced loss, under- or overachievement, and a variety of other subjects. A situational group would be one that occurs as a result of an experience of certain students.

Example: I ran a single-session group for students who were on a class trip and their teacher died of a heart attack while on the trip with them. This situational group met only once since they were with the teacher at the time of his death.

Support groups, task facilitation groups, psychoeducational groups, counseling groups, brief groups, and psychotherapy groups are the variety of groups used by social workers. Some are used more in the school environment than others.

Support Groups

The main thrust of support groups is mutual aid, help with life stressors, and enhancement of coping skills. Focusing on participants' strengths and allowing the expression of feelings are the responsibilities of the therapeutic leader. Each participant interacts with each other in an effort to normalize the experience that is being coped with and to give advice on dealing effectively with the situation (Toseland & Rivas, 2005). The concept of hope is essential to develop in these groups. Mutual support aids in this procedure. Many times these groups are helpful for cancer survivors or in school for children whose parents are suffering with the disease or have died from the disease. Children from single family homes or nontraditional family units as well as from LGBQT homes can also benefit from such a group. These examples are just a few of the many groups that may be found in the school environment.

Example: In a group of students from divorced families, the group would share the stressors surrounding the issues dealing with sharing holidays with their parents. The students usually shared some of the same feelings of ambivalence toward leaving one parent and spending the holiday with the other. The support they were able to give each other worked well, and feedback after the holiday was positive.

Task Facilitation Groups

These are formed around a task to be accomplished. They might be community organizing, task forces, study groups, discussion groups, and so on. These groups have in common first and foremost a clearly stated purpose. Process and content are developed. It is characterized by mutual respect, cooperation, and comradery; feedback is essential; conflicts are confronted and dealt with; members can be a source of information; and group issues are addressed in the present (Corey & Corey, 2006). The group develops along the lines of "warm-up, action, and closure" (Corey & Corey, 2006, p. 11).

Example: A group or coalition was formed by the Parent Faculty Organization to combat the use of alcohol by adolescents. Sharing of experiences, brainstorming of ideas to curtail the problem, and the use of community resources to educate and communicate with other parents in the community were all outgrowths from this group experience.

Psychoeducational Groups

These are groups for emotionally well-adjusted people who need help in the area of group focus. The group is structured and addresses the area of concern on a cognitive basis. The main purpose of this group is to give information, discuss the issues, and integrate the material. Often, a questionnaire is distributed before the group begins to assess what is needed in the area of concern. Some of the psychoeducational issues for which groups might be developed include (a) stress over homework, (b) dealing with the burdens of honors classes, (c) balancing activities with school work, (d) dealing with suicidal friends, and (e) learning to deal with drugs and alcohol.

Since school is an educational setting, this type of group meshes with the school agenda. It is an effective way to help children and adolescents develop social and emotional skills in the school setting.

Example: A group was run in my high school for students who were in honors classes and being overwhelmed by assignments and pressures for excellence. The students in this group decided to ask the administration to have teachers give tests in their subject areas on assigned days so that the students wouldn't have more than one major test on a given day. That effort was successful.

Counseling Groups

This type of group setting is conducive to problem-solving. It is a process that helps people deal with the conscious thoughts and concerns that they are considering.

Interpersonal, social, professional choice, and concerns about issues of their own development are all discussed in counseling groups. These groups are usually short-term in focus and try to help the participants resolve problems in the here and now. Feedback from group members and the leader is important in this modality. The purpose of this group is to develop coping skills and understand the strengths that one has through the group process. Using the skills developed in the group to generalize real life issues as well as aiding in behavioral changes are important outcomes of this group experience. These groups can be beneficial to elementary and high school-aged students. The group leader should be cognizant of the developmental issues of the students he or she is serving and the areas of difficulty that are common to the age group at hand (Corey & Corey, 2006). It is suggested that the counselor (social worker) is trained in treatment issues that confront children and adolescents in particular.

Example: A group was initiated for students who had difficulty with peer social relationships. Many of these students were isolated and not involved in extracurricular activities. The primary goal of this group became for members to support each other in getting involved in at least one extracurricular activity while the group was convened.

Psychotherapy Groups

This modality arose out of a shortage of counselors around 1950. It has proven to be a successful intervention because it gives support of multiple participants, an atmosphere of concern, and the ability to confront clients in an effort to escalate positive behavioral change (Corey & Corey, 2006).

It differs from counseling groups because the participants are experiencing a significant emotional disturbance and/or mental problems. These groups are not likely to be used in a school environment because the level of emotional investment and time involved to alleviate the symptoms is more time consuming than what can be offered in the school. Generally, the level of training for the therapist is also greater, and more in depth skills are needed to successfully achieve changes.

Example: I was the case manager for a class of emotionally difficult students in a self-contained class. We met on a weekly basis to discuss feelings and behaviors that each had experienced in the previous week. At times, there were great expressions of anger and sadness. These were encountered by the other group members with support and appropriate responses to the behaviors exhibited. At times, students would express their anger with hostility, and the other members would temper and caution the subject by showing empathy or sharing with them the consequences that they had dealt with in similar situations.

Brief Groups

These are time-limited sessions that can last from 8 to 12 weeks (Corey & Corey, 2006). Each of the aforementioned groups can be formatted as a brief group encounter. The conditions or rules of the group are set out immediately so that each person participating will know what is expected and what the parameters of the group are. For the purpose of efficiency in therapy, brief work is used more readily than it was in the past. When time limits are placed on a modality, it appears that interventions are more successful. In the school environment, brief work is very beneficial and often used. Students as well as faculty respond well to the concept of limited time. The issue of missing class time is also a consideration in school. Using brief therapy addresses that concern and takes a minimum of class time. Children and adolescents respond well to time contracts. The procedure is then adhered to, and the development of the group can follow sequentially. In my experience with children of divorce, the group flows well when structured by a predetermined time limit. If the time is not long enough, recontracting for more time is an option.

SINGLE-SESSION GROUPS

Single-session groups exist, are not usually seen in a therapeutic setting, and are usually educational in nature. A relaxation or stress reduction group helps participants learn how to use techniques and skills after the group ends. A suicide awareness group imparts knowledge to students on the signs and symptoms of the suicidal person as well as examining their own feelings for danger signs.

In the area of counseling groups, I have seen single-session groups run for terminally ill patients who have difficulty getting to group sessions. These groups move through the exploratory, transitional, action, and termination phase in the one session that they exist. In rural areas, with elderly people, and even with adolescents, this type of group can be helpful to the participants.

Support groups can also run as single-session groups. Examples of these might be adult children of alcoholics, people who are retiring, those who have lost their job, high school students learning to deal with a death of a classmate, single adolescent fathers, and so on.

STAGES OF GROUPS

Gazda Model

According to Gazda, a group progresses through four specific stages: exploratory, transition, action, and termination.

Exploratory Stage

This stage is characterized by getting to know one another, developing goals, and setting ground rules. At this point in the group development, personal disclosure is not recommended. It is a time when people can "put their best foot forward" and establish their place in the group. It is important at this time for the therapist leader to disclose something about himself or herself and to set the tone for acceptance, care, and empathy for the group members. Mutual respect, caring, and trust must be built in this stage (Gazda, 1984).

Transition Stage

At this time in the process, some of the members begin to self-disclose. It sets the stage for what is to follow but often is met with resistance by other group members, and attempts are made to return to more comfortable social group interactions. The therapist must be able to make the environment safe for disclosure while containing the anxiety of those who are resisting it. To move to the next level, the therapist has to begin to model some disclosure himself or herself (Gazda, 1984).

Action Stage

In this stage, the counselor encourages a move to action to facilitate the change effort. Confrontation is a skill most needed by a counselor in this stage. Clients must not only "talk the talk" but also "walk the walk." Feelings about the group process are explored during this stage. The next part of this process is for the participants to confront each other (Gazda, 1984).

Termination Stage or Phase

In this part of the group process, new areas are not developed. There is usually a preset date so that all group members are aware of the group coming to an end. Feedback is given during this phase as well as what the group has meant to the individual members and what goals they have achieved. The counselor must point out the gains made by the group members and how the group process has achieved its goals (Gazda, 1984).

Crespi Model

Another sample model for the stages of groups specifically in schools from Crespi is as follows:

Stage 1: The Forming Stage

Courtesy: Meet, greet, and develop rapport.

Confusion: Following basic instructions, members operate with little direction.

Caution: There is concern about statements outside boundaries.

Commonality: Bonds of similarity among members emerge.

Stage 2: The Storming Stage

Concern: No member should harm another.

Conflict: As bonds of similarity arise, dissimilarity appears.

Confrontation: Members learn how to confront others.

Criticism: As lack of progress occurs, criticisms emerge.

Stage 3: The Norming Stage

Cooperation: Members address basic rules.

Collaboration: As rules emerge, agreement is needed on process.

Cohesion: Togetherness emerges.

Commitment: As a group unit, they move forward.

Stage 4: The Performing Stage

Challenge: Members feel increased responsibility for the group.

Creativity: New methods of communication emerge.

Consciousness: With increased openness, member self-recognition increases.

Consideration: Increased awareness of self and others emerges.

Stage 5: The Adjourning Stage

Compromise: Members recognize unresolved issues and strive for balance.

Communication: An awareness of changes through communication occurs.

Consensus: Members deal with conflict through compromise.

Closure: Reluctantly at times, members face closure and termination (Crespi, 2009, pp. 275–276).

GROUP TIME AND PLACE

The important considerations in finding a place where the group can meet are privacy and allowing for face-to-face sessions. Sitting in a circle is the preferred seating arrangement for a group. Temperature of the room is also important. Rooms that are too cold or stifling hot prevent normal interaction and are also distracting. I find with children and adolescents that offering them a snack or a cold drink often helps lower the anxiety level of the participants. It affords the students the opportunity to move freely in the room and supports social interaction.

The meeting room should have a door that closes and prevents people from looking in. It should be located in a quiet area of the school to alleviate distractions. The chairs should be comfortable but not cushy or fluffy. Observation of body language is important to the group process and can be noted more easily when people are seated in an upright position. The room should be cheerfully colored but not with distracting ornaments or pictures. Simplicity is best.

The group in a school milieu should probably meet on a weekly basis for one class session (usually 40 to 45 minutes). Staggering group sessions is another way of dealing with time. Some groups might meet once a week for 4 weeks, then once every 2 weeks for the next 2 weeks, and then once per month for a few months. This format might be helpful in a school environment where time out of class is an issue.

COGNITIVE-BEHAVIORAL GROUPS

Cognitive-behavioral therapy has been shown to be quite effective with children and adolescents. It is an evidence-based modality so that its efficacy has been substantiated. The integration of thoughts, feelings, and behaviors is the thrust of cognitive-behavioral group therapy. The therapist functions as an instructor teaching members about dysfunctional, irrational thinking, and how to evaluate one's cognitions. According to Corey, ". . . members are taught to recognize, observe, and monitor their own thoughts and assumptions, especially their negative automatic thoughts" (2004, p. 376). Catastrophizing is a mechanism that many people use in everyday life: that is, looking at the worst case scenario and dwelling on it. The group leader can help the individual change that thinking pattern. As group members identify these patterns in others, they learn how they too are using them. Realistic thinking is reinforced in the group process. Supporting or refuting core beliefs is another area where group members can help each other develop better ways of coping with reality. Evidence weighing is a basic ingredient to this form of therapy and helps the participants gain insight into behaviors and thoughts. Some of the other procedures used in this modality are Socratic dialogue (very direct and specific questioning) with the therapist, homework assignments, accumulating information on the assumptions that one makes, and keeping records of behaviors (Corey, 2004). Through the process of "guided discovery" the student realizes the relatedness between thinking, feeling, and acting

(Corey, 2004). It is a here-and-now form of therapy in the group process and usually is time-limited. It can be considered both task-oriented and brief.

SOLUTION-FOCUSED GROUPS

This format for group therapy follows the principles of the modality used in individual and family work. In this modality, the therapist first tells the group what solution-focused therapy is and that it is oriented to finding solutions to problems experienced in the present and then focuses on the future. The miracle question focuses group members on what life would be like if the miracle occurred and specifically what changes would they envision. The ability to picture the specific changes that would be present motivates participants to move toward those changes. The question asked to follow up this one is "how" would those changes be made? The scaling question is another technique commonly used in solution-focused treatment. That is, asking on a scale of 1 to 10 how would you rate yourself now in evaluating yourself in light of those changes? This question is asked regularly in group meetings to see if improvement exists.

Ron Banks (2005) describes a solution-focused treatment process. He proposes that the language in the sessions should be positive, respectful, and creative. Actions needed are the essence of the session, and the therapist needs to ask questions that keep the group functioning on a positive course. Problems should be challenged, and only one at a time should be focused on. The therapist needs to ask unique questions that reframe the problems into a positive framework (Banks, 2005).

He outlines six steps in the process of group solution-focused group therapy. First, there needs to be a clear and concise description of the problem area by the client in question. Next, any group member is permitted to ask questions to clarify the problem being described. Pathology or viewing the presented problem through a labeling process must be avoided. This is the responsibility of the therapist (leader). Third, each group participant is asked to express understanding and empathy for the member's problem. Other members may choose to share their own similar experiences. The client's strengths and abilities to deal with the problem should be emphasized. The fourth step is the miracle question and future plans. How will your life be after this problem is resolved, and how is it 5 years later? The therapist uses the group to reinforce his or her positive view of the client's strengths and resiliency. Step 5 involves looking at improvements that have been made from the time the problem was at its worst. It might be helpful for other members to help the client see his or her progress in this situation. Complementing the client and pointing out others' positive responses to the client is in order at this step and time. The last step is asking the client for feedback, including what the next step is that the client will take. Thanking all participants is the last part of this process (Banks, 2005).

EVALUATION

The evaluation of groups by participants is very helpful to the group leader, and the essential feedback prepares the leader for future group development. Evaluative instruments range from the simple to the very complex and research-based. The following are examples of these scientific measures.

GROUP COUNSELING EVALUATION

We would like your feedback on your group experience at the Counseling Center. This information is voluntary and will be kept confidential. We appreciate your honesty and ask that you do not put your name on the sheet so that your responses will remain anonymous. Your feedback will help us improve our group counseling services. Fill out the form and return it to your group leader.

For #1–9, please circle the number along the scale that best represents your counseling experience:

Not Applicable	Strongly Agree	Neither Agree or Disagree	Agree	Disagree	Strongly Disagree
N/A	5	4	3	2	1

1. I made progress toward my personal goals in group counseling. N/A 5 4 3 2 1
2. I can work more effectively on my personal problems. N/A 5 4 3 2 1
3. I can better understand my problems/issues. N/A 5 4 3 2 1
4. I can better communicate my thoughts and feelings. N/A 5 4 3 2 1
5. I am more sensitive to, and accepting of, differences in others. N/A 5 4 3 2 1
6. Group counseling helped me stay in school. N/A 5 4 3 2 1
7. I feel that I can better handle my feelings and behavior. N/A 5 4 3 2 1
8. I have healthier relationships with others. N/A 5 4 3 2 1

9. I am satisfied with my overall group counseling experience. N/A 5 4 3 2 1
   (If disagree, please explain) ______________________________
   ____
   ____

10. What were the best features of this group? ______________________________
    ____
    ____

11. What didn't you like or how might the group be changed? ______________________________
    ____
    ____

12. How could the group counselor/leader improve? ______________________________
    ____
    ____

13. Further comments on any of the above scales or about your group experience at the Counseling Center (use the back of this form if you need more room): __________
    ____
    ____

Number of group sessions I have already had this semester: Semester ..Fall ..Spring Year__ _____

..1 – 2 ..3 – 5 ..6 – 9 ..10+

Group Counselor/Leader's name ____________________

rev. August '05

(www.wcu.edu.wncln.wncln.org/, 2005)

Therapeutic Factors Inventory-S ID #_________ Group Session # _________

(Continued)

(Continued)

Please rate the following statements as they apply to your experience in your group by circling the corresponding number, using the following scale:

1 = Strongly Disagree to 7 = Strongly Agree

1.	Because I've got a lot in common with other group members, I'm starting to think that I may have something in common with people outside group, too.	1	2	3	4	5	6	7
2.	Things seem more hopeful since joining group.	1	2	3	4	5	6	7
3.	I feel a sense of belonging in this group.	1	2	3	4	5	6	7
4.	I find myself thinking about my family a surprising amount in group.	1	2	3	4	5	6	7
5.	Sometimes I notice that in group I have the same reactions or feelings as I did with my sister, brother, or a parent in my family.	1	2	3	4	5	6	7
6.	In group I've learned that I have more similarities with others than I would have guessed.	1	2	3	4	5	6	7
7.	It's okay for me to be angry in group.	1	2	3	4	5	6	7
8.	In group I've really seen the social impact my family has had on my life.	1	2	3	4	5	6	7
9.	My group is kind of like a little piece of the larger world I live in: I see the same patterns, and working them out in group helps me work them out in my outside life.	1	2	3	4	5	6	7
10.	Group helps me feel more positive about my future.	1	2	3	4	5	6	7
11.	It touches me that people in group are caring toward each other.	1	2	3	4	5	6	7

12.	I pay attention to how others handle difficult situations in my group so I can apply these strategies in my own life.	1	2	3	4	5	6	7
13.	In group sometimes I learn by watching and later imitating what happens.	1	2	3	4	5	6	7
14.	This group helps me recognize how much I have in common with other people.	1	2	3	4	5	6	7
15.	In group, the members are more alike than different from each other.	1	2	3	4	5	6	7
16.	It's surprising, but despite needing support from my group, I've also learned to be more self-sufficient.	1	2	3	4	5	6	7
17.	This group inspires me about the future.	1	2	3	4	5	6	7
18.	Even though we have differences, our group feels secure to me.	1	2	3	4	5	6	7
19.	By getting honest feedback from members and facilitators, I've learned a lot about my impact on other people.	1	2	3	4	5	6	7
20.	This group helps empower me to make a difference in my own life.	1	2	3	4	5	6	7
21.	I get to vent my feelings in group.	1	2	3	4	5	6	7
22.	Group has shown me the importance of other people in my life.	1	2	3	4	5	6	7
23.	I can "let it all out" in my group.	1	2	3	4	5	6	7

(Permission granted by authors for the reproduction of this scale)

SUMMARY

Group work in schools is an ideal method of reaching a maximum number of students. Groups can be situational or topic-oriented. Group selection, statement of goals and purpose, and issues of confidentiality are essential for a successful group process.

Evidenced-based interventions such as solution-focused and cognitive-behavioral can be used in group settings. The various types of groups: support, task facilitation, psycho-educational groups, counseling groups, brief groups, and psychotherapy groups were presented and examples of each were given. How members are chosen for a group and the dynamics (i.e., planning, informing educators of absences in class to attend groups, protecting confidentiality) of working with groups in schools were discussed in this chapter. A few group models were also presented. Group evaluation was explained.

ACTIVITIES

Activity 1: Level 1: When dealing with students who have underachievement issues, what type of group would be best suited? Why?

Level 2: Discuss a group that you have been involved with in your practicum. How was the group structured? Please explain the statement of purpose and the goals of the group. Is the group still in progress? What evidence-based interventions have you used that have worked?

Activity 2: Level 1: How would you deal with confidentiality in a group setting if confidence was broken by one of the participants?

Level 2: Give an example of a topic-oriented group that you would develop in the school and describe a time-limited ten session plan.

Level 2: As an intern or novice in the field of school social work describe in detail a group with whom you would use one of the aforementioned interventions.

SELF-REFLECTION QUESTIONS

1. Do you think group participation is more effective with certain age groups? If so, which ones and why?

2. What are some of the advantages and disadvantages of open groups?

CLASS DISCUSSION QUESTIONS

1. What kind of group would you classify your class as?

2. Give an example of a topic-oriented group that you would develop in the school and describe a time-limited ten session plan.

3. Present/describe an example of a group that would best achieve its goals through a single-session group. Include the stages of the group process.

Chapter 11

STUDIES, ANALYSIS, AND DISCUSSION FROM AN AUTHENTIC SCHOOL PRACTICE PERSPECTIVE

INTRODUCTION

In this chapter, specific case studies are reviewed from authentic situations. As a professor, I encouraged and assigned practice tasks that would help the students transition from the school situation to the college classroom. The particular cases presented take into consideration socioeconomic, ethnic, racial, culture, and locale diversity. The vignettes chosen from professional practice are indicative of cases dealing with students classified according to IDEA. Examples from specific treatment modalities were also selected. It is essential for the student intern to bring his or her cases to the classroom keeping in mind the limits of confidentiality.

STUDENT INTERN INTERVENTIONS

The following vignettes were actual experiences that my college students in School Social Work have had in their placements. These were supervised by licensed clinicians in the field of social work.

Mary

An example of such a case was written by one of my students. It was chosen for its poignancy and application to urban school students. It is as follows:

Mary is an 8-year-old African-American female currently in the third grade. Last year, while in the second grade, Mary experienced a tragic, life-altering event in her life. The following is her story. Mary was living with her mother for the duration of 7 years. During those 7 years Mary's mother had been diagnosed with cancer and was adamant about finding Mary's biological father. Mary's mother brought one of the men she suspected to be Mary's father to the hospital for a paternity test. When they went to the hospital for the results of the test, Mary's mother collapsed and died of a massive heart attack. On that same day, Mary also found out that the man who had been tested was in fact her father. Mary had to live with this man (a stranger) after her mother's death. After a few months, Mary had missed her mother so much that she tried to throw herself in front of a car. When asked why, Mary responded, "I want to go to heaven to be with my mommy." The mobile crisis unit was called and determined that Mary would benefit from outside counseling with her father. Mary is currently in a bereavement group, improving academically, and getting along very well with her father. Although she has vocalized that she still misses her mother, she has not had any suicidal ideations.

The student social worker was asked to see this student after the mobile crisis unit had decided that Mary needed counseling. Although she used supportive techniques that helped the child, this child could be counseled using attachment-based therapy practice. This modality has been used to help children in the schools, especially after a significant loss has occurred in that child's life. Although it is not an evidence-based modality, it has shown significance in a study by Arthur Becker-Weidman (2006).

This intervention would be used with Mary after the mobile crisis unit has determined that she was not in imminent danger. The attachment-based approach would be a team effort of both the teacher and school social worker.

The school is an ideal environment to encourage a secure base after a disruption has occurred. The social worker realizes that children who experience these emotional disruptions will have difficulty learning. *Attachment* is defined as an emotional link that connects to another person. It is basic to human nature (Ornstein & Moses, 2002). Mary would be considered an ambivalently attached child. For her, not knowing boundaries and becoming frustrated or using dangerous behavior to cope would be allayed by the intervention of the social worker. The social worker must be available and predictable. The school environment would also be stable, and the teacher would be helped to be empathic and benevolent.

The social worker would coach the teacher and problem-solve with him or her to maximize the intervention. Mary's teacher must develop consistent rules and responses in the classroom so that the child knows what to expect. In individual sessions, the therapist would help Mary feel comfortable expressing her feelings especially about the loss of her mother. Mary might be encouraged to use a narrative to tell her story. Journals, autobiographies, family trees, or pictures would help Mary express her feelings. When there are vacations, Mary might develop a memory box to help her understand that the social worker will be in her thoughts and memory. A small focus group might help Mary as well as other peers experiencing loss to see that they are not alone. The social workers might help the school develop policies for dealing with children who have experienced such emotional bond disruptions (2002).

Joe

Joe is a 15-year-old male of Latino background from an inner city neighborhood and was admitted to a local county hospital for psychiatric evaluation. His parents were substance abusers, and his mother used cocaine and alcohol during her pregnancy. He was supervised in the first 15 months of life by an older sibling who was in second grade. Joe showed early signs of emotional disturbance, and at 10 years old was himself sexually abused. His history before hospitalization was one of severe behavioral disorder and school expulsion. He threatened another student with a knife. His diagnoses included bipolar disorder, oppositional-defiant disorder, as well as a learning disability (NOS) and ADHD. Some of Joe's strengths included verbal articulation, insight, sense of humor, motivation, and having a solid support system.

The interventions used by the school social worker prior to his hospitalization were in-school counseling, therapy in the community, a harm assessment, and a violence prevention assessment. The harm assessment by the school psychologist ascertained whether or not Joe was a threat to himself or others. The violence prevention assessment evaluates the degree of risk associated with a violent threat. The four categories in this assessment included:

1. Characteristics of the threat: direct or indirect; specific or detailed; impulsive or premeditated; and veiled, conditional, or implied. (Answers to these questions help determine the severity of the threat and whether or not the student is in the state of crisis.)

2. Predisposing characteristics: personal and family history, unstable home environment, and history of aggression.

3. Precipitating characteristics: interpersonal instability, and drug or alcohol use.
4. Psychosocial factors: maladaptive emotional or behavioral characteristics such as depression, aggression, alienations, and egocentrism; exposure to violence in the past; or mistreatment by others (*School violence threat risk assessment using Acute Petra*, n.d.).

Other issues to address in school violence assessment are (a) lack of insight, (b) seeking to obtain a weapon, (c) lack of family communication, and (d) modeling of violent behavior to name just a few. Some of the formal assessment tools that can be used are as follows: "The Historical Clinical, and Risk Management-20, Version 2 (HCR-20; Webster et al., 1997); The SAVRY (Borum et al., 2003); and the Early Assessment Risk Checklist [for boys and for girls] (EARL-21B and 21G; Levine et al., 2001)" (cited in Bernes & Bardick, 2007, p. 423).

It was determined that Joe was a threat to others and was suspended for 10 days. Thereafter, the intake reevaluation found him still a threat, and he was sent to the psychiatric facility for evaluation and observation. In the hospital, Joe received individual therapy twice per week, group therapy 3 times per week, and Dialectical Behavioral Therapy (DBT), family therapy, medication (lithium and geodon—a newer drug used for the treatment of bi-polar disorder), recreational and play therapy, and a structured school program. The DBT program included five modules of skills training. These were (1) mindfulness (reasonable, emotional, and wise mind), (2) interpersonal skills (dealing with conflict, and self-respect), (3) emotional regulation (skills), (4) distress tolerance (tolerating crises), and (5) dialectical counseling (diary cards and individual counseling to modify reactions) (Lynch et al., 2006). DBT is a form of cognitive-behavior therapy used with borderline personality disorder. (A good article for reference is "Dialectical Behavior Therapy Ways of Coping Checklist: Developmental and Psychometric Properties" [Neacsiu, Rizvi, Vitaliano, Lynch, & Linehan, 2010].)

Miriam

Miriam is a 17-year-old Latina female. She lives in an inner city neighborhood with her mother, grandmother, stepfather, three sisters, and two brothers. She is enrolled in an alternative high school in an inner city. Her presenting problems include anger and verbal aggression; interpersonal issues with her stepfather; inability to manage time, leading to feelings of being overwhelmed and frustrated; and a history of truancy through tenth grade. Although her profile is multiproblematic, her strengths include intelligence, insightfulness, and ambition to make her life better for herself. The intervention used by the school social worker was a family intervention using the dyad of mother and child with the rationale that Miriam felt that her parents were having excessive emotional effects on her. Solution-focused therapy was utilized. The social worker asked each person in the session what they admired about each other and what concerned them most about each other. Miriam said that she admired her mother for always having a positive outlook on life and worried that her mother would side with her stepfather and blames her for the recent argument they had. Her mother admired Miriam for being focused and persevering on any endeavor she pursued. She worried that Miriam had changed her motivation for going to college and becoming a therapist. Miriam talked about how her stepfather told her siblings how evil she was and that she was "trouble." Her mother expressed how awful she felt to be caught between her husband and her daughter. Miriam admitted that she wasn't as serious about continuing school and going to college. The goal for Miriam then became to get serious about school and prove to her mother that she wanted to graduate and go on to college. Miriam expressed how badly she felt about having the emotional closeness between them erode. They agreed to work on strengthening their relationship (Corcoran, 1998).

Sam

Sam is a Caucasian eighth grader who is 14 years old. He is placed in a school for children with severe emotional and mental problems. He suffers from ADHD and was hospitalized after an uncontrollable rage where he threw and broke a chair in the classroom. He has also shown symptoms of agitation, anxiety, and depression. After leaving the hospital, he promised and did comply with his medication regimen. Thus, the school social worker developed a plan to work with him using solution-focused therapy. Sam showed insight into his anger issues, and the therapist used scaling to assess his motivation and hopefulness. Dealing with solutions for his problems helped Sam focus on the present. His strengths include showing insight into his problems and utilizing his inner resources. Thus, he became empowered. To create a balance for Sam in his environment, systems level changes had to be developed. He needed to continue to comply with his medication and focus on his strengths such as baseball, soccer, and music. On a mezzo level having Sam receive resources from Care Plus Crisis Unit of New Jersey will help him deal with and control his anger. The mobile crisis unit provides services in the community, mobile crisis, anger management, home visits, and so on (*Direct Services*, 2009). (Refer to Appendix B for tools on solution-focused treatment in schools.)

James

James is a Latino 17-year-old boy who lives in an inner city neighborhood and is on house arrest for threatening to kill specific teachers in his school. He is presently attending an alternative school program during school hours. He generally behaves dangerously, has poor impulsive control, and impulsive behavior. He claims he has negative obsessive thoughts that have been recurring for years and thus self-medicates with multiple drugs: marijuana, in particular, and some prescription drugs as well. The school social worker in this case chose a course of short-term cognitive therapy treatment. The goals of treatment are to help control distorted patterns of thinking, increase self-control, and deal with his behaviors. The focus of treatment for James is for him to understand the antecedents and consequences of his behavior. That is, he needs to understand the idea of terroristic threats toward his teachers and the consequences of this behavior. James (and his group) was challenged by another gang group in his school to kill specific teachers. Since he and his friends received this challenge and because they felt socially isolated and labeled as "losers," they chose to carry out the act. Solutions were focused on how to create a better self-image and gain insight and knowledge into his character. Several goals were developed: to learn how to problem-solve and come up with socially acceptable solutions, and to improve judgment and self-control. He also needed to have his distorted patterns of thinking challenged and develop new ones that were satisfactory. He must learn how to function as a member of mainstream society and therefore develop a more realistic and positive self-image. James believed that an impulse overcame him when he decided to write the terroristic note that precipitated so much trouble for him. He, thus, needed to develop coping skills to monitor his impulses and develop more prosocial reactions (Goldstein, 1999). James benefited from identifying anger, understanding the intensity of it, and learning the physiological signs of distress. He used the Hassle Log (see Appendix C) to better understand the triggers and learned methods of managing the responses through breathing, relaxation, and imagery. Problem-solving and learning new ways of communicating to resolve conflict was suggested (Feindler & Engel, 2011). Group training (such as Anger Management Training [2011]) is another viable treatment modality.

Carol

Carol is a 16-year-old Caucasian girl who receives special education in a comprehensive public high school setting. She has several learning disabilities, which include the birth defect of athetoid cerebral palsy. As part of her special education-related services, she is required to attend in-school counseling with the social worker. Her parents are recently divorced, which brings her newly into the school district. One of the issues she brings to therapy is that she feels responsible for her parents' divorce. (In reality, her father had abandoned the family.) She currently lives with her mother and stepfather. She has become very dependent on her stepfather and suffers from separation anxiety when he leaves for business trips. Carol also had difficulties developing relationships with her peers. The school social worker chose solution-focused therapy as the modality to work with Carol. This modality is used in schools because of its evidence-based significance and its efficiency. The usual range is from 5 to 7 sessions with 30- to 45-minute periods (Franklin, Moore, & Hopson, 2008).

Carol was challenged to reevaluate her preexisting perceptions in her interpersonal relationships and identify more productive ways to cope with her relationships in the present (Corcoran, 1998). This effort was made to develop on her strengths and within a short period of time see significant changes in her relationships. A person involved in solution-focused treatment feels empowered when they can derive his or her own solutions thus permitting him or her to see important results (Dane et al., 2001). Carol set three goals for therapy: (1) to attend all her classes daily, (2) to participate in one extracurricular activity, and (3) to reduce separation anxiety because of her stepfather's absence. Her first goal was achieved through setting and completing her short-term goal of attending all classes for a consistent period of time. She realized that her isolation was one cause of lack of peer involvement. Her second goal was achieved when she began to attend a newly formed Animal Rights Club. With the social worker's help, Carol was able to make the connection that her stepfather was not like her father and that he would come back when he went on a business trip as opposed to her father's circumstances. (Refer to Appendix B for an outline for individual solution-focused sessions in the school.)

PERSONAL VIGNETTES AND REFLECTIONS FROM ACTUAL SCHOOL SOCIAL WORK PRACTICE

The following are vignettes from my actual practice experience in the high school (I also worked at the junior high and elementary school levels). The students were all middle class White students from various ethnicities. They are all basically true stories with changes made to protect the identity of the students and families involved. As with every practice, some situations culminate in success and others do not. As I look back on my practice of school social work, the care and attention given to these students may have contributed to their successes. One thing that I can emphasize is that no one in my experience committed suicide or any other violent crimes while they were under the child study team's (CST) watchful attention. As you read through the stories, you will notice that some cases will end after high school graduation and others will not. Students, whose life one has an impact on, will often continue the relationship (on a different level) after high school is completed. Parents, as well, will often decide to contact the school social worker to inform him or her of the events in the student's life or to ask for guidance. I've been involved not only in the happy events but also in the sad ones. Last year, I received a call from a parent that one of my students at the age of 34 had committed suicide. These experiences have a lasting effect on us. On another note, I have been invited to weddings as well as birth (of their children) celebrations. Overall, the practice has been extremely gratifying. I try to recount as many different students from a variety of special education classifications as possible. You may notice some that are missing because I may not have been a case manager for a person with that classification.

Alicia: A Case of Emotional Disability

Alicia was self-referred as a freshman in high school. At first she presented as an acting-out, rebellious teen, but this façade masked an anxious depression with suicidal ideation. Alicia was doing poorly academically, and after contacting her mother, I learned that Alicia was acting out at home to her parents' dismay. A crisis occurred when she began to break objects in her room and raged uncontrollably. Her mom called 911, and Alicia was hospitalized for several months and given medication. Her diagnosis was that of an anxious depression with separation anxiety. When she returned to school, the hospital professionals suggested that she be evaluated by the child study team for assistance with her academics. This was done, and she was classified as being emotionally disturbed. She was placed in a resource room for support, and the IEP called for her to receive counseling services from the social worker. Through these supportive sessions in which attachment therapy was utilized, Alicia developed ego strengths that helped her cope. Alicia's father left the family home at about this time. He blamed Alicia for his leaving and refused to see or speak to her. Her teachers were alerted to her difficulties and became the replacement figures in her life along with her social worker. Predictability and consistency were the cornerstones of the treatment process, and she began to excel academically and emotionally. The weaning process was initiated, and in her senior year she was seeing me once per week for about one-half hour. She received the most improved student award at high school graduation. She no longer needed a resource room as of her junior year and was declassified. Her goal was to attend college and reside there. She was able to do this and eventually graduated and left the area to live in the Midwest where she married and began her adult life. Alicia was able to cope with the loss of her father who remained estranged from her through her college attendance.

Leon: A Case of Emotional Disability

Leon was a seemingly happy-go-lucky young sophomore when I met him. He was a football player who had been identified for being overly aggressive both physically and verbally on the football field. After our conversation, I realized that he was very much bullied by his father. By the next time I met with him, his father had been killed in a motor vehicle accident. Leon was distraught. His mother brought him and his other siblings to a counselor for crisis and bereavement treatment. Nonetheless, Leon did not overcome his feelings. They became sublimated into acting out behaviors. Leon was fun loving, so he spent much of his time cutting classes and being part of the group that cut school and "hung out" in the adolescent constructed shack in his friend's back yard. They would drink, smoke marijuana, and have parties with young freshman girls. The administration wanted him out of the school since he was involving other students in his acting out behaviors and because he did poorly academically. After an incident where he threatened to beat up his girlfriend, he was suspended pending CST evaluation. I was his case manager. After completion of his classification conference and individual education program, he was placed in an alternative school for students who were bright but had emotional difficulties. His IEP included therapy on a weekly basis in school. It was given in that alternative school. The treatment modality was psychodynamically oriented, but his insights were not very accessible. He easily graduated from that school and went on to college. What seemed to happen to Leon was a progression of depression (never having resolved his father's death) and drug abuse. There were periods in his life when he was sober but would always fall back into use. I was in touch with him throughout his life after high school and had a very close professional relationship (more as a consultant) with him. He married and had a child during a period when he was sober. He again began to fall into his old habits, and his mother saw to it that he had residential placement and rehabilitation. All these efforts failed. He threatened suicide often while he was bingeing, and eventually his mother found him dead in a lonely hotel room. His story could have had another ending, but the illnesses of depression and drug addiction could not be overcome by him. It is an example of how clients determine their own destiny. I realized that even though I intervened in every way I could I was not always successful in my efforts and that saddened me.

Seth: A Case of Other Health Impaired

Seth was a 14-year-old freshman when he became my case management responsibility. He was from a professional family who realistically knew what the problems were and had the ability to handle the situation. I was told that my responsibilities included informing the teachers of his modifications and helping him get his coat on in the afternoon. Seth suffered from muscular dystrophy. He was in a wheelchair and had limited use of his hands when I met him. Without the disability, he would have been a college prep student who was not involved in special education. As it was, he was a college prep student who took school and life quite seriously. He was elected to the student council in his freshman year. He was aware of his illness and his limitations (which is not the norm for a high school student). We developed a wonderful relationship, spending much time together since he did not eat lunch and could not have any extracurricular activities outside of student government. Part of my job was to get him to accept the help that he needed and getting the teachers and staff to make the necessary accommodations for him because of his disability. These tasks became daunting since, as his high school years went by, he became less able to fulfill his obligations as a student in college prep classes without significant modifications. These became more extensive as time wore on because of the disease progression. His IEP would sometimes have to be revised during the school year instead of annually. His cognitive ability began to wane as well, so it was difficult to modify the work based on the special needs. It was no longer time that was extended but the content began to become hard for him to remember and comprehend. I must say that most of the professionals cooperated and his parents were exemplary. He completed high school with great success and was scheduled to begin college in the fall. He never got to college because he died that summer. I was greatly touched by his passing and felt compelled to do whatever I could to relay his message. Each year I return to the high school and give his memorial scholarship award. This was my way of coping with his loss.

Ana: A Case of Neurological Impairment (Specific Learning Disability)

Ana was a young girl, a 14-year-old freshman who had suffered from spinal meningitis in infancy that left her with a disability that was labeled by the child study team as neurological impairment. Her IEP included weekly counseling sessions by the school social worker. Although her intellect was in the below average range, she was not able to take advantage of the cognitive therapy that was offered. Ana was told of her disability but chose to deny its existence. She wanted to be in college preparatory classes because she idolized her older sister who did in fact attend college. Although cognitive behavioral techniques were employed, Ana refused to accept the fact that she would not pursue a career in biology as did her sister. Her irrational thinking was difficult to change. Her family was realistic about her ability and tried to explain her limitations to her with the idea that she could pursue a career that was more technical than academic. The counseling sessions with me were also focused on the strengths that she possessed. She liked animals, was socially adept, and had good relationships with her family and teachers. Ana became depressed, which compounded her academic difficulties. She was absent a great deal. In her sophomore year, she was brought for a visit to the technical school (satellite school) where she had many choices. Included in these choices were small animal care, horticulture, cosmetology, skin care and esthetics, medical office assistant training, and culinary arts. These programs were available in an afternoon program, and the morning would be spent in the regular high school setting. Although Ana agreed and began the program, she did not continue. Her neurological difficulties were compounded by her emotional overlay, and she became truant. This phenomenon is one that sabotages the therapeutic relationship and impedes the counseling process. She got pregnant and decided to quit school and take care of her child. Unfortunately, the ability to accept her limitations and embrace the possibilities of being successful in a technical field was not acceptable to her.

Nicky: A Case of Visual Impairment

Nicky was a 14-year-old student who came to the high school classified as visually impaired. He suffered with the disease Retinitis Pigmentosa. This condition was characterized by the slow progressive loss of vision. Nicky was a typical teen in denial of what was to happen to him. At that point, his vision loss was not interfering with his functioning. He enjoyed socializing and being involved with his peers. He loved to sing and play the guitar in his leisure time.

His mother was very involved with accessing services for him. Nicky resisted these interventions, particularly working with the Commission for the Blind. The representative would come on a bimonthly basis and try to give him Braille lessons. He refused to comply with the practice and sometimes would not come to those sessions. His IEP required a one-half hour counseling session per week by the school social worker. Cognitive therapy was the modality of choice. Linking thoughts, feelings, and behaviors was important for Nicky. Understanding the link between behaviors and consequences was essential in this case. If he did not prepare for the future, it would make his life more difficult. Understanding the consequences helped him try to accept the help and work through some of the feelings attached to the problem he faced. Addressing his sadness and his ability to acknowledge those bodily sensations helped him realize that he needed to comply with the program that would enhance his life in the future. He did comply and eventually graduated and went on to college. His vision loss was a slow process and did not cause significant changes in his life after graduation from high school. The last I heard, he was working as a counselor for an organization in New York City that helped visually impaired people.

Jack: A Case of Social Maladjustment

Jack was a 15-year-old male who was referred by his teachers for uncooperative and acting out behavior. His family was known to the school system since his mother had been in trouble in school as well, and his aunt was classified with Mild Cognitive Impairment. According to the social history, his mother had been impregnated by her father having Jack as a result of that union. His sister, who was younger, was also a product of that incestuous relationship. The family (Jack, sister, and mother) resided in the home of his grandparents (father and grandmother). Jack was a pleasant person on the surface. On interview, he discussed the idea of assassinating a public figure for the purpose of notoriety. He hoped to be famous someday for an infamous deed. When questioned further, it was ascertained that he had no distinction of moral values and could not discern anything wrong with his ideas. He was sent to our psychiatrist for a second opinion and for issues of classification. Our consultant felt that Jack was a danger to others and recommended residential placement. He was placed in Bonnie Brae School (New Jersey) for boys with behavioral problems. It is a residential school that serves this population and provides behavior modification and therapy. I felt that was the best intervention that we could provide.

Matt: A Case of Orthopedically Handicapped

Matt was identified by the high school child study team when he was still in eighth grade. He had cerebral palsy. He was highly impaired by this affliction as a result of a birth trauma. He worked with a private speech and occupational therapist, both of whom were part of the annual planning of his IEP as well as his monthly team meetings. Each year at the beginning of the school term, his new teachers, his individual aide, his case manager, and the specialists mentioned above would meet to review the safety issues involved in his program. There were certain foods that might cause him to choke, so the Heimlich maneuver had to be learned by each professional who worked with him. Lists of foods that couldn't be given in class and that he could not have in the cafeteria were also explained. He needed individual help on a one-to-one basis for tutorial since he couldn't take notes himself. He also needed to use a laptop computer in class for tests. He was extremely proficient with technology. He had an individual aide who went to class with him and took notes when Matt was unable to do it. All these were accommodations developed from his IEP (Present Levels of Performance) and therefore, were provided by the school district. The IEP was strictly adhered to, since this was such an extraordinary situation. The monthly meetings included going over his IEP and making the necessary accommodations as well as discussing his progress with his individual teachers. Matt was a self-advocate. He had learned early on that advocacy was an important part of his education. On the other hand, he had a wonderful sense of humor and wanted to be an active member of the student body, which included extracurricular activities such as Spanish Club and Student Council. Without the disability, Matt would have been a regular high school college prep student. He had friends and would socialize with them on the weekends. He was a computer whiz and therefore was involved with those students who were interested in that activity. He did participate in a special computer programming class. Overall, his high school experience was successful, and the IEP and the accommodations to the regular program made this a positive experience for him. The cooperation between the school and the family in this case was essential and greatly contributed to his successful completion of high school.

Carla: A Case of Multiple Disabilities

Carla was a multiply disabled young girl who came to us as a freshman in high school. She was one of the students who I case managed and who was well-adjusted and able to deal with her handicapping condition. I attribute most of the success of this student to her parents. They were realistic about her abilities and were able to negotiate the public school program to maximize her success. Carla was in special education self-contained classes for English and mathematics. She was mainstreamed for all other subjects. Her parents realized her limits, which were a perceptual visual impairment as well as a hearing impairment, and were able to accept her placement in modified curricula. Carla had a particular interest in pets. She had a cat, and her parents realized that this interest could be used to help her create a career and eventually economic independence. In her sophomore year in high school, she was accepted into the half-day vocational program where she learned small animal care. She excelled. At the same time, she began to work after school in a pet grooming center where she learned even more skills and got invaluable experience. As the end of high school arrived, the transition plan was developed in her IEP, and the need for clarifying her next step was essential. Everyone involved in the process was realistic about her abilities and strengths as well as her limitations. She could have gone directly into a career of pet care and grooming, but it was decided that Carla wanted to be a veterinarian technician. This career required a two-year community college experience. It is a rigorous program that involves biology, chemistry, and other subjects that Carla had not been exposed to in the high school program. A decision was made by Carla and her parents to begin the program and take just one or two courses per semester; it didn't matter how long it took her to complete the program but that she did complete the program. She continued to work at a local groomer and also started her own pet sitting business. It did take her about 7 years to complete the program with help of the special services department at the community college, but tenacity and support were the ingredients that enabled her success.

Marian: A Case of Developmental Disability

Having a child with limited intellectual functioning is a difficult task for a parent to accept. Many parents refuse to accept the limitations of their child and continue to advocate for more academic learning. At the high school level, the task of the case manager is often to help those parents accept their child's limitations and to develop a program that can contribute to that child's maximum capacity for a successful life.

Marian was a youngster who was considered a higher functioning person with Down's Syndrome. Her parents felt that her capacity for intellectual and academic learning was indeed much higher than the testing and school professionals concluded. She was given academic learning until the age of 16, when it became obvious that she had reached her limit of learning at about a first- or second-grade level. It becomes the difficult task of the case manager to assess and communicate to the parents that the child has "maxed" out. In Marian's case, her parents could not accept this inevitability. They advocated for her to receive more academic work and did not want her to be placed in the training for a sheltered workshop where she would learn the skills needed to function in a productive lifestyle. As time passed and it became more realistic to them that she would need to learn those skills if she were to function in the real world after high school, they reluctantly accepted her fate. At the age of 21, as high school came to a close for this special education student, her parents began to request more services. The child herself began to have an overlay of emotional problems that were exhibited in depression. She even spoke of suicide on an elementary level. The special education team and I (the case manager) were as supportive as possible and recommended counseling for Marian and her family. This recommendation was never accepted and after Marian's graduation at the age of 21, she remained at home with her parents, who at that point had retired from work. The gains she had made through her training were lost because her parents refused to have her enter a sheltered workshop. They claimed it was in a "bad" neighborhood and not safe enough for her. Recently, a colleague of mine saw Marian walking with her mother down the road. She is approximately 45 years old at this time. She remains at home now just living with her mother. This story has a sad ending for a young woman who could have had some interaction with the outside world but was prevented from having a more productive life.

James: A Case of Profound Intellectual Disability

During my tenure as an elementary school social worker, I performed many social and developmental histories. One of these was done on a profoundly intellectually disabled young child. He was so impaired that he did not have the ability to speak, sit, walk, or talk. He communicated through expression and sounds. James attended a special program that we had for children who were profoundly intellectually disabled. I met with his mother to update his developmental history and to see if there had been any changes to his condition. At that point there hadn't. He enjoyed being given affection such as being hugged, and although he could not raise his arms to respond, his mother knew through his expression that it was pleasurable.

The home had been refurbished to accommodate the stretcher (where he stayed during his waking hours). The bathroom was fixed so that there would be easy access for the parents to bathe this young man as he got older and heavier. I do remember the positive attitude that his mother had, and although she did not have any other children, she cherished this boy deeply. His parents tried to provide him with the most normal life possible. I recall that he could not urinate and defecate on his own, and his parents were involved in these procedures on a daily basis. Their lifestyle had been altered to accommodate the needs of this profoundly needy young boy.

Epilogue: I later found out that the child's father suffered from cancer and died in early middle age. Not long after that James died as well. No information was given on this mother.

Larry: A Case of Traumatic Brain Injury

Larry was from a single-parent home living with his mother and his sister. He was a classified student with the label of learning disabled. Larry was a typical high school student who went to vocational school in the afternoon and did his academics in the morning in a resource room setting. So many high school students feel omnipotent and impulsively take chances with their lives. Larry was just that type of student. His mother allowed him to use a moped to go from the high school to the afternoon vocational program. On one of these journeys, he was hit by a car and sustained severe head injuries. He was in a coma for a few weeks and his fate was not known at that time. We were told by the doctors that he might not live. I was his case manager and spent a great deal of time with his mother and sister supporting them during this time of tremendous crisis. Fortunately, Larry survived but was not the same as before the accident. He was extremely depressed, and his cognitive ability was damaged as a result of the accident. As you may know, traumatic brain injury often results in various stages of depression. He was then placed in a rehabilitation hospital where he spent the next year of his life working on efforts to regain what was lost physically, emotionally, and mentally. As a result of his brain injury, he was clinically depressed and received both medication and therapy for that affliction. He never accepted the limitations that were caused by the accident, and after that year decided to get a job without completing high school. We tried to give him a work study program but he refused that as well. Little is known of the adult life of this student.

EMOTIONAL TOLL ON SOCIAL WORKERS

As you can see from the preceding vignettes, working with clients takes a great toll on social workers and interns as well. *Burnout* is sometimes experienced. This is defined as: "emotional exhaustion, depersonalization or cynicism, and diminished personal accomplishment" (Kim, Ji, & Kao, 2011, p. 258). We learn that both physical and emotional components comprise burnout. Supervisors and administrators need to help social workers avoid these problems. Family members and peer support as well as self-help groups are necessary for those of us who work with clients (Kim et al., 2011). Moore, Bledsoe, Perry, and Robinson (2011) found that for social work interns journaling was a viable method of alleviating some of the toll taken on their physical and mental processes. Physical activity and proper nutrition were components of the physical care needed. Communicating with family and friends, watching TV, napping, and gardening are some of the activities that allay emotional stress because of working as social work interns (Moore et al., 2011). Overall, self-care is essential when we practice social work.

SUMMARY

This chapter basically contains vignettes from real practice situations. The purpose is to acquaint the student with issues faced on a daily basis by school social workers. In the student oriented vignettes, more emotional and situational issues are shown through experience. The hope is to give students the practical understanding of theory to practice. The practitioner based vignettes explained more about the students who were given counseling or case management under the auspices of the Individual Education Program.

ACTIVITIES

Activity 1: Levels 1 & 2: Ask your supervisor if he or she would share one incident where an intervention was not successful and one that was. Review the cases and decide what was positive and negative about each.

Activity 2: Level 1: What treatment modality would you apply to a child who has just lost a parent? Why?

Level 2: Can you describe a case in your caseload where you could apply attachment-based or attachment therapy as an intervention with a student or group? For each modality, the social work student would be asked to describe an intervention for a particular student. Explain specifically the steps you would follow.

SELF-REFLECTION QUESTIONS

1. As a new social worker, what are the best methods to use supervision effectively?
2. If you disagree with your supervisor on specific interventions, what is your recourse? How would you handle it?

CLASS DISCUSSION QUESTIONS

1. Can you describe a case in your caseload where you could apply solution-focused therapy as an intervention with a student or group?
2. Can you describe a case where an evidence-based practice was used? Explain specifically the steps you would follow.
3. Recount a case that you deem successful and explain the case as well as the steps of intervention that you feel contributed to the success.

Chapter 12

SCHOOL POLICY, PROGRAM DEVELOPMENT, AND EVALUATION

INTRODUCTION

A review of existing policies (i.e., truancy, possession of illegal substances, and involvement in physical fights) should be examined by the incoming social worker in the school. Agency policies such as crisis and trauma plans need to be incorporated into the school's policies if they do not exist. Instruction on the development of policy is described and a plan to address its implementation is highlighted. Several examples of school policies are given. A discussion of informal versus formal policies is reviewed.

Many schools do not have programs that are needed for children. Such programs as child abuse or sexual abuse (prevention and identification procedures or protocols), alcohol and drug awareness and occurrence, bullying, suicide prevention, drop-out, truancy and school failure prevention, adolescent pregnancy, single-parenting, assertiveness training, and peer mediation are some of the programs that are discussed in this chapter. Planning, developing, and implementing such programs are the focus of this chapter. Students are asked to demonstrate competency in development through implementation of a program relevant to the problem areas. Special education program development and implementation are examined.

WHAT AN INTERN CAN DO TO DEVELOP NEEDED PROGRAMS

When an intern enters a placement, it is important to evaluate the policies and program plans in place for the above-mentioned situations. Students need to ask the supervisor for copies of such programs. If these programs and policies don't in fact exist, it is incumbent on the intern to initiate plans for such actions with the help and support of his or her supervisor. The school is the place where the largest segment of children can be reached. Therefore, it is my suggestion that prevention programs are most helpful and can reach the largest segment of children and adolescents.

Needs assessments can be very helpful in eliciting the support of the administration for many of these policies and programs. Another useful procedure is to solicit information from surrounding school districts or ones with similar populations to see the policies and programs that they have in place and to use this information to reinforce your case for the need in your school. The Internet is a wonderful resource to find such programs. Many times other school districts will even share their information, which makes the research and development of your plans simpler.

ALCOHOL AND DRUG AWARENESS AND OCCURRENCE

Substance abuse in adolescents is an ongoing problem. According to the U.S. Department of Health and Human Services, Substance Abuse and Mental Health Services Administration, "In 2010, an estimated 22.1 million persons (8.7% of this age group) aged 12 or older (in the 12- to 17-year- old age range) were classified with substance dependence or abuse in the past year. Of these, 2.9 million were classified with dependence or abuse of both alcohol and illicit drugs, 4.2 million had dependence or abuse of illicit drugs but not alcohol, and 15.0 million had dependence or abuse of alcohol but not illicit drugs" (http://www.samhsa.gov/data/NSDUH/2k10NSDUH/2k10Results.htm#7.1.2).

Of those who do receive treatment, recidivism is another significant problem. It is important that substance abuse gets identified and treated in the schools, since the impact is not only on the young person who experiences the problem but also it increases the risks for auto accidents and suicide. Those who experience substance abuse in adolescence are eight times more likely to develop substance dependency in adulthood.

Griswold, Aronoff, Kernan, and Kahn explain that the Substance Abuse and Mental Health Services have categorized stages of substance use as follows:

1. Use when minimal or experimental has few or minimal consequences
2. Regular use has several and more severe consequences
3. Substance use disorders are maladaptive patterns of use accompanied by clinically significant impairment or distress (2008, p. 331).

Some of the comorbid disorders in adolescent substance abusers were depression, ADHD, PTSD, and conduct disorder as well as oppositional defiant disorder (2008).

A screening tool suggested for adolescent substance abuse is the CRAFFT survey and can be seen in Chapter 9.

Some suggest that cognitive-behavioral therapy is most effective since substance abuse originates in the interaction of person and environment. Substances both illicit and legal are easily available in the adolescents' environment. Marijuana is said to be easily accessible to teens and the third most commonly used drug by adolescents in the United States (Burrow-Sanchez, 2006).

To work effectively in schools with adolescents, the counselor or social worker must develop an alliance with the teen, assess the severity of the problem (keeping in mind that it is part of adolescence to experiment with substances), identify a treatment plan that would work, and acknowledge from the onset that relapse is possible (2006). A good instrument to use for global assessment would be the Problem-Oriented Screening Instrument (Rahdert, 1991, cited in Burrow-Sanchez, 2006). It is a general screening tool to uncover problems in such areas as substance abuse, violence and bullying, school and academic issues, mental and physical health, family and peer relations, vocations, and special education. Looking at the person in environment is essential for treatment to be effective. It can be downloaded at http://cart.rmcdenver.com/instruments/problem_oriented.pdf. Burrow-Sanchez (2006) explains that outpatient family treatment is assessed to be the most effective for substance abuse.

Prevention programs in school on a yearly basis would at least make pre- and adolescents aware of the warning signs and symptoms. Having recovering addicts address students is one way to bring the message home. Many adolescents can relate to other young people who have suffered with substance abuse and/or addiction. In the high school where I worked, we had a gamut of programs ranging from individual speakers such as former users to experts talking on the subject. We had both small groups and lecture hall sized programs. Each has its pros and cons, but the emphasis is on the exposure to the material and information about where to get help if it is needed.

SUICIDE PREVENTION

Although suicide has declined in the United States for 15 to 19 year olds, it is important that we remain vigilant in our efforts to continue on this course. The use of screening surveys has been seen as useful, but whom you administer these to and when becomes problematic. The Columbia University Suicide Screen has a 75% success rating in identifying students at risk (Ciffone, 2007). Throughout my career as a school social worker, I found that the use of school-based prevention programs are most helpful in identifying those at risk as well as having peers get involved in bringing at-risk students to the attention of the professionals. At my high school, we did a prevention program every year for the freshman. It resulted in many referrals and may have prevented several serious suicide attempts. After every prevention program that was provided to students, at least one student would come forward to reveal his or her own suicide experience or that of a peer.

Ciffone in his 2007 article describes the components of the suicide prevention program used in his high school district (South Elgin High School) Suicide Prevention Program (http://www.u-46.org/sehs/spp/). He explains that the research has suggested that suicide is the result of mental illness, specifically depression, and not caused by the ups and downs of normal adolescence. The following are the components of the South Elgin prevention program:

- Written intervention policies for the staff
- Freshman orientation presentations by an on-site school social worker with all 9th-grade students to reduce access barriers and stimulate self- and peer referrals to the same school social worker
- Easy access to school social workers, on-site from September through June, for assessment, intervention and referral
- Structured classroom discussions on mental health, mental illness, and suicide to all 10th-grade students in health class [in Illinois, the health class is a graduation requirement and seems to be the most legitimate class to provide for this type of discussion]
- Prevention information materials for distribution to all 10th-grade students
- Formal and informal evaluations of prevention message effectiveness
- Follow-up screening mechanism for pro-suicide attitudes
- Post-vention component to be used following any student death (Ciffone, 2006, cited in Ciffone, 2007).

Ciffone used the survey: "SEHS (South Elgin High School) Survey Questions and Desired Responses." The survey questions and desired answers are as follows:

1. I would counsel a suicidal friend without getting help from someone else. (No)
2. If my friend appeared suicidal and asked me not to tell anyone, I . . . (Tell anyway)
3. If a friend said he or she was "thinking of suicide" and it seemed like they were saying it to get sympathy or attention from me, I probably . . . (Take them seriously)
4. If a friend came to school in a bad mood and said, "My family would be better off without me," I would encourage him or her to get help from a professional counselor. (Yes)
5. If suicidal thoughts crossed my mind regularly, I would seek out and talk to a friend about those thoughts. (Yes)
6. If I was very upset and suicidal thoughts crossed my mind, I would be willing to talk with a professional counselor about those thoughts. (Yes)
7. Suicide is the result of (choose the most accurate)—stress or certain thinking errors? (Certain thinking errors)
8. Most teens who killed themselves were probably suffering from mental illness. (Yes) (Ciffone, 2009, p. 44).

In the article, Ciffone cites the fact that teens are more affected by the program than they were originally. He also ascertained that even when given by another presenter the results were consistently effective (2009). See Appendix D for a sample of a school-based suicide checklist for counselors.

COLUMBIA UNIVERSITY SUICIDE SCREEN

The Columbia University Suicide Screen (CSS) is a 43-question written scale that includes 32 general health questions and 11 global items that discuss the risks for adolescent suicide. It is used in conjunction with the availability of a mental health professional and was developed by David Schaffer, MD (Schaffer et al., 2004). He works at Columbia University College of Physicians and Surgeons with funding coming from the Center for Disease Control. There is no cost involved in using the instrument. Assent from the student and consent from his or her parent(s) must be obtained before using the survey. The names of the participants are kept confidential, and if they screen positive, a secondary evaluation takes place by a mental health professional. The screening takes about 15 minutes, but the secondary evaluation depends on the individual screener and the participant. There is a separate survey for males and females. (see Appendix E).

TRUANCY AND SCHOOL FAILURE PREVENTION

Truancy or unauthorized absences is often preceded by absenteeism (Reid, 2010). This issue occurs because of the many variables to which a youngster is subject. It may begin as a protracted illness, but without community and school support the absenteeism may evolve into school truancy and even school drop-out. Truancy may also begin because of environmental or personal deficits that arise. It may be the result of antisocial behavior such as sexual behaviors; substance use, abuse, or addition; and delinquency. Some environmental issues that contribute to this behavior are dysfunctional family problems, poor transportation, bad weather, and/or unsupportive school milieu (Teasley, 2004). Truancy differs from absenteeism in that the absence is unexcused and usually unknown to the parents. Poverty often contributes to truancy and absenteeism as well. The inability to have proper nutrition and/or appropriate clothing or school supplies can contribute to a student's nonattending behavior. As school social workers, our job is to assess the issues that contribute to the phenomenon and seek to prevent or intervene when these issues arise. Some of the school factors that contribute to truancy are schools with lower socioeconomic students, inconsistent school policies, poor communication between school and family, nonsupportive teachers and administrators, poor teaching skills, low expectations, teacher absenteeism, and lack of sensitivity to diverse populations (Teasley, 2004). Sometimes the needs of a student haven't been met in school so they stop attending. Examples of these needs might be English Language Learners, undiagnosed learning disability, or even social isolation. Some of the personal factors involved include low academic performance, falling behind in the schoolwork, and emotional difficulties including phobias (Teasley, 2004). Truancy usually develops in adolescence, possibly as a result of sexual activity, antisocial or criminal behaviors, and/or substance abuse involve ment. Parents play a key role in the issues surrounding truancy. More involved parents seem to have children who exhibit higher academic performance. Parents who are involved in their children's education and cognitive development as well as motivate their children to achieve in school guide their children toward academic success. Often they are role models who have achieved in school. Stability of attending the same school is highly desirable. Having a time and place for school work at home is also helpful. Parents who are involved in school activities and communicate with school professionals ward off lack of school attendance for their children. Parental supervision is also key, regardless of the student's age. As structure in the home decreases, the rate of absenteeism and truancy increases. Lack of ethnic and racial sensitivity in schools seems to coincide with higher rates of truancy and absenteeism (Teasley, 2004).

School social workers must be aware of state laws regarding absenteeism and truancy as well as school policies in this area. The causes of absenteeism and truancy are complex. No single cause can be cited as the highest contributing factor to the dilemma. As a school social worker, one must assess the cause of the problem before developing an intervention.

Interventions

Academic interventions to help a student whose grades are low or in the failing range may ward off truancy or absenteeism. Peer tutoring, that is, having an older student helping a younger student, might be successful on two levels: academic and the development of a positive role model. Mentoring by an adult or older student would also be another opportunity. It helps when a person can coach or encourage the young person to attend school.

School interventions might include parental workshops, communicating with minority families more effectively, school counselor or attendance officer intervention, making home visits (school social workers are most effective in communicating through home visits with students and families), and a Cognitive Behavior Therapy (CBT) system of rewards for school attendance (Teasley, 2004).

Family interventions should include assessment of family values, open communication between school personnel and families, and having parents understand the laws involved as well as their responsibilities to their child's school attendance. Referral to a community-based organization for supportive family services might be helpful after the assessment is complete.

Minority and ethnic groups respond to learning applications to the real world with respect for their diversity. Teachers should be aware of understanding the difference in values, learning styles, and cultural needs of their diverse students. School social workers can make teachers aware of these issues and help guide them to multicultural responsive educational practices.

Community interventions include availing the help of agencies, organizations, and social groups that may contribute to keeping students in school. Having meetings and conferences when parents are available is essential. Also having outside agencies aware of the problems of truancy and absenteeism is important so that they may be more sensitive to the needs of the families dealing with the issues of these problems (Teasley, 2004). Collaboration is the key to preventing and intervening in the areas of truancy and absenteeism. These conditions lead to the next issue we examine, which is school dropout.

Several programs in Colorado have been successful. The Truancy Reduction Program and Project Start have used multidimensional approaches to combat truancy. Several components are essential for these projects to work. Included in the programs are: a commitment on the part of the school system to keep at-risk students in school; collaboration with community resources such as the juvenile courts; a continuum of support, which outlines rewards and consequences; parental involvement; and constant evaluation (Fantuzzo, Grim, & Hazan 2005).

DROPOUT

Dropout or push out is the conundrum. Many students are forced to leave school by the risk factors that arise and put them up "against the wall." Such issues as suspensions, which lead to failure; expulsion; and flagrant infractions of the attendance policies as well as humiliation by teachers and administrators often lead a student to drop out of school. These issues would be considered "pushouts" (Dupper, 2003). It is often the purview of the school social worker to intervene and find alternative educational environments for these students. It is the right of every child in the public school system to graduate from high school. Who has really failed when a student drops out of school? The school as an institution, the community, and the local and state governments all play a role in the loss of a student through dropout. They also pay the price of caring for that person through public assistance programs through the years. According to Jonson-Reid (2011), 1.2 million students in the United States drop out of school before graduating. In New York City, the dropout rate was reduced to 37% in 2009 as opposed to earlier rates of 50% to 54% (http://schools.nyc.gov/). It costs the community to train and employ these young people if in fact they do get work. The societal costs of increased substance abuse and delinquency are also a factor. According to the study by Fagan and Pabon (1990), males claimed they left school because of needing a job and losing interest in it. Pregnancy is a major reason for both males and females dropping out of school (1990). Swaim, Beauvais, Chavez, and Oetting (1997) report that dropouts are higher users of substances than those who remain in school. Ethnicity did not seem to be a variable in substance use among students in good standing. In yet another study by Mayer and Mitchell (1993), the variables of tutoring, an intensive summer program focusing on English, math, assertiveness, study and test preparation, and career development were helpful in reducing the dropout rate. All the information in the research found that the punitive approach to education was a contributor to school drop-out rates. Supportive programs had a much more positive result (Swaim et al., 1997). In a more updated study published in 2004, it was found that a drop-out prevention program worked because of students forming close relationships with tutors who showed care and concern. The adult role model also contributed to the reduction of dropouts (Somers & Piliawsky, 2004).

Poverty often causes a student to drop out of school to help with the family finances. Low maternal educational level also plays a part in students' attendance and drop-out rate (Allen-Meares, 2004). Children of migrant workers also have a higher risk of dropping out. These children usually don't make close ties and develop relationships in school, since they're transients. Since the Elementary and Secondary Education Act of 1965, funds have been provided to states for the development of programs for children of migrant workers (Allen-Meares, 2004). How successful this intervention was is not clear. The fact that the government has tried to help these children and has brought the issue to the awareness of the country is an important step toward intervention.

Although the number of teenage parenting statistics has declined since the 1990s, teen pregnancy and parenting still account for a portion of the adolescent drop-out rate in schools. It is hoped that if pregnancy prevention programs begin early (possibly in elementary school) and include problem-solving techniques and social skills, pregnancies may be avoided in adolescence (Allen-Meares, 2004). One must keep in mind the cultural aspects of teen pregnancy as well. With programs to help single, adolescent mothers continue their education, drop-out potential may be averted.

VIOLENCE PREVENTION APPROACHES

In recent years, violence in schools has been a grave problem. We have seen school shootings, suicide, suicide pacts, and weapons in schools emerging as very significant problems. All these issues involve both perpetrators and victims. Violence involving firearms in the United States is 15 times higher than in a sampling in European countries (Vazsonyi, Belliston, & Flannery, 2004). The identification of the individuals at risk for violent behaviors is an issue that needs to be addressed. Some behaviors that can predict future violence potential are: (a) school truancy and rule offenders, (b) substance abuse, (c) fighting in school, (d) gang membership, (e) antisocial behavior, (f) acting out behavior in classrooms, (g) animal cruelty, and so on. Example: One of my students had gone into the school field at lunchtime and stepped on all the Canadian goslings and eggs. His behavior went without consequence except for my chiding of him. Later that school year, he was arrested for beating his mother and sister.

BULLYING

Bullying is also referred to as *peer victimization*. Since this behavior is seen in the school as well as the community, it should be dealt with comprehensively. Cyberbullying sometimes takes place off school grounds, but the effects spill over to the school building. Both the victim and the perpetrator can experience long-lasting effects from this behavior. Since peer victimization is not exclusively reserved for the school environment, a comprehensive program that includes multiple systems should be employed. An ecological approach seems most practical. Social workers seem to be the best professionals to deal with the problems and address solutions. It is not limited to our culture. It can be seen in different cultures throughout the world. The statistical estimates are that 5% to 15% of children experience this type of victimization (Mishna, 2003).

Bullying is defined as, " . . . repeated, intentional, harmful, and aggressive behavior inflicted by a person or group with seemingly more power on a person or group with lesser power" (Ferguson, San Miguel, Kilburn, Sanchez, & Sanchez, 2007).

Olweus suggests that bullying is caused by reaction patterns and personality characteristics as well as physical ability. Its causes are multidimensional. Olweus also suggests that teachers' attitudes as well as class environment can contribute to the continuation of such behaviors. He gives certain principles that are needed to curtail bullying behaviors. These are:

- [interactions] characterized by warmth, positive interest, and involvement by adults;
- firm limits to unacceptable behavior;
- where nonhostile, nonphysical negative consequences are consistently applied in cases of violations of rules and other unacceptable behaviors; and
- where adults act as authorities and positive role models (Olweus & Limber, 2010, p. 126)

Olweus, Limber, and Mihalic (1999) contends that the first condition for a successful program is that the adults involved are aware of the program and willing to intervene in making a change. He believes the message to the students must be: Bullying is unaccepted in our schools, and it must be stopped. Classroom activities must involve clear rules against bullying and review of those rules repeatedly. Role playing, writing exercises, and small group discussions are important. On an individual basis, interventions should include dealing with the bully, parental involvement, and support for the victim (1999).

Dan Olweus has done extensive work on developing and testing bullying prevention programs. The survey questionnaire includes 40 items, some of which are

(7) I was hit, kicked, pushed, shoved around, or locked indoors.

(8) Other students told lies or spread false rumors about me and tried to make others dislike me.

(12a) I was bullied with mean or hurtful messages, calls or pictures, or in other ways on my cell phone or over the Internet (computer).

(25) I called another student(s) mean names and made fun of or teased him or her in a hurtful way. (2007)

This survey includes items of both the victim and the abuser. Through this procedure, one can determine whether or not an abuser was also a victim and vice versa. We appreciate the permission of Hazelton Press for use of these several questions.

The restorative justice model is also being suggested as a method of dealing with the bullying situation. This type of experience includes a face-to-face meeting with the bully and victim to express regret and to stage an environment for reconciliation and forgiveness (Ferguson et al., 2007).

Presently, we see an increase in both interest in bullying and the long-range effects of the process. Getting prevention measures to both the perpetrator and the victim is essential. Treatment, not punishment, is the key to solving the problem.

CHILD AND SEXUAL ABUSE

Child and sexual abuse are areas of deep concern for our country. It is a hidden problem that permeates all levels of socioeconomic strata and in every family constellation. The abuse in itself is problematic, but what complicates the problem is the need of the child to protect the abuser either out of love and loyalty or fear of repercussions. When these situations surface in the media, we see the actual horror that our children are subjected to. Our schools are on the front lines of these problems and need to be vigilant and prepare our faculty and staff about the warning signs and symptoms. School social workers hold a paramount position in the school in prevention, and referral, as well as treatment of children who have been sexually abused. We are often at the forefront of such programs. If these don't exist in a school setting, it is the responsibility of the school social worker to implement them.

According to Fieldman and Crespi, one of every four girls and one out of ten boys are sexually abused (2002). *Sexual abuse* can be defined as nonconsensual physical contact with a person under 18 years old which includes attempted or consummated intercourse or touching, grabbing, and kissing a child. It also includes photographing the child nude, exposing oneself to a child, or having the child view a sexual behavior. School difficulties often result in this apparent experience.

Intervention by school social workers, counselors, and psychologists through prevention programs can greatly help sexual abuse victims. Through programs for teachers and school personnel, recognition of behavioral or physical symptoms exhibited by these victims and how to respond to these victims are provided. Children who participated in such programs were more likely to disclose their experiences of abuse (Fieldman & Crespi, 2002). Open discussion that occurs in such programs for children allow for the communication of experiences in an open fashion. Children are taught skills and coping mechanisms when confronted with sexual situations. Parents, too, could benefit from prevention programs. It is felt that such education would help the participants be aware of the methods used by such offenders. Some basic characteristics of victims include shyness, lack of self-esteem, loners, and those experiencing family dysfunction.

In Texas public schools, the prevention program for students includes:

- *Concepts*: appropriate touch, identifying who is safe to be with, how to recognize an offender, defining what sexual abuse is, and what their rights are as children.
- *Skills/coping mechanisms*: how to communicate with others, refusal skills, empowerment, and how to disclose the experience and/or the offender.
- *Methods used*: videos and pamphlets for the older children (junior high and high school), role playing, activity books, drawing and coloring, and puppetry for the younger children (preschool through elementary school).
- *Who to seek help from*: social workers, psychologists, counselors, nurses, a teacher, or any safe person (Lanning, Ballard & Robinson, 1999).

It wasn't until 1974 that the federal government passed laws that would prevent children from experiencing physical or emotional abuse at the hands of their caretakers. This was the Child Abuse Prevention and Treatment Act (PL93–247). It also made provisions for the National Center on Child Abuse and Neglect (Kohl, 1993). Some programs now focus on potential perpetrators of the abuse. It appears that programs actually increase the reporting of such cases by the victims. According to Kohl, the most important concepts taught were those that developed self-esteem, the fact that it is OK to say "No," what touch is inappropriate, personal safety, and one's own body integrity (p. 145). The remedies that sought to help children are support and resisting such abusive advances (p. 145). Usually these preventive sessions occur on 1 day for about 1 hour. It also might be helpful to conduct parental (guardian) workshops to help them teach their children about inappropriate touch. In some cultures, it is difficult for parents to speak to their children about such issues, but if they are guided through the school social worker, it may support them. Example: I once saw an intellectually marginal student who molested his 7-year-old cousin. The 16-year-old perpetrator explained to me that he had been sexually abused by an uncle also at the age of 7. He said he wanted to know what it felt like to do it to somebody.

Child abuse and neglect, in general, appears to be a problem that has plagued our society for a very long time. Child protection service workers are understaffed and underpaid. The issues come to the surface when a child brutally dies at the hands of his or her caretaker. Does this have to occur again and again? Prior to 1875, no protection was afforded to children. The Illinois Supreme Court decided that inhumane treatment of children was unacceptable. From 1875 to 1962, child protection became an issue. It was the Society for the Prevention of Cruelty to Animals that first recognized and acted on helping abused children. In the 1960s, physicians became interested in the battered child, and thus the media became involved. The Children's Bureau started to look at the issues of child abuse and neglect, which culminated in the creation of the Child Abuse Prevention and Treatment Act of 1974 (mentioned above). This federal act mandated states to provide funds and take a more active role in prevention, treatment, and action involving child abuse and neglect (Myers, 2008).

Child protection is within the purview of the schools. Mandated reporting of suspected child abuse or neglect is the law in most states. If a school professional does not report a suspected case, they can be fined and/or prosecuted. They are also given immunity from legal suits from the accused. School programs for all children must be provided to ensure that children know what acceptable treatment is and who they should tell if it is not. Schools should also offer parenting classes for parents and teen parents during after school hours to educate and inform them of proper behavior, where they can get help, and a system of support (Massey-Stokes & Lanning, 2004).

PEER MEDIATION AND CONFLICT RESOLUTION

Prevention programs that focus on anger management, peer mediation, prosocial behaviors, and group esteem sessions were those that I used at the high school level. It can also be helpful on an elementary and junior high level. On a macro level, school programs that encourage positive social activities can help curtail violence. Many times when working with a student who had aggressive tendencies, an extracurricular activity would be encouraged. Playing sports sometimes defused a potentially violent student and gave him or her the ability to expend the negative energy on a playing field (Shannon, 1999). Violence prevention should begin in the elementary school. There are many programs that schools enlist to help develop self-esteem and prosocial behaviors.

Examples:

- PeaceBuilders Violence Prevention Program is a schoolwide program that uses cognitive-behavioral methods to target antecedents of the negative behavior. It provides for a system of rewards to encourage positive behaviors. The five main concepts are as follows:

  1. Praise good behaviors
  2. Avoid put downs
  3. Find people who are logical/wise
  4. Recognize the pain you have caused
  5. Seek to recompense for the wrong behaviors (Vazsonyi et al., 2004).

Although long-term effects of this program did not provide the data that should produce continued significance, it was an important step for targeted whole school populations (Vazsonyi et al., 2004).

- Peace by Peace is a program that I supervised in my high school in the 1999–2000 school year. The program was developed earlier and involved student selection by a faculty nomination process. The next step in the process was the training program which took place over a 2-day period. Students were able to learn the six-step process. These steps included:

  1. Open the session
  2. Gather information
  3. Focus on common interests
  4. Create options

5. Evaluate options and choose a solutions
6. Write the agreement and close the session

Conflict resolution is defined as two or more people having a dispute over something. Its resolution involves identifying and implementing solutions to the problems or the context of the conflict. Conflict resolution is assumed to be nonviolent, meeting the needs of the individuals involved, and the possibility of improving the relationship as a result of the resolution. The program involves giving individuals the skills for dealing with such situations.

The student volunteers are taught five conflict resolution styles:

1. Standing up for what is believed correct. This position is nonnegotiable.
2. Collaborating - working with someone to negotiate the disagreement and finding a mutually acceptable solution.
3. Compromising - seeking a solution with each combatant giving up something
4. Accommodating - departing from your position for the sake of peace or giving in today for postponed gratification
5. Avoiding - postponing the confrontation or withdrawing from the conflict.

The following 10 ways to deal with conflict are also taught to the student volunteers: (1) share, (2) take turns, (3) use chance, (4) compromise, (5) expand the pie, (6) negotiate, (7) postpone, (8) abandon the issue, (9) ask for help, and (10) apologize. The basic steps in conflict resolution are to define the problem, brainstorm solutions, and evaluate the options and choose one method and try it out.

Students are then taught to read nonverbal cues. Examples of such cues that the students will learn are leaning forward as an aggressor, avoiding eye contact, crossing arms and legs, and pulling at ears or hair.

Listening is essential in resolving a conflict. Through listening we receive information as well as defusing the charged emotions. When we listen we communicate our understanding through our tone of voice, gestures, posture, facial expressions, and so on. It is very important that empathy is shown to the subjects so that they feel supported and understood.

There are three myths about conflict:

1. *Conflict is always bad* - Not necessarily. It is a natural part of human communication. Through it, we gain growth and progress.

2. *Conflict is always a contest*—that is, one person wins and one loses. Some conflicts can be resolved with a win-win conclusion.

3. *Only one way to deal with a conflict is possible*. There are different styles to use and one must learn the most appropriate style to use for efficient solutions (see styles above).

A complete copy of the Peace by Peace packet can be found in Appendix F.

DOMESTIC AND PARTNER VIOLENCE PREVENTION

Primary prevention in this area is most effective. Children and teens who experience domestic violence are often victims themselves. Public schools are vital in the preparation of students for dealing with such violence. Teen dating violence is an important area of concern for adolescents especially ones who become sexually active at an early age (by age 14) (van Wormer & Roberts, 2009).

The following is a teen survey to determine if a relationship is likely to become violent.

1. Does your date or boyfriend brag about beating up or intimidating people?

2. Does he ever suggest that he knows how to kill, for example, by playfully putting his hands on your neck, then say he was only joking?

3. Does he own or have access to a gun, or show a fascination with weapons?

4. Has he ever forced you to kiss or have sex? Does he show an awareness of your wishes and feelings?

5. Does he use illegal drugs, especially amphetamines, speed, meth or crack?

6. Does he get drunk on a regular basis or brag about his high tolerance for alcohol? Does he push you to drink alcoholic beverages or take illicit drugs?

7. When you are with him, does he control how you spend your time? Is he always the one to drive or criticize you severely if you take the wheel?

8. Is he constantly jealous? Does he control your friendships with other people and seem to want to have you all to himself?

9. Is he rapidly becoming emotionally dependent on you; for instance, does he say things like "I can't live without you"? Is he thinking of an all-or-nothing pattern (either you are his best friend or his worst enemy-often about past relationships)?

10. Do you have the feeling that only you understand him? That others do not or cannot?

11. Note the relationship between his parents. Is his mother very submissive to his father? Is there heavy drinking and/or lots of tension in his family?

12. Is there a history of past victimization by his father?

13. Is there a history of animal abuse in his background?

14. Has he ever struck you? Have you known him to lose control of his anger for certain periods of time?

15. Has he ever threatened or tried to commit suicide?

16. Does he get out of patience quickly with children or is he verbally abusive toward them?

____Total "Yes" answers.

If you have answered yes to two or more items, you should talk to a mature person before pursuing this relationship further (van Wormer & Roberts, 2009, pp. 154–155).

ADOLESCENT PREGNANCY

The United States has the highest rate of teen pregnancy among developed countries (Minnick & Shandler, 2011). Birth rates had declined between the years 1993 and 2000, and this was seen across racial and ethnic groups. With the inception of welfare reform (Personal Responsibility Reconciliation Act, 1996), which is the basis of Temporary Aid to Needy Families (TANF), research has shown that it does not have an effect on teen pregnancy. The findings of the Hao and Cherin 2004 study were that welfare reform did not have the intended effect of reducing teen pregnancy and school dropout rates. It was found that teens in welfare families were more likely to have births in the new era of welfare reform. It is also noted that teens from low income families were more likely to drop out of school since the inception of welfare reform. The problem of mothers not being available to monitor the whereabouts or behaviors of their teen daughters because of "welfare to work" obligations may impact on the pregnancy rates of those girls from welfare families. Supervision and fear of financial difficulties are the variables that may be responsible for teen pregnancy and school dropout (2004).

Prevention programs in schools are often unable to reach those teens who seem to be at greatest risk, since they have higher absentee rates than other teens and often drop out of school early. It was found that pregnancy prevention programs took place in the community (especially in working class communities) where parents are more available. The best programs that reduce teen pregnancy are those that promote parental-child communication and parental monitoring. Community programs that involve after school activities and supportive peer groups are also helpful (Allen, Philliber, & Hoggson, 1990). Decision-making skills and knowledge about sexual risk factors are also deterrents to pregnancy risk. A multilevel program seems to work best. In the Clarke et al. study, the use of community facilities in a housing project seemed to work best (2011).

In another program (Teen Voices/Teen Choices) researched by Minnick and Shandler, the successful teen pregnancy program was a one-session intervention. It was delivered by teen single mothers in schools who discussed their pregnancy, labor, and experiences as parents. They also discussed the health risks and the fallacy of the romantic view that a baby would enhance their relationship with their boyfriend and reduce those feelings of being lonely and isolated (2011). The program was set up as a one-session experience because of the lack of school attendance among the at-risk adolescents for teen pregnancy. It proved successful. The perception of the adolescent participants about teen pregnancy was positively altered by this intervention. Perhaps an intervention with parents and their children highlighting better communication skills might also help. There seems to be a higher incidence of teen pregnancy in African-American and Latino communities. Help should be targeted in these communities.

ASSERTIVENESS TRAINING

Assertive training is an area of school prevention that may help allay problems in many areas including sexual abuse, bullying, anger management, depression, withdrawal, and even adolescent pregnancy. When children and adolescents learn how to assert their rights and privileges, many abuses may be prevented. Yet little is seen in the school literature dealing with assertiveness training. It is often mistaken for aggressive behaviors. There is a distinct difference. An *assertive response* is defined by Sprague and Thyer as "a response that was forthright and honest without being threatening or abusive was considered an assertive response" (2002, p. 68).

According to Massat, Constable, McDonald, and Flynn, assertion skills include the following:

1. Initiates conversations with others;
2. Acknowledges compliments;
3. Invites peers to play; invites others;
4. Says and does nice things for self; is self-confident;
5. Makes friends;
6. Questions unfair rules;
7. Introduces self to new people;
8. Appears confident with opposite sex;
9. Expresses feelings when wronged;
10. Appropriately joins ongoing activity/group (2009, p. 627).

Kolb and Griffith explain that there are three different styles of communication: Aggressive, passive, and assertive. Aggressive communication involves using power and position to get their needs met. Passive individuals take a hopeless position fearing confrontation and giving in to the aggressor. They are at the mercy of external forces. Assertive individuals get their needs met by stating their wishes clearly, by using good eye contact, and speaking clearly and confidently. They have an internal locus of control. Strategies for developing assertiveness are as follows:

1. Respond calmly and directly as soon as you realize that your rights have been violated
2. Focus on the specific behavior that compromised your rights by using "I" statements
3. Share the feelings you experienced as a result of the behavior
4. Describe your preferred outcome and discuss how to handle future situations (Kolb & Griffith, 2009, p. 33).

The techniques taught in this program are (a) refusing to discuss the issue, (b) compromise, (c) taking the offense, and (d) fogging. The first might entail walking away. Compromise is giving up part of what you want when the other person does it as well. Taking the offense is taking charge of the discussion and planning the offense. Fogging is obfuscating the situation until you get help or seek guidance. These techniques are often taught through role playing (2009).

Some cultures, both religious and ethnic, may discourage assertiveness and impact on the student's ability to fully engage in such a training program. It might also cause familial conflict because of a family's cultural differences.

SPECIAL EDUCATION PROGRAM DEVELOPMENT

Developing a program for students with special needs can be a daunting task. An evidence-based model is an excellent method of undertaking such a task. The problem statement would be how to best educate a child who suffers from a debilitating problem. This might be severe emotional difficulty that impedes the youngster's education. Research has shown that a comprehensive approach might work best (Vernberg, Roberts, & Nyre, 2008). The approach used in this research was multifaceted and based on the following principles:

1. Children are deeply embedded in their network of relationships: Attend to cross setting linkages and events.

2. Children do best if adults involved in their lives agree: Collaborate with everyone involved with the child.

3. Personal skills (self-regulation, perspective taking) are intimately linked to developmental status: Match interventions to the child's developmental level.

4. Children should function in natural social settings: Maintain placement in home and neighborhood school.

5. Warmth and positive attention are essential: Cultivate authoritative style for all adults

6. Evidence-based treatments should be used: Utilize a core menu of treatment options for syndromes and disorders.

7. Cognitive and behavioral skill development are key goals: Focus on the acquisition and use of specific skills.

8. The use of cognitive and behavioral skills depends on the social environment: Devote energy to focused, sustained efforts in real-world settings.
9. Multiple outcomes are possible from similar backgrounds, and there are multiple pathways to similar outcomes: Maintain a flexible, data-driven view of the causes and maintainers of SED [serious emotional disorders] symptoms (Vernberg et al., 2008, p. 172).

This program called the Intensive Mental Health Program was implemented and evaluated as per the evidence-based model. The outline for service delivery is as follows:

- 3 hours daily (M–F) specialized classroom in regular elementary building
- 3 hours daily (M–F) in neighborhood school
- 24-hours per day behavior program
- 2 individual, 4 group therapy sessions weekly
- Regular Core Team meetings with everyone involved with the child
- In-home parenting consultation and family therapy
- Graduated transition to neighborhood school (Vernberg et al., 2008, p. 174).

The evaluation of this program showed significant improvements in all areas for children in this program. Seventy-five percent of the participants showed significant improvement, but 25% needed continued services in this program. It appears that chronic emotional disturbance is a challenge to all involved and continued treatment is essential (Roberts, Vernberg, Biggs, Randell, & Jacobs, 2008).

Example: I headed a team for the development of a special education class for juniors and seniors with SED at the high school level. These six students would have dropped out if they had not been in the program. It was housed in the comprehensive high school, and the program was researched investigating many models. The model adopted consisted of a morning group period to plan the day and review the previous day. Four special education (self-contained core courses) classes, lunch, and elective classes in the mainstream composed the rest of the day along with individual counseling sessions on a biweekly basis. The school social worker led a weekly group for the students and a bimonthly evening group for parents (considering parental convenience). It was evaluated at the end of the school year, and all but one student remained in school. Two students graduated successfully from school at the end of the first year.

SUMMARY

The aim of this chapter was to prepare school social workers for critically reviewing programs and policies on entering a school system as an intern or as a professional school social worker. Examples of areas where programs would be necessary were given along with specifics of the programs and their development. Several evaluative instruments were appended at the end of the book because of their length. Each program given and instrument provided has been reviewed and implemented successfully in a real school environment.

ACTIVITIES

Activity 1: Level 1: As a new intern, what method would you use to evaluate policies in your placement?

Level 2: What steps would you take to inform the administration of the need for a policy in a certain area? How and to whom would you present this need?

Activity 2: Levels 1 & 2: Review the current policies that are in place in your practicum. What components would you look for in a successful plan?

Activity 3: Level 1: What action would you take to implement a needed school program or policy?

Level 2: Your school does not have a drug and alcohol awareness program. Describe the method you would use and the steps involved in developing and/or implementing such a program.

SELF-REFLECTION QUESTIONS

1. Are school social workers often on policy committees?
2. What are the effective, positive impacts of school programs for problem areas such as those discussed in this chapter?

CLASS DISCUSSION QUESTIONS

1. Are there any programs or policies that you see in your placement that are inadequate?
2. How often do you think school policies should be evaluated and updated?

3. When should new policies or programs be introduced?

4. After examining the programs and policies in the school where you are placed or employed, please describe the method of needs assessment and the steps you would implement in the process of developing a needed program or policy.

HELPFUL WEBSITES

http://www.schoolmediation.com/

http://www.projectbullyfreezone.com/workplace_information.html

http://www.childwelfare.gov/preventing/programs/types/sexualabuse.cfm

http://www.sprc.org/library_resources/sprc

www.clafh.org

Chapter 13

PRACTICE EVALUATION

INTRODUCTION

Practice Evaluation in the schools is one of the hardest tasks especially if one is to produce quantitative data. Parental feedback is usually qualitative but when Middle States Evaluations (or other outside districtwide evaluative processes) are done, surveys are sent to all parents and to the community with quantitative evaluation taking place. Outcome and process evaluation is discussed. Standards for School Social Work as per the NASW are presented. Evaluation surveys are examined and suggested to evaluate practice. Students of social work are asked to evaluate their own practice in their internship. As we know, the trend in social work is toward evidence-based practice. It behooves us as school social workers to quantify our work showing the benefits of its practice.

MACRO PRACTICE EVALUATION

The National Center for Education Evaluation and Regional Assistance (NCEE) sponsored by the U.S. Department of Education conducts large-scale research on programs and practices in schools and is sponsored by federal money (National Center for Education Evalaution and Regional Assistance, 2009). It also supplies technical assistance to schools and hopes to spread the information about the evaluative research throughout the United States. It is a resource for educators to use and adapt educational programs to their schools.

What Works Clearinghouse

The What Works Clearinghouse (WWC) organization is part of the NCEE and began in 2002 by the U.S. Department of Education's Institute of Educational

Sciences. Its purpose is to give educators, researchers, and the community a source of proven educational research. It contains databases and reports that give people reviews of evidence-based research programs including products, practices, and policies that are instituted to help students become successful (National Center for Education Evalaution and Regional Assistance, 2009). It should be noted that there is a dearth of research in the field of school social work, and it needs to be enhanced. It is our duty to add to this body of knowledge, since social workers are so vital to our schools.

Education Resources Information Center

The Education Resources Information Center (ERIC) provides research and information electronically of 1.2 million records of educational material including journal articles to interested parties (students, teachers, and the public) in education. It has been in operation for the last 30 years. I have found it extremely useful in all my research dealing with education (National Center for Education Evalaution and Regional Assistance, 2009).

National Library of Education

The National Library of Education (NLE) provides educational information to the public. It includes information on current and historical programs, activities and publication provided by the U.S. Department of Education. It also includes federal educational policy (i.e., No Child Left Behind, etc.), educational research, and statistical information. The services are accessed via phone, Internet, fax, or U.S. mail (National Center for Education Evalaution and Regional Assistance, 2009).

Regional Educational Laboratory Program

This is a network of 10 laboratories that provide access to supported scientific educational research. They do this through the use of applied research and projects, studies, and technical assistance (National Center for Education Evaluation and Regional Assistance, 2009).

MIDDLE STATES EVALUATION

Many states have adopted the Middle States Evaluation process for self-study of their school's programs, policies, and curricula. The states of Delaware, Maryland, New Jersey, New York, Pennsylvania, and the District of Columbia,

U.S. Caribbean, Europe, Middle East, Asia, and Africa have used the Middle States evaluative body. There are three accrediting commissions:

1. Commission on Higher Education
2. Commission on Secondary Schools
3. Commission on Elementary Schools (Standards for Accreditation for Schools, 2009).

According to the Commission on Secondary Schools, *accreditation* is defined as the following:

> ". . . the affirmation that a school provides a quality of education that the community has a right to expect and the education world endorses. Accreditation is a means of showing confidence in a school's performance. When the Commission on Secondary Schools accredits a school, it certifies that the school has met the prescribed qualitative standards of the Middle States Association within the terms of the school's own stated philosophy and objectives" (Commission on Secondary Schools: Middle States Association of Colleges and Schools, 2006).

The entire school is subject to scrutiny not just college preparatory programs. The only programs that are not involved are those records that are kept confidential by law.

The reason that many schools get involved in this program is to have a structure for self-evaluation. This is a very positive component of school policy since the entire community is involved in the process. Community, parents, students, administrators, faculty, and staff are all involved in this evaluation process. There are many reasons that schools use such an evaluative process. The process lends itself to clarification of policies, development of relationships, broader participation of school personnel, and structure for planning changes or improvements to provide a better educational environment and programs.

NASW STANDARDS FOR SCHOOL SOCIAL WORK PRACTICE

NASW had developed the standards for school social work practice in 1978. They were revised in 2002 and again in 2012. These professional standards include some of the following concepts:

- A school social worker should follow the ethics and principles set forth in the NASW Code of Ethics;

- should have a graduate degree in social work from an accredited MSW program and fulfill the state requirements for school social work;
- set aside time to fulfill the responsibilities of the job description;
- provide consultation to faculty, administrators, and staff as well as board members and the community;
- practice with multicultural understanding that enhance students' learning environment;
- shall conduct assessments of individuals, families, and organizations;
- should understand and implement evidence-based practice;
- maintain accurate records;
- organize their workload to fulfill their duties efficiently and within the school's guidelines;
- pursue professional development to enrich their practice in the field;
- work with the school administration to enhance the services they provide;
- use the empowerment perspective to help students and their families access resources in the school and the community;
- maintain confidentiality and explain the limits of confidentiality in the school setting
- advocate for students;
- mobilize services and resources to help students;
- develop workshops and training to meet the goals of the institution;
- maintain accurate data to help in the planning and delivery of services;
- develop intervention plans that help students maximize their educational facilities;
- address areas of need and develop appropriate services to bridge the gaps; and
- develop mediation and conflict resolution skills to enhance interpersonal relationships (NASW Standards for School Social Work, 2002 &2012).

These concepts should form the basis against which we evaluate our programs and policies in schools. The later version (2012) includes many more aspects of assessment and evaluation.

QUANTITATIVE AND QUALITATIVE RESEARCH

Both quantitative and qualitative research can be used to evaluate both the students and families and the systems in the school environment. Outcome evaluations are of interest to us in the schools. *Outcome evaluations* refer to the end result of the intervention. Some would suggest that process evaluations are also important. *Process evaluations* refer to what the components of the intervention were. Depending on your school and what your needs are, you can choose one or both of these forms of evaluation. The following will focus on outcome evaluations.

In a recent article evaluating school social work practice, general global areas of concern were addressed. Such variables as decreased problematic behavior, lessening of concerns of both parents and teachers, and family well-being were the issues evaluated by both parents' and teachers' pre- and postintervention. Burk's behavior rating scale and Individual Treatment Concerns of Parents and Teachers (a form developed by the author of this article) were the surveys used. Changes were noted from baseline to 1-month, 3-month, and 6-month intervals. Significant improvements were seen in the areas under investigation showing that school social work services did contribute to improvement (Diehl, 2009).

The Student and Families

Student's progress can be seen in his or her interpersonal relationships improving and in academic achievement. Measures like absences from school or tardiness are indicators or evaluators of progress. Grades and comments from teachers about behavior are also indications of improvement or deterioration. These items are somewhat measureable, but measuring changes are not quantifiable. These changes would be considered qualitative changes.

In an Individual Education Plan (IEP) there are goals that need to be measured. These are usually given a numerical condition.

Example: The goal might be for Johnny to come to school 80% more often than he is attending at the present time. Another goal might be to hand in assignments 50% more often than he is handing them in presently. These are goals that are measureable and can support his (a student's) progress. IEP goals are developed from a student's Present Level of Performance. When these are used correctly, they can support a student's progress.

Other individual goals are harder to support. Whether or not a student is progressing emotionally is difficult to assess. Using evidence-based practice can help a clinician evaluate the progress. Such interventions as giving a depression scale before each session might be used to assess the success of the treatment process. Such scales as the *Children's Depression Inventory* and *Anxiety Scale for Children and Adults* are just two of many scales designed to evaluate the progression of the therapeutic intervention (Dupper, 2003). Refer to Chapter 9 in this text for a complete list of assessment tools. Looking at student's previous history can also be a guide to helping establish whether or not progress has taken place.

Individual scales could also be devised to assess what you desire to know about a student. Using a Likert scale, one could assess the intensity of a child's feelings as he or she progresses through the treatment process. Such feelings as anger, sadness, happiness, frustration, well-being, and so on can be assessed on a weekly basis. Using the scaling question in Solution-Focused Therapy, can also be a tool to assess feeling level. Keeping a chart of this scale can help guide treatment and assess the significance of change taking place during the time period of therapeutic intervention.

Example: Creative Therapy Associates (1994) in Cincinnati, OH has developed a *"Feelings Poster"* chart that displays people exhibiting different feelings. A child might be asked which picture appropriately tells how he or she is feeling. This chart comes in individual sizes and in a large poster size. It could even be used at home to help parents understand what a child is feeling and maybe even keep an account of the number of times a child feels a certain way during the week. This can be used with younger children since reading ability is not necessary.

Evaluation of Student by Teacher, Student, Parent, and Family

CONFIDENTIAL

INDIVIDUAL CONCERNS: TEACHER FORM (IC-T) ©

Diehl, D. (2007)

Student's name or ID #: ____________________ Date: ____________________

Grade: Pre K 1 2 3 4 5 6 7 8 9 10 11 12 Class: ____________________

Person completing form: ____________________ Relation to child: ____________

School Social Worker:____________________ School:____________________

In behavioral terms, please identify the primary concerns you have with this student. After identifying these concerns, please rate from 1 to 7 the frequency with which the student engages in this behavior. You will be asked to do a similar rating in 1 month, 3 months, and 5 months. At those times, you are to base your observations on the frequency of behavior you have observed in the student since the last observation.

1 = Never 2 = Very Rarely 3 = Rarely 4 = Half the Time

5 = Frequently 6 = Very Frequently 7 = Always

Concern/Problem	**Initial Referral** *Date*:	**1 month** *Date*:	**3 months** *Date*:	**5 months** *Date*:
Example: *Peter has been physically aggressive toward classmates (e.g., hitting, and pushing others).*	7	7	2	4
(1) ______________________ ______________________ ______________________				
(2) ______________________ ______________________ ______________________				
(3) ______________________ ______________________ ______________________				
Intensity Score (For social work purposes only)				

(Continued)

(Continued)

***Examples* of specific concerns defined in behavioral terms** (Stein, 2007):

- Out of seat excessively
- Easily distractible
- Does not attend to subject matter
- Has a hard time accepting authority
- Does not follow directions well.
- Isolates self from others
- Refuses to cooperate with class room or home rules
- Sneaks around/lies
- Peer conflicts
- Worrisome nature and is specifically worried about ____________________ ______________________________
- Alcohol or other drug use
- Appears anxious
- Verbalizing self-negatives
- Needs frequent reassurance
- Appears sullen/depressed
- Hits or pushes peers/teachers/siblings
- Yells at or makes rude remarks to teachers/peers/parents
- Stares into space/daydreams
- Has emotional outbursts in class/at home
- Needs redirection
- Controlling with peers/adults

CONFIDENTIAL

INDIVIDUAL CONCERNS: STUDENT FORM (IC-S) ©

Diehl, D. (2007)

Student's name or ID #: ____________________ Date: ____________________

Grade: Pre K 1 2 3 4 5 6 7 8 9 10 11 12 Class: ____________________

Person completing form: ____________________ Relation to child: ________________

School Social Worker: ______________________ School: ____________________

In behavioral terms, please identify the primary concerns you have for yourself. After identifying these concerns, please rate from 1 to 7 the frequency with which you engage in this behavior. You will be asked to do a similar rating in 1 month, 3 months, and 5 months. At those times, you are to base your observations on the frequency of behavior you have observed in yourself since the last observation.

1 = Never　　2 = Very Rarely　　3 = Rarely　　4 = Half the Time

5 = Frequently　　6 = Very Frequently　　7 = Always

Concern/Problem	**Initial Referral** *Date*:	**1 month** *Date*:	**3 months** *Date*:	**5 months** *Date*:
Example: *I have trouble concentrating in class.*	7	7	2	4
(1) ______________________ ______________________ ______________________				
(2) ______________________ ______________________ ______________________				
(3) ______________________ ______________________ ______________________				
Intensity Score (For social work purposes only)				

(Continued)

(Continued)

***Examples** of specific concerns defined in behavioral terms* (Stein, 2007):

- I feel worried and nervous
- I say negative things about myself (e.g., I'm stupid, or I'm ugly)
- I need to be told I'm doing OK more than most kids
- I don't smile much and keep my head down
- I hit or shove others whenever I feel like it
- I yell or say rude things to people whenever I feel like it
- I daydream/ stare off in space
- I throw a big fit when things don't go my way
- I need to be reminded to stay on task
- I have to have my own way
- I am using alcohol or other drugs
- I have trouble sitting still
- I get distracted easily
- I have trouble paying attention to the teacher/ my parents
- I don't like authority
- I don't follow directions very well
- I keep to myself and don't talk to others much
- I don't follow rules at school/home
- I am dishonest more than the average kid
- I have trouble getting along with other students
- I worry a lot especially about ______ ______________________

CONFIDENTIAL

INDIVIDUAL CONCERNS: PARENT FORM (IC-P) ©

Diehl, D. (2007)

Student's name or ID #: ____________________ Date: ____________________

Grade: Pre K 1 2 3 4 5 6 7 8 9 10 11 12 Class: ____________________

Person completing form: ____________________ Relation to child: ____________________

School Social Worker: ____________________ School: ____________________

In behavioral terms, please identify the primary concerns you have for your child. After identifying these concerns, please rate from 1 to 7 the frequency with which your child engages in this behavior. You will be asked to do a similar rating in 1 month, 3 months, and 5 months. At those times, you are to base your observations on the frequency of behavior you have observed in your child since the last observation.

1 = Never 2 = Very Rarely 3 = Rarely 4 = Half the Time

5 = Frequently 6 = Very Frequently 7 = Always

Concern/Problem	**Initial Referral** *Date*:	**1 month** *Date*:	**3 months** *Date*:	**5 months** *Date*:
Example: *Peter is physically aggressive with his sister (e.g., hits, kicks).*	7	7	2	4
(1) ____________				
(2) ____________				
(3) ____________				
Intensity Score (For social work purposes only)				

(Continued)

(Continued)

***Examples* of specific concerns defined in behavioral terms** (Stein, 2007):

- Easily distractible
- Has a hard time accepting authority
- Does not follow directions well.
- Isolates self from others
- Refuses to cooperate with home rules
- Sneaks around/lies
- Peer conflicts
- Worrisome nature and is specifically worried about ______________________________
- Alcohol or drug use
- Appears anxious
- Says negative comments toward self
- Needs frequent reassurance
- Appears sullen/depressed
- Hits or pushes peers/teachers/siblings/parents
- Yells at or makes rude remarks to peers/teachers/siblings/parents
- Stares into space/daydreams
- Has emotional outbursts in class/at home
- Needs redirection
- Controlling with peers/adults

CONFIDENTIAL

INDIVIDUAL CONCERNS: FAMILY FORM (IC-F) ©

Diehl, D. (2007)

Student's name or ID #: ____________________ Date:____________________

Grade: Pre K 1 2 3 4 5 6 7 8 9 10 11 12 Class: ____________________

Person completing form: ____________________ Relation to child: ______________

School Social Worker: ____________________ School: ____________________

In behavioral terms, please identify the primary concerns you have for your family. After identifying these concerns, please rate from 1 to 7 the frequency with which your family engages in this behavior. You will be asked to do a similar rating in 1 month, 3 months, and 5 months. At those times, you are to base your observations on the frequency of behavior you have observed in your family since the last observation.

1 = Never　2 = Very Rarely　3 = Rarely　4 = Half the Time

5 = Frequently　6 = Very Frequently　7 = Always

Concern/Problem	**Initial Referral** *Date:*	**1 month** *Date:*	**3 months** *Date:*	**5 months** *Date:*
Example: *We don't have a place to live.*	7	7	2	4
(1) ______ ______ ______				
(2) ______ ______ ______				
(3) ______ ______ ______				
Intensity Score (For social work purposes only)				

(Continued)

(Continued)

Examples of specific concerns defined in behavioral terms (Stein, 2007):

- Need housing or shelter
- Conflict between siblings
- Poor communication
- Need food
- Need clothing
- Aggressive behaviors between the kids
- Do not have a job/employment
- Family member using alcohol or other drugs
- We don't have transportation
- No health insurance
- Family lacks structure and rules
- Financial problems
- Family has health issues
- Parent and child arguments
- Family doesn't spend time together

SYSTEM'S EVALUATION

The discussion of system's evaluation is of major importance to the school social worker. This would include (a) the performance of the social worker; (b) how many new evaluations (for special education) he or she chaired; (c) how many students were seen either individually or in groups; (d) how he or she functioned as a member of the team; and (e) the impact of prevention programs such as bullying, child abuse, and suicide prevention. System's evaluation can be either process or outcome in nature.

Evaluation of the School Social Work Services

An evaluation of the school social worker services from parents and students should also be part of the evaluation process. How does one obtain such information? A short survey may be sent to community members. It might include satisfaction level with the programs provided by the social worker; quality of interaction between child, parent, and social worker; satisfaction with the services provided by the individual social worker; parental attitudes toward the school after involvement with the social worker, and so on. Many of these instruments can be developed by the social worker and given pre- and postinteraction. This would give validity to the research data and establish evidence-based information. For programs, one might develop a survey prior to the program as to how much information is known on the topic and compare that with the posttest evaluation of knowledge. This would be outcome-based. Overall, evaluation of the social worker and services provided help solidify the position and enrich the school's programs. It is essential that this work be done.

Accountability factors that are viewed by the community in the importance of the role of school social workers are as follows:

- adolescent pregnancy
- family preservation and youth foster care placements
- homelessness
- juvenile crime
- emotional and behavioral problems
- substance abuse
- youth employment and readiness for adult employment
- violence, child abuse, and suicide (Dibble, 1999)

Priorities for school social worker accountability for the *schools* are different. These are as follows:

- academic achievement and grades
- graduation rates
- students continuing to postsecondary education
- cooperation and good work habits
- violence and/or aggression
- linkage for the child with outside services
- suspensions and/or expulsions
- referrals for misbehavior and learning problems (Dibble, 1999)

Viewing both of these lists, one can see that school social workers' accountability is very extensive and varied. Depending on the needs of those being interviewed, the priorities differ.

Many of us fear evaluation. If it is conducted systematically and periodically, it can enhance the school social worker's position and effectiveness. Knowing the needs of our constituents empowers us and helps us provide what is needed in our school community. Thinking we know what is needed without input from those we serve lessens our ability to serve.

We should also seek evaluation from administrators, peers (teachers), and school board members. This information should also be sought out regularly so that we can adjust our work to perform more efficiently. This information can also be obtained whether by objective survey or by open-ended questions. We should keep in mind that anything we ask of our professional colleagues should be short and not take more than a few minutes. The following is a simple evaluation form that can be used by administrators, faculty, and community members.

ST. JOHN PARISH SCHOOL SYSTEM SJBP 129

School Social Worker Evaluation Form

Evaluatee: School or Work Site:

Evaluator: Position:

Evaluation Period: Date of Evaluation:

Total Number of Observations: Conferences

Directions: Using the rating scale below, evaluate job performance in each task area by marking the column appropriately as indicated in the rating scale below:

Rating Scale: **S** – Satisfactory **NI** – Needs Improvement **U** – Unsatisfactory

Satisfactory Meets expected levels of performance most of the time.

Needs Improvement Performance is below that expected by the St. John parish School Board and deficiencies must be eliminated. Written documentation is required.

Unsatisfactory Performance is of such a serious nature as to terminate employment if substantial improvement is not shown. Written documentation is required.

PERFORMANCE RESPONSIBILITIES	Rating	Comments

1. Explains and interprets school social work services to parents, teachers and other members of the parish school system.
2. Facilitates communication between the home and school, seeking to involve families in the educational process.
3. Provides consultation, counseling services and/or training programs for parents either on an individual or group basis.
4. Serves as a liaison between the school, home, and community agencies through reciprocal referral arrangements, collaboration on cases, and assistance to families in obtaining and utilizing community resources.

5.	Produces a written report of any social work assessments or other services provided to students.
6.	Provides or assists in the inservice training of school personnel in the areas of responsibility and expertise.
7.	Participates in SBLC.
8.	Maintains accurate case records on all students regarding their referral, evaluation, and any other services provided by the social worker in accordance with the requirements of parish, state, and federal laws, regulations, and/or policies.
9.	Attends staff, professional and interagency meetings as assigned.
10.	Provides individual and group counseling and guidance.
11.	Assists with the scheduling of students.
12.	Discusses future course requirements, training programs, and career plans with students and parents.
13.	Checks incoming cumulative records, evaluates transcripts for completeness, and prepares records to be sent to other schools.
14.	Completes surveys and profiles for students, including a follow up survey after students exit the school.
15.	Completes all required reports of the parish and the state department of education.
16.	Participates in professional growth and development activities.
17.	Works cooperatively in sharing knowledge, skill, and expertise with others.
18.	Displays proper respect for superiors.
19.	Observes professional lines of communication at all times with individuals inside and outside of the school system.
20.	Maintains the confidentiality of school and student records.
21.	Attends work regularly and arrives punctually.
22.	Follows rules and regulations of the St. John the Baptist Parish School Board.

(Continued)

(Continued)

23. Notifies supervisor promptly in case of absence, and communicates in advance the date of return so that proper provisions can be made.
24. Makes use of constructive criticism and avoids the use of sarcasm, undue criticism, inappropriate language and behavior, and the use of racial and/or ethnic slurs when dealing with others.
25. Accepts other job duties as may be assigned which are related to the scope of the job.

The evaluatee is recommended for continued employment: Yes_____ No_____

REMARKS:

Evaluator: Date:

The signature below indicates the evaluatee has seen and been provided with a copy of the evaluation.

It does not indicate either agreement or disagreement with the results of the evaluation.

Evaluatee: Date:

School Social Worker Evaluation (SJBP 129) Page 3 Rating Scale: S – Satisfactory NI –Needs Improvement U – Unsatisfactory PERFORMANCE RESPONSIBILITIES Rating Comments

(School Social Worker Evalaution Form) (www.stjohn.k12.la.us/form)

Student Evaluation of Field Instruction

Name of your agency: ______________________________

Name of your Field Instructor: ______________________________

Items (using a 5-point Likert scale from strongly agree to strongly disagree):

1. The placement allowed me to integrate classroom knowledge with a variety of practice opportunities.
2. The placement provided an atmosphere conducive to learning.
3. The placement helped me develop skills as a beginning social work professional.
4. The agency made me aware of diversity issues.
5. There was adequate opportunity to participate in activities with other professional staff.
6. The assignments given were appropriate to my educational level and learning needs.
7. My office space at the agency was adequate.
8. My field instructor helped me recognize and assess my own reactions to the work.
9. My field instructor helped me develop beginning generalist social work skills.
10. My field instructor helped me address the ethical and value dimensions of my work.
11. I received supervision weekly.

Self-Evaluation

- I submitted my learning contract after developing it with my supervisor.
- I handed in all my process recordings on time.
- I was able to show application of my supervision in my process recordings.
- I was punctual, and my attendance was excellent.
- I was able to identify areas of self-strength.
- I was able to articulate learning needs.
- I was able to express self-awareness and be self-reflective in my supervision sessions.
- I was aware of ethical dilemmas and addressed these with my supervisor.
- I was aware of ethnic and cultural diversity in my school placement.
- I presented myself in a professional way (Raab & Pratt, Dominican College, 2010).

Qualitative research can be had through personal interview, unsolicited feedback, and letters submitted to the school administration as well as data obtained from surveys with open-ended questions. Anonymity and confidentiality must be ensured by those administering any survey instrument to reassure participants' candid and honest answers and to maintain its validity. Review of past data can also be used to compare to the present and/or use for baseline purposes.

The experts cite the school social work evaluations that should be investigated for evaluation of services. These are: data such as school records, observations, tests, surveys, questionnaires, simulations, interviews, self-evaluations, and rating behavioral changes (Dibble, 1999). These areas range from quantitative to qualitative evaluation.

SUMMARY

This chapter's goal was to give students various methods of evaluation for practice. Without evaluation, our profession would lack substance and efficacy. Practice evaluation in the schools is a daunting task especially if one is to produce quantitative data. Community, parental, and student feedback are necessary to produce evidence-based practice. Outcome and process evaluation have been discussed. Standards for School Social Work as per the NASW were presented as a springboard for evaluation. Sample evaluation surveys were presented and suggested to evaluate practice. Students of social work must be mindful of the importance of practice evaluation to support the need for evidence-based practice in our field.

ACTIVITY

Activity: Levels 1 & 2: Ask your school administrator if you might see the results of a Middle States or other evaluative body evaluation. What would you look for to assess the strengths and weaknesses of your school placement?

SELF-REFLECTION QUESTIONS

1. What is the most effective way of receiving feedback from students and families?
2. What can you offer to the school district as an evaluative tool for your position?
3. What are some of the systems evaluations and how are they evaluated: process/outcome?

CLASS DISCUSSION QUESTIONS

1. Discuss the time necessary (and if you think it is feasible) to complete evaluations in your district.
2. What do you do with the information obtained from the completed evaluations?
3. How do you assess the validity of the instruments that you will use?
4. Develop a short survey to be completed by students, parents, and colleagues. Ask questions either qualitative or quantitative about your practice of school social work.
5. Prepare a report discussing positive outcomes, using numbers to justify the effectiveness of social work within schools. With so much going on in schools with losing funding, a report of this caliber could help add and save jobs.

Chapter 14

Global Issues in School Social Work

INTRODUCTION

According to the United Nations Convention on the Rights of the Child, the aim of education "... should be the development of respect for human rights and fundamental freedoms, and preparation for responsible life in a free society, in the spirit of understanding, peace, and tolerance" (cited in Sossou, 2002, p. 91). These are the goals to which we aspire, but they are not always achieved in the various countries of the world. Children have been treated harshly in schools and have not been afforded the rights to which they are entitled. Efforts are being made around the world to improve the school conditions, and with the help of school social workers it may be achieved.

The world is shrinking. With the advent of technology and economic globalization, there has been a growing interdependence of countries. With specialized knowledge throughout the world, it is incumbent on social workers to seek out and help each other improve our services for all children in schools. The sharing of thoughts and ideas as well as policies and methods enhance our ability to improve our profession.

Another phenomenon resulting from the changing world is the influx of immigrants to our country. Whether or not they are documented, they attend our schools and are part of our cultural fabric. Shifts in economies and world disasters (natural and otherwise) present us with new encounters with people from other countries. An example of this was presented in the *International Network for School Social Work April 2011.* In the borough of Queens in New York City, it was noted that 46% of the population was born in another country, and there are 138 languages spoken (http://internationalnetwork-schoolsocialwork). School social workers in their professional capacity are best equipped with skills and knowledge of services to ease the transition and help these newcomers with academic, social, and emotional needs. We, therefore, need to know what is happening in other countries.

Presently, there is an International Federation of Social Workers. It originated in 1956 and supplanted an earlier organization: the International Permanent Secretariat of Social Workers, which began in 1928 and was active until the beginning of World War II. The present organization has put forth efforts to unite educators and practitioners, get involved in political action, develop a common agenda for all those involved in social work worldwide, and strategize about the common actions and development of the profession (http://www.ifsw.org/f38000378.html). There are member organizations around the world including the National Association of Social Workers in the United States.

A BRIEF HISTORY OF INTERNATIONAL SCHOOL SOCIAL WORK

School social work developed as the issue of compulsory education came to fruition in many countries. The United States, Canada, and England were able to pass compulsory education into law by the late 19th and early 20th centuries. The steps in the development of compulsory education started with minimum years of required education to at least attain literacy. As the adjustment and economics are expanded, children will receive a higher level of schooling. The problem arises in the poverty-stricken countries where there is a level of education available but children are needed to work to attain a subsistence level for family survival (Huxtable & Blyth, 2002).

The need for social work services in schools evolved from a need for parents to be helped and guided to send their children to school. Children needed to be in school to get an education. Schools in England hired what began as attendance (welfare) officers, and in the United States they were called *visiting teachers*. They would visit the home and work with families to encourage school attendance. They explained the purpose of education and helped families adapt to the new institution. In the Scandinavian countries, the school social worker was referred to as a *school curator* meaning one who cares (Huxtable & Blyth, 2002). These professionals were guidance counselors as well as those who helped students with problems and guided them through the use of supportive services.

Many nations now have school social workers and have adopted this school position over the 20th century. In the United States, it began with the visiting teacher in 1906. Canada began school social work in the 1940s. In Ghana, the inception of the profession began in the 1950s. Food distribution enhanced the attendance in schools and became a part of the work of the school social worker. The most recent countries to provide school social work services during the 1980s were Austria, New Zealand, Switzerland, Saudi Arabia, Sri Lanka, Macedonia, Russia, Latvia, Hungary, and Estonia. Japan has begun a program, but it is in its early stages (Huxtable & Blyth, 2002). Many of these countries are still in the infant stages of development and are recognizing and developing programs based on their unique needs. We should keep in mind that new programs need to be explained and introduced with clear and accurate communication so that the understanding of faculty, staff, parents, and students will be comprehended.

There seems to be a lack of knowledge about school social work in many countries in southern Europe, Asia, and Africa. In Australia, there are limited services usually only available during crises (Huxtable & Blyth, 2002). With knowledge and interaction comes power and support. School social work is a growing profession, and there are 27,000 school social workers worldwide with 14,000 in the United States alone (2002). The profession has evolved from the roots of compulsory education and is either supported by government agencies or nongovernment agencies. It is a fledgling field in many countries but growing with the needs of students and communities.

Canada

Canada was chosen since it is our neighbor to the north and shares many similarities with us. Canada is much less populated (than we are) with 30 million people. There are 8 million school-aged people in Canada, and the schools are run by provinces and territories, which are quite diverse in size, ethnicity, and types of communities. The country has a reputation for accepting diversity and has a humanitarian outlook. Some of the flaws that need to be worked on are the poverty of women and children, homelessness, and illiteracy (Loughborough, Shera, & Wilhelm, 2002). These are some of the same issues that we are dealing with in the United States. There are six major regions in Canada: the Northlands (4/5ths of the territory) with 51% of the population being Native Inuits; the Atlantic Region, Quebec, the Bilingual and Multicultural Belt, Upper Canada, and the West comprise the other regions. The Atlantic Region has mostly European descendants. Quebec residents are 95% of French ancestry. In the Bilingual and Multicultural Belt, there are differences particularly between urban and rural centers. This is a hub of business and industry and has 25% of the country's population. Toronto is considered the most culturally diverse city in the world (Rees, 1998 cited in Huxtable & Blyth, 2002).

The schools are governed by the individual provinces with no centralized agency overseeing the programs, policies, or curriculum. Thus, the schools are plagued with disputes involving uniform curriculum, special education, and the need and degree of parental involvement in schools (Loughborough, Shera, & Wilhelm, 2002). Their system is much like ours with free public school education through high school. Violence and aggression are areas of concern for the schools and areas where the school social worker becomes involved. Some districts hire their own school social workers, but other social workers are obtained through mental health facilities. The systems view of school social work was adopted in the 1970s with the importance of the problem-solving approach involving macro, mezzo, and micro systems being utilized. There are approximately 750 school social workers in seven provinces (2002). Most are contracted through the local boards of education, but some are based in community mental health centers. Some provinces including Newfoundland, Prince Edward Island and the territories of Yukon, the Northwest Territories, and Nanavut do not have school social workers.

Most school social workers function as case managers but with the very large client responsibility. It is nearly impossible to carry a case load and see students regularly. Crisis intervention is the main role of the school social worker. The services of the school social worker in different provinces vary. The density of the population and the rural areas create hardships for providing services as well as distance coverage for the social workers.

Most students come to the attention of the school social worker through problems involving some of the following issues: academic issues; social, emotional, and economic problems; family and parenting situations; mental and physical difficulties; and school attendance (Loughborough, Shera, & Wilhelm, 2002). The social worker is a liaison between the home and school. Recent history finds school social workers more involved with therapeutic interventions than becoming an administrative extension.

The Identification, Placement, and Review Committee (IPRC) and the Child Study Team (CST) in the United States have similar functions. The committee identifies those students who are having difficulties or those of high achievement and places them in a variety of settings from self-contained to fully mainstreamed (Loughborough, Shera, & Wilhelm, 2002). There are different methods of teamwork used in different provinces, but the overall goal is to identify the students with special needs and help them function to full potential. As in the United States, the thrust is toward inclusive education as much as is possible for the individual student.

Prevention is another aspect of school social work in the Canadian provinces. Educational programs include child abuse prevention, conflict resolution, social skills, bereavement, and divorce programs. These are just some of the areas that school social workers become involved with regarding prevention. If prevention does not work, then intervention is the next order of work for the social worker.

Most school social workers in Canada hold a master's degree. The credit hours required for those who hold a bachelor's degree in social work to receive a master's is similar to the United States. There are 36 social work programs in Canada, and the governing organization is the Canadian Association of Schools of Social Work (CASSW) (Loughborough, Shera, & Wilhelm, 2002).

Ghana

Ghana was chosen as an example of an African nation that is thriving. Ghana is located on the west coast of Africa. It was a former British colony that gained independence in 1957. There are approximately 18 million people with 51% of the population below the age of 18 (UNICEF, 1998, cited in Huxtable & Blyth, 2002). Most people live in rural areas, and there are at least 100 various ethnicities and 50 languages spoken in Ghana (Roe et al., 1992, cited in Huxtable & Blyth, 2002). English is the official language, although one can anticipate the problems that arise in schools with the large number of languages spoken in this country. There are 10 regions in Ghana divided into 110 districts. Farming is the most prevalent occupation in this country.

Unlike Canada, Ghana has a central national agency responsible for all levels of education. At the end of the primary level (first 6 years), students are tested to decide whether or not they will continue to the next level of education. There are two such levels (3 years of junior high and 3 years of high school) and then students can apply for entrance into the university. There are five universities, teachers' colleges, and polytechnical schools in the country that rely on admissions testing for acceptance (Sossou, 2002).

Free compulsory education was instituted in 1996, but universal education has not yet been achieved (Sossou, 2002). Because of the large number of school-age children, a "split session" was initiated with morning and afternoon sessions (Sossou & Daniels, 2002). This procedure has been used successfully in the United States as well. More boys than girls attend school, and the percentage differences widen as the level of education increases. Special education exists for those with intellectual and sensory impairment, but those children with physical problems are integrated into the mainstream. These children receive services for vocational training and physical education in specialized environments. No special accommodations are made for those children with learning disabilities. Teachers must adapt their methods to help these children learn. The teachers use practical methods rather than anything based on scientific evidence (Sossou & Daniels, 2002).

The problems most evident and significant in Ghana that are affecting children are child labor, poverty, and homeless children ("street children"). Poverty is the overriding problem that prevents children from being successful in school. Lack of money to pay for school supplies and in many instances, lack of food and shelter cause children's absence from school and is often the cause of school dropout. Child abuse also is a difficulty that exists in Ghana. Corporal punishment is used both at home and at school. Caning, slapping, and whipping are the methods commonly used in schools on elementary and junior high school students. The ideas that children must be submissive and willful children and should have their willfulness inhibited are common notions in Ghana. This philosophy emerged from the early Christian missionaries who used corporal punishment to control students. The reasons for corporal punishment include poor academic performance, tardiness, absences, and/or poor behavior (Sossou, 2002).The expectations for children are often too high, as well as the idea that the children are possessed by demons. This notion comes out of the African Pentecostal Movement which finds demonization of unacceptable behavior as a valid rationalization (Hachett, 2003). As in other parts of the world, divorce and domestic violence are issues that cause difficulties for children in school as well as home (Sossou & Daniels, 2002).

School social work services in Ghana were initiated in the 1950s under the auspices of the Department of Social Welfare. The responsibilities of the school social worker include (a) assisting children to reach their academic potential, (b) helping delinquents modify their behavior, (c) administering social services to school children as well as faculty and staff, (d) developing liaison with families and school, (e) reaching out to community institutions as resources, and (f) establishing parent-teacher organizations (Sossou, 2002). Special services are under the auspices of the school welfare officer. Helping the faculty and staff with problems they are experiencing in social, emotional, and economic areas is an admirable service. The philosophy of the welfare officers is that well-adjusted teachers help students and schools be successful (Sossou & Daniels, 2002). This concept is one that would enrich the schools in other countries if it were adapted. Prevention is another aspect of the social workers' purview.

The University of Ghana and the Ghana Education Service are working together to give professional training in social work for the welfare officers. There is a 2-year training program that yields a degree in social administration, and a 10-week field experience is mandatory. This degree is acknowledged by the state and the International Council for Social Work Education. In 1990, a 3-year bachelor's level course in social work was established at the University of Ghana. There are plans for a master's level program (Sossou & Daniels, 2002).

Japan

Japan is a unique society that has arisen from the defeat of war to become a world leader. Although it is part of the Asian continent, it is an exception in many respects. Japan is a small nation made up of 120 million people living on four main islands. Most people live along the coast, and urban life is most prevalent. Buddhism has contributed to religion, the arts, and culture. Shintoism is the most popular religion. Much of the lifestyle has been adopted from the West, which fosters the sense of isolation from the rest of the continent. The Tokugawa government in the 17th century promoted isolation, and this remained in place until the mid-1800s with a new government and socioeconomic changes as well a constitution. Industrialization and universal education were encouraged by the militant government, which included aggressive invasion into other countries. This philosophy brought the Japanese into the World War II conflict (Yamashita, 2002). Cultural changes have arisen since the war with differences between generations. The younger generation has a democratic worldview while the older cohort believes in the monarchical form of government. What is best for the nation not the individual is seen as the preferred way of life by the older generation (2002).

The social work profession arose out of the need for a professional group that could deal with emerging social issues in the 1950s. The origins of the profession in Japan emanate from the United States and European models, but social workers were mainly concerned with legislation and services to the elderly. In recent times, the Japanese family resembles that of the West. Most people live in nuclear families with mothers being the primary caretakers of children. Social work services to children in schools have not been seen as necessary, since poverty and health needs were not issues. Recently child abuse has been acknowledged in Japan, but there is no prescribed way of reporting it (Yamashita, 2002).

Universal education was established in the late 19th century. The education system is comprised of 6 years of elementary school (required), 3 years of junior high school (compulsory), and 3 years of high school which is optional. About half the students who complete high school go on to higher education with most attending academic colleges. The school curriculum in public schools is nationally established and strictly adhered to by school personnel (Yamashita, 2002). The students must wear uniforms and follow the school rules where lack of adherence is penalized with sometimes severe punishment including corporal punishment. Some problems facing Japanese schools are school refusal behaviors, bullying, and violence. There is a great deal of emphasis on education in Japan, which causes fierce competition that begins as early as kindergarten. Absenteeism is rampant in the schools, and since the 1980s counseling centers have been set up in school districts to cope with this problem. Those who attend school sometimes become aggressive exhibiting behaviors such as attacking teachers, bullying and destroying school property (Yamashita, 2002). In Japan, teachers usually have been the professionals who deal with these problems. Recently, the school nurses and school counselors are helping children with problems.

School social workers have recently been placed in public schools. In 1999, the School Social Work Association of Japan was initiated to give the public knowledge about the profession and how it can help with school problems. The philosophy of the educators is discipline and strict rules with punitive solutions to the problems faced. Mothers (usually the parent who gets involved with the school) are not willing to criticize or disagree with teachers for fear of retribution on their children (Yamashita, 2002). Hierarchical issues and fear of stigma have prevented parents from taking a more active role especially with children in special education. Parents feel the need for school social workers who are caring and empathic to their children. These are the qualities that engender trust in the social workers. Traditionally, special education has taken place in segregated schools. The children placed in these schools are those with physical disabilities, developmental disabilities, and visual and/or auditory difficulties (Kayama, 2010). In the 1990s, reform began in Japanese special education which included children with learning disabilities, attention deficits, and autism. Disabilities of these categories were added between the years 2006 and 2008. Inclusion in regular education became available modeling the U.S. special education laws. The school social worker in Japan can now be a liaison between the community, parents, and schools. Although school social work is not universal in Japan and the special education coordinators are not usually social workers, they are becoming trusted and accepted by the parents and school officials (2010). The parents seek an emotional connection with the school social worker, and hopefully this will occur to enhance and empower school social workers' position in the schools. The philosophy and problem-solving techniques of the social worker would mitigate the harsh treatment of students in schools. Being a liaison between school and students in problem solving would benefit the system greatly (Yamashita, 2002).

Japanese social work education includes a masters' degree in social work. There is also certification granted after passing a national examination (http://www.jassw.jp/birdeye/pdf/birdeye-english.pdf).

Republic of Korea

Korea is an example of an Asian country which has survived occupation, division and war to become a thriving nation. The Republic of Korea (which I will refer to as Korea) was established after World War II. The country was divided with the southern portion (now known as the Republic of Korea) being democratic and capitalistic, and the northern portion (now known as the Democratic People's Republic of Korea) governed by communism. This section of the chapter will describe only South Korea. Prior to the war, Korea was occupied by Japan from 1910 to 1945.

The population of Korea is decreasing with the child and adolescent group becoming lower and the elderly population increasing. Since the 1960s population's rapid growth, the government has instituted incentives to lower the birth rate. Tax exemptions have helped keep the birth rate down. The population in cities is increasing with 25% of people living in Seoul. Even though the younger population is reduced the migration to the cities causes overcrowding in schools with classroom size being over the average of the U.S. schools (49 students per classroom in Korea as opposed to 23 in the United States). The economy is strong with little investment in social welfare programs (Kim, 2002).

Social welfare services in Korea were not begun until the 1960s. At the time, social security was initiated and aid to the poor began. In the same time frame, the poor received help only on an emergency basis and the help came from foreign missionary services. The poor suffered greatly. With rapid economic growth came more prosperity and recognition of the needs of the poor. Human rights were recognized. As a result of the rapid growth came many problems. Urbanization and growth of industry lead to fewer unskilled jobs, increased unemployment, family problems, criminal behavior and youth delinquency. As a result, the government increased their welfare services: Revised Child Welfare Act, Welfare Act for the Elderly, Welfare Act for the Handicapped, Act on Education for Preschool Children, and so on. During this period of the 1980s the government also regulated the profession of social work. There were three levels defined based on education and experience. The purpose of hiring 3000 social workers at that time was to evaluate people for social services, develop policy, and give assistance to the poor. Community welfare centers were established which included services such as: psychotherapy, rehabilitation, job training and financial support (Kim, 2002).

Education in Korea evolved from 372 CE. It began as a place to educate male nobility. As the Christian missionaries influenced the country, more children were given an education. Even so, only 30% of children were attending elementary school as of the mid-20th century. It was in 1949 that changes occurred with an education system becoming more equal. It consisted of a 6-year elementary school, a 3-year middle school experience, a 3-year high school experience, and 4 years of college or university instruction. Only elementary school is compulsory, and there is tuition for the middle and high school students unless you are the rural poor. Tutoring is very popular and used to enhance test scores. There is much competition and pressure in the school system for achieving academic excellence (Kim, 2002).

The purpose of education in Korea is getting into a *good* college. Education revolves around examinations and test scores. The emotional well-being of students has not been a factor (Young & Jung, 2002). Issues that have evolved as a result of this focus are school dropout (3%), mental health issues, and emotional difficulties along with family problems. Behavioral problems, substance abuse, and learning and poor adjustment became evident. The need for school social work was obvious. The purpose of school social work in Korea is to assist children and adolescents to achieve academic success (Kim, 2002). It was difficult to get the Korean schools to allow social workers entry into the schools. A survey of a significant number of students revealed that the students were suffering from test anxiety, depression, eating disorders, and self-esteem issues as well as stealing, substance abuse, and gang involvement. Almost 10% of the participants claimed that they had thought about suicide. (According to Huxtable and Blyth, the total percentage of suicidal considerations is 21 for middle and high school students and 43 for seniors in high school.) The Ministry of Education decided to put a school social work pilot project in place. These social workers helped the students with interpersonal relationships, school adjustment, and taught the skills involved in problem solving. Techniques used were psychodrama, group work, and individual counseling (Young & Jung, 2002). Overall, the response was very positive, and more school social workers were hired. It should be noted that the hiring is not mandated and based on grant money that may be taken away. In 2002, there were 12 schools employing school social workers (Young & Jung, 2002).

Social workers in Korea must pass a test to practice. Licensure is now being used to ensure that credentialed professionals are working as social workers (http://www.kasw.or.kr/site/global/globalEng.jsp).

Some of the areas that Korean school social workers may focus on in the future are as follows:

- Creating better communication between students and teachers
- Having a mental health prevention program
- Helping students with eating disorders
- Student support when transferring or potential dropouts
- Group work for students experiencing emotional difficulties (Young and Jung, 2002)

Germany

Germany is included in this chapter as an example of a country that has risen up from the defeat of war and occupation to a thriving, successful, and stable country. Germany is another country whose history was impacted by World War II. After the defeat of Germany in this war, the country was divided into east and west sections. The occupation of West Germany was under the auspices of the western allies, while the eastern portion (East Germany) was under the direction of the USSR and communism. The reunification came about in October, 1990. Many social, political, and economic changes have come about since this occurrence.

Land and population size has increased. Germany has the lowest birth rate in the entire world, and there is (as in other countries) an increase in the elderly population (Wulfers, 2002).

The educational system in this country varies, because the 16 provinces are independently responsible for the educational system. The literacy rate is almost 100% and there are 9 to 10 years of required compulsory education. The kindergarten, which is the first level, is optional and is given to children between the ages of 3 and 6 years old. Primary education is for grades one through four. There are two levels of secondary education: Students can leave school after 10th grade with a general certificate or go into the second level for ages 15 to 18. This latter level of study can be either vocational or academic (gymnasium). The next level of education is either technical/vocational or university (Wulfers, 2002). It appears that a very small percentage of German students are going to the next level of university study. Most are slated for one of three vocational tracks. These are either in school or immediately out to business settings for training. The first two offer a combination of school and vocational training, and the second offers training in healthcare or the social sciences (social work). The third option is for disadvantaged students who are usually directed out to business and have been enduring a difficult time in recent years in finding a position (Schmidt, 2010). Companies are becoming more selective, and this leads to youth unemployment.

There are 104 independent universities in Germany and 300 higher education facilities. Special education is a separate entity for those with intellectual, language, sensory, and behavioral difficulties. Psychologists rather than social workers are involved in decision making, which includes determining the placement of special needs students. As in the United States and other countries, there is a direction of mainstream education taking place in Germany. It is in the early stages (Wulfers, 2002).

The family structure has been changing in the last few decades. Fewer siblings and single-parent homes have impacted the social lives of children. Divorce and reconstituted families have also changed the landscape of family life. There is also a movement against foreigners that is fostering right wing groups. It appears that some adolescents who are unsure of their future form a subculture that not only use alcohol and drugs but also are forming neo-Nazi groups and are showing intolerance and aggressive behavior toward foreigners (Pennekamp & Porschke, 2002). The economics have also changed. Less money is put aside for social programs and many students are dropping out of school leaving them unqualified for work and unemployed. Drug use and criminal activity are also increasing among young people (Wulfers, 2002).

Social work in Germany seems to be community-based. Social workers are responsible for whole populations in towns working with children, youth, and families rather than individual clients. The cities and county welfare departments work together to provide these services. The communitywide scope does provide for more systemic coverage of those in need. The majority of school social workers are assigned to upper middle and high schools. The majority of their work concerns those who are not going on to the university but rather are either in technical or apprenticeship programs (Pennekamp & Porschke, 2002). As in the other forms of social work in Germany, the school social workers stress a systems approach. The schools are helped through their intervention in responding to the stressors experienced by children rather than enforcing compliance. The school social worker usually spends time with those students who are at risk for deviant and/or illegal behaviors, behavioral problems, and/or emotional difficulties. School social workers work with the systems affecting the students and network with outside agencies to provide services for children and families. A problem-solving approach is the prevalent method of helping in the schools. Some of these duties include helping students acquire jobs, take part in leisure time activities, and become involved in clubs. The philosophy of the educational system is to partner teachers (cognitive focus) and school social workers (social and emotional emphasis) in giving students optimal opportunity for success. Since the reunification, a new Child and Youth Welfare Law was enacted that in part focused on the inclusion of school social workers (Wulfers, 2002).

In Germany, the preparation for a career in social work includes a 3-year technical college and a 1-year internship at an approved agency. There is no specific curriculum for the specialty of school social work (Wulfers, 2002).

Hungary

Hungary is included as an example of a country that has come from totalitarian rule to democracy. Hungary is considered to be a Central European nation with a history of conquest and communism, which ended at the beginning of the 1990s. This sociopolitical era stands as the backdrop of the present form of government and culture of the country today. Hungary lost approximately 66% of its land and about 50% of its citizens to neighboring countries, after World War II. Even though the country has been expanding economically including during communist rule, it still has had difficulty with the transition to a democratic form of government. It now has a democratic parliament, with open elections and a multiparty system. The open elections have experienced political swings from the right to the left and again to the right. The change in systems resulted in a difficult transitional situation leading to inflation, unemployment, and reduction of services to the poorer people. Poverty rose affecting 33% of the population (Hare, 2002).

Health issues in the very young are handled through the schools. As children get older, there is less consistency in the provision of healthcare. Children who drop out of school are those least provided with health care. Poor nourishment as well as lack of physical activity and unhealthy behaviors (drinking and smoking) are the problems most faced by youth in Hungary. This country ranks the highest in alcoholism among the people of the world. The highest suicide rate among adult men is also a concern for Hungary (Hare, 2002).

Since the end of the communist period in Hungary, school control has shifted from a rigid central government to a local form of school governance. The Public Education Act of the 1990s gave this autonomy to 3000 local governments comprising the country. Local funding as well as federal grants supply the revenue for schools. Compulsory education ranges from ages 5 and 7 to 18. Secondary education has also changed with less delineation between general and vocational curricula. In 1995, a National Core Curriculum was established with requirements in content at the end of 4th, 6th, 8th, and 10th grade. Private schools are now permitted and property formally taken by the government was returned to the religious communities (Hare, 2002).

Unlike other Central and Eastern Block countries, Hungary has provided decent opportunities for their special needs students. In the primary schools, they educated special needs students in 200 centers. Integration of special education students into the mainstream has now begun. Few opportunities exist for special education students in the secondary programs. There is discrimination in schools against a group of people called *Roma* or *Romani*. These people are also known as *Gypsies* and have their roots in India. Many do not enter secondary school in Hungary, and many do not complete primary school. Programs are needed to help this group succeed in school so that they may become productive contributors to the society in which they reside. The general population discriminates against them, which contributes to their unfortunate circumstances (Hare, 2002).

There are school social workers in special needs schools but not in mainstream schools. The welfare of children after the change of government was very important, and welfare services are now provided for children in schools (not school social workers). In the 1990s, *family assistance centers* did assign social workers to schools. They dealt with school attendance and social and emotional difficulties of students. This did not continue, and now there are teachers appointed to the position of child protection officers in schools and are trained to report abuse to child welfare authorities. Hungarian children rank fourth in the world (according to the World Health Organization) in their dislike for school. School social workers assigned to schools might mitigate this situation (Hare, 2002).

Social work was abandoned during the communist rule. The government was in charge of caring for the needs of children. The Eotvos Lorand University in Budapest first offered social work education in 1985. Now social work courses are part of the college and university curriculum throughout the country (Hare, 2002).

Malta

Malta is included as an example of an island community that has experienced colonial rule. Malta is a group of Mediterranean islands about 60 miles south of Sicily. Malta is the largest island, and the object of this report. As an island community dating back to 4000 BCE, it has been occupied by various cultures that invaded it. These included North African and southern and northern European civilizations as well as ancient ones. The Maltese language, which is of Semitic origin but has Romantic aspects, is now the official language. Malta's culture and traditions are uniquely their own. English and Italian are also spoken by most inhabitants. This island community was ruled by England until it got independence in 1964. As a result of business and industrial growth, the standard of living is much improved. In the late 1940s, Malta's welfare system emerged issuing pensions, clearing slums, building schools, and increasing the minimum wage. Education is an important priority in this country and is heavily subsidized by the government (Pace, 2002).

Compulsory education in Malta is required for children from the ages of 5 to 16. The primary level, from ages 5 to 10, is coeducational, but thereafter, secondary school children from ages 11 to 16 are separated by gender. At about age 11, children take a test to decide whether they attend a Junior Lyceum (academic pursuit) or an Opportunity Center. After that, schooling called *sixth forms* is given to those who wish to attend from the ages of 16 to 18 or older who have qualified through an examination. This level prepares students for the university, but a qualifying exam also must be taken for university entrance. Other schools that are available after sixth forms are vocational, technical, and other forms of adult education. There are also private schools both secular and religious (Roman Catholic), which are seen as a better alternative than public institutions (Pace, 2002).

As school problems have increased, the number of auxiliary professionals has remained the same. There are seven school social workers on the island with a student population close to 63,000. That means that each social worker is responsible for 9,000 young people. There are approximately 6,000 teachers in the private and public school sectors.

There are nine separate special education schools in Malta. The students are served in these schools according to their disability. These include developmental disabilities, behavioral disabilities, learning problems, physical disabilities, visual and hearing impairments, and those with multiple disabilities. Inclusive education is beginning in Malta for those students with physical, behavioral, sensory, and intellectual disabilities. As noted before, social work services are limited and thus impact on mainstreaming these students. Homebound instruction is made available for those students who are temporarily confined to their homes. Social workers are often asked to evaluate the progress of such students and decide whether or not to keep the child on home instruction. School social workers are as available to special schools as they are to regular education schools (Pace, 2002).

As in other countries around the world, Malta has problems related to drug use, childhood employment, and poverty. Drug use was established through a survey of 12- to 18-year-old students. Almost 5% of those students admitted to using drugs such as marijuana. Many times, those families experiencing financial stressors employ their own children to the exclusion of school attendance. Often, the school social worker is called in to help the family find an alternate for their problems. Social workers also help those who are in need of welfare benefits, which are given through the taxation of the working community (Pace, 2002).

In 1974, the Education Act #39 gave the government the power to employ Education Welfare Officers who would go into homes and help children with problems (particularly lack of attendance). It wasn't until 1993 that these professionals were called school social workers. A diploma in social work is granted by the University of Malta. The coursework includes academic as well as practicum experience. There are four levels of social work in Malta: (1) principal, (2) senior, (3) accredited, and (4) registered II and registered I social worker (Pace, 2002). As in many countries, the school social worker began with the responsibility of helping with absent students and dropouts. These social workers are trying to create a home and school community and are the liaisons of such a structure. They presently serve families with stress, informing families about the importance of education, helping families with small businesses to send their children to school, families who have children with learning disabilities, and those families who have a sick member. Much of their work is preventative and involves primary care. If children break the law, the school social worker is often called on to help that child and family rather than employing punitive practices. School social workers also set up and deliver antibullying programs for the school community (Pace, 2002). School social workers deliver individual counsel to children, support parents, and help teachers deal with classroom issues. A research project, Focus, has provided a needs assessment for social workers that resulted in the inclusion of incorporating group counseling in schools; helping students with learning difficulties to be proactive on their own behalf; advocating for students to the administration; and acting as mentors to parents, teachers, and students (2002). Other projects such as Tomorrow's Teachers Project help nurture the relationship between the university and the teacher or mentors. The educational change has gone from individual focus to interpersonal relationship. This aspect prepares the teacher to be open-minded, motivated, and cooperative with students, families, and other professionals (vanVelzen, Bezzina, & Lorist, 2008).

Scandinavian and Nordic Countries

The Scandinavian and Nordic Countries (Denmark, Finland, Norway, Sweden, and Iceland) are included in this segment, since they are a group of countries that follow along similar social policies. They present an excellent example of a society that is welfare centered. The welfare of the underprivileged is taken seriously, and child welfare is a high priority. On a continuum of countries presented in this chapter, they are considered the most liberal and socialist in economy and politics. They consider it a right of the people to use social welfare services (Andersson, Poso, Vaisanen, & Wallin, 2002). The government is essential in providing care from "cradle to grave." Services for children are offered from infancy through school completion. Corporal punishment has been banned by law. There is a strong emphasis on prevention, and some criticize this as not enough actual services and tools available to social workers for the investigation and treatment of child maltreatment cases (2002).

The Nordic countries all have compulsory education that is free. It spans from ages 6 to 16 for the basic education. Upper level education usually spans from ages 16 to 19. A comprehensive exam is administered at this point. The next level can be vocational, technical, or academic (university level). A bachelor's degree takes 3 years to achieve, and a master's takes up to 5 years (Andersson et al., 2002).

Much governmental financial support is given to education. Illiteracy is not an issue in the Nordic countries. Child welfare was expanded to include school social workers and psychologists in the mid-20th century. Although school social work is not mandated by law, most municipalities use the services of these professionals especially with adolescents and older children. Preventative work is the first priority, but social workers in schools also do individual counseling, group work, consultation with all concerned with students both in and out of schools, and work on changing policies and programs to fit the needs of the students. Special education usually takes place in small classes or special settings. Inclusive education has begun in some of these countries (Andersson et al., 2002).

The training of school social workers varies. There is no specific curriculum for schools as a specialty. Social workers sometimes have a bachelor's or master's degree but since there is no uniformity in certification, the credentials of the social workers vary. Many attend special seminars and training sessions to enhance their skills (Andersson et al., 2002). Research development is sorely needed in these countries. As social workers in schools become a more vital part of school life, the need for problem solving approaches and clinical skills will be addressed (2002).

PROBLEMS FACED BY THE WORLD'S CHILDREN

After the review of the aforementioned countries, one can observe that there are similar challenges and issues facing the world's children in general and the school social work profession. Poverty is the overriding problem faced by children throughout the world. It limits children's ability to succeed in life as well as their ability to receive a basic education. Approximately, 130 million children of primary school age throughout the world are not in school (Huxtable & Blyth, 2002). These are the adults of the future who will be responsible for the global world as it progresses. Poverty is the main factor that keeps them in this position. *Economic stagnation* in developing countries seems to be maintaining poverty (Seipel, 2003, p. 195). There is sustained inequity among the world's population regarding wealth. The rich control a substantial amount of the wealth of a country as opposed to the poor. The ratio of wealth between the rich and poor countries is now 60:1 as opposed to what it was in the 19th century, when it was 9:1 (Seipel, 2003). Poverty has caused illiteracy, malnutrition, disease, famine, and death for many children in developing countries.

Violence against children is an area of worldwide concern. Wars, domestic violence, bullying, and corporal punishment are just some of the difficulties that children face with violence. We see how wars in Iraq and Afghanistan have disrupted children's lives and made many of these children victims and casualties of the situation. Children are used for suicide bombing, and boys as young as 10 years old have been inducted into armies to fight as soldiers on the front lines of battles. In war-ridden countries, schooling is many times suspended, and children lose their ability to participate in the normal tasks assigned to that developmental stage in life. Posttraumatic stress disorder is often experienced by these children and is one example of psychological damage inflicted on children (van Wormer, 2006).

Domestic violence takes its toll on children both physically and psychologically. Women around the world have been abused or neglected. Many children have witnessed the violent death of a parent as well as been victims of a parent who is vindictive against his or her partner. Children have been beaten or starved to death in all countries, even the affluent ones. The UN Convention on the Rights of the Child (1989) says that children have the right to due process, to be protected from violence and being exploited, and the right to healthy living and proper nutrition. This document was ratified by every country in the

UN except the United States and Somalia (van Wormer, 2006). The reason for lack of U.S. congressional ratification was the fear that there would be government involvement in family life, no provisions for the unborn, restrictions on the execution of minors, and prohibition of physical discipline on children (van Wormer, 2006).

Corporal punishment is used as a way of controlling children in schools. The inflicting of such punishment (on the body) is the result of many different infractions. It is sometimes done for lack of attendance, tardiness, or poor academic performance as well as controlling poor behavior (Sossou, 2002). Corporal punishment is practiced in schools in many countries including Korea, Japan, and Ghana. Some of the practices are barbaric and include whipping, caning, and even using irritants in genital areas (Ghana) (2002).

Bullying is a universal issue experienced by children, adolescents, and adults throughout the world. "Bullying is defined as any repeated negative activity or aggression intended to harm or bother someone who is perceived by peers as being less physically or psychologically powerful than the aggressor" (Glew, Fan, Katon, & Rivara, 2008, p. 123). With children, it is usually more prevalent in junior and senior high school students. It had been an issue predominantly seen in boys, but in recent years girls have also participated. It is an extremely damaging phenomenon that in schools leads to poor academic performance, absenteeism, dropping out, and in very severe cases to suicide. In the United States, the issue has been brought to the fore with the recent suicide of a student from New Jersey who jumped off the George Washington Bridge to his death as a direct result of cyber-bullying. The state of New Jersey has issued a policy on school bullying as have other states and countries. It is called the Anti-Bullying Bill of Rights. A school safety team that reviews all complaints is to be established in each school district, and the penalties for bullying are more severe. That is, if you encourage or support the bullying in any way, there are consequences under the bullying policy (http://www.nj.com/news/index.ssf/2011/01/gov_christie_signs_anti-bullyi.html).

With the Internet and other technology, more bullying is seen firsthand by students and adults alike. Two-thirds of the 37 school shootings in the United States (since 1974) have been associated with the assailants being bullied prior to the shooting events (Glew et al., 2008). Although the rates of reported bullying vary around the world, it is seen worldwide. For example, in a U.S. study with children in grades four through 12, 45% of those students said they had been involved in bullying. In South Africa, a similar cohort of students surveyed said that 90% had been exposed to bullying (McGuinness, 2007). Different forms of bullying include verbal, physical, relational, and cyber (2007).

Homelessness worldwide gives rise to street children. These are children who are roaming the streets in different countries often experiencing violence, prostitution, and rape. Many come from single-parent homes and are of the lower socioeconomic status. The attitude of these children is negative and hopelessness prevails. They often use drugs such as inhalants to escape the stark reality of their lives. Ill health and AIDS are conditions on the rise among these children. The urbanization and industrialization of countries creates socioeconomic conditions that are adverse to many poverty-stricken children and may lead to homelessness. The decrease of extended families often creates a situation where no support is available to parents, and thus the children are left to their own devices on the streets. Lack of schooling or failure in school also lends impetus to children living on the streets. Many of these children in developing countries have no parental contact and rely on each other for help. The street children usually range from 6 to 17 years of age. There are 100 million street children worldwide (leRoux & Smith, 1998). The roots of homelessness appear to be in poverty. Loss of jobs, cutbacks in social service support, privatization, and deregulation of mega industries as well as loss of low-cost housing seem to present ideal conditions for homelessness. The need to care for all humanity and realize that providing dignity through jobs, health care, and low-cost housing will enhance the entire world community (Wright, 2000).

Prevention and immunization programs throughout the world have reduced illness (mental and physical) for children. The efforts of school social workers and public health initiatives have contributed to this positive change. Some issues globally remain of considerable concern. These include tuberculosis, AIDS, and malaria (which are the leading illnesses of preschool children in Africa). Vitamin A deficiency is the cause of 40 million children suffering from compromised immune systems, and iodine deficiency leads to 20 million born with mental problems (van Wormer, 2006). The government providing universal health care is an issue left undecided in many countries including the United States. Preventative care is another topic that is discussed, but in many countries it is not a priority.

Drug use and abuse is on the rise in many countries and has become a concern among young people. Some of the countries where such concerns exist include Canada, Great Britain, Malta, Germany, and even Finland. In Finland, concern over suicides related to drug use in adolescents has prompted this concern (Huxtable & Blyth, 2002). The drug trafficking business is a $500 billion per year industry worldwide (McConville, 2000). The ease of access and lower cost provides adolescents more accessibility to such drugs. Cannabis is the most widely used of these illicit drugs (Degenhardt et al., 2011).

FUTURE GOALS FOR SCHOOL SOCIAL WORK

As we review the changes in the various countries that have taken place and how we can learn from each other, the need for international school social work in the 21st century is apparent. The development of an international organization of social workers such as the International Network for School Social Work and the International Federation of Social Workers encourages our professionals to reach out to others and share our knowledge and skills. It is essential that we connect with each other to support and render new ideas in the service of our students and school communities. With the newfound ability in technology, the ease of this communication is enhanced.

School social workers are somewhat new in many countries throughout the world. Inclusive education and prevention programs are areas that need to be developed. The sharing of ideas and existing programs are key to improving the lives of children. School social workers are equipped with skills and techniques that can facilitate these services. In the United States, there are many successful programs for prevention as well as the use of inclusive education. In Ghana, social workers' availability in schools to faculty and staff is an ideal intervention to keep the entire school community functioning better. These should be shared.

This chapter points out some of the difficulties as well as the similarities of countries across the world to deal with the problems and issues that arise among our student population and schools in general. As we look toward the future, it behooves us to consider all the world's children and how our knowledge, skills, and techniques can be shared to improve the lives and education of our youth. Policies and programs that are successful need to be distributed and disseminated worldwide.

SUMMARY

The aim of this chapter was to examine international school social work from its onset. The similarities and differences among the countries presented were highlighted as well as some of the positive aspects that others could adopt in their countries. The countries of Canada, Ghana, Japan, Republic of Korea, Germany, Hungary, Malta, and the Scandinavian and Nordic countries were included. Each country was selected for a particular unique quality that it possesses. The need for our understanding of other nations' school social work programs is essential with the influx of immigrants and the communication that is now available through technology. Some of the shared problems that face children universally are violence, drug abuse, child abuse, homelessness, and mental and physical health difficulties. The care and education we give to the world's children is essential, since they will be the caretakers of our collective future.

ACTIVITIES

Activity 1: Levels 1 & 2: Choose a country that was discussed in this chapter and find something unique about the school social work program that would be helpful in your present or former school placement.

Activity 2: Level 1: Do you think that you can offer a policy or program from your school to one of the above countries? What would that policy or program be?

Level 2: How would you suggest it would impact that country?

SELF-REFLECTION QUESTIONS

1. Are there common issues that children in schools face internationally?
2. In the UN Convention on the Rights of Children, the United States was one of two countries that did not sign the agreement. What are your thoughts on our lack of support for this initiative?

CLASS DISCUSSION QUESTIONS

1. Are there any ideas found in other countries that might enhance our own school environments?
2. Which countries seem to share common educational values with the United States?

APPENDIX A

FROM THE INDIVIDUALS WITH DISABILITIES EDUCATION ACT

(E) Manifestation Determination.3,

(i) **In General.** Except as provided in subparagraph (B), **within 10 school days of any decision to change the placement** of a child with a disability **because of a violation of a code of student conduct,** the local educational agency, the parent, and relevant members of the IEP Team (as determined by the parent and the local educational agency) **shall review all relevant information** in the student's file, including the child's IEP, any teacher observations, and any relevant information provided by the parents to determine–

(I) **if the conduct** in question **was caused by, or had a direct and substantial relationship to, the child's disability;** or

(II) **if the conduct** in question **was the direct result of the local educational agency's failure to implement the IEP.**

59 Look at subsection (b) (c) and (d) of 300.530 for the distinctions between change of placement, a 0 day removal for one incident, a series of additional 0 day removals in one school year, and cumulative removals that exceed 0 days in one year. See Commentary in the *Federal Register,* pages 474 to 479.

0 If the school suspends the child with a disability for more than 0 days and determines that the child's behavior was not a manifestation of the disability, they may use the same procedures as with non-disabled children, but they must continue to provide the child with a free appropriate public education (FAPE). (Section 42(a)()(A)) If the child has a Section 504 plan, and the behavior was not a manifestation of the disability, the school may suspend or expel the child. The child is not entitled to receive a free appropriate public education.

The school is obligated to provide a free, appropriate public education to the child, even if the child has been suspended or expelled.

1. If the school district suspends a child with a disability for more than 10 days, regardless of severity of the child's misconduct (i.e., violation of a code of conduct v. possession of a weapon), the child must continue to receive FAPE (see Section 42 (a) () (A)), so the child can participate in the general education curriculum, make progress on the IEP goals, and receive a functional behavioral assessment, behavioral intervention services and modifications to prevent the behavior from reoccurring.
2. The IEP Team must review all information about the child and determine if the negative behavior was caused by the child's disability, had a direct and substantial relationship to the disability, or was the result of the school's failure to implement the IEP.
3. If you are dealing with a discipline issue, you need to obtain a comprehensive psycho-educational evaluation of the child by an evaluator in the private sector who has expertise in the disability (i.e., autism, attention deficit, bipolar disorder, Asperger's syndrome, auditory processing deficits). The evaluator must analyze the relationship between the child's disability and behavior. If there is a causal relationship, the evaluator should write a detailed report that describes the child's disability, the basis for determining that the behavior was a manifestation of the disability, and recommendations for an appropriate program. If you are dealing with a manifestation review, ask the evaluator to attend the hearing to explain the findings and make recommendations about alternative plans. Your goal is to develop a win-win solution to the problem.

(ii) **Manifestation.** If the local educational agency, the parent, and relevant members of the IEP Team determine that either subclause (I) or (II) of clause (i) is applicable for the child, the conduct **shall be determined to be a manifestation of the child's disability.**

(F) Determination That Behavior Was a Manifestation. If the local educational agency, the parent, and relevant members of the IEP Team make the determination that the conduct was a manifestation of the child's disability, **the IEP Team shall–**

(i) **conduct a functional behavioral assessment, and implement a behavioral intervention plan** for such child, provided that the local educational agency had not conducted such assessment prior to such determination before the behavior that resulted in a change in placement described in subparagraph (C) or (G);

(ii) in the situation where a behavioral intervention plan has been developed, review the behavioral intervention plan if the child already has such a behavioral intervention plan, and **modify** it, as necessary, **to address the behavior;** and

(iii) except as provided in subparagraph (G), return the child to the placement from which the child was removed, unless the parent and the local educational agency agree to a change of placement as part of the modification of the behavioral intervention plan.

(G) Special Circumstances. School personnel may remove a student to an interim alternative educational setting for **not more than 45 school days** without regard to whether the behavior is determined to be a manifestation of the child's disability, in cases where a child–

(i) **carries or possesses a weapon** to or at school, on school premises, or to or at a school function under the jurisdiction of a State or local educational agency;

(ii) **knowingly possesses or uses illegal drugs,** or sells or solicits the sale of a controlled substance,[7] while at school, on school premises, or at a school function under the jurisdiction of a State or local educational agency; **or**

(iii) **has inflicted serious bodily injury** upon another person while at school, on school premises, or at a school function under the jurisdiction of a State or local educational agency

(H) Notification. Not later than the date on which the decision to take disciplinary action is made, the local educational agency shall notify the parents of that decision, and of all procedural safeguards accorded under this section.

(2) Determination of Setting. The interim alternative educational setting in subparagraphs (C) and (G) of paragraph () **shall be determined by the IEP Team.**

5 If the child's behavior did not involve weapons, drugs, or serious bodily injury (see Section 45(k) () (G)), the child should return to the prior placement.

Section 45(k) (7) (C) clarifies that the term "weapon" means a "dangerous weapon" capable of causing death or serious bodily injury.

7. If a doctor prescribes a controlled substance for the child, and the child has possession of the medication at school, this is not illegal possession or illegal use. The school may not expel or suspend the child for

possessing prescribed medication. If the child attempts to sell or solicit the sale of the controlled substance, this "special circumstance" warrants a suspension for 45 school days and possible criminal prosecution.

8. See Section 45(k)(7) for the statutory differences between "controlled drugs" (Schedule I - V) and "illegal drugs," and definitions of "weapon" and "serious bodily injury."

9. If the child's behavior involves a dangerous weapon, illegal drugs, or serious bodily injury, the child may be suspended for 45 school days even if the behavior was a manifestation of the disability. The child is still entitled to FAPE pursuant to Section 42(a)()(A) and Section 45(k)()(D).

70 The decision to place a child into an interim alternative educational setting shall be made by the IEP Team, not by an administrator or school board member. This is mandatory. The educational setting is an interim placement, not a permanent placement. Remember: parents are full members of the IEP Team" (Wright & Wright, 2007, pp.119-120).

Appendix B

SOLUTION-FOCUSED THERAPY IN THE SCHOOLS

First session

- Inquire into the child's life.
- Clarify problem behaviors (Why do you think you are here?).
- Ask relationship questions to see how others view the problem.
- Track exceptions to the problem.
- Scale the problem. . . .
- Ask the miracle question to develop solutions.
- Take a session break to reflect, develop compliments and formulate tasks.
- Deliver compliments and tasks.

Subsequent

- Warm-up.
- Begin the work of the session by tracking new exceptions to the problem.
- Use relationship questions to track how the client perceives that others have not responded to the changes and to amplify the client's belief in the power of the changes.
- Ask the scaling question to see where the client has moved on the scale.
- Return to the use of the miracle question or its variation.
- Break to formulate thoughts and develop compliments and tasks.
- Deliver the compliments to reinforce positive behaviors and assign new task

---

(Franklin et al., 2008, p. 21).

Appendix C

HASSLE LOG

Name:__________________ Date:__________________ Time:_______________

Where were you? __Home __School __Outside __Car/Bus __Other

What Happened: __Teased __Told to do something __Someone stole from me
__Someone started a fight with me __I did something wrong
__Other_________________________

Who was that somebody? __Friend __Sibling __Another student
__Parent __Teacher __Another adult
__Therapist/Counselor __Other_____________
____

What did you do: __Hit back __Ran away __Yelled __Cried
__Ignored __Broke something __Was restrained
__Told adult __Walked away calmly __Talked it out
__Told friend

How did you handle yourself: __Poorly __Not so well __OK __Good
__Great

How angry were you: __Burning mad __Really angry __Moderately angry
__Mildly angry __Not angry at all

Notes:____

____

(Feindler & Engel, 2011).

APPENDIX D

A COUNSELOR CHECKLIST FOR SCHOOL-BASED SUICIDE

(Check the appropriate box.)

PROGRAM COMPONENTS	Yes	No	Not Sure
Program construction			
Support for the program has been given by the administration.			
The district school board has approved the program.			
A policy that describes explicit procedures for intervention with potentially suicidal students has been published.			
Community mental health resources for referral, training, and consultation have been identified.			
A needs assessment has been conducted to determine the knowledge and attitudes of teachers and students regarding youth suicide.			
Multidisciplinary teams have been formed as part of the program.			
An outside mental health consultant has been made available.			
In-service training regarding suicide has been implemented for teachers, counselors, and staff. Qualified professionals with a special focus on adolescent suicide have been made available in the event of a crisis.			

(Continued)

(Continued)

Crisis prevention			
The administration conducts psychometric screening to identify students at risk and conducts an appropriate follow-up of these students.			
Students with substance, academic, or family problems are identified.			
Supportive counseling for at-risk students is available.			
Suicidal students are immediately referred to a mental health professional.			
Classroom and group discussions on teen suicide are conducted by mental health professionals competent in suicide prevention skills.			
Handouts, pamphlets, and wallet cards with suicide prevention information are distributed to students and parents.			
POSTVENTION			
The school policy			
Individual and group counseling will be provided for students.			
A specialized consultant will work with the school's prevention team.			
A single spokesperson will address the media.			
A prepared written statement regarding the death will be read to the students by the teachers.			
Memorial activities will not exceed what the school custom is for acknowledging the death of a student.			
Assemblies to discuss the death will not be held.			
Students who want to attend the funeral may do so with parental permission.			
The school will stay open during the funeral for those students not attending the funeral.			
Referrals for "survivors of suicide" counseling will be made.			
TOTAL			

(Malley & Kush, 1994, p. 191).

Appendix E

THE COLUMBIA SUICIDE SCREENING

The CSS is a 43 question written scale that includes 32 general health questions and 11 global items that discuss the risks for adolescent suicide. It is used in conjunction with the availability of a mental health professional and was developed by David Shaffer, M.D. He works at Columbia University: College of Physicians and surgeons with funding coming from the Center for Disease Control. There is no cost involved in using the instrument. Assent from the student and consent from his/her parents must be obtained before using the survey. The names of the participants are kept confidential and if they screen positive a secondary evaluation takes place by a mental health professional. The screening takes about 15 minutes but the secondary evaluation is dependent on the individual screener and the participant. There is a separate survey for males and females. Both are being included in this chapter.

The female survey is as follows:

School #: __________ [1-2]
I.D. #: __________ [3-6]
Card #: __________ [7-8]

COLUMBIA UNIVERSITY HEALTH SURVEY FOR HIGH SCHOOL STUDENTS (females)

This survey has been designed by researchers at Columbia University in Order to learn about the physical and emotional health of high school students.

- Your responses to the questions are **confidential**.
- Your name appears only on the cover sheet, which has been removed, and will be stored in a locked file cabinet separate from the questionnaire.
- You will be contacted **only** if you indicate that you would like help in any area, or if your responses to certain questions are of interest to the project staff, In either case, a member of the staff will contact you **privately**.

PLASE **ANSWER ALL QUESTIONS**, EVEN IF YOU FEEL THEY DON'T APPLY TO YOU.

1. Today's date: Month _____ Day _____ Year _____ [9-14]
2. Your date of birth: _____ Month _____ Day _____ Year _____ [15-20]
3. Your age at last birthday: _____ [21-22]
4. Your sex: M _____ F _____ [23]
5. Do you regard yourself as . . . (check one) White _____ Black _____ Hispanic _____ Asian _____ Other _____ [24]
6. Your grade: 9th _____ 10th _____ 11th _____ 12th _____ [25-26]
7. Have you seen any of the following health professional during the past year? (check all that apply)

Pediatrician/Family physician	___ yes	___ no	[27]
Eye doctor	___ yes	___ no	[28]
Dentist	___ yes	___ no	[29]
Phychiatrist	___ yes	___ no	[30]
Phychologist	___ yes	___ no	[31]
Social worker	___ yes	___ no	[32]
Social worker	___ yes	___ no	[33]
Counselor	___ yes	___ no	[34]
Other medical doctor (such as orthopedist, neurologist, etc)	___ yes	___ no	[35]
Other (not listed above)	___ yes	___ no	[36]

Instruction

Place a mark in the box next to your answer to the question. Then follow the arrow from that box to find the next question you are to answer.

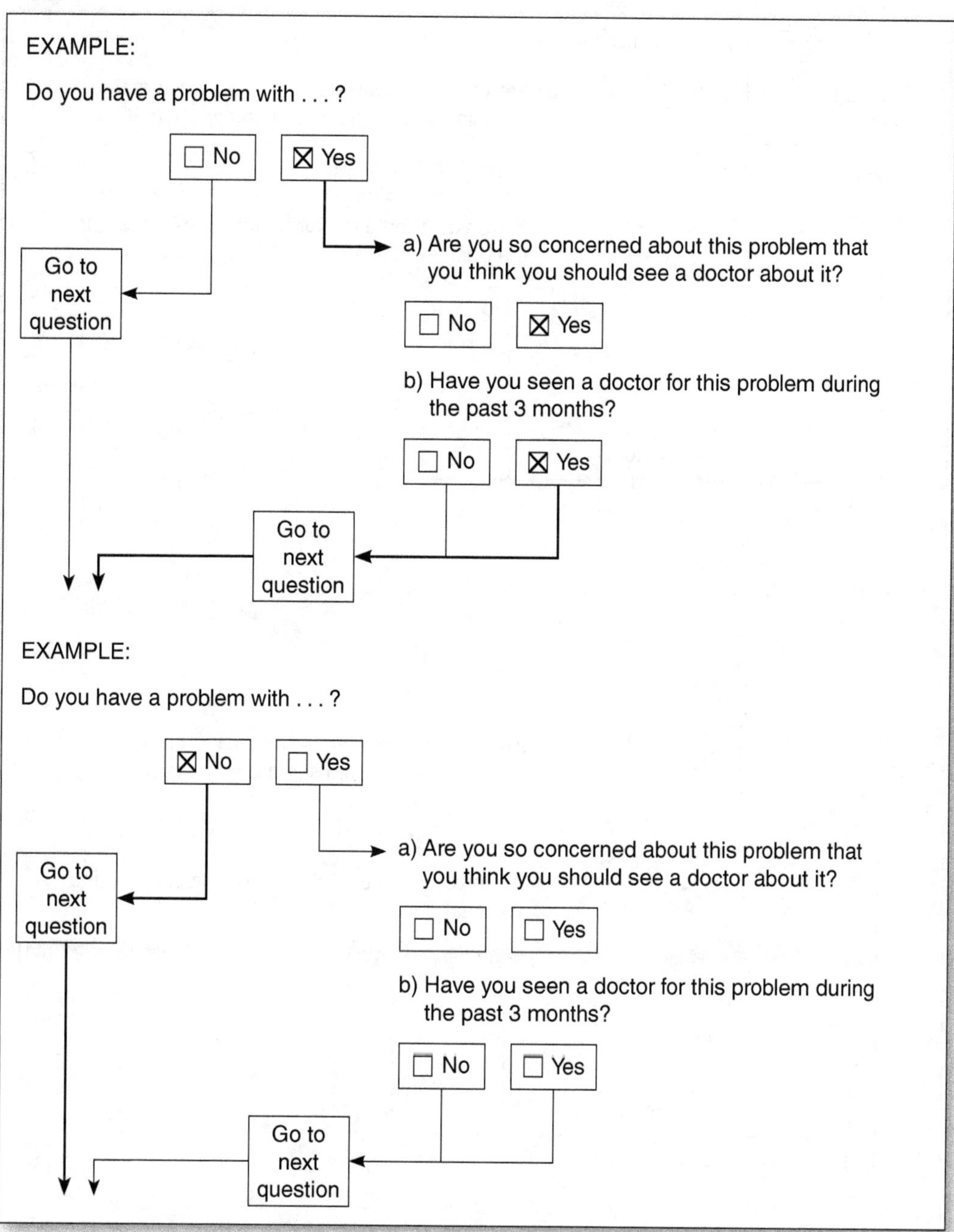

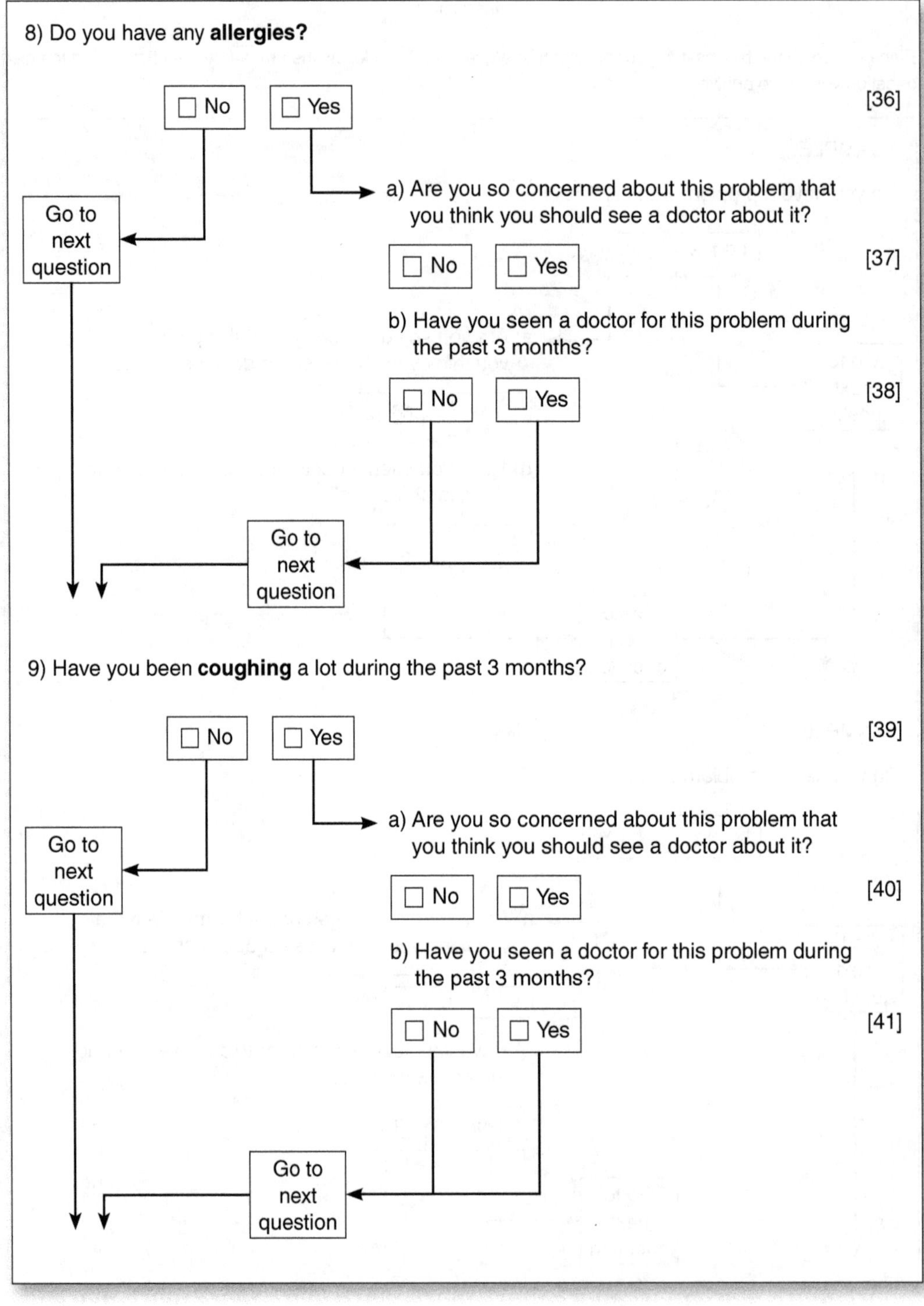
8) Do you have any **allergies?**

☐ No ☐ Yes [36]

No → Go to next question

Yes → a) Are you so concerned about this problem that you think you should see a doctor about it?

☐ No ☐ Yes [37]

b) Have you seen a doctor for this problem during the past 3 months?

☐ No ☐ Yes [38]

No / Yes → Go to next question

9) Have you been **coughing** a lot during the past 3 months?

☐ No ☐ Yes [39]

No → Go to next question

Yes → a) Are you so concerned about this problem that you think you should see a doctor about it?

☐ No ☐ Yes [40]

b) Have you seen a doctor for this problem during the past 3 months?

☐ No ☐ Yes [41]

No / Yes → Go to next question

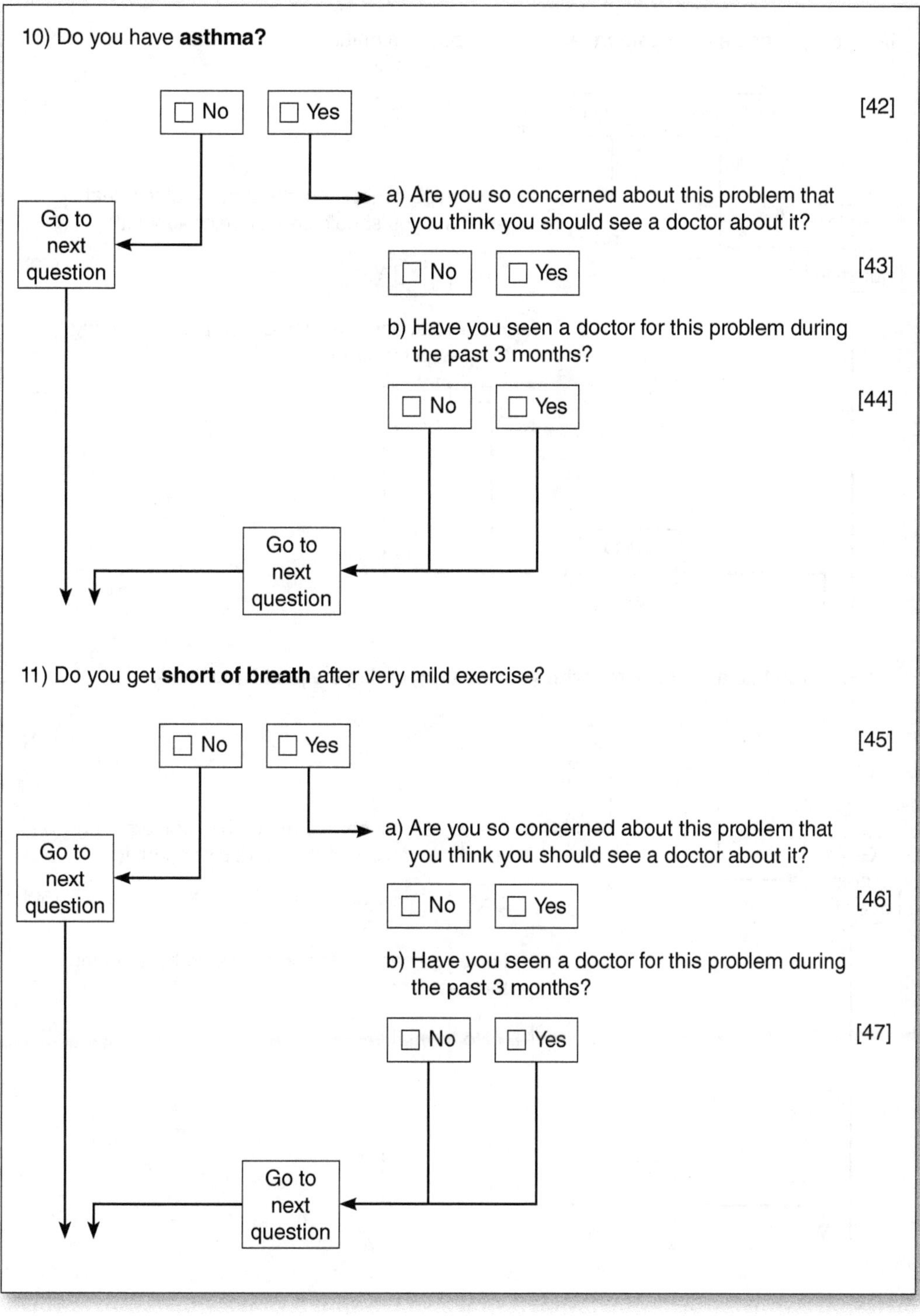

10) Do you have **asthma?**

☐ No ☐ Yes [42]

No → Go to next question

Yes → a) Are you so concerned about this problem that you think you should see a doctor about it?

☐ No ☐ Yes [43]

b) Have you seen a doctor for this problem during the past 3 months?

☐ No ☐ Yes [44]

No / Yes → Go to next question

11) Do you get **short of breath** after very mild exercise?

☐ No ☐ Yes [45]

No → Go to next question

Yes → a) Are you so concerned about this problem that you think you should see a doctor about it?

☐ No ☐ Yes [46]

b) Have you seen a doctor for this problem during the past 3 months?

☐ No ☐ Yes [47]

No / Yes → Go to next question

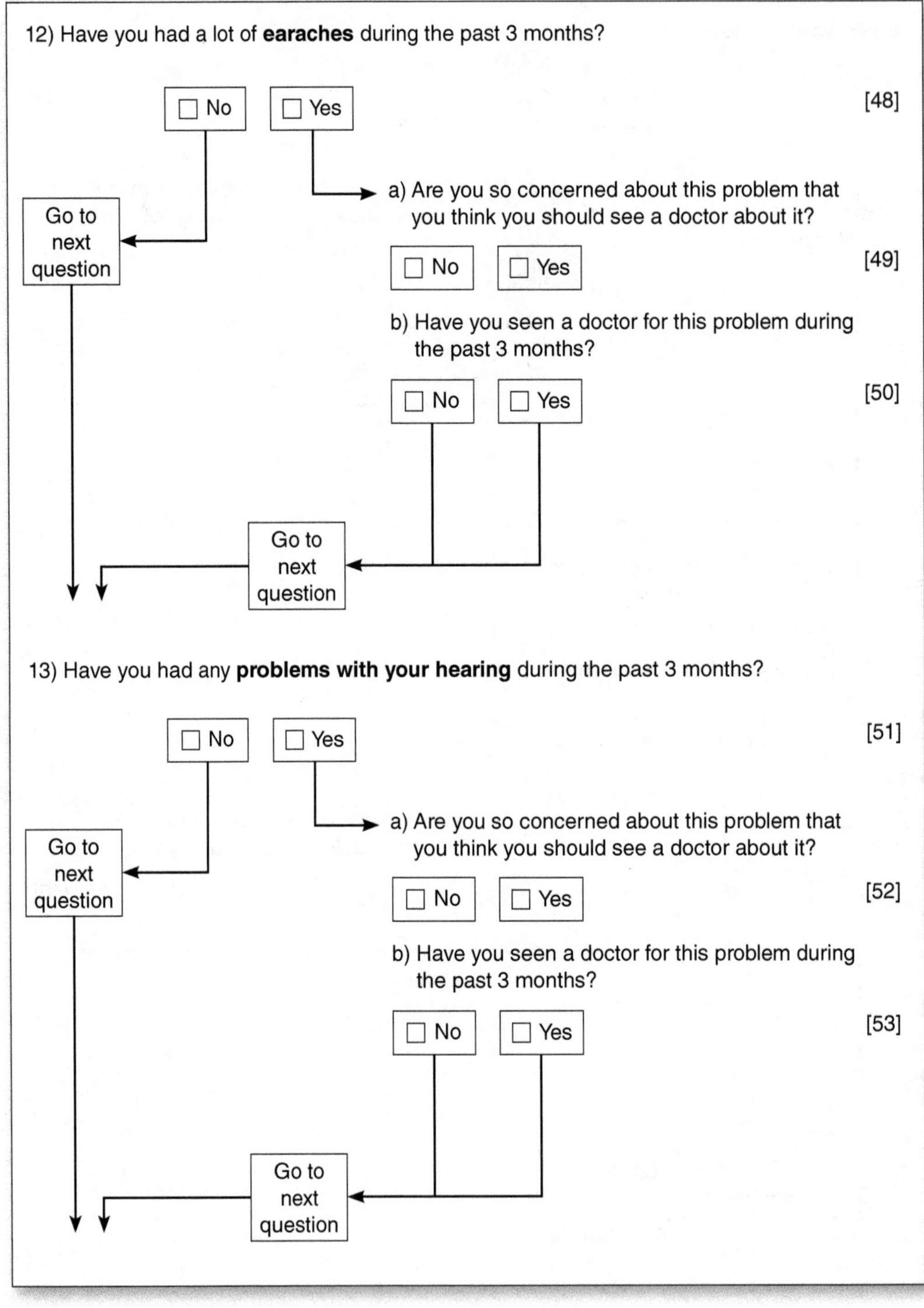

12) Have you had a lot of **earaches** during the past 3 months?

☐ No ☐ Yes [48]

No → Go to next question

Yes → a) Are you so concerned about this problem that you think you should see a doctor about it?

☐ No ☐ Yes [49]

b) Have you seen a doctor for this problem during the past 3 months?

☐ No ☐ Yes [50]

No / Yes → Go to next question

13) Have you had any **problems with your hearing** during the past 3 months?

☐ No ☐ Yes [51]

No → Go to next question

Yes → a) Are you so concerned about this problem that you think you should see a doctor about it?

☐ No ☐ Yes [52]

b) Have you seen a doctor for this problem during the past 3 months?

☐ No ☐ Yes [53]

No / Yes → Go to next question

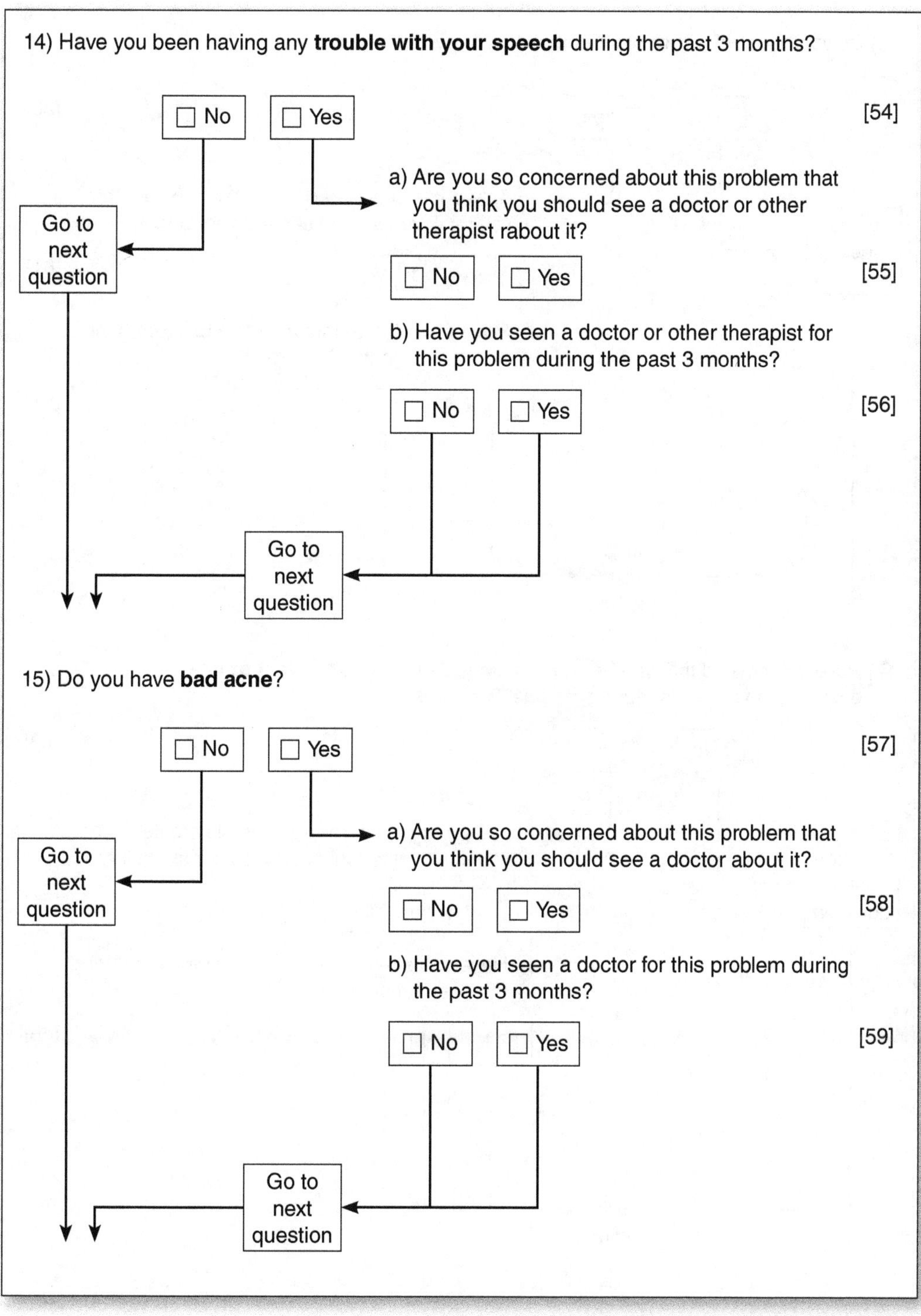

14) Have you been having any **trouble with your speech** during the past 3 months?

☐ No ☐ Yes [54]

No → Go to next question

Yes → a) Are you so concerned about this problem that you think you should see a doctor or other therapist rabout it?

☐ No ☐ Yes [55]

b) Have you seen a doctor or other therapist for this problem during the past 3 months?

☐ No ☐ Yes [56]

Go to next question

15) Do you have **bad acne**?

☐ No ☐ Yes [57]

No → Go to next question

Yes → a) Are you so concerned about this problem that you think you should see a doctor about it?

☐ No ☐ Yes [58]

b) Have you seen a doctor for this problem during the past 3 months?

☐ No ☐ Yes [59]

Go to next question

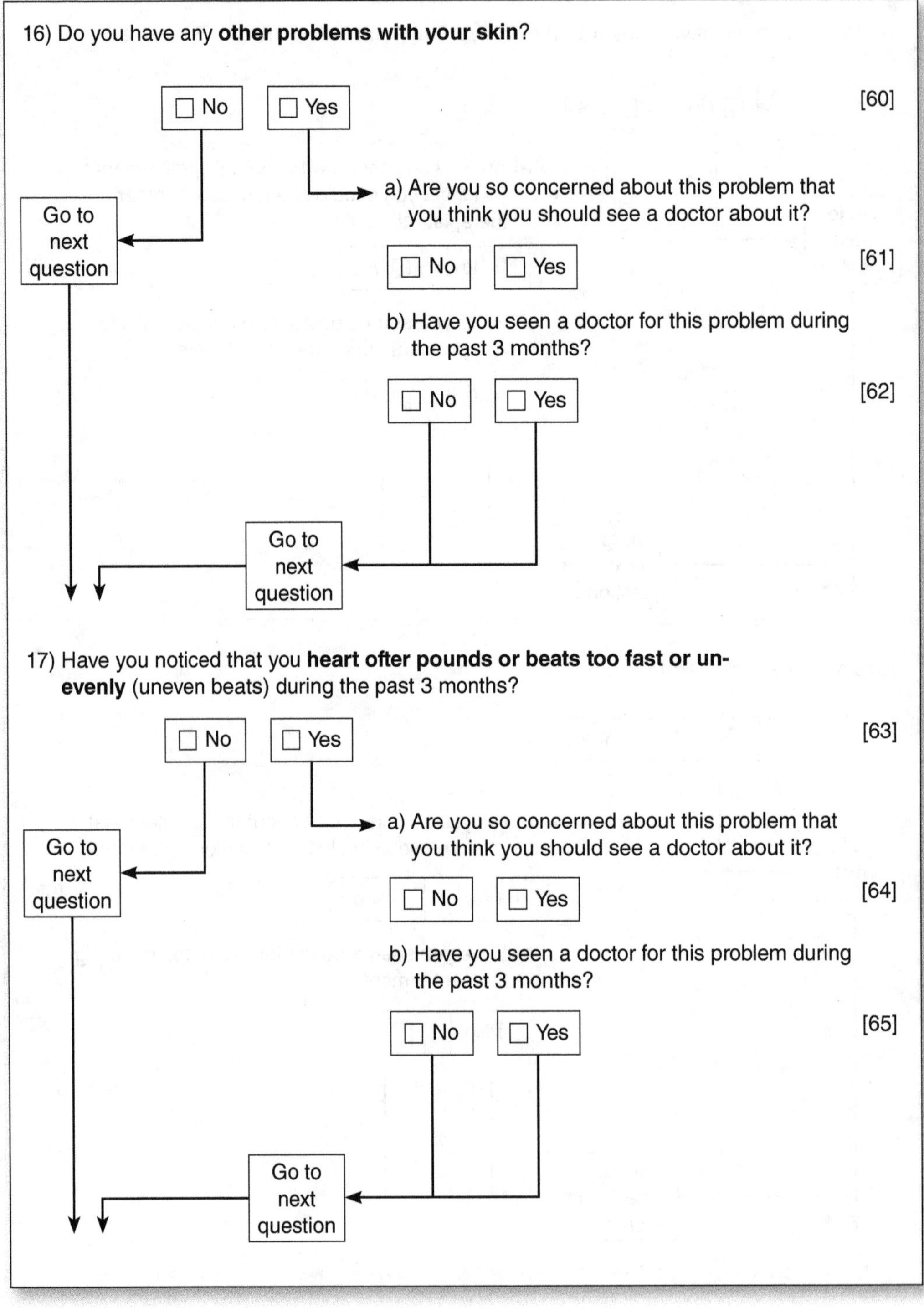

16) Do you have any **other problems with your skin**?

☐ No ☐ Yes [60]

Go to next question

a) Are you so concerned about this problem that you think you should see a doctor about it?

☐ No ☐ Yes [61]

b) Have you seen a doctor for this problem during the past 3 months?

☐ No ☐ Yes [62]

Go to next question

17) Have you noticed that you **heart ofter pounds or beats too fast or unevenly** (uneven beats) during the past 3 months?

☐ No ☐ Yes [63]

Go to next question

a) Are you so concerned about this problem that you think you should see a doctor about it?

☐ No ☐ Yes [64]

b) Have you seen a doctor for this problem during the past 3 months?

☐ No ☐ Yes [65]

Go to next question

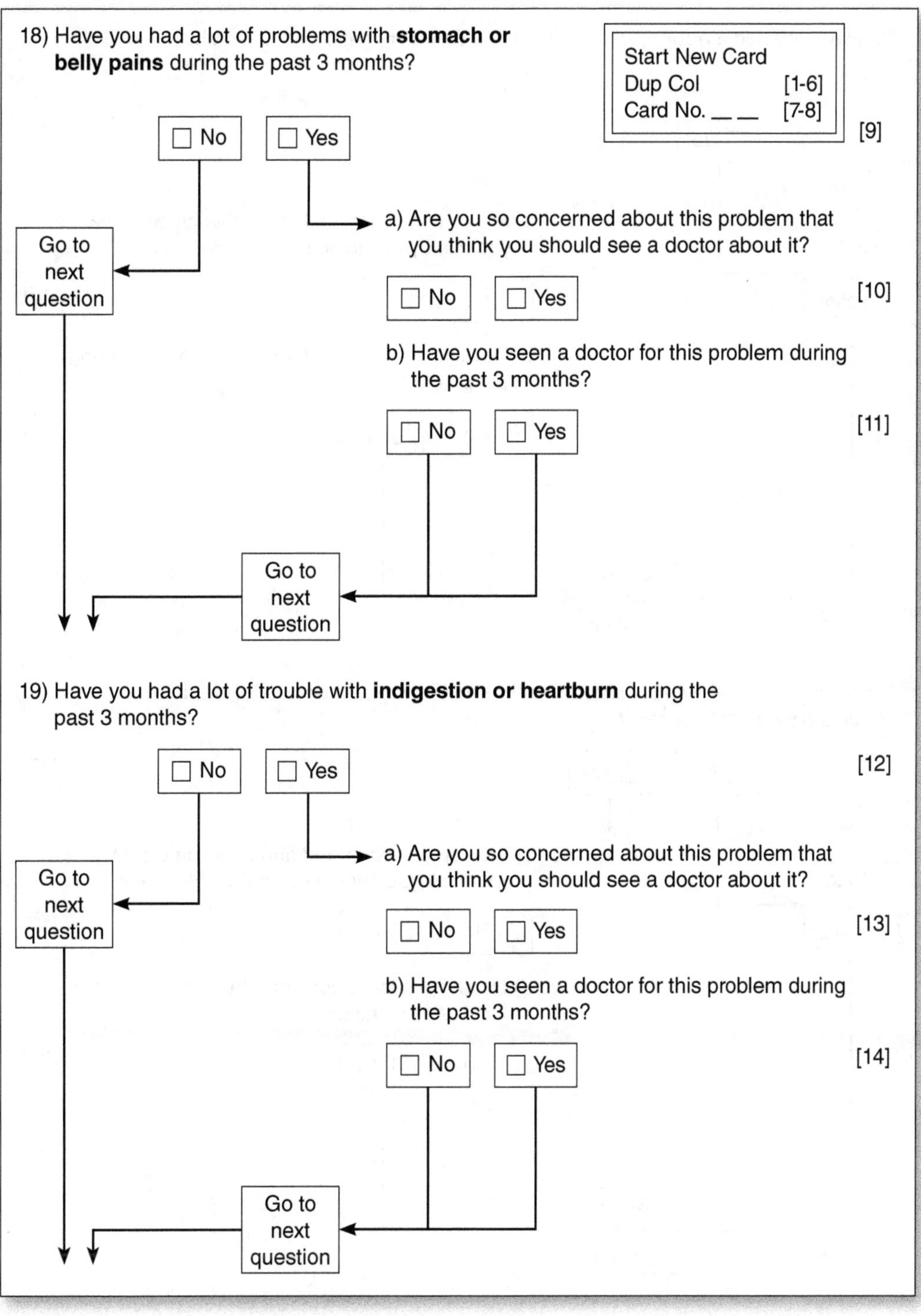

18) Have you had a lot of problems with **stomach or belly pains** during the past 3 months?

Start New Card
Dup Col [1-6]
Card No. __ __ [7-8]

☐ No ☐ Yes [9]

Go to next question

a) Are you so concerned about this problem that you think you should see a doctor about it?

☐ No ☐ Yes [10]

b) Have you seen a doctor for this problem during the past 3 months?

☐ No ☐ Yes [11]

Go to next question

19) Have you had a lot of trouble with **indigestion or heartburn** during the past 3 months?

☐ No ☐ Yes [12]

Go to next question

a) Are you so concerned about this problem that you think you should see a doctor about it?

☐ No ☐ Yes [13]

b) Have you seen a doctor for this problem during the past 3 months?

☐ No ☐ Yes [14]

Go to next question

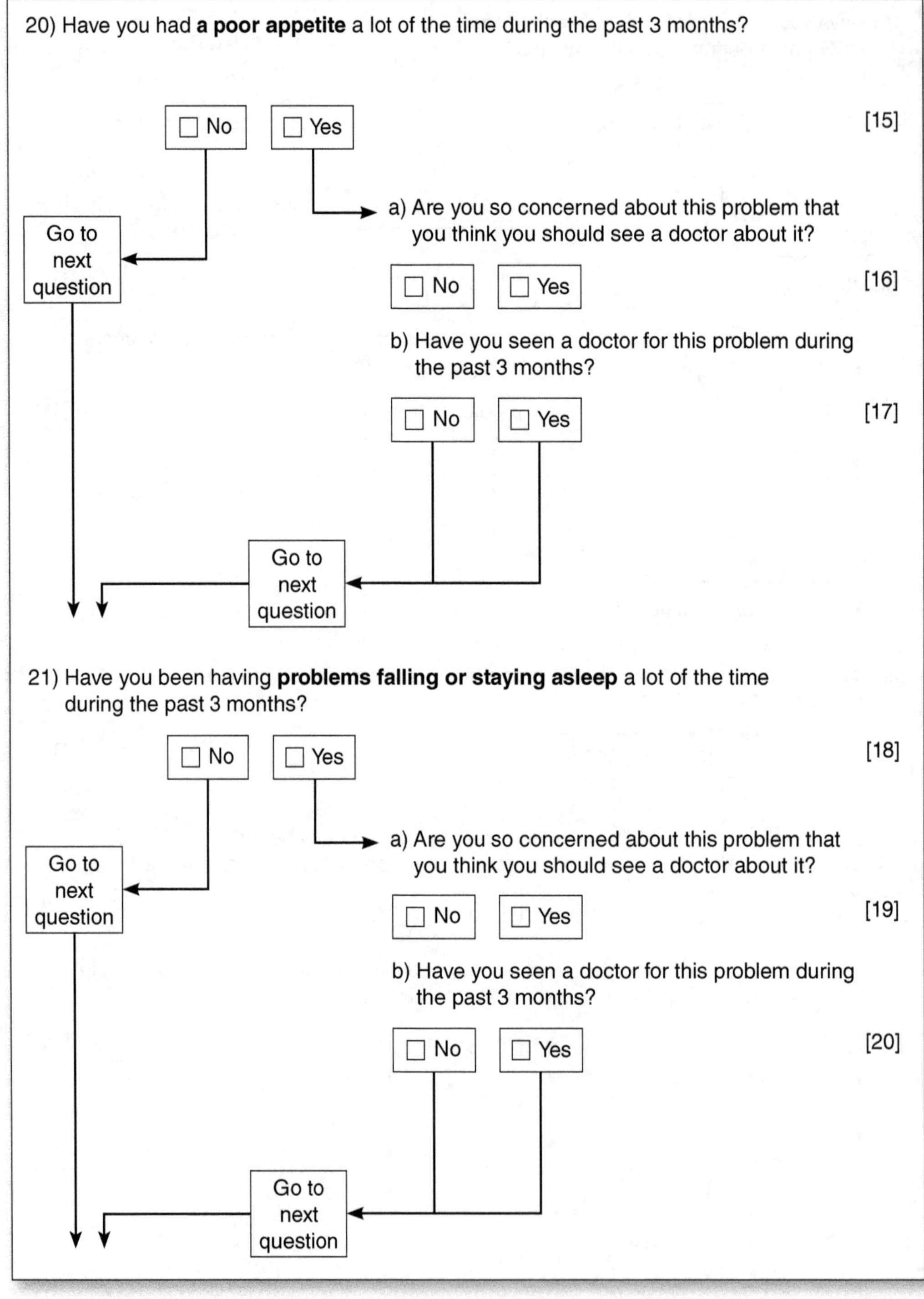
20) Have you had **a poor appetite** a lot of the time during the past 3 months?

☐ No ☐ Yes [15]

Go to next question

a) Are you so concerned about this problem that you think you should see a doctor about it?

☐ No ☐ Yes [16]

b) Have you seen a doctor for this problem during the past 3 months?

☐ No ☐ Yes [17]

Go to next question

21) Have you been having **problems falling or staying asleep** a lot of the time during the past 3 months?

☐ No ☐ Yes [18]

Go to next question

a) Are you so concerned about this problem that you think you should see a doctor about it?

☐ No ☐ Yes [19]

b) Have you seen a doctor for this problem during the past 3 months?

☐ No ☐ Yes [20]

Go to next question

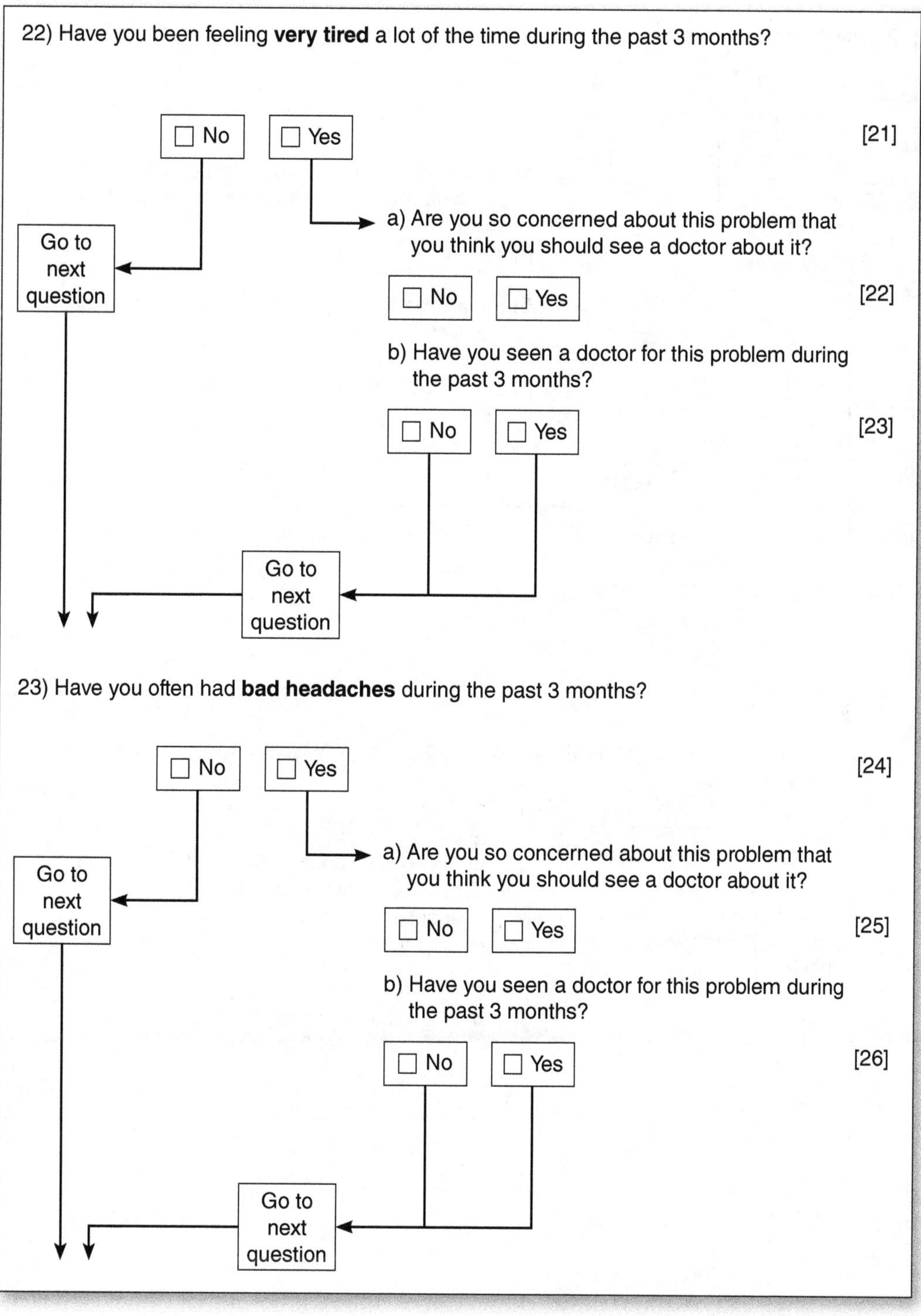
22) Have you been feeling **very tired** a lot of the time during the past 3 months?

☐ No ☐ Yes [21]

Go to next question

a) Are you so concerned about this problem that you think you should see a doctor about it?

☐ No ☐ Yes [22]

b) Have you seen a doctor for this problem during the past 3 months?

☐ No ☐ Yes [23]

Go to next question

23) Have you often had **bad headaches** during the past 3 months?

☐ No ☐ Yes [24]

Go to next question

a) Are you so concerned about this problem that you think you should see a doctor about it?

☐ No ☐ Yes [25]

b) Have you seen a doctor for this problem during the past 3 months?

☐ No ☐ Yes [26]

Go to next question

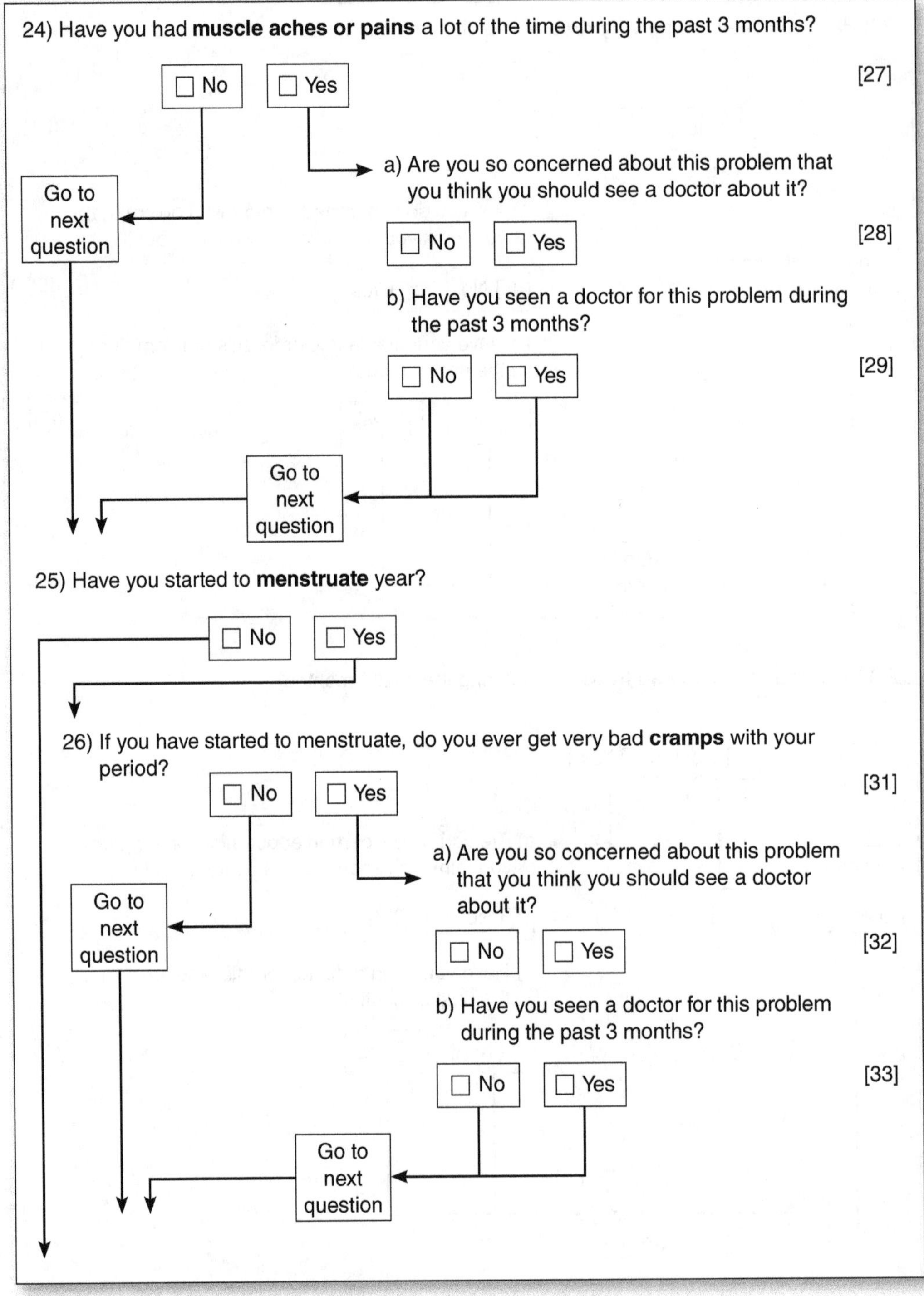
24) Have you had **muscle aches or pains** a lot of the time during the past 3 months?

☐ No ☐ Yes [27]

Go to next question

a) Are you so concerned about this problem that you think you should see a doctor about it?

☐ No ☐ Yes [28]

b) Have you seen a doctor for this problem during the past 3 months?

☐ No ☐ Yes [29]

Go to next question

25) Have you started to **menstruate** year?

☐ No ☐ Yes

26) If you have started to menstruate, do you ever get very bad **cramps** with your period?

☐ No ☐ Yes [31]

Go to next question

a) Are you so concerned about this problem that you think you should see a doctor about it?

☐ No ☐ Yes [32]

b) Have you seen a doctor for this problem during the past 3 months?

☐ No ☐ Yes [33]

Go to next question

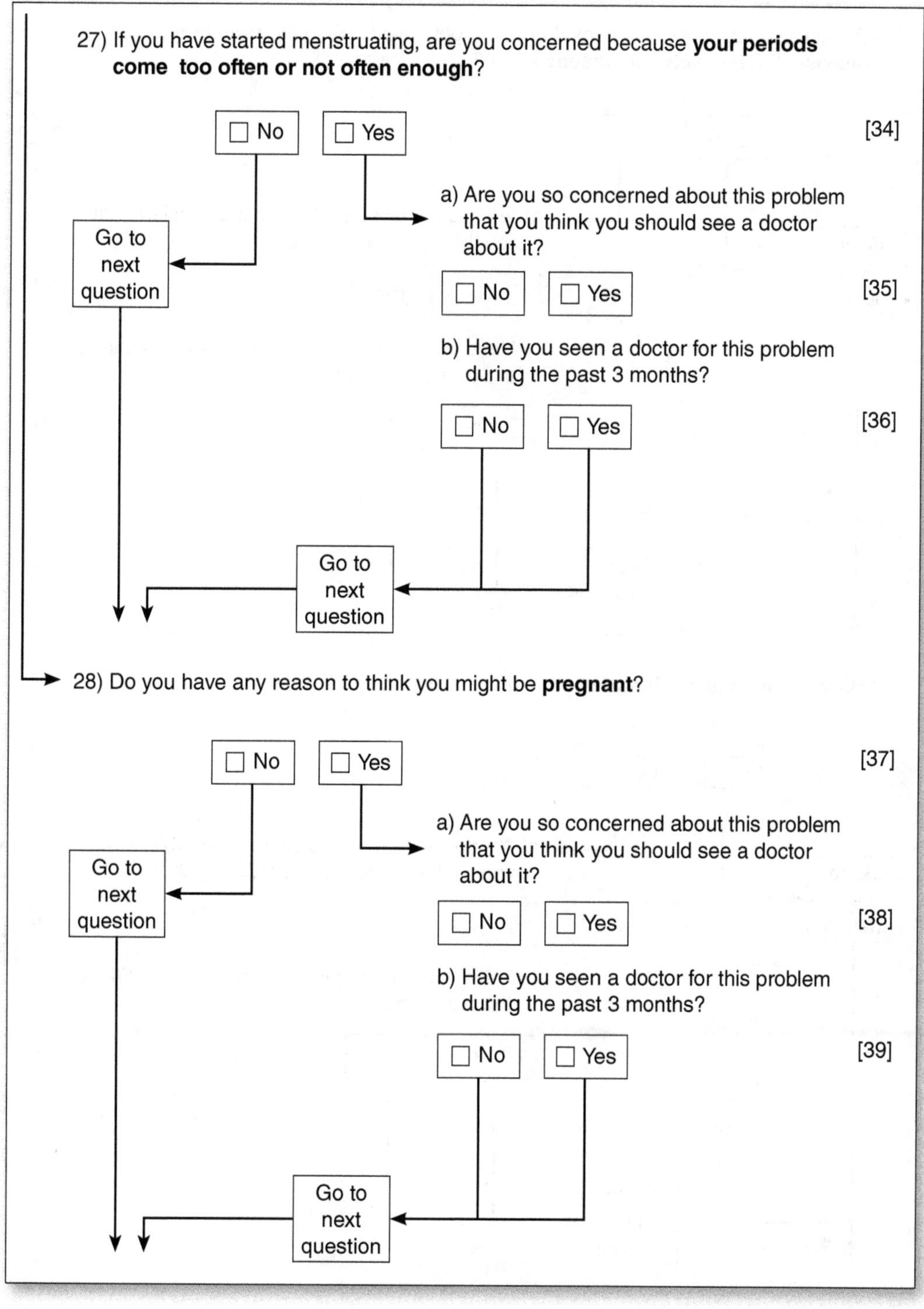
27) If you have started menstruating, are you concerned because **your periods come too often or not often enough**?
No
Yes
[34]
a) Are you so concerned about this problem that you think you should see a doctor about it?
Go to next question
No
Yes
[35]
b) Have you seen a doctor for this problem during the past 3 months?
No
Yes
[36]
Go to next question
28) Do you have any reason to think you might be **pregnant**?
No
Yes
[37]
a) Are you so concerned about this problem that you think you should see a doctor about it?
Go to next question
No
Yes
[38]
b) Have you seen a doctor for this problem during the past 3 months?
No
Yes
[39]
Go to next question

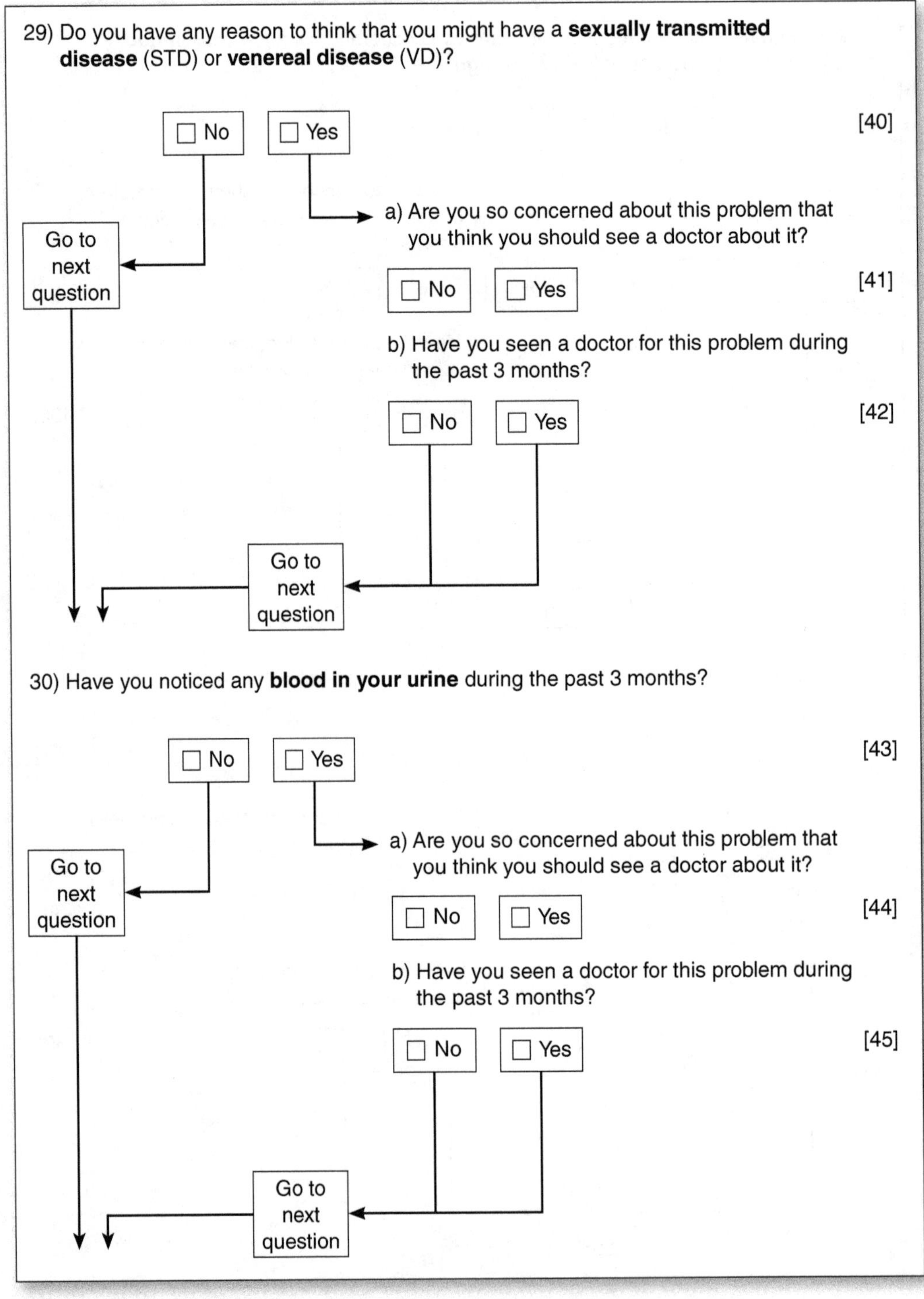

29) Do you have any reason to think that you might have a **sexually transmitted disease** (STD) or **venereal disease** (VD)?

☐ No ☐ Yes [40]

No → Go to next question

Yes → a) Are you so concerned about this problem that you think you should see a doctor about it?

☐ No ☐ Yes [41]

b) Have you seen a doctor for this problem during the past 3 months?

☐ No ☐ Yes [42]

Go to next question

30) Have you noticed any **blood in your urine** during the past 3 months?

☐ No ☐ Yes [43]

No → Go to next question

Yes → a) Are you so concerned about this problem that you think you should see a doctor about it?

☐ No ☐ Yes [44]

b) Have you seen a doctor for this problem during the past 3 months?

☐ No ☐ Yes [45]

Go to next question

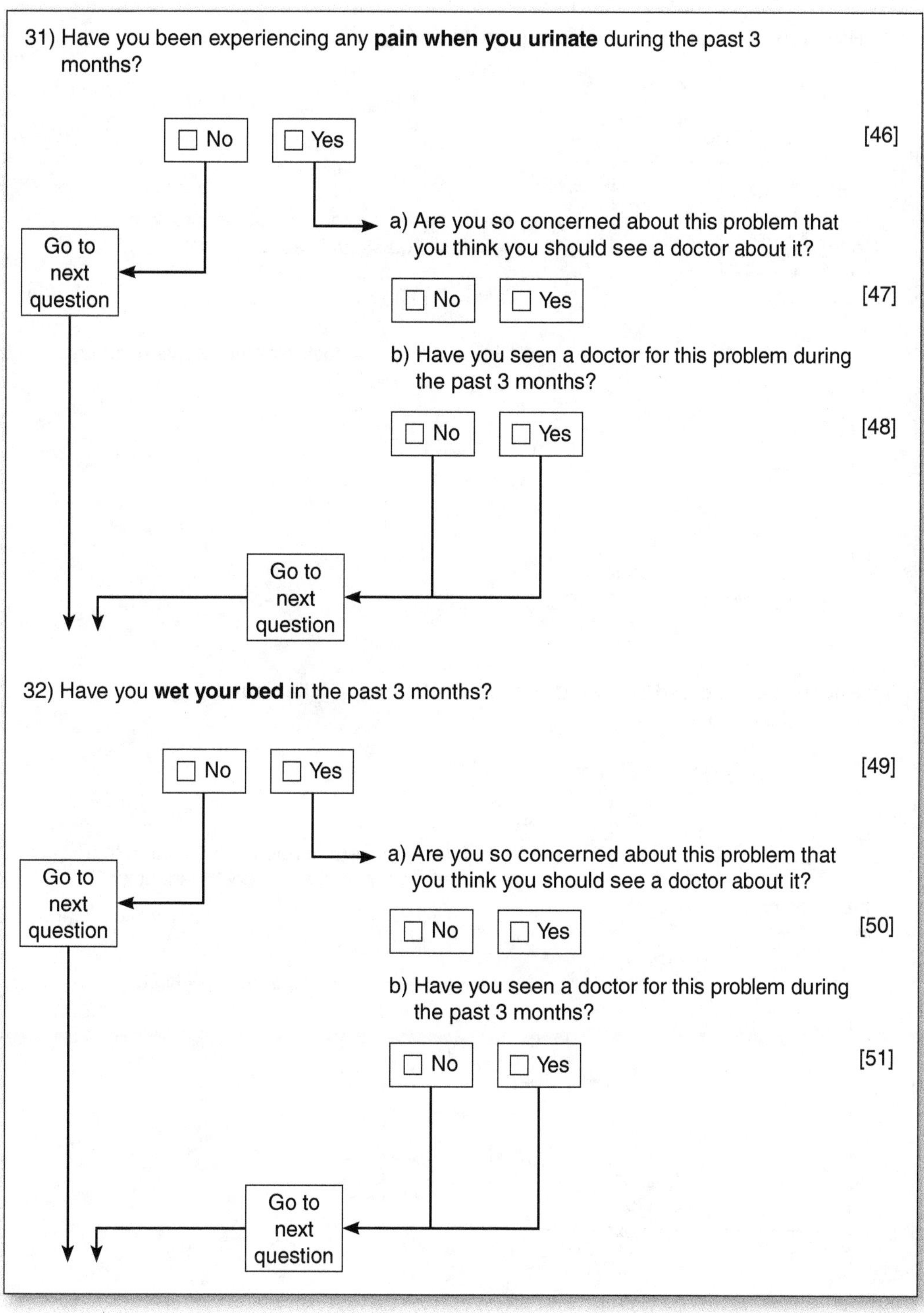
31) Have you been experiencing any **pain when you urinate** during the past 3 months?

☐ No ☐ Yes [46]

a) Are you so concerned about this problem that you think you should see a doctor about it?

☐ No ☐ Yes [47]

b) Have you seen a doctor for this problem during the past 3 months?

☐ No ☐ Yes [48]

32) Have you **wet your bed** in the past 3 months?

☐ No ☐ Yes [49]

a) Are you so concerned about this problem that you think you should see a doctor about it?

☐ No ☐ Yes [50]

b) Have you seen a doctor for this problem during the past 3 months?

☐ No ☐ Yes [51]

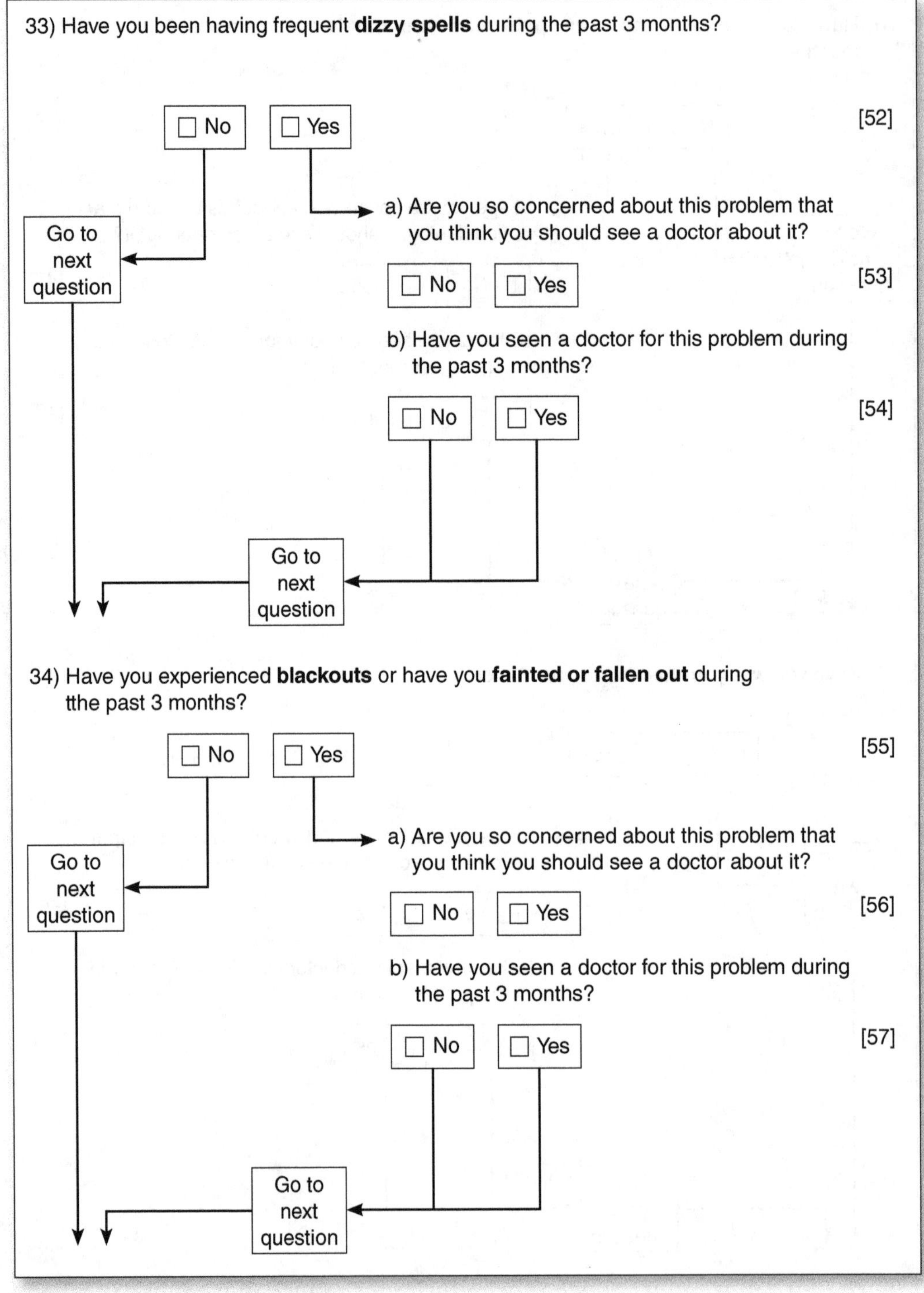

33) Have you been having frequent **dizzy spells** during the past 3 months?

☐ No ☐ Yes [52]

Go to next question

a) Are you so concerned about this problem that you think you should see a doctor about it?

☐ No ☐ Yes [53]

b) Have you seen a doctor for this problem during the past 3 months?

☐ No ☐ Yes [54]

Go to next question

34) Have you experienced **blackouts** or have you **fainted or fallen out** during tthe past 3 months?

☐ No ☐ Yes [55]

Go to next question

a) Are you so concerned about this problem that you think you should see a doctor about it?

☐ No ☐ Yes [56]

b) Have you seen a doctor for this problem during the past 3 months?

☐ No ☐ Yes [57]

Go to next question

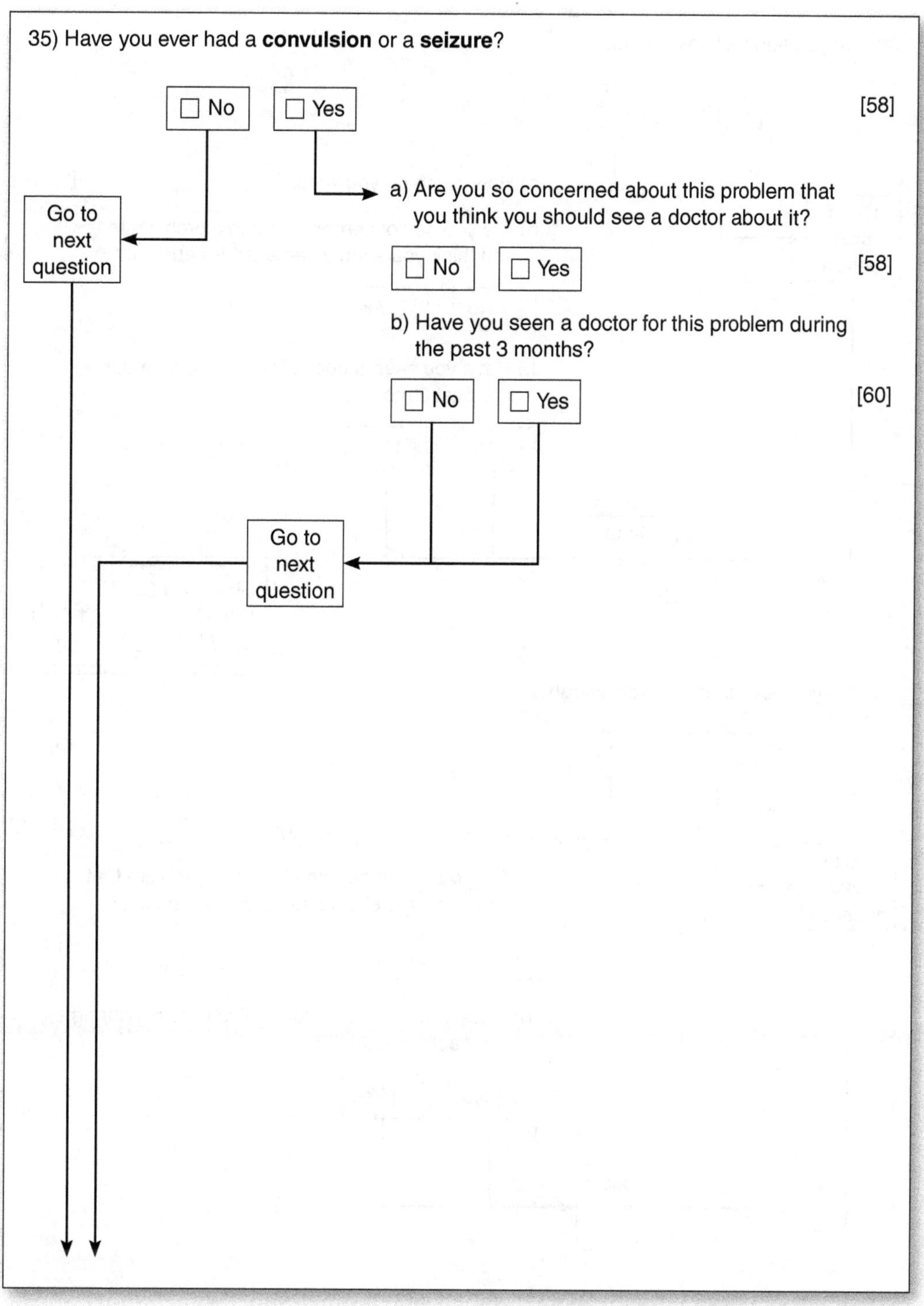

35) Have you ever had a **convulsion** or a **seizure**?

☐ No ☐ Yes [58]

a) Are you so concerned about this problem that you think you should see a doctor about it?

☐ No ☐ Yes [58]

b) Have you seen a doctor for this problem during the past 3 months?

☐ No ☐ Yes [60]

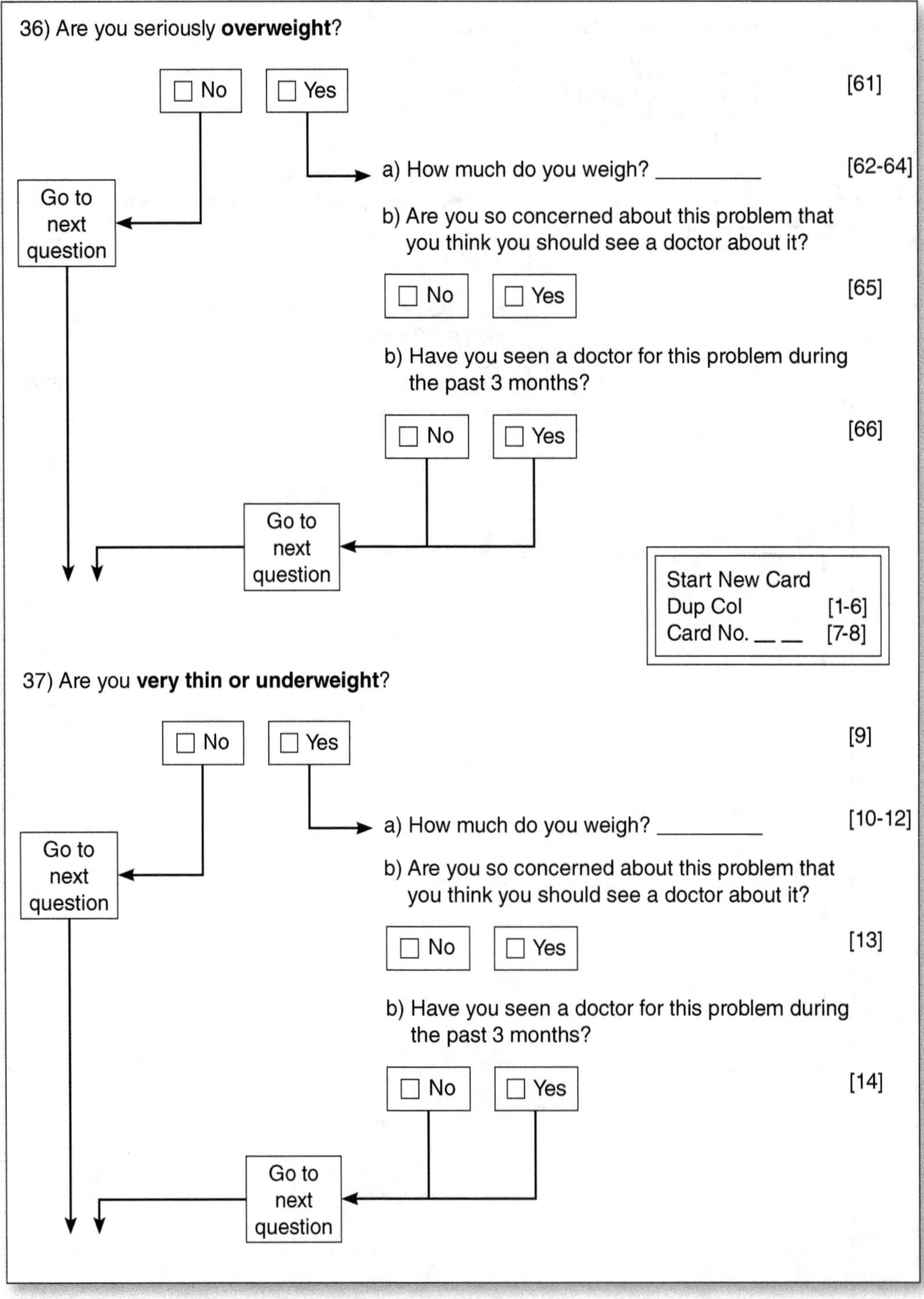
36) Are you seriously **overweight**?

☐ No ☐ Yes [61]

Go to next question

a) How much do you weigh? __________ [62-64]

b) Are you so concerned about this problem that you think you should see a doctor about it?

☐ No ☐ Yes [65]

b) Have you seen a doctor for this problem during the past 3 months?

☐ No ☐ Yes [66]

Go to next question

Start New Card
Dup Col [1-6]
Card No. __ __ [7-8]

37) Are you **very thin or underweight**?

☐ No ☐ Yes [9]

Go to next question

a) How much do you weigh? __________ [10-12]

b) Are you so concerned about this problem that you think you should see a doctor about it?

☐ No ☐ Yes [13]

b) Have you seen a doctor for this problem during the past 3 months?

☐ No ☐ Yes [14]

Go to next question

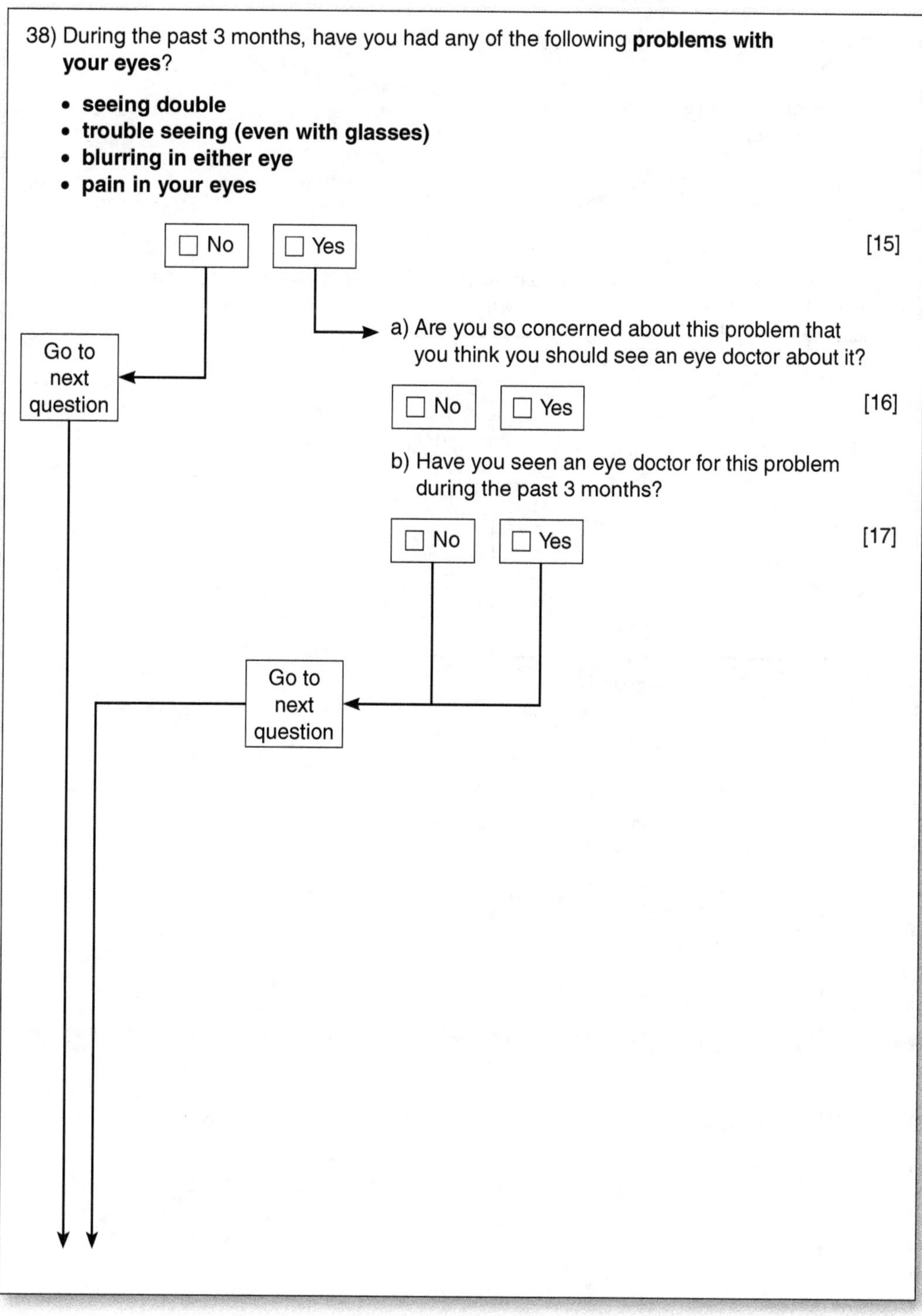

38) During the past 3 months, have you had any of the following **problems with your eyes**?

- **seeing double**
- **trouble seeing (even with glasses)**
- **blurring in either eye**
- **pain in your eyes**

☐ No ☐ Yes [15]

Go to next question

a) Are you so concerned about this problem that you think you should see an eye doctor about it?

☐ No ☐ Yes [16]

b) Have you seen an eye doctor for this problem during the past 3 months?

☐ No ☐ Yes [17]

Go to next question

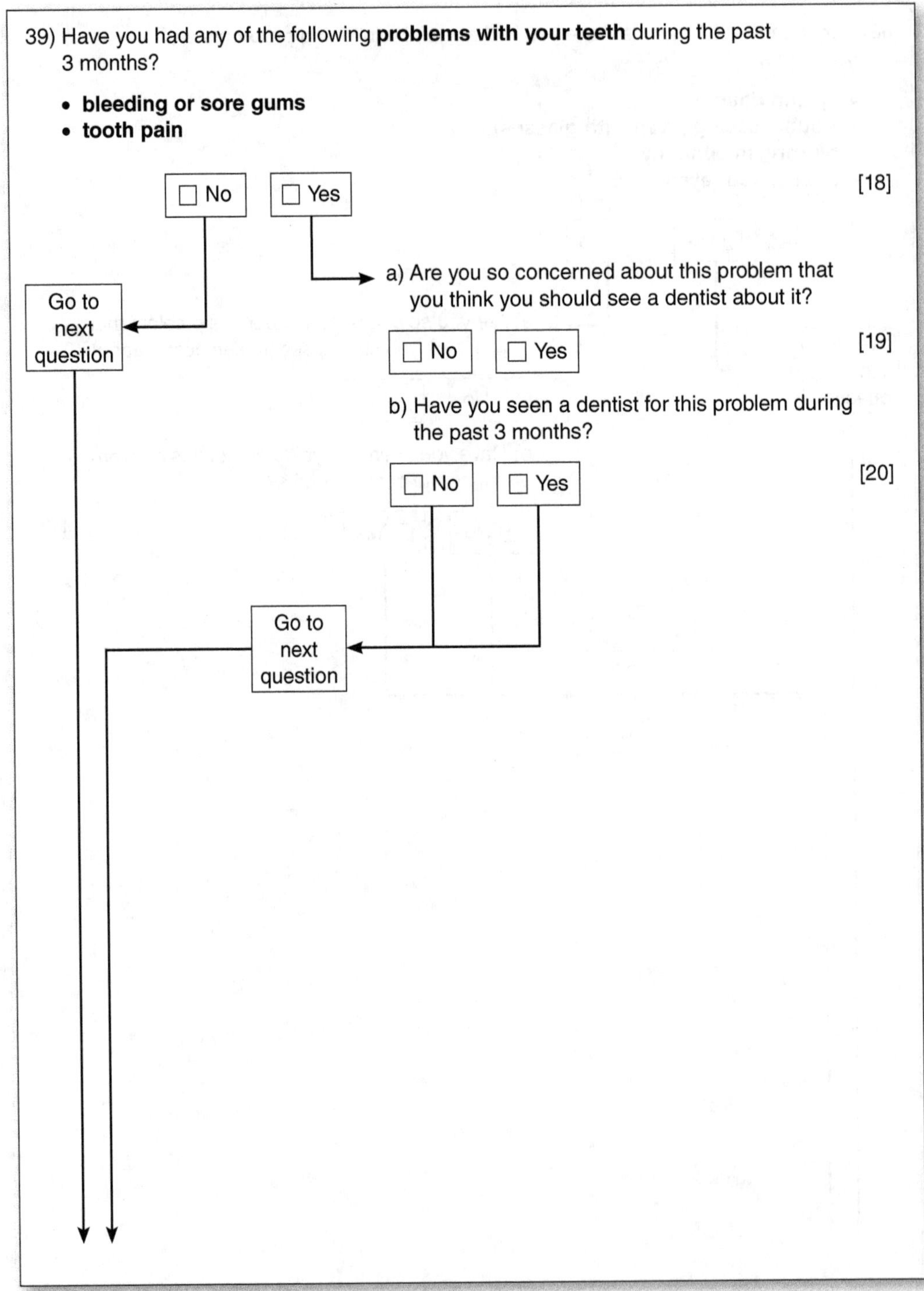

39) Have you had any of the following **problems with your teeth** during the past 3 months?

- **bleeding or sore gums**
- **tooth pain**

☐ No ☐ Yes [18]

a) Are you so concerned about this problem that you think you should see a dentist about it?

☐ No ☐ Yes [19]

b) Have you seen a dentist for this problem during the past 3 months?

☐ No ☐ Yes [20]

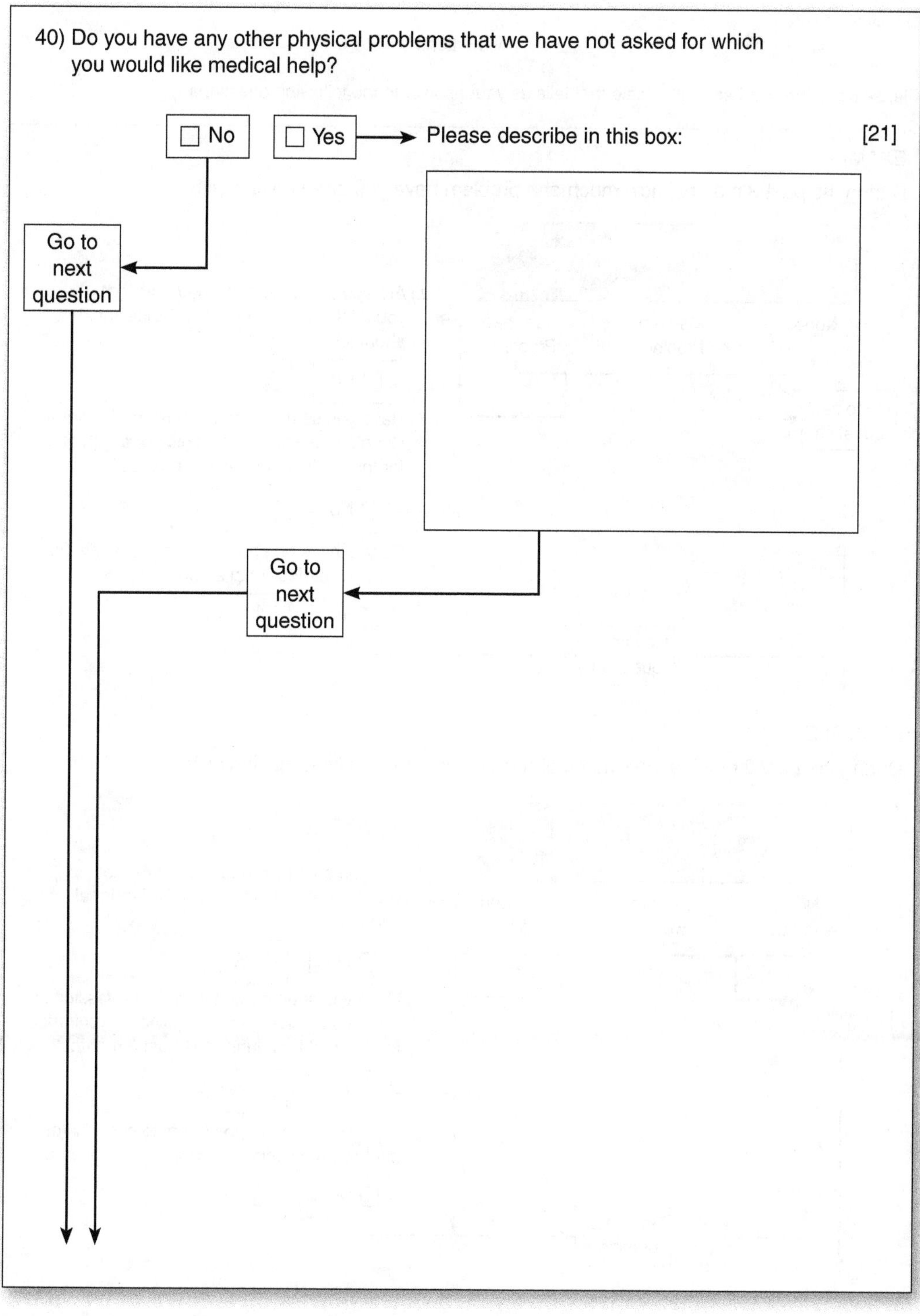
40) Do you have any other physical problems that we have not asked for which you would like medical help?

☐ No ☐ Yes → Please describe in this box: [21]

Go to next question

Go to next question

Questions 41–51

Instructions

Please circle the number on the scale that tells us your answer to the following questions.

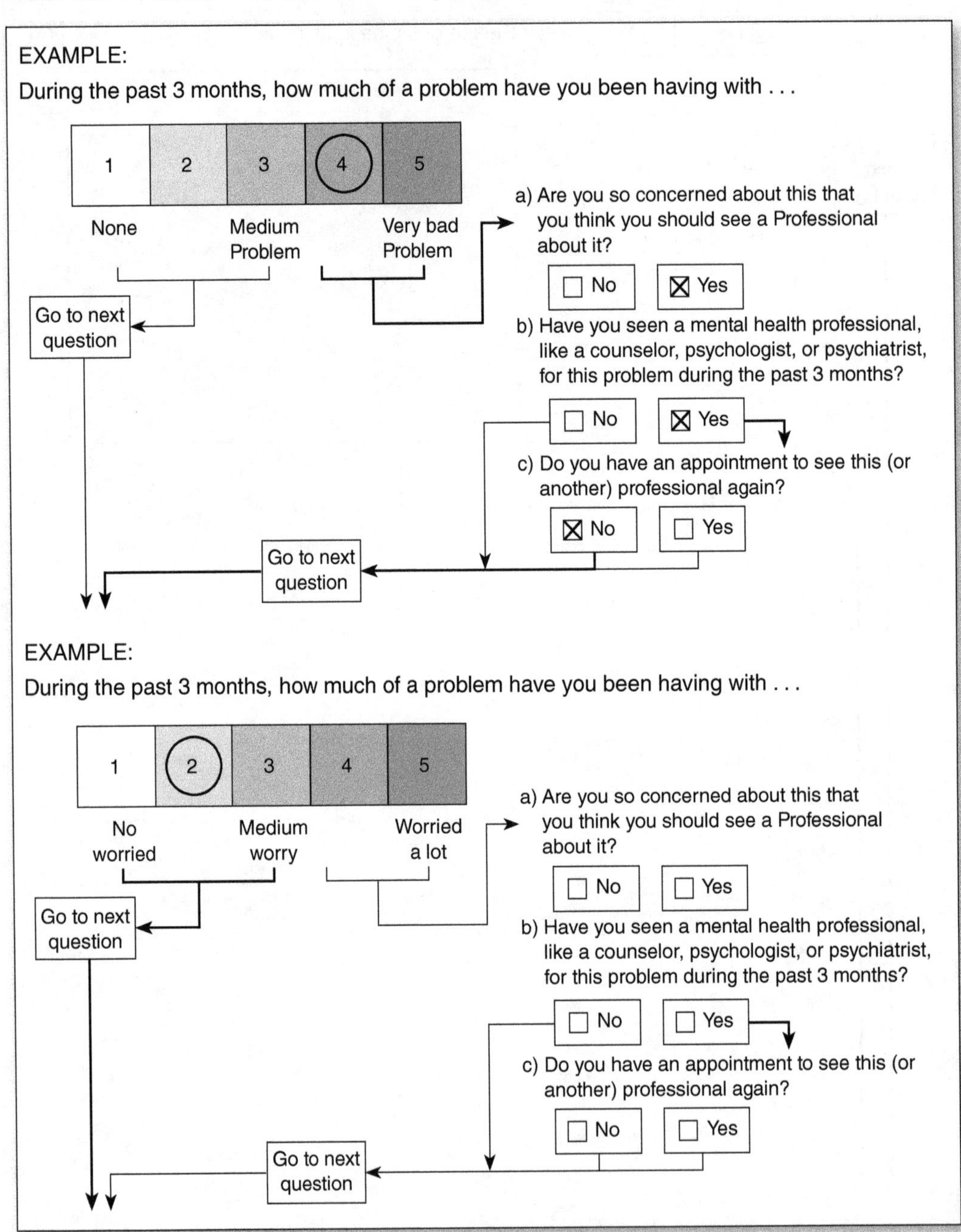

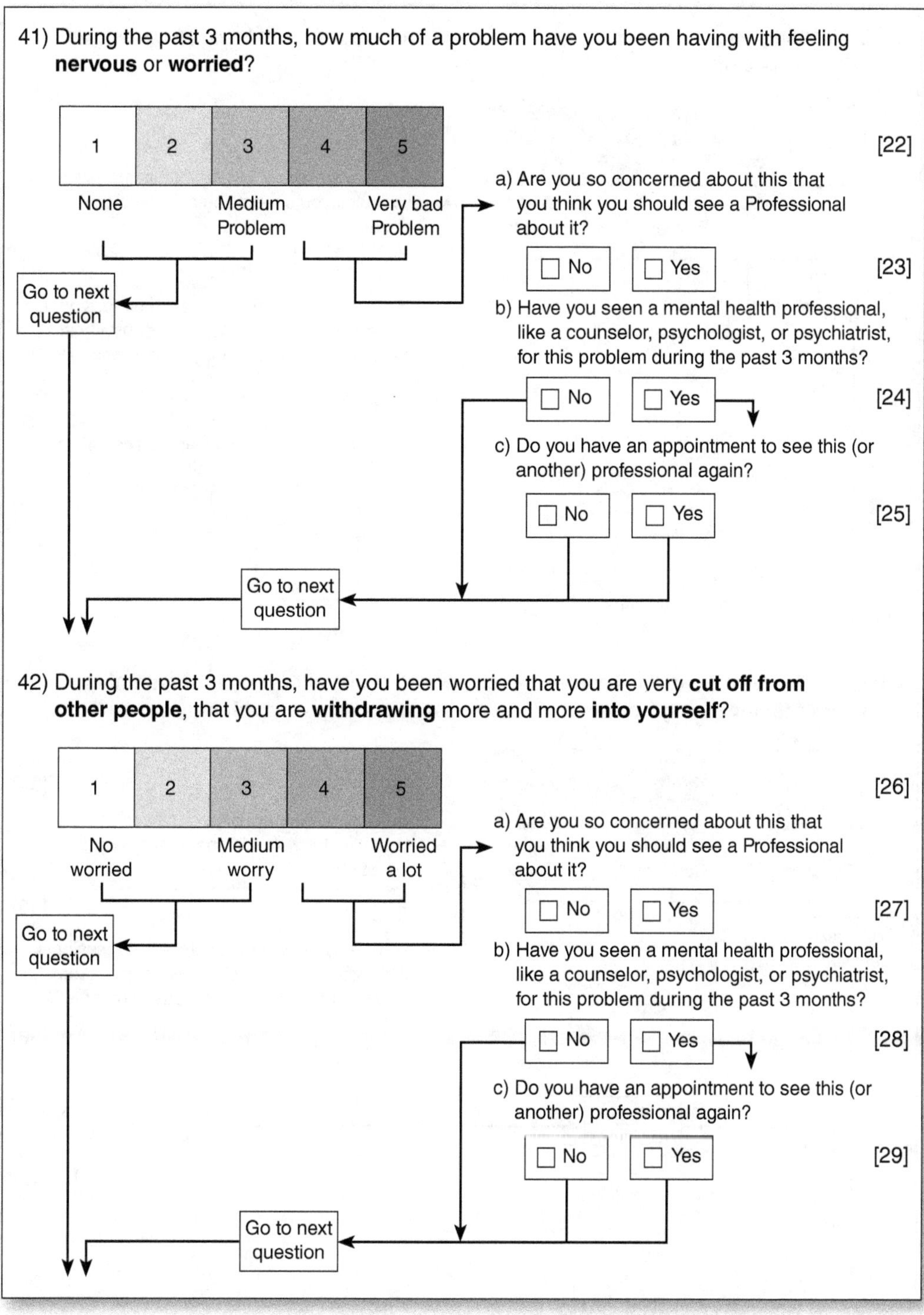

41) During the past 3 months, how much of a problem have you been having with feeling **nervous** or **worried**?

1	2	3	4	5
None		Medium Problem		Very bad Problem

[22]

1–3: Go to next question

4–5: a) Are you so concerned about this that you think you should see a Professional about it?

☐ No ☐ Yes [23]

b) Have you seen a mental health professional, like a counselor, psychologist, or psychiatrist, for this problem during the past 3 months?

☐ No ☐ Yes [24]

No: Go to next question

Yes: c) Do you have an appointment to see this (or another) professional again?

☐ No ☐ Yes [25]

Go to next question

42) During the past 3 months, have you been worried that you are very **cut off from other people**, that you are **withdrawing** more and more **into yourself**?

1	2	3	4	5
No worried		Medium worry		Worried a lot

[26]

1–3: Go to next question

4–5: a) Are you so concerned about this that you think you should see a Professional about it?

☐ No ☐ Yes [27]

b) Have you seen a mental health professional, like a counselor, psychologist, or psychiatrist, for this problem during the past 3 months?

☐ No ☐ Yes [28]

No: Go to next question

Yes: c) Do you have an appointment to see this (or another) professional again?

☐ No ☐ Yes [29]

Go to next question

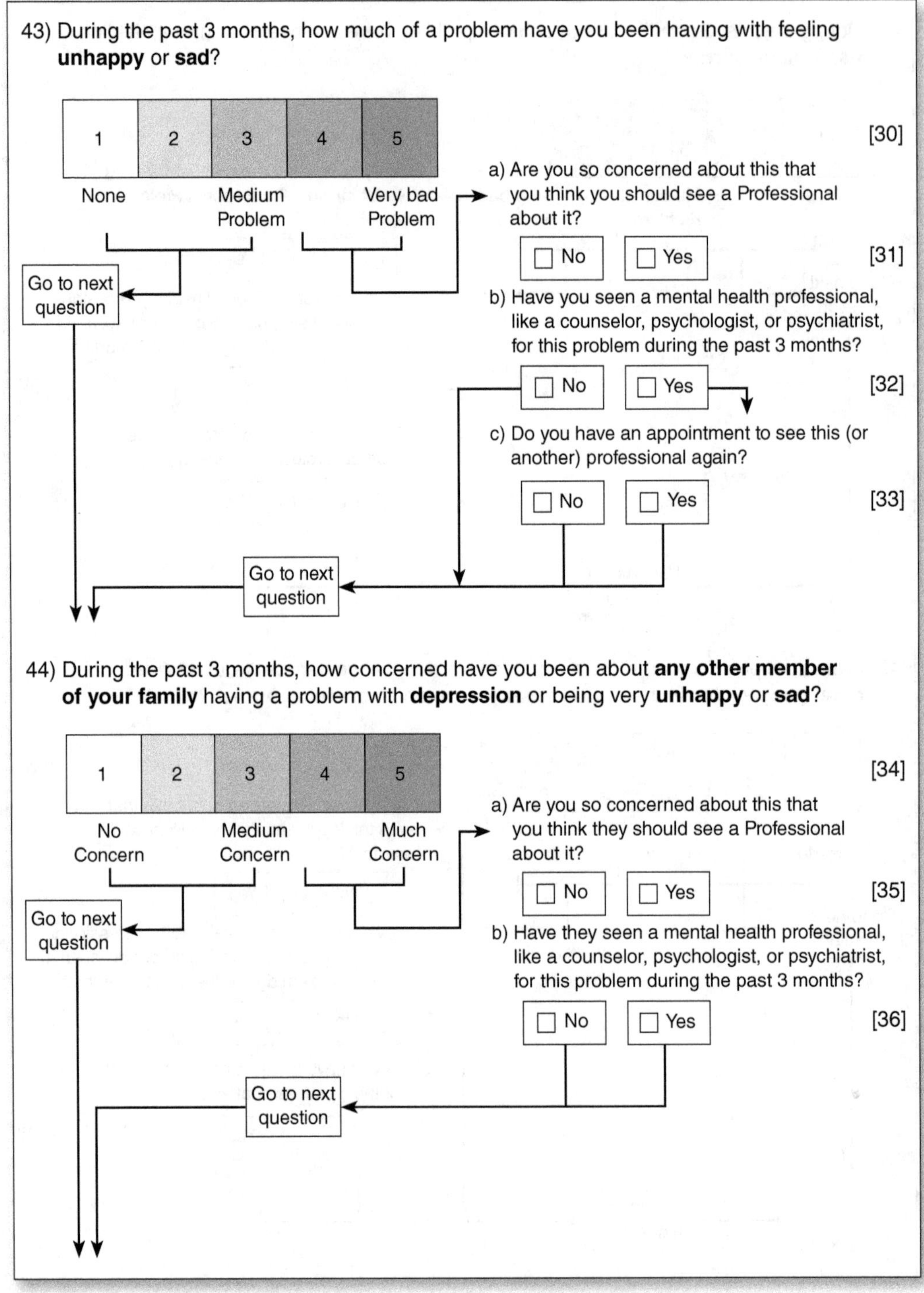

43) During the past 3 months, how much of a problem have you been having with feeling **unhappy** or **sad**?

44) During the past 3 months, how concerned have you been about **any other member of your family** having a problem with **depression** or being very **unhappy** or **sad**?

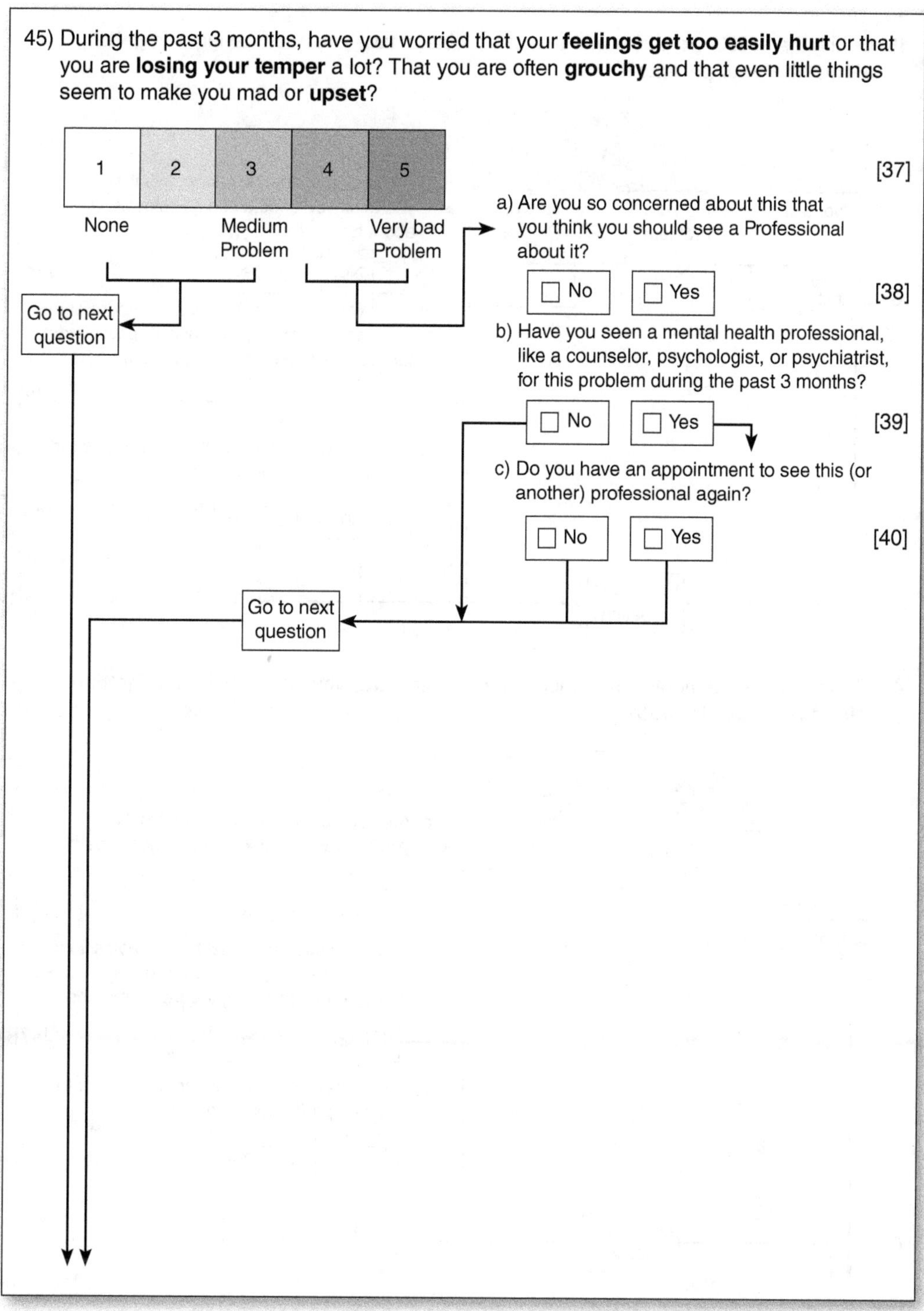

45) During the past 3 months, have you worried that your **feelings get too easily hurt** or that you are **losing your temper** a lot? That you are often **grouchy** and that even little things seem to make you mad or **upset**?

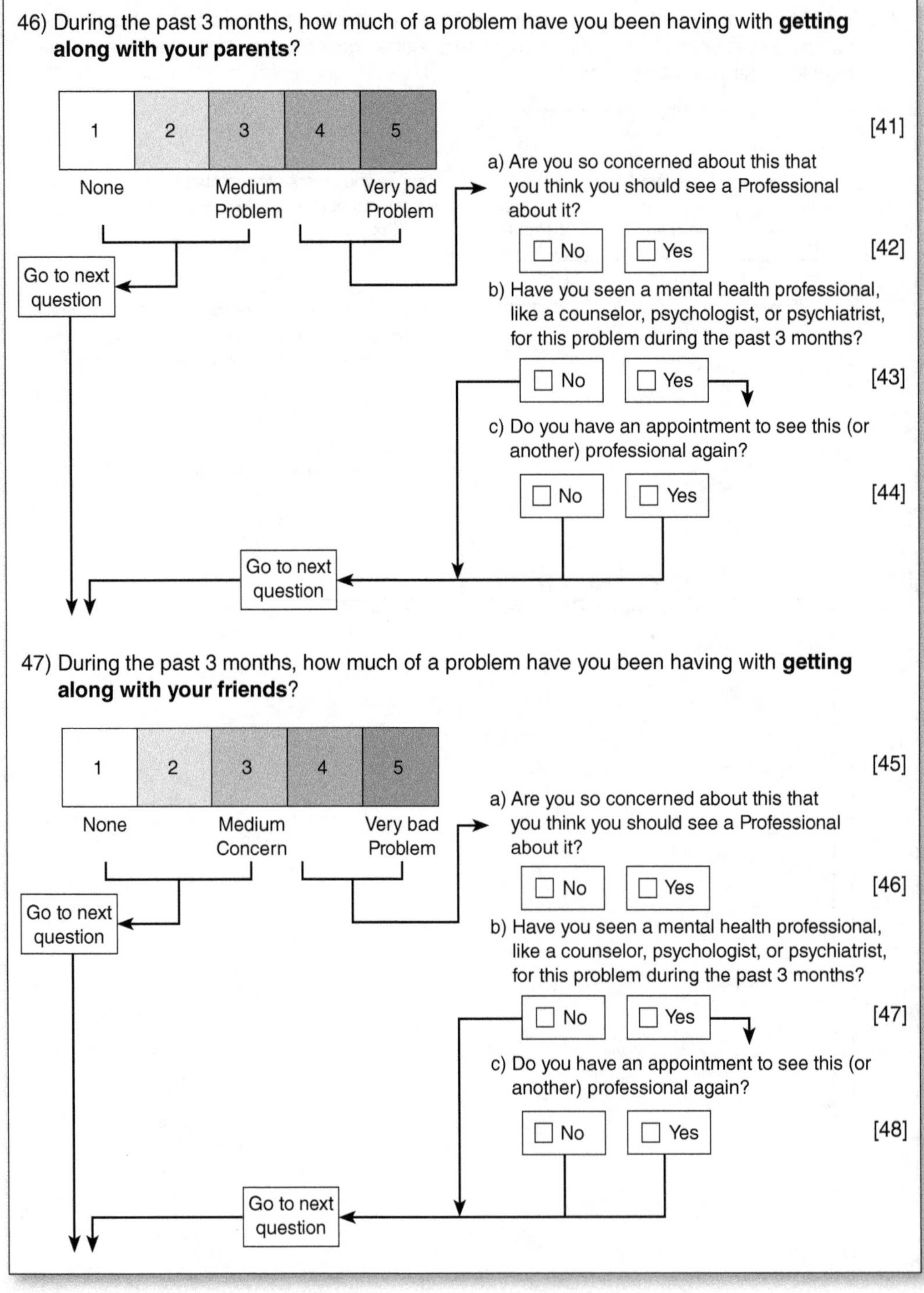
46) During the past 3 months, how much of a problem have you been having with **getting along with your parents**?

1	2	3	4	5
None		Medium Problem		Very bad Problem

[41]

None–Medium Problem: Go to next question

a) Are you so concerned about this that you think you should see a Professional about it?

☐ No ☐ Yes [42]

b) Have you seen a mental health professional, like a counselor, psychologist, or psychiatrist, for this problem during the past 3 months?

☐ No ☐ Yes [43]

c) Do you have an appointment to see this (or another) professional again?

☐ No ☐ Yes [44]

Go to next question

47) During the past 3 months, how much of a problem have you been having with **getting along with your friends**?

1	2	3	4	5
None		Medium Concern		Very bad Problem

[45]

None–Medium Concern: Go to next question

a) Are you so concerned about this that you think you should see a Professional about it?

☐ No ☐ Yes [46]

b) Have you seen a mental health professional, like a counselor, psychologist, or psychiatrist, for this problem during the past 3 months?

☐ No ☐ Yes [47]

c) Do you have an appointment to see this (or another) professional again?

☐ No ☐ Yes [48]

Go to next question

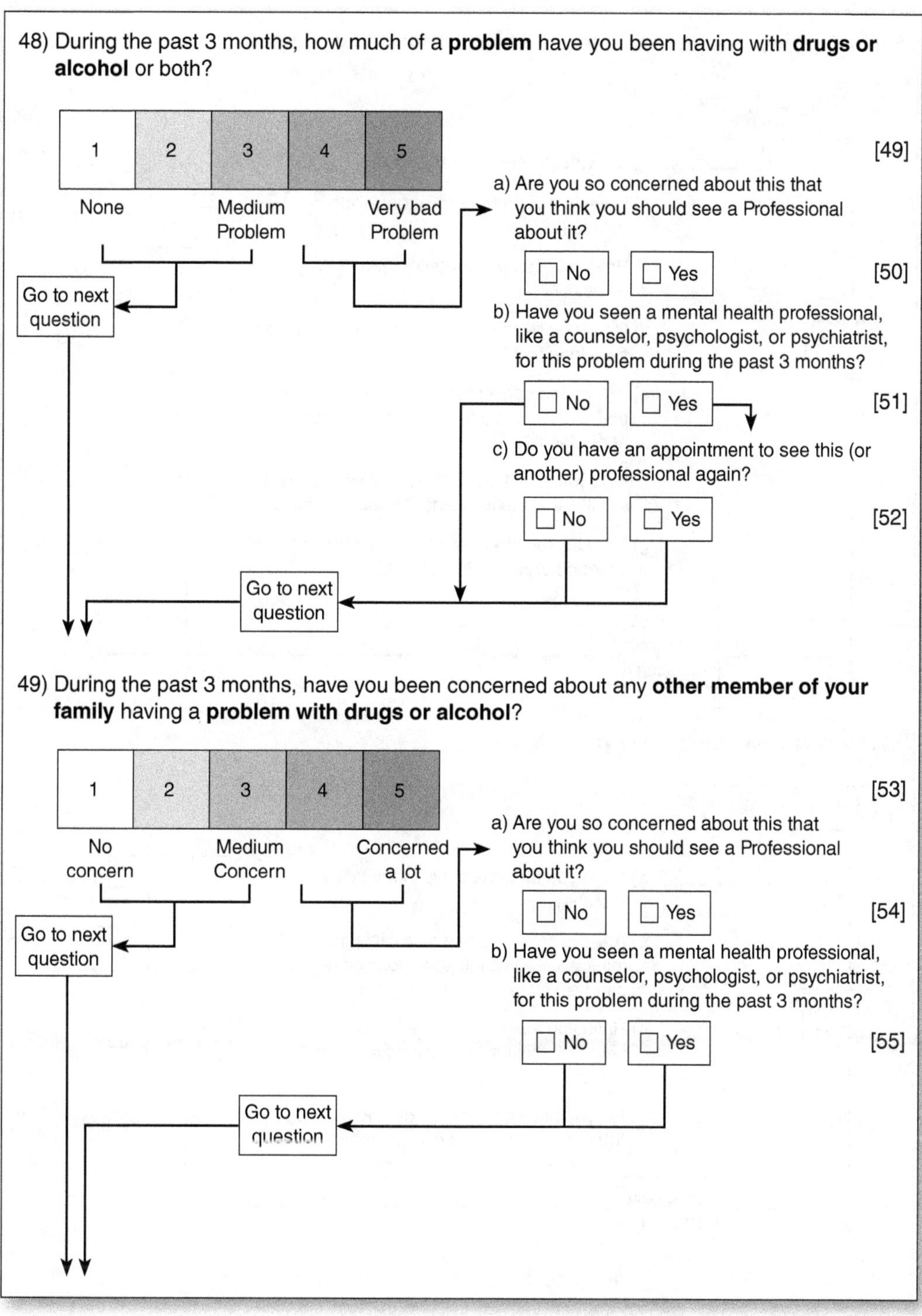

48) During the past 3 months, how much of a **problem** have you been having with **drugs or alcohol** or both?

1	2	3	4	5

None — Medium Problem — Very bad Problem [49]

None / Medium Problem → Go to next question

Very bad Problem →

a) Are you so concerned about this that you think you should see a Professional about it?

☐ No ☐ Yes [50]

b) Have you seen a mental health professional, like a counselor, psychologist, or psychiatrist, for this problem during the past 3 months?

☐ No ☐ Yes [51]

No → Go to next question

Yes →

c) Do you have an appointment to see this (or another) professional again?

☐ No ☐ Yes [52]

→ Go to next question

49) During the past 3 months, have you been concerned about any **other member of your family** having a **problem with drugs or alcohol**?

1	2	3	4	5

No concern — Medium Concern — Concerned a lot [53]

No concern / Medium Concern → Go to next question

Concerned a lot →

a) Are you so concerned about this that you think you should see a Professional about it?

☐ No ☐ Yes [54]

b) Have you seen a mental health professional, like a counselor, psychologist, or psychiatrist, for this problem during the past 3 months?

☐ No ☐ Yes [55]

→ Go to next question

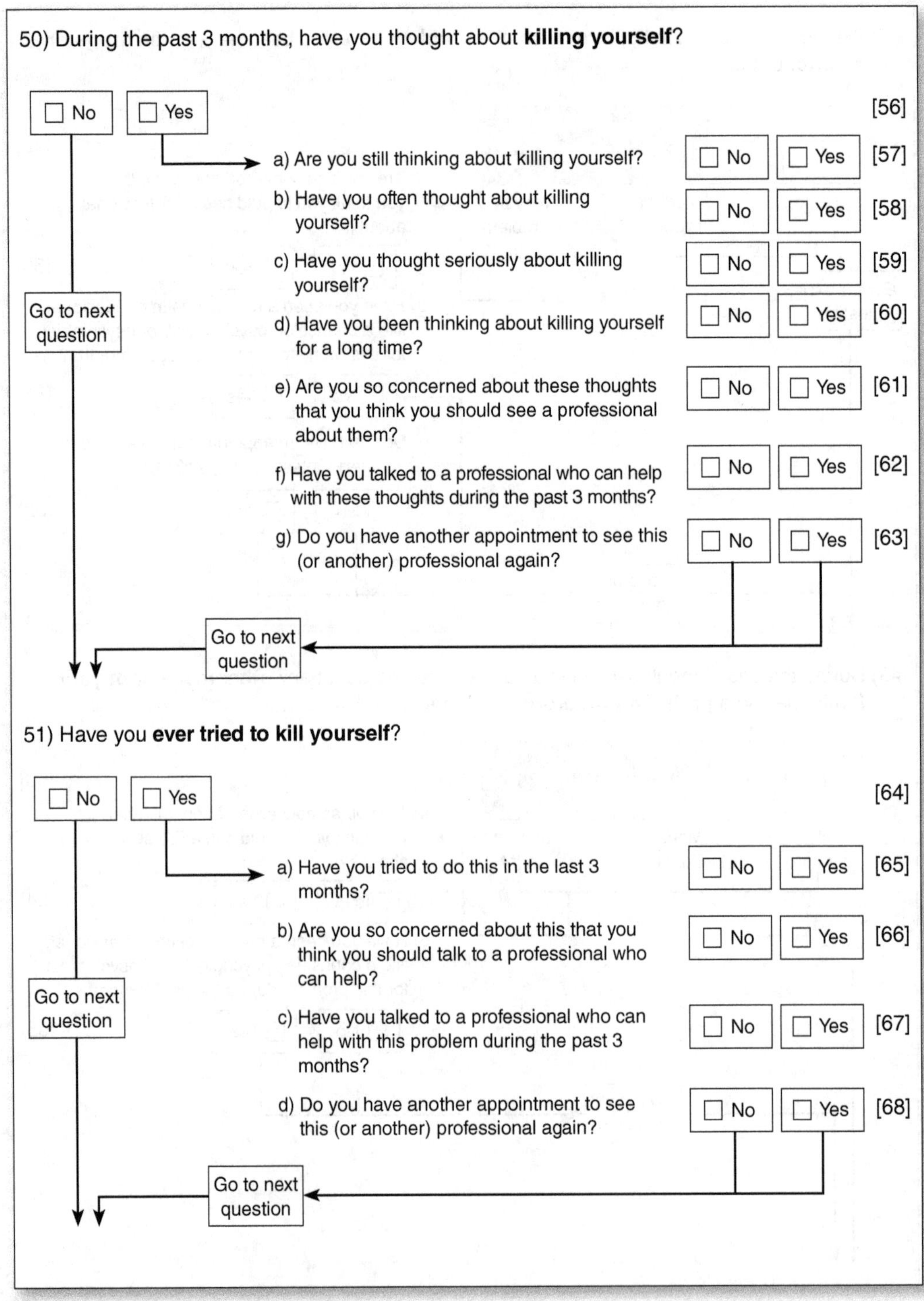

50) During the past 3 months, have you thought about **killing yourself**?

☐ No ☐ Yes [56]

a) Are you still thinking about killing yourself? ☐ No ☐ Yes [57]

b) Have you often thought about killing yourself? ☐ No ☐ Yes [58]

c) Have you thought seriously about killing yourself? ☐ No ☐ Yes [59]

d) Have you been thinking about killing yourself for a long time? ☐ No ☐ Yes [60]

e) Are you so concerned about these thoughts that you think you should see a professional about them? ☐ No ☐ Yes [61]

f) Have you talked to a professional who can help with these thoughts during the past 3 months? ☐ No ☐ Yes [62]

g) Do you have another appointment to see this (or another) professional again? ☐ No ☐ Yes [63]

Go to next question

Go to next question

51) Have you **ever tried to kill yourself**?

☐ No ☐ Yes [64]

a) Have you tried to do this in the last 3 months? ☐ No ☐ Yes [65]

b) Are you so concerned about this that you think you should talk to a professional who can help? ☐ No ☐ Yes [66]

c) Have you talked to a professional who can help with this problem during the past 3 months? ☐ No ☐ Yes [67]

d) Do you have another appointment to see this (or another) professional again? ☐ No ☐ Yes [68]

Go to next question

Go to next question

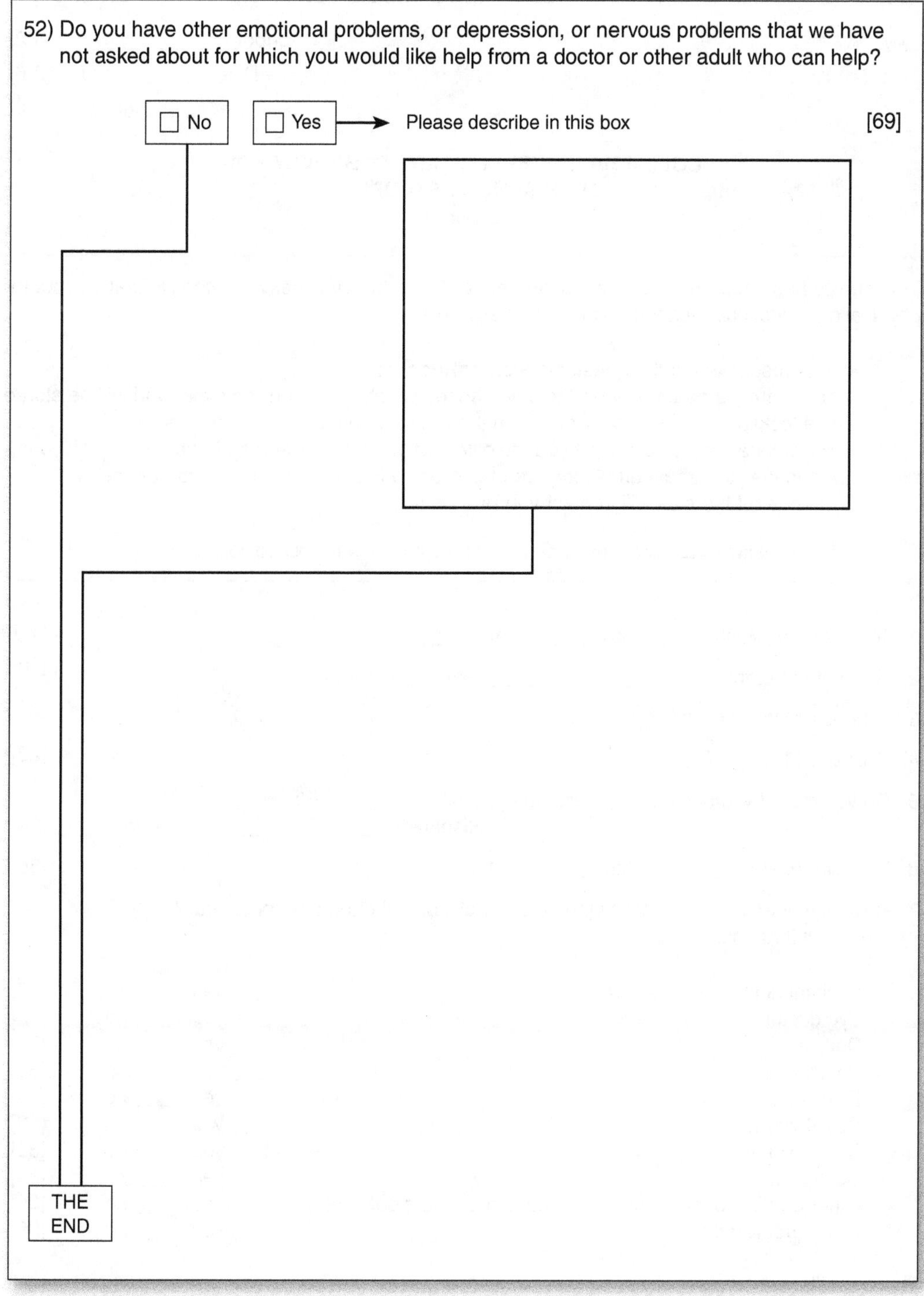

52) Do you have other emotional problems, or depression, or nervous problems that we have not asked about for which you would like help from a doctor or other adult who can help?

☐ No ☐ Yes → Please describe in this box [69]

THE END

School #: __________ [1-2]
I.D. #: __________ [3-6]
Card #: __________ [7-8]

COLUMBIA UNIVERSITY HEALTH SURVEY FOR HIGH SCHOOL STUDENTS (males)

This survey has been designed by researchers at Columbia University in Order to learn about the physical and emotional health of high school students.

- Your responses to the questions are **confidential**.
- Your name appears only on the cover sheet, which has been removed, and will be stored in a locked file cabinet separate from the questionnaire.
- You will be contacted **only** if you indicate that you would like help in any area, or if your responses to certain questions are of interest to the project staff, In either case, a member of the staff will contact you **privately**.

PLASE **ANSWER ALL QUESTIONS**, EVEN IF YOU FEEL THEY DON'T APPLY TO YOU.

1. Today's date: Month _____ Day _____ Year _____ [9-14]
2. Your date of birth: Month _____ Day _____ Year _____ [15-20]
3. Your age at last birthday: _____ [21-22]
4. Your sex: M _____ F _____ [23]
5. Do you regard yourself as . . . (check one) White _____ Black _____ Hispanic _____ Asian _____ Other _____ [24]
6. Your grade: 9th _____ 10th _____ 11th _____ 12th _____ [25-26]
7. Have you seen any of the following health professional during the past year? (check all that apply)

Pediatrician/Family physician	___ yes	___ no	[27]
Eye doctor	___ yes	___ no	[28]
Dentist	___ yes	___ no	[29]
Phychiatrist	___ yes	___ no	[30]
Phychologist	___ yes	___ no	[31]
Social worker	___ yes	___ no	[32]
Social worker	___ yes	___ no	[33]
Counselor	___ yes	___ no	[34]
Other medical doctor (such as orthopedist, neurologist, etc)	___ yes	___ no	[35]
Other (not listed above)	___ yes	___ no	[36]

Instruction

Place a mark in the box next to your answer to the question. Then follow the arrow from that box to find the next question you are to answer.

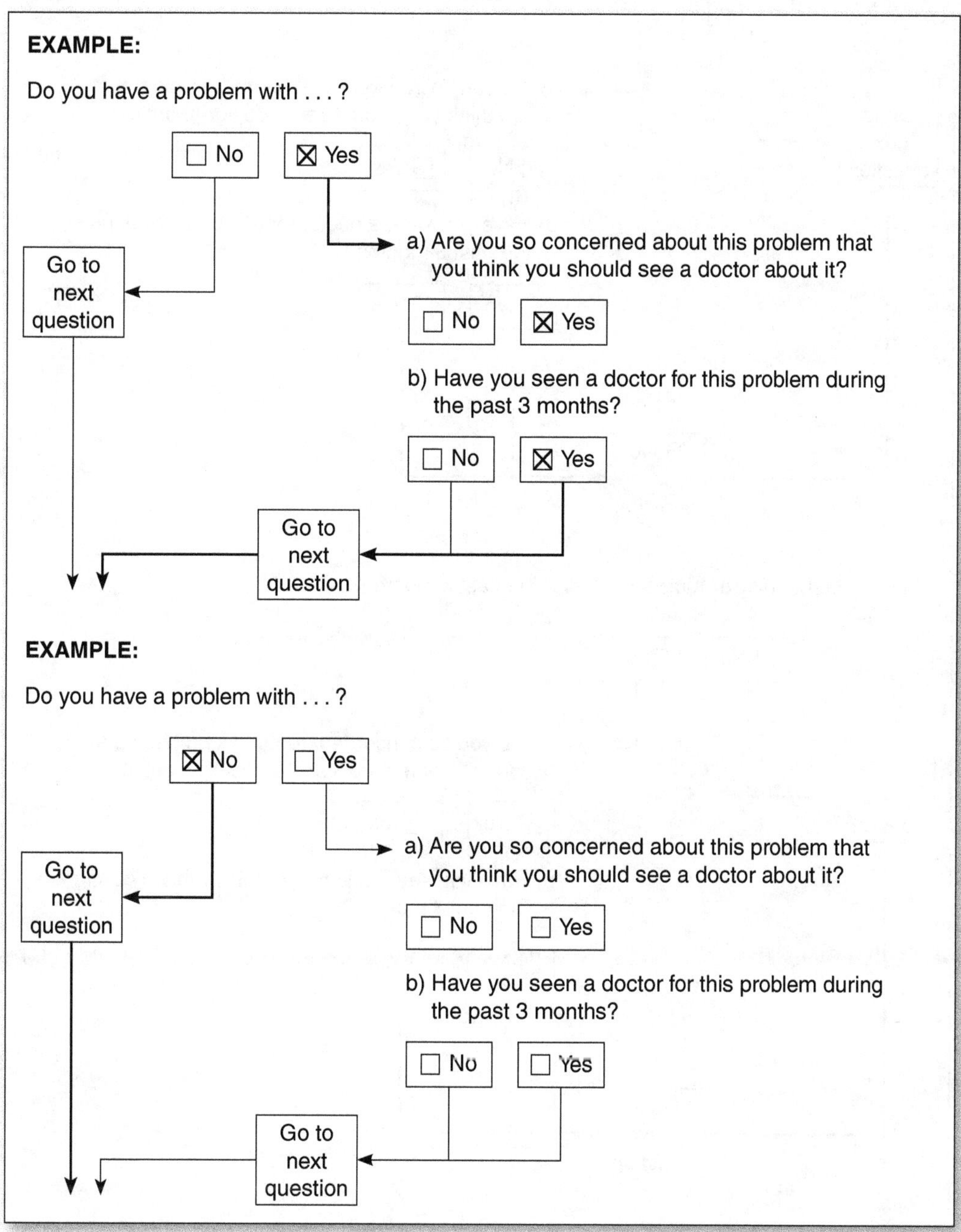

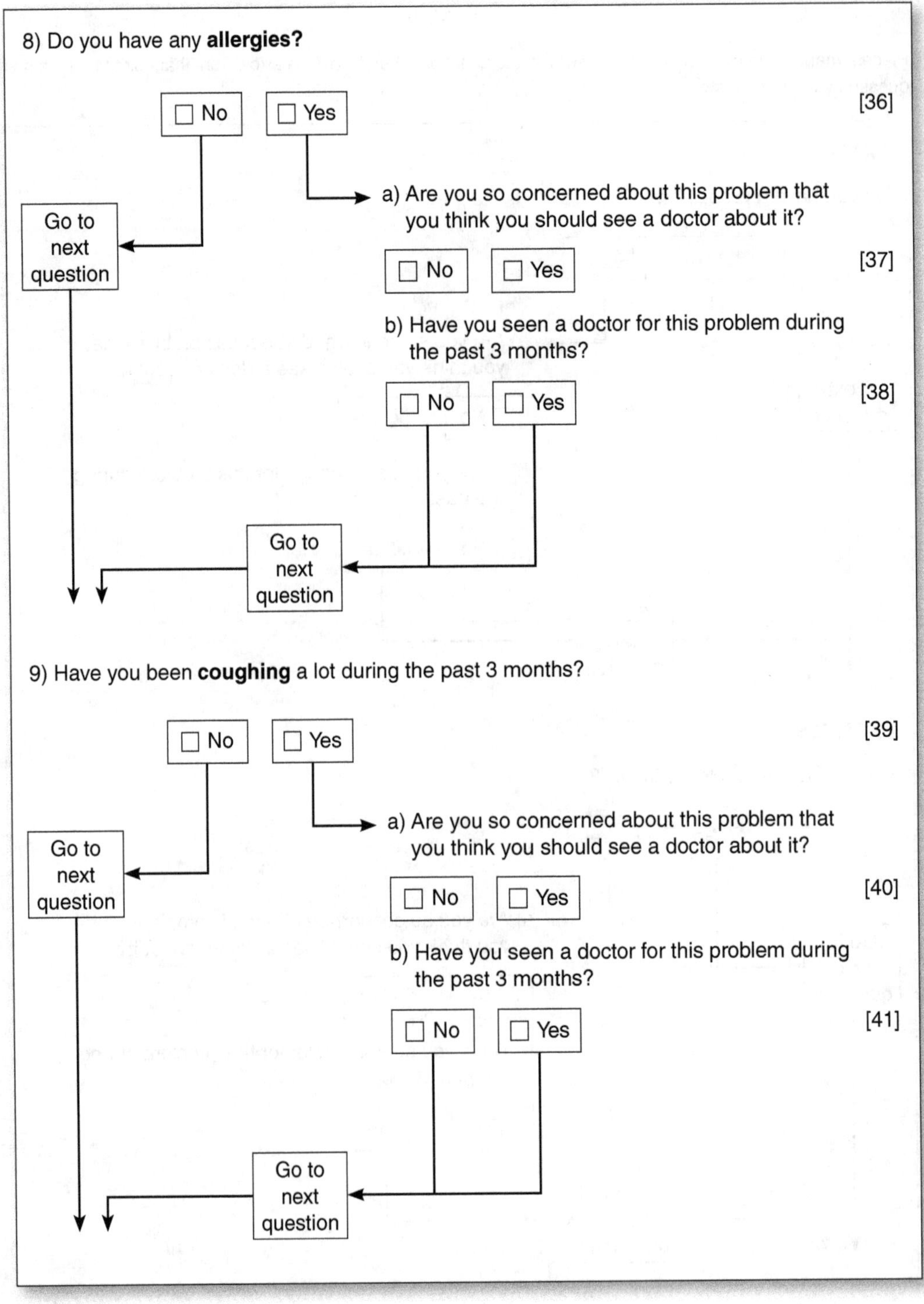
8) Do you have any **allergies?**

☐ No ☐ Yes [36]

No → Go to next question

Yes → a) Are you so concerned about this problem that you think you should see a doctor about it?

☐ No ☐ Yes [37]

b) Have you seen a doctor for this problem during the past 3 months?

☐ No ☐ Yes [38]

No / Yes → Go to next question

9) Have you been **coughing** a lot during the past 3 months?

☐ No ☐ Yes [39]

No → Go to next question

Yes → a) Are you so concerned about this problem that you think you should see a doctor about it?

☐ No ☐ Yes [40]

b) Have you seen a doctor for this problem during the past 3 months?

☐ No ☐ Yes [41]

No / Yes → Go to next question

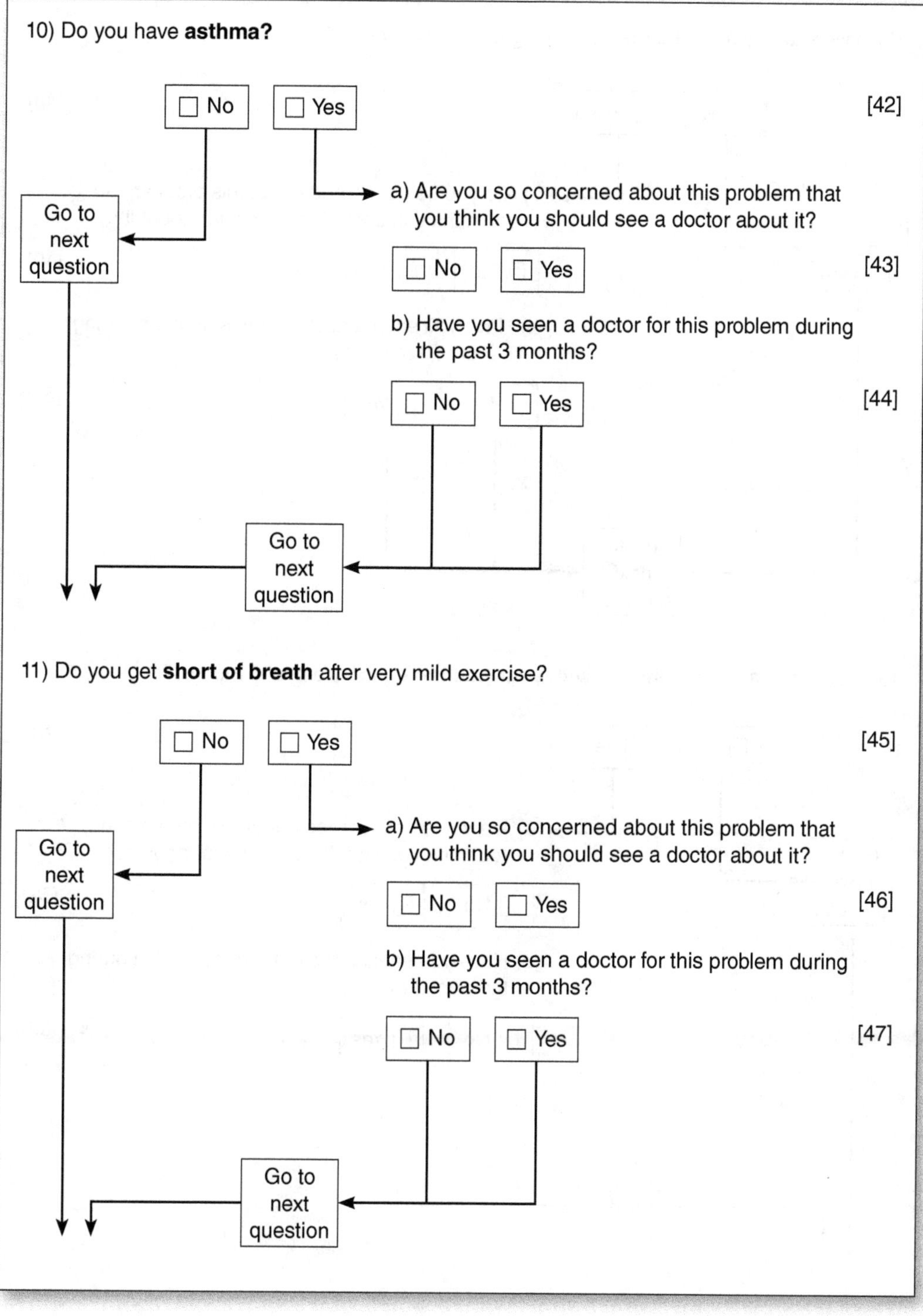
10) Do you have **asthma?**

☐ No ☐ Yes [42]

Go to next question

a) Are you so concerned about this problem that you think you should see a doctor about it?

☐ No ☐ Yes [43]

b) Have you seen a doctor for this problem during the past 3 months?

☐ No ☐ Yes [44]

Go to next question

11) Do you get **short of breath** after very mild exercise?

☐ No ☐ Yes [45]

Go to next question

a) Are you so concerned about this problem that you think you should see a doctor about it?

☐ No ☐ Yes [46]

b) Have you seen a doctor for this problem during the past 3 months?

☐ No ☐ Yes [47]

Go to next question

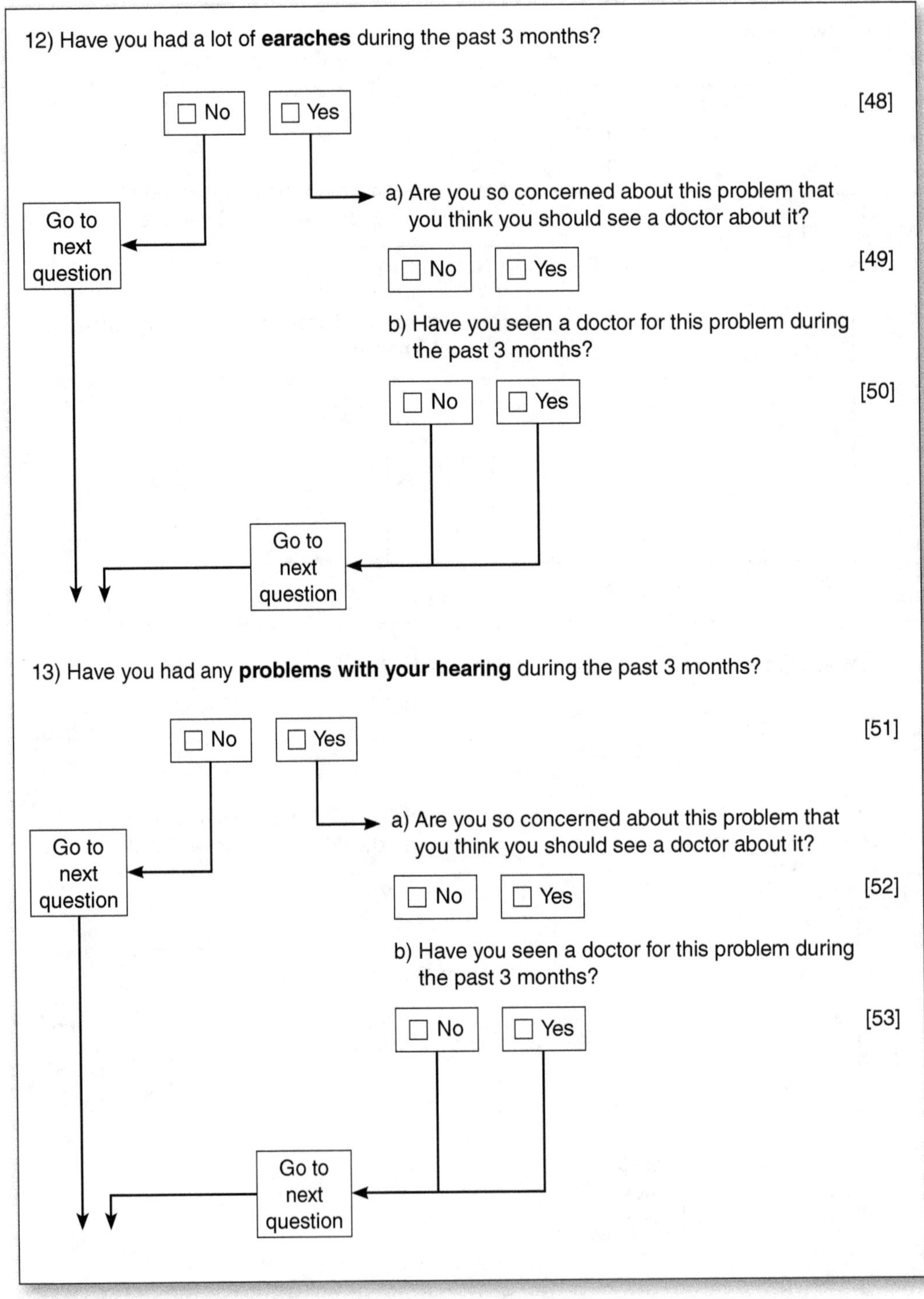
12) Have you had a lot of **earaches** during the past 3 months?
☐ No
☐ Yes
[48]
Go to next question
a) Are you so concerned about this problem that you think you should see a doctor about it?
☐ No
☐ Yes
[49]
b) Have you seen a doctor for this problem during the past 3 months?
☐ No
☐ Yes
[50]
Go to next question
13) Have you had any **problems with your hearing** during the past 3 months?
☐ No
☐ Yes
[51]
Go to next question
a) Are you so concerned about this problem that you think you should see a doctor about it?
☐ No
☐ Yes
[52]
b) Have you seen a doctor for this problem during the past 3 months?
☐ No
☐ Yes
[53]
Go to next question

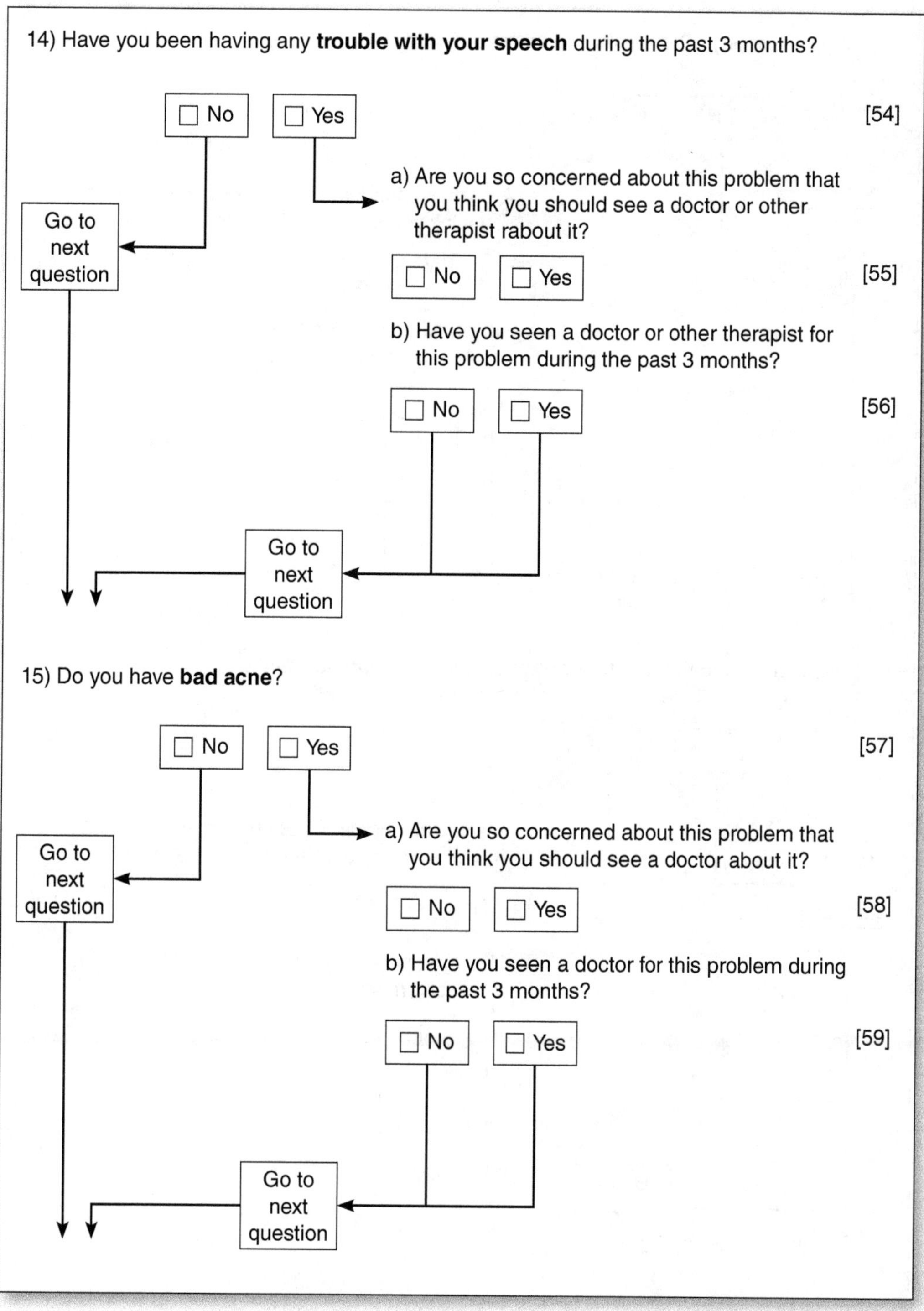

14) Have you been having any **trouble with your speech** during the past 3 months?

☐ No ☐ Yes [54]

No → Go to next question

Yes → a) Are you so concerned about this problem that you think you should see a doctor or other therapist rabout it?

☐ No ☐ Yes [55]

b) Have you seen a doctor or other therapist for this problem during the past 3 months?

☐ No ☐ Yes [56]

Go to next question

15) Do you have **bad acne**?

☐ No ☐ Yes [57]

No → Go to next question

Yes → a) Are you so concerned about this problem that you think you should see a doctor about it?

☐ No ☐ Yes [58]

b) Have you seen a doctor for this problem during the past 3 months?

☐ No ☐ Yes [59]

Go to next question

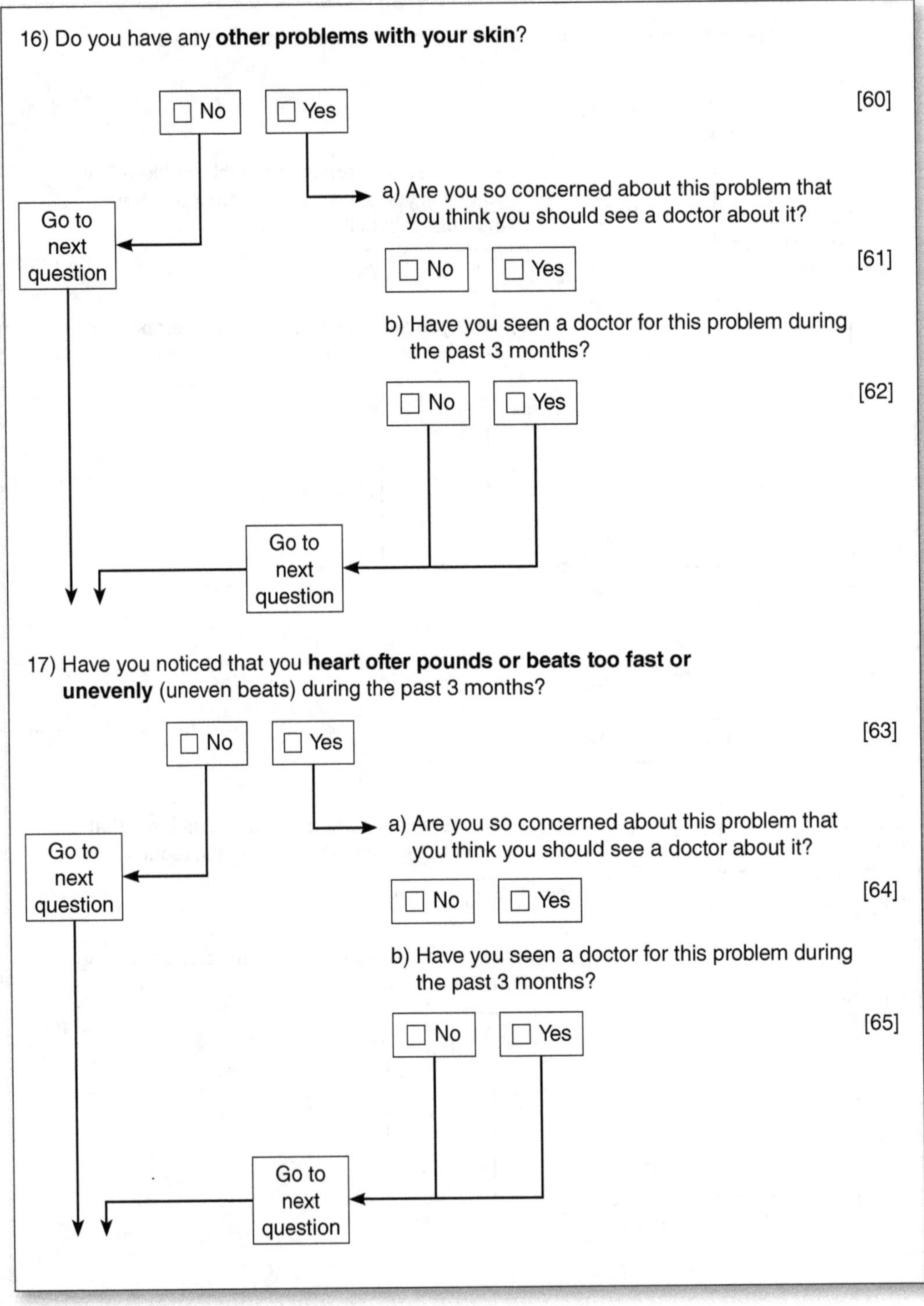
16) Do you have any **other problems with your skin**?

☐ No ☐ Yes [60]

Go to next question

a) Are you so concerned about this problem that you think you should see a doctor about it?

☐ No ☐ Yes [61]

b) Have you seen a doctor for this problem during the past 3 months?

☐ No ☐ Yes [62]

Go to next question

17) Have you noticed that you **heart ofter pounds or beats too fast or unevenly** (uneven beats) during the past 3 months?

☐ No ☐ Yes [63]

Go to next question

a) Are you so concerned about this problem that you think you should see a doctor about it?

☐ No ☐ Yes [64]

b) Have you seen a doctor for this problem during the past 3 months?

☐ No ☐ Yes [65]

Go to next question

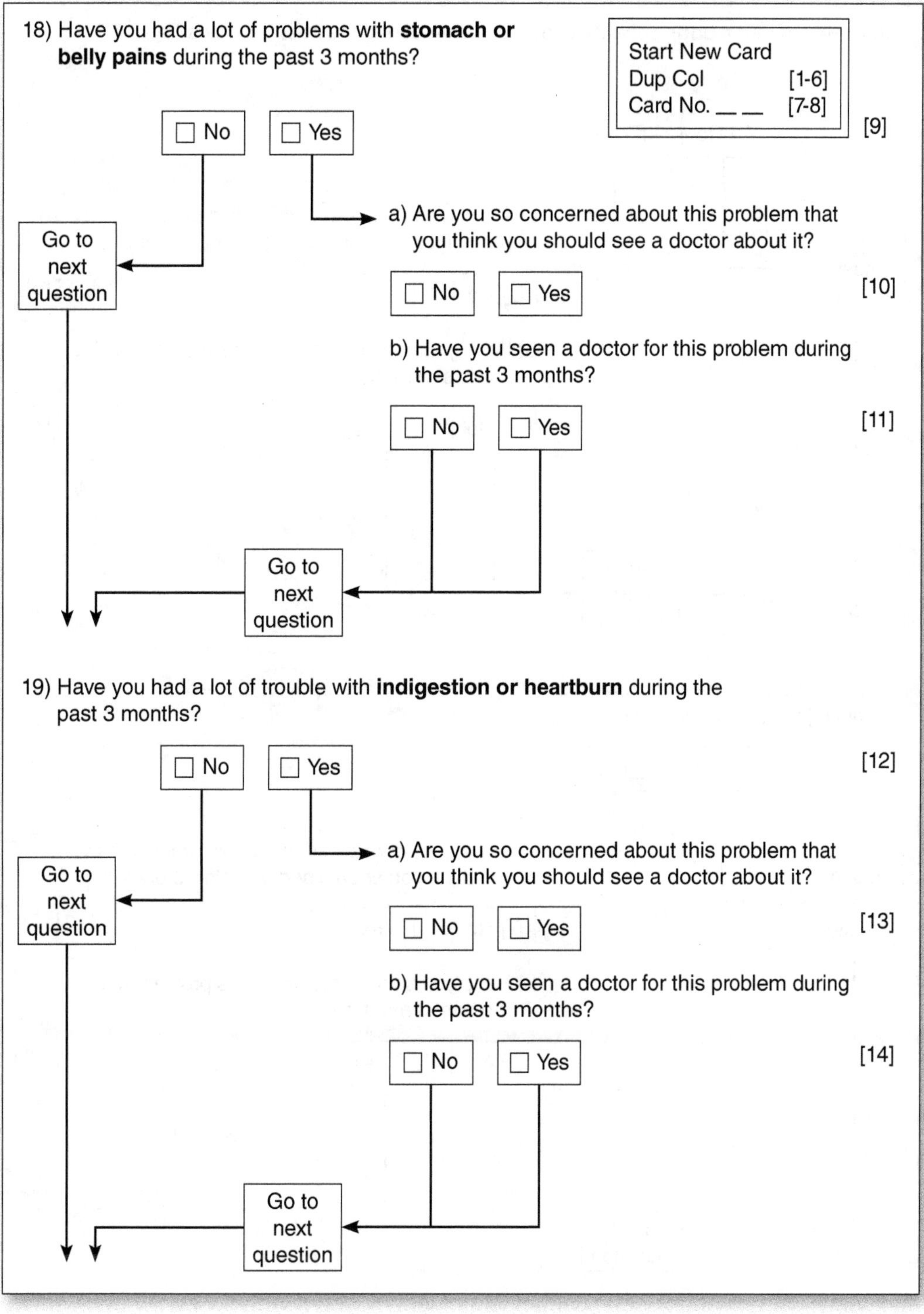
18) Have you had a lot of problems with **stomach or belly pains** during the past 3 months?

Start New Card
Dup Col [1-6]
Card No. __ __ [7-8]

☐ No ☐ Yes [9]

Go to next question

a) Are you so concerned about this problem that you think you should see a doctor about it?

☐ No ☐ Yes [10]

b) Have you seen a doctor for this problem during the past 3 months?

☐ No ☐ Yes [11]

Go to next question

19) Have you had a lot of trouble with **indigestion or heartburn** during the past 3 months?

☐ No ☐ Yes [12]

Go to next question

a) Are you so concerned about this problem that you think you should see a doctor about it?

☐ No ☐ Yes [13]

b) Have you seen a doctor for this problem during the past 3 months?

☐ No ☐ Yes [14]

Go to next question

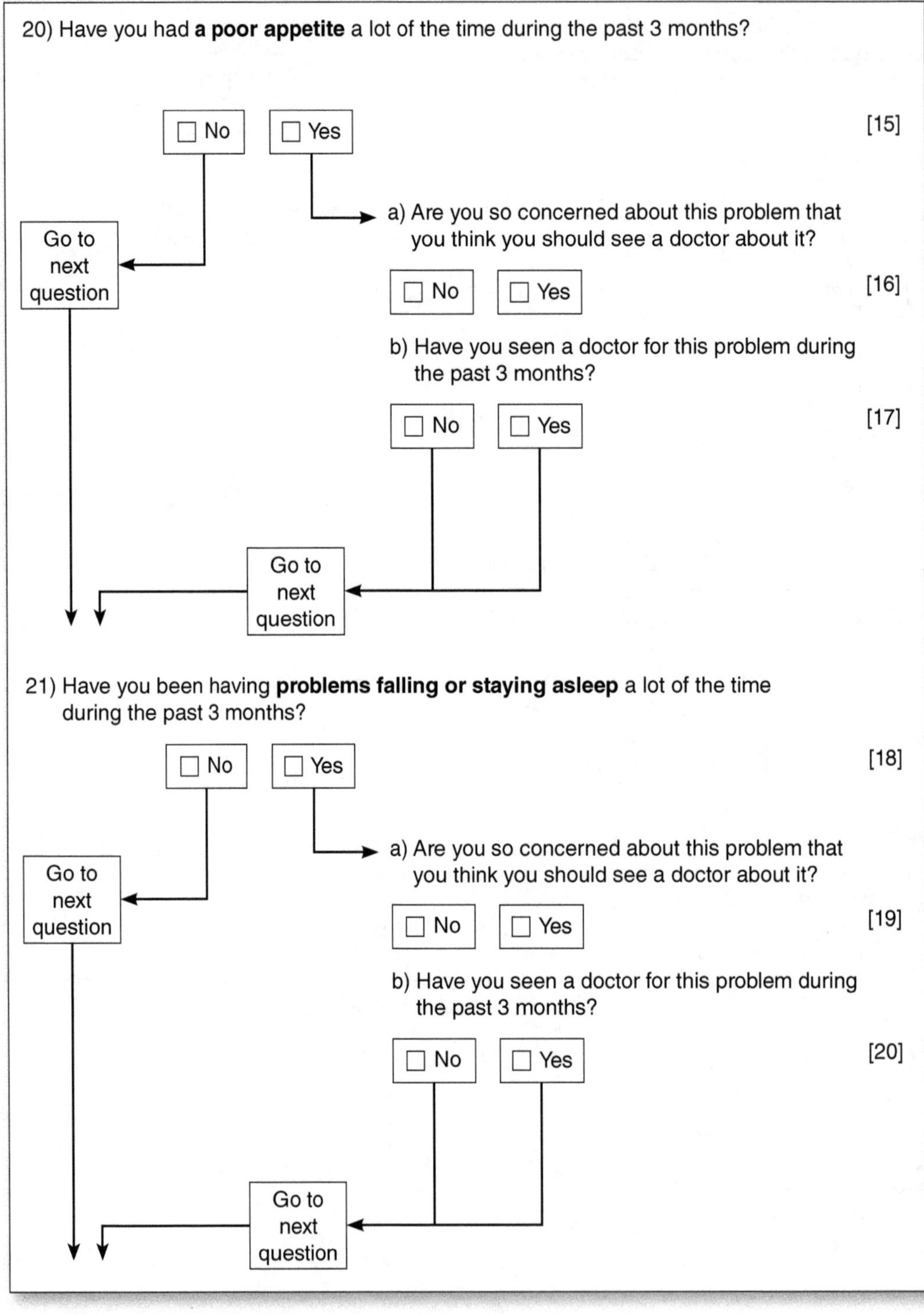

20) Have you had **a poor appetite** a lot of the time during the past 3 months?

☐ No ☐ Yes [15]

No → Go to next question

Yes → a) Are you so concerned about this problem that you think you should see a doctor about it?

☐ No ☐ Yes [16]

b) Have you seen a doctor for this problem during the past 3 months?

☐ No ☐ Yes [17]

No / Yes → Go to next question

21) Have you been having **problems falling or staying asleep** a lot of the time during the past 3 months?

☐ No ☐ Yes [18]

No → Go to next question

Yes → a) Are you so concerned about this problem that you think you should see a doctor about it?

☐ No ☐ Yes [19]

b) Have you seen a doctor for this problem during the past 3 months?

☐ No ☐ Yes [20]

No / Yes → Go to next question

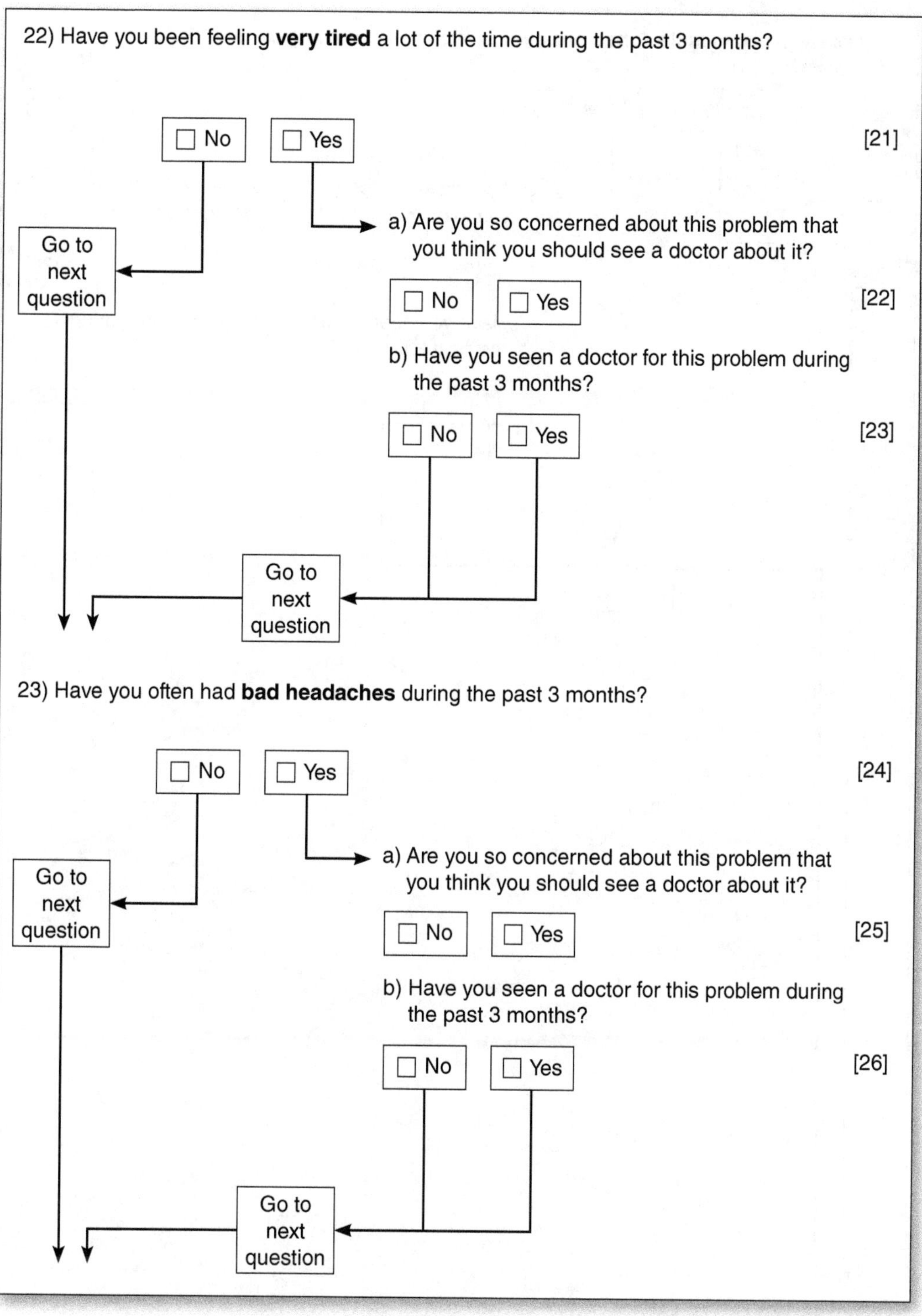
22) Have you been feeling **very tired** a lot of the time during the past 3 months?

☐ No ☐ Yes [21]

Go to next question

a) Are you so concerned about this problem that you think you should see a doctor about it?

☐ No ☐ Yes [22]

b) Have you seen a doctor for this problem during the past 3 months?

☐ No ☐ Yes [23]

Go to next question

23) Have you often had **bad headaches** during the past 3 months?

☐ No ☐ Yes [24]

Go to next question

a) Are you so concerned about this problem that you think you should see a doctor about it?

☐ No ☐ Yes [25]

b) Have you seen a doctor for this problem during the past 3 months?

☐ No ☐ Yes [26]

Go to next question

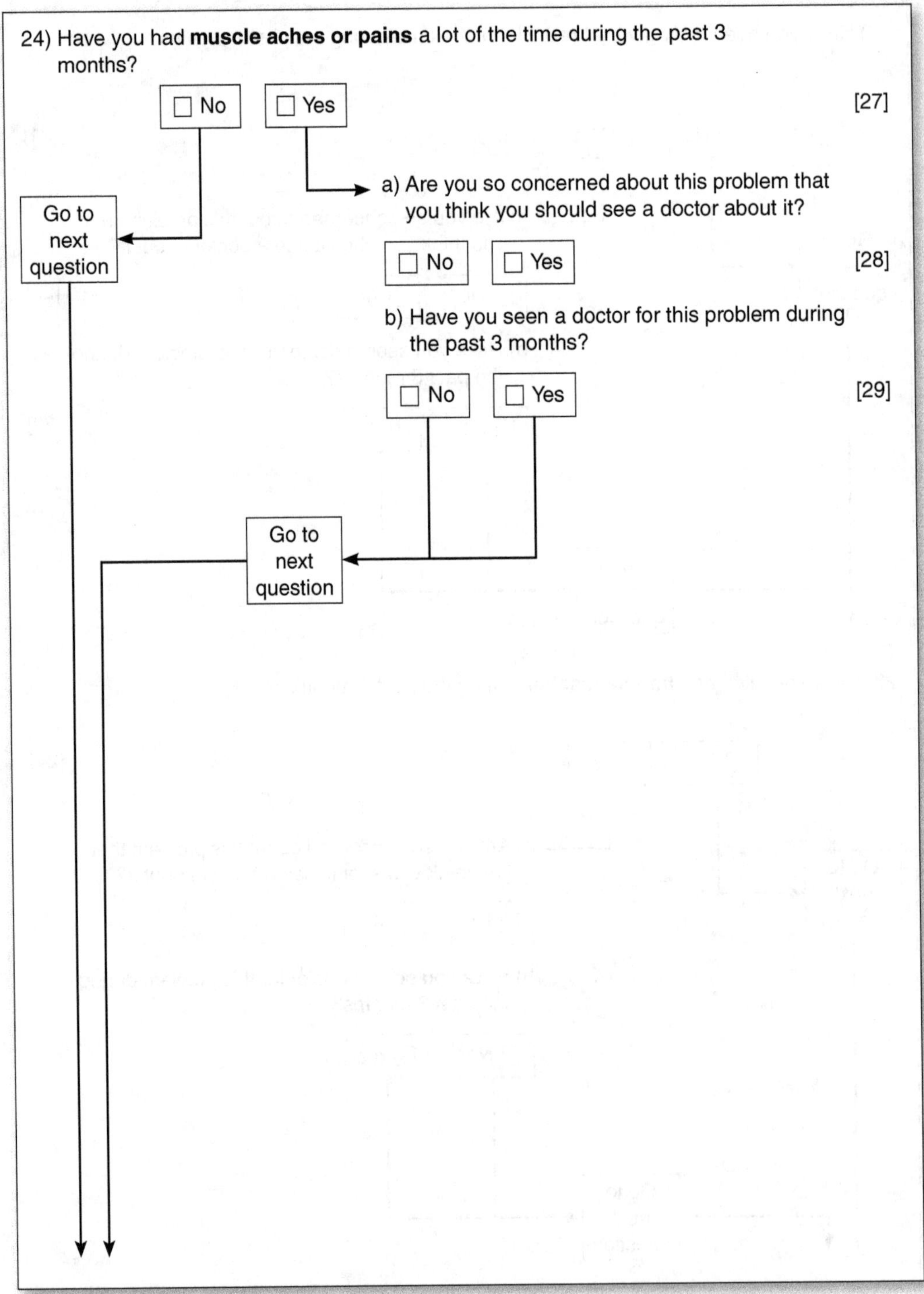

24) Have you had **muscle aches or pains** a lot of the time during the past 3 months?

☐ No ☐ Yes [27]

a) Are you so concerned about this problem that you think you should see a doctor about it?

☐ No ☐ Yes [28]

b) Have you seen a doctor for this problem during the past 3 months?

☐ No ☐ Yes [29]

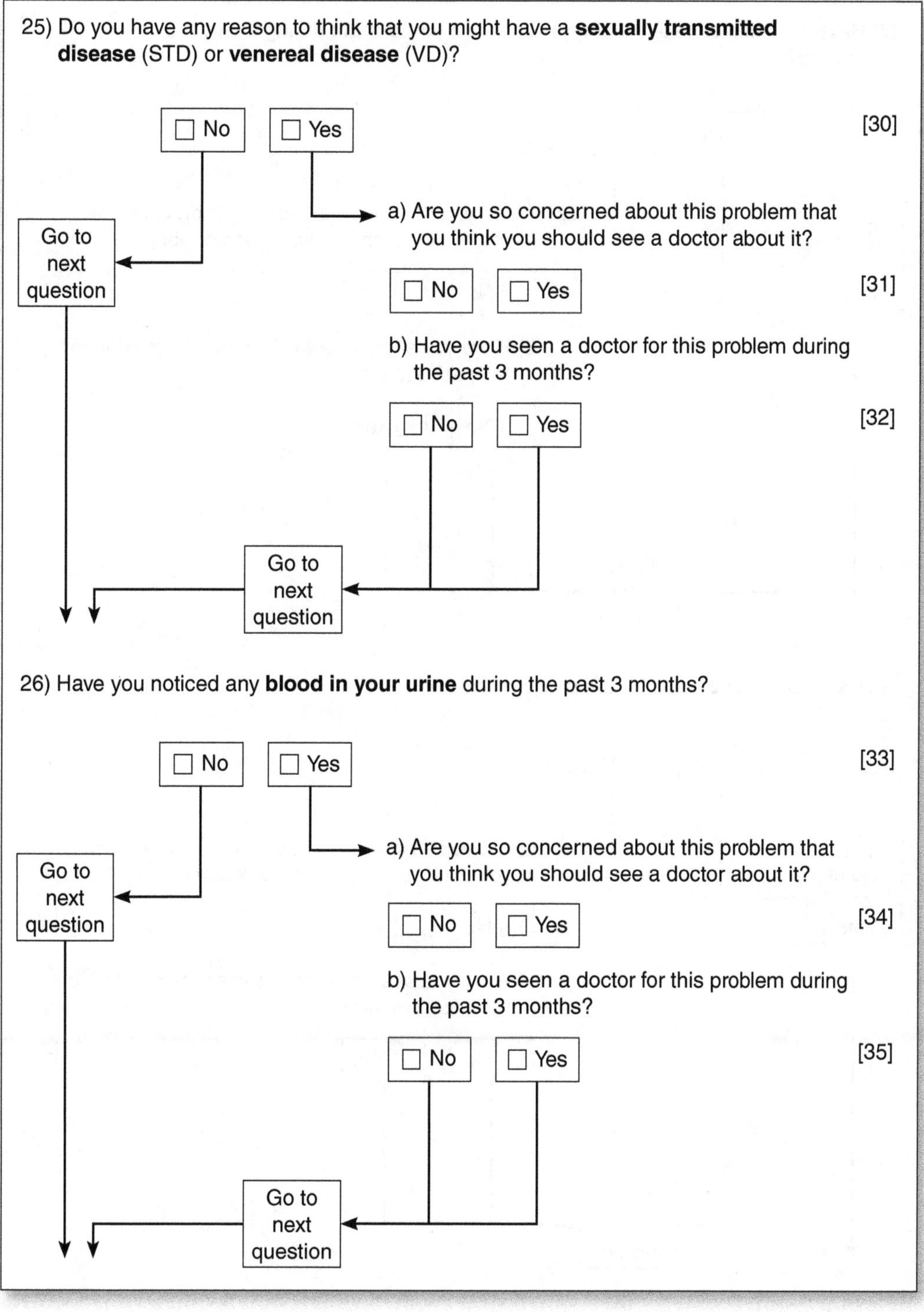

25) Do you have any reason to think that you might have a **sexually transmitted disease** (STD) or **venereal disease** (VD)?

☐ No ☐ Yes [30]

a) Are you so concerned about this problem that you think you should see a doctor about it?

☐ No ☐ Yes [31]

b) Have you seen a doctor for this problem during the past 3 months?

☐ No ☐ Yes [32]

26) Have you noticed any **blood in your urine** during the past 3 months?

☐ No ☐ Yes [33]

a) Are you so concerned about this problem that you think you should see a doctor about it?

☐ No ☐ Yes [34]

b) Have you seen a doctor for this problem during the past 3 months?

☐ No ☐ Yes [35]

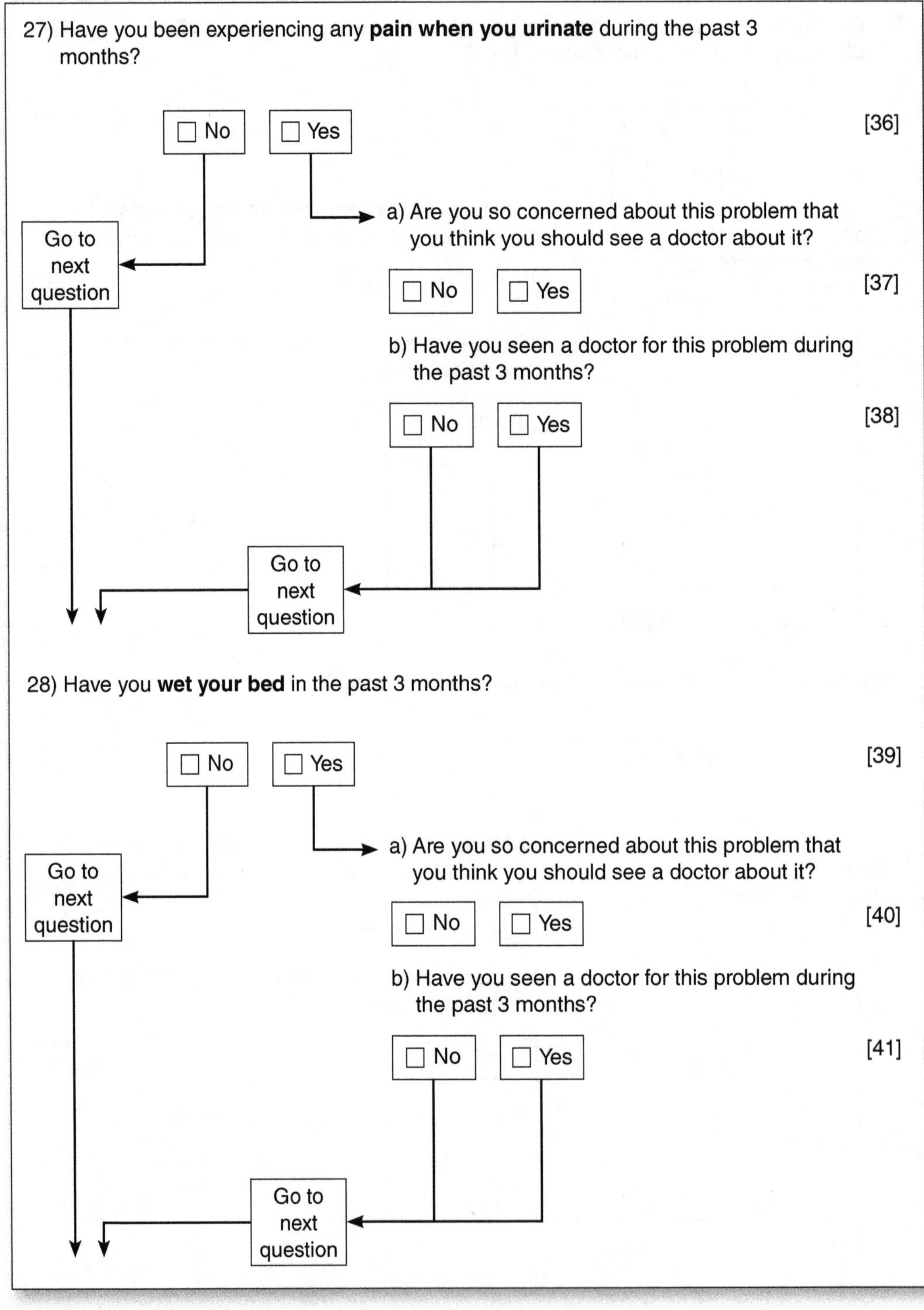

27) Have you been experiencing any **pain when you urinate** during the past 3 months?

☐ No ☐ Yes [36]

Go to next question

a) Are you so concerned about this problem that you think you should see a doctor about it?

☐ No ☐ Yes [37]

b) Have you seen a doctor for this problem during the past 3 months?

☐ No ☐ Yes [38]

Go to next question

28) Have you **wet your bed** in the past 3 months?

☐ No ☐ Yes [39]

Go to next question

a) Are you so concerned about this problem that you think you should see a doctor about it?

☐ No ☐ Yes [40]

b) Have you seen a doctor for this problem during the past 3 months?

☐ No ☐ Yes [41]

Go to next question

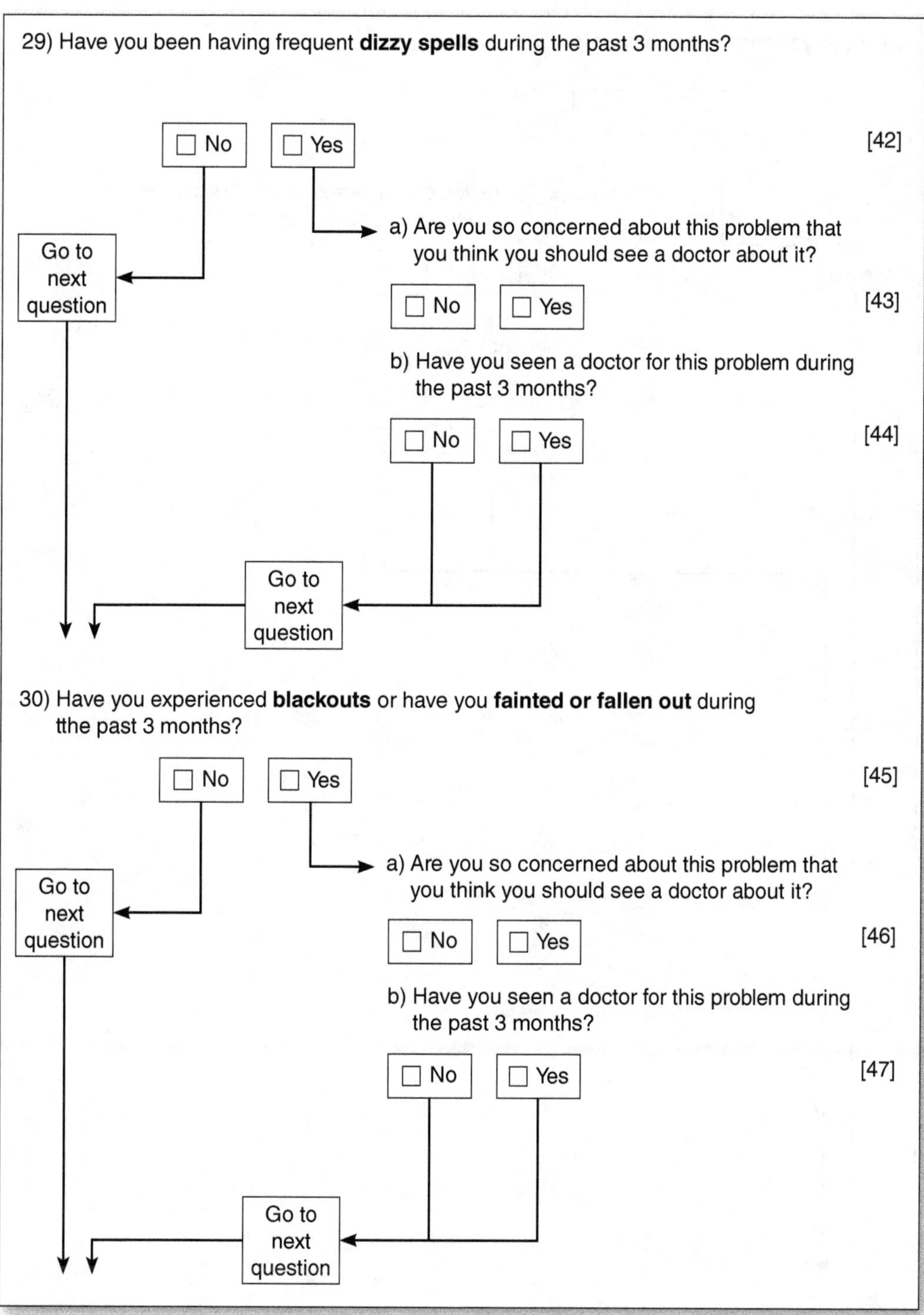

29) Have you been having frequent **dizzy spells** during the past 3 months?

☐ No ☐ Yes [42]

No → Go to next question

Yes → a) Are you so concerned about this problem that you think you should see a doctor about it?

☐ No ☐ Yes [43]

b) Have you seen a doctor for this problem during the past 3 months?

☐ No ☐ Yes [44]

Go to next question

30) Have you experienced **blackouts** or have you **fainted or fallen out** during tthe past 3 months?

☐ No ☐ Yes [45]

No → Go to next question

Yes → a) Are you so concerned about this problem that you think you should see a doctor about it?

☐ No ☐ Yes [46]

b) Have you seen a doctor for this problem during the past 3 months?

☐ No ☐ Yes [47]

Go to next question

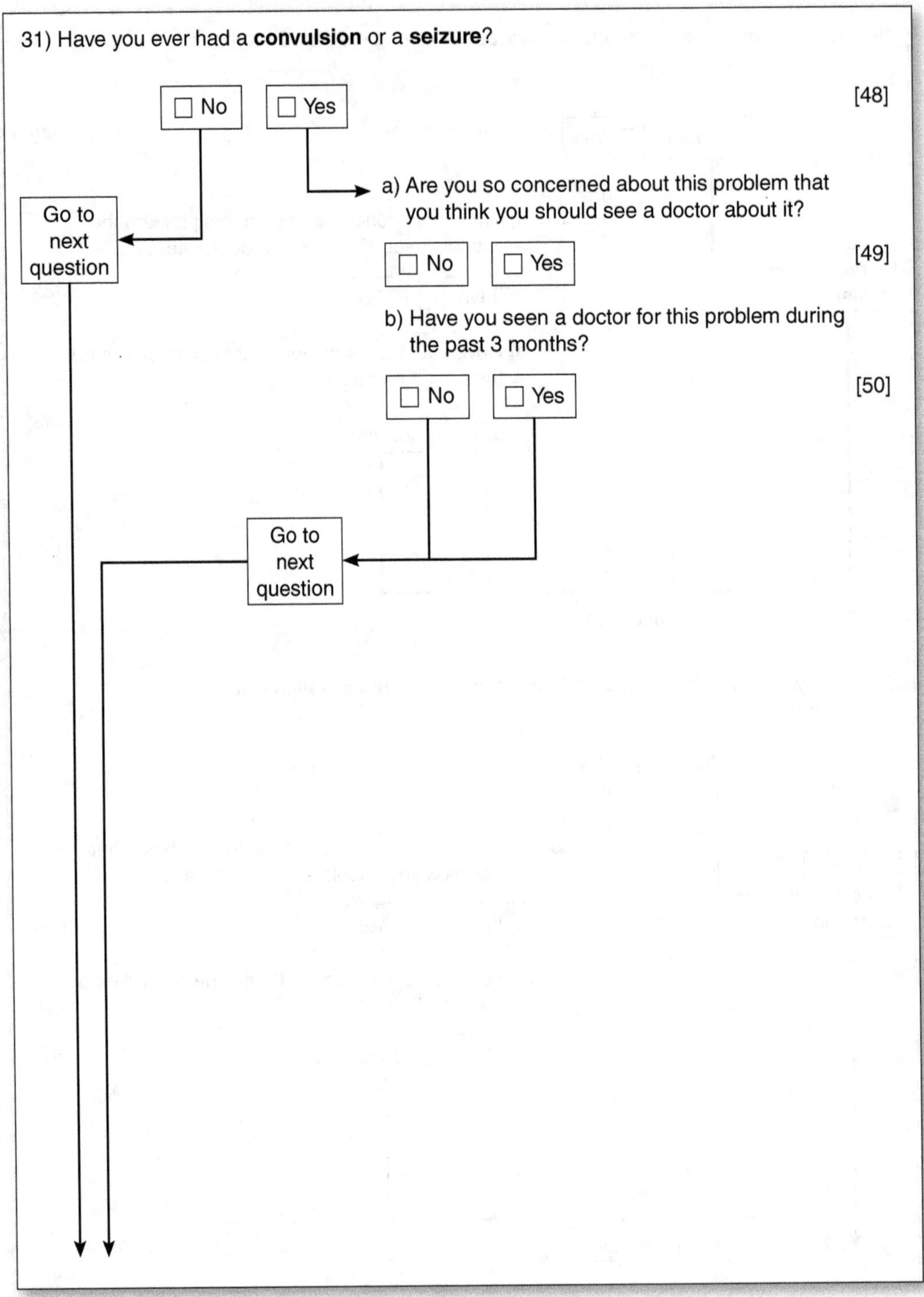

31) Have you ever had a **convulsion** or a **seizure**?

☐ No ☐ Yes [48]

a) Are you so concerned about this problem that you think you should see a doctor about it?

☐ No ☐ Yes [49]

b) Have you seen a doctor for this problem during the past 3 months?

☐ No ☐ Yes [50]

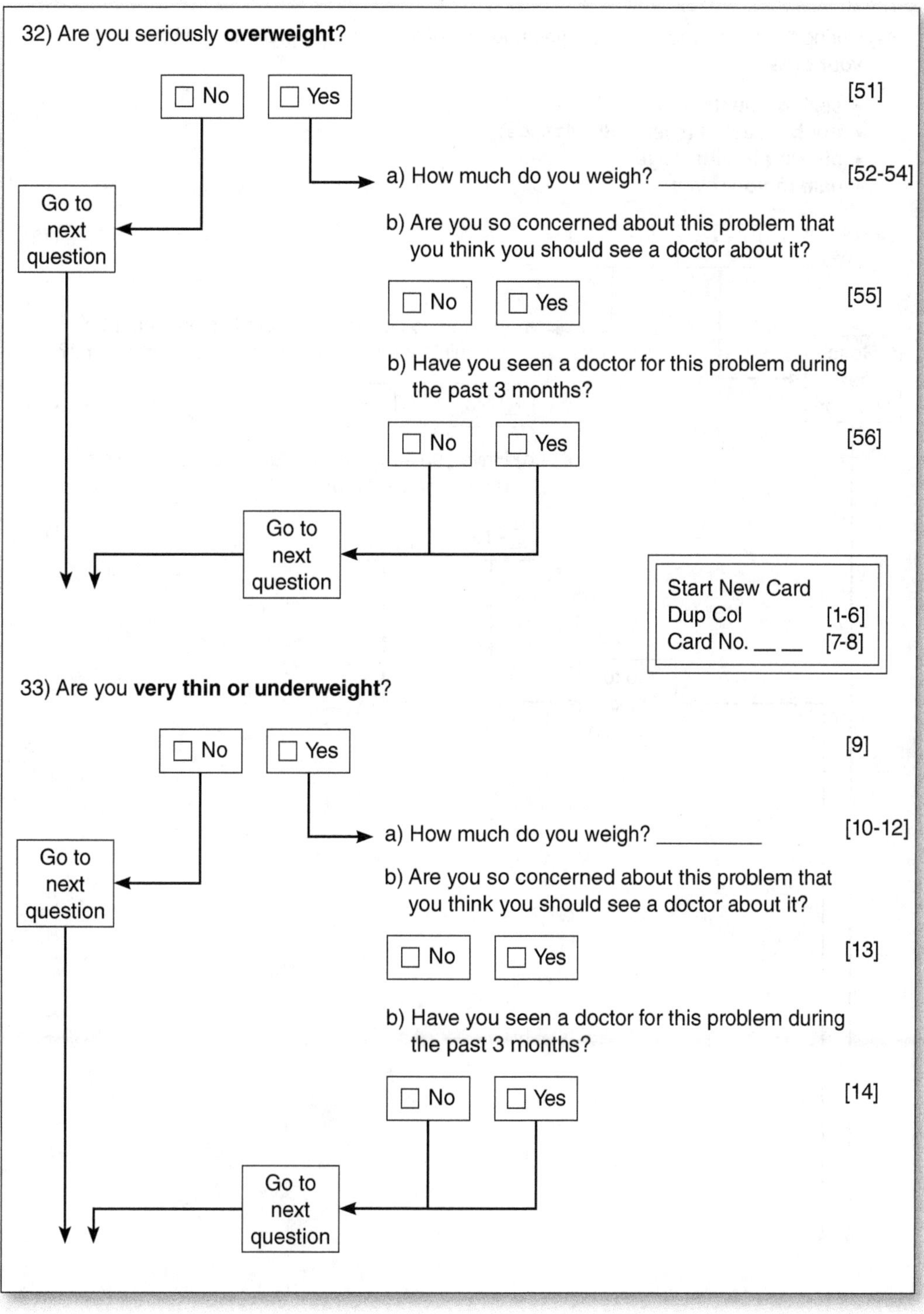

32) Are you seriously **overweight**?

☐ No ☐ Yes [51]

Go to next question

a) How much do you weigh? __________ [52-54]

b) Are you so concerned about this problem that you think you should see a doctor about it?

☐ No ☐ Yes [55]

b) Have you seen a doctor for this problem during the past 3 months?

☐ No ☐ Yes [56]

Go to next question

Start New Card
Dup Col [1-6]
Card No. __ __ [7-8]

33) Are you **very thin or underweight**?

☐ No ☐ Yes [9]

Go to next question

a) How much do you weigh? __________ [10-12]

b) Are you so concerned about this problem that you think you should see a doctor about it?

☐ No ☐ Yes [13]

b) Have you seen a doctor for this problem during the past 3 months?

☐ No ☐ Yes [14]

Go to next question

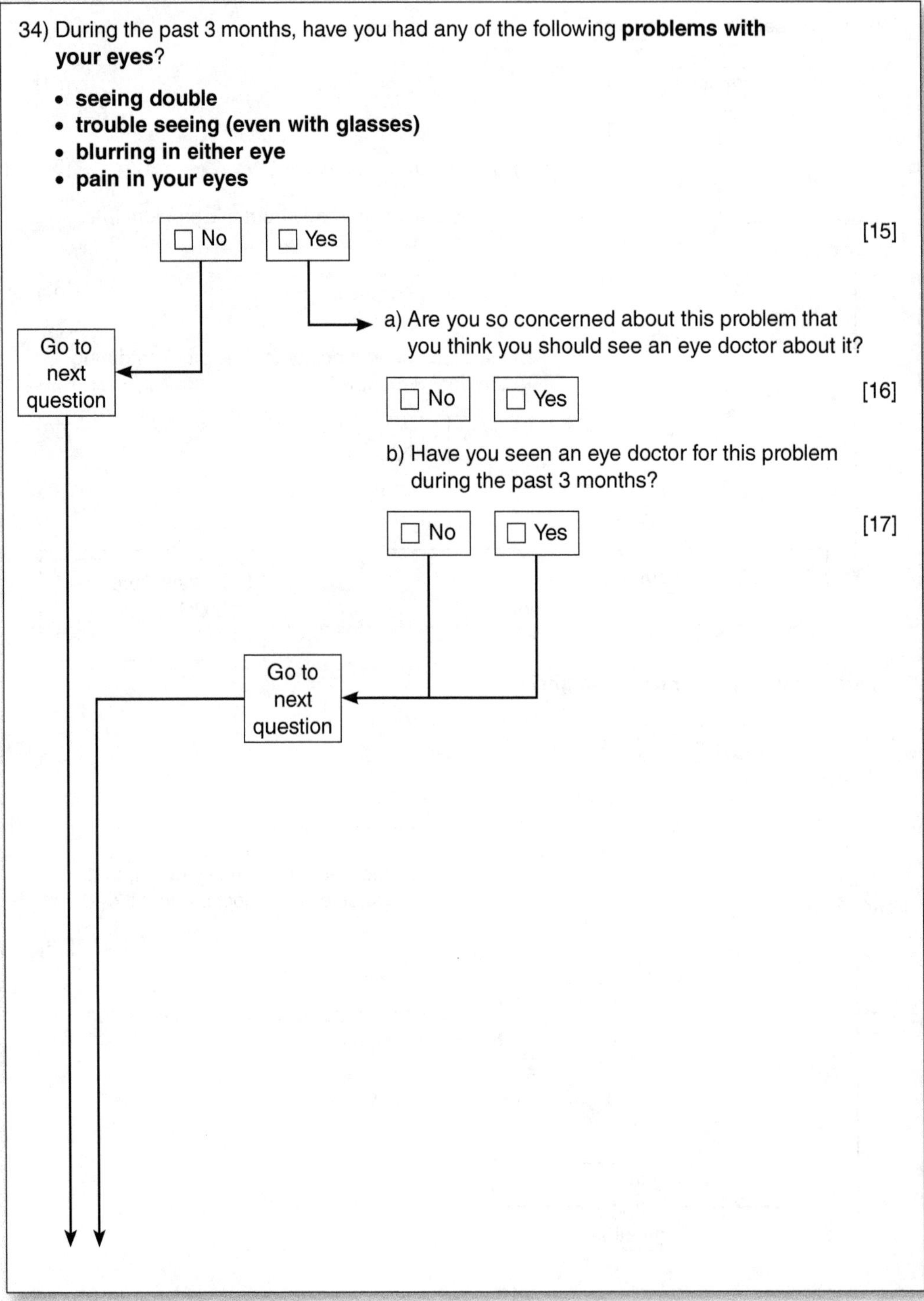

34) During the past 3 months, have you had any of the following **problems with your eyes**?

- **seeing double**
- **trouble seeing (even with glasses)**
- **blurring in either eye**
- **pain in your eyes**

☐ No ☐ Yes [15]

No → Go to next question

Yes → a) Are you so concerned about this problem that you think you should see an eye doctor about it?

☐ No ☐ Yes [16]

b) Have you seen an eye doctor for this problem during the past 3 months?

☐ No ☐ Yes [17]

No / Yes → Go to next question

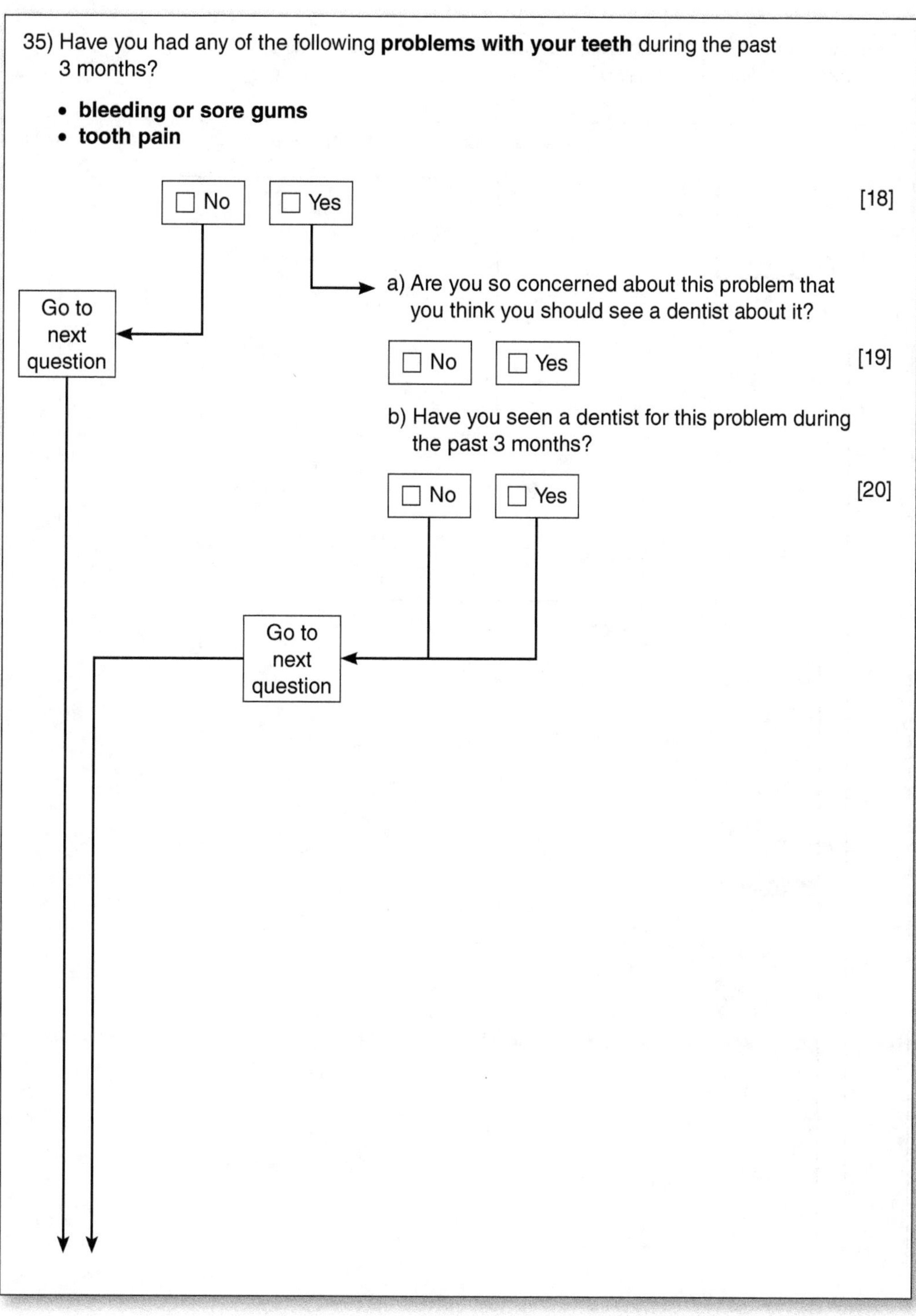
35) Have you had any of the following **problems with your teeth** during the past 3 months?

- **bleeding or sore gums**
- **tooth pain**

☐ No ☐ Yes [18]

No → Go to next question

Yes → a) Are you so concerned about this problem that you think you should see a dentist about it?

☐ No ☐ Yes [19]

b) Have you seen a dentist for this problem during the past 3 months?

☐ No ☐ Yes [20]

No/Yes → Go to next question

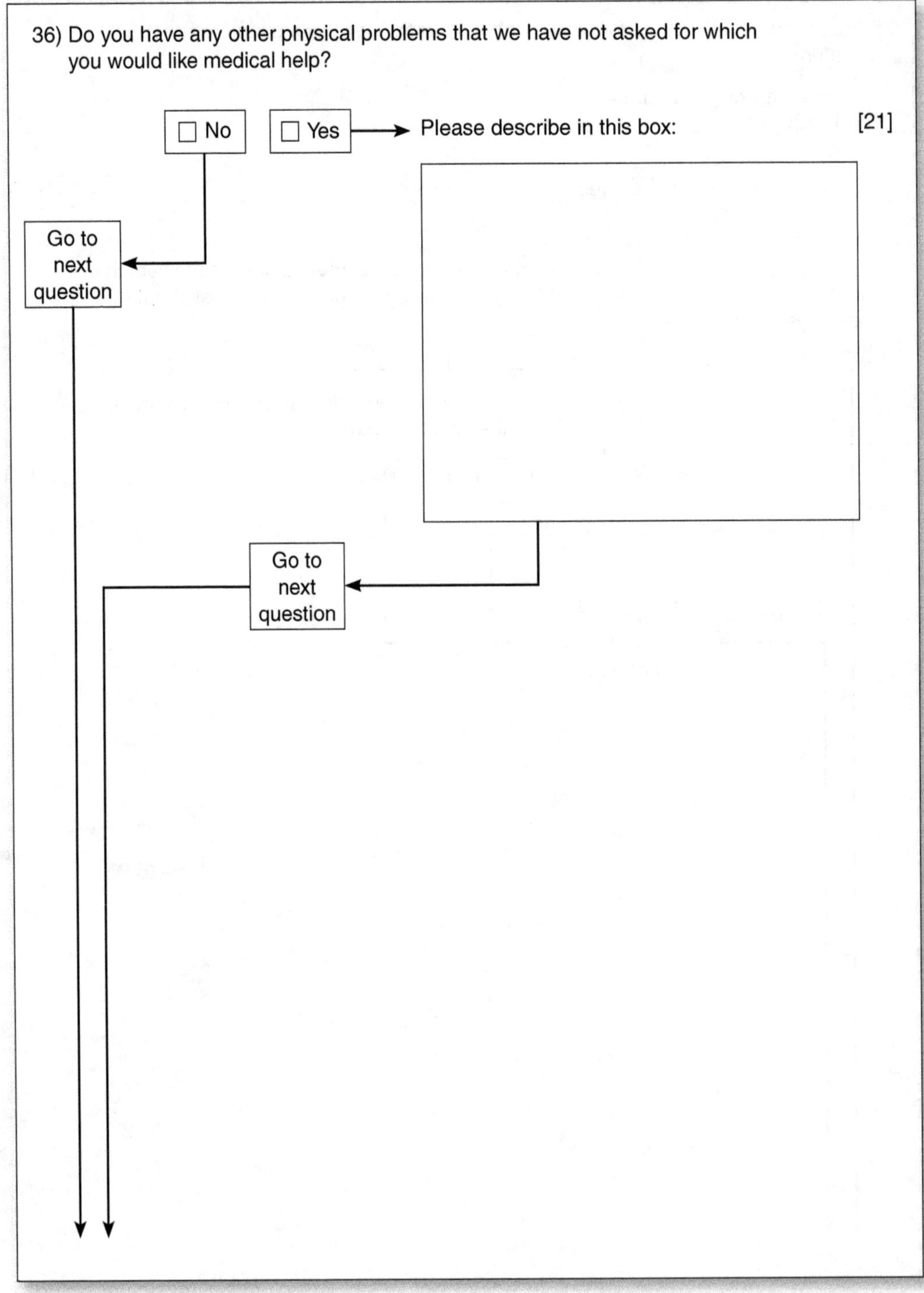

36) Do you have any other physical problems that we have not asked for which you would like medical help?

☐ No ☐ Yes → Please describe in this box: [21]

Questions 37–48

Instructions

Please circle the number on the scale that tells us your answer to the following questions.

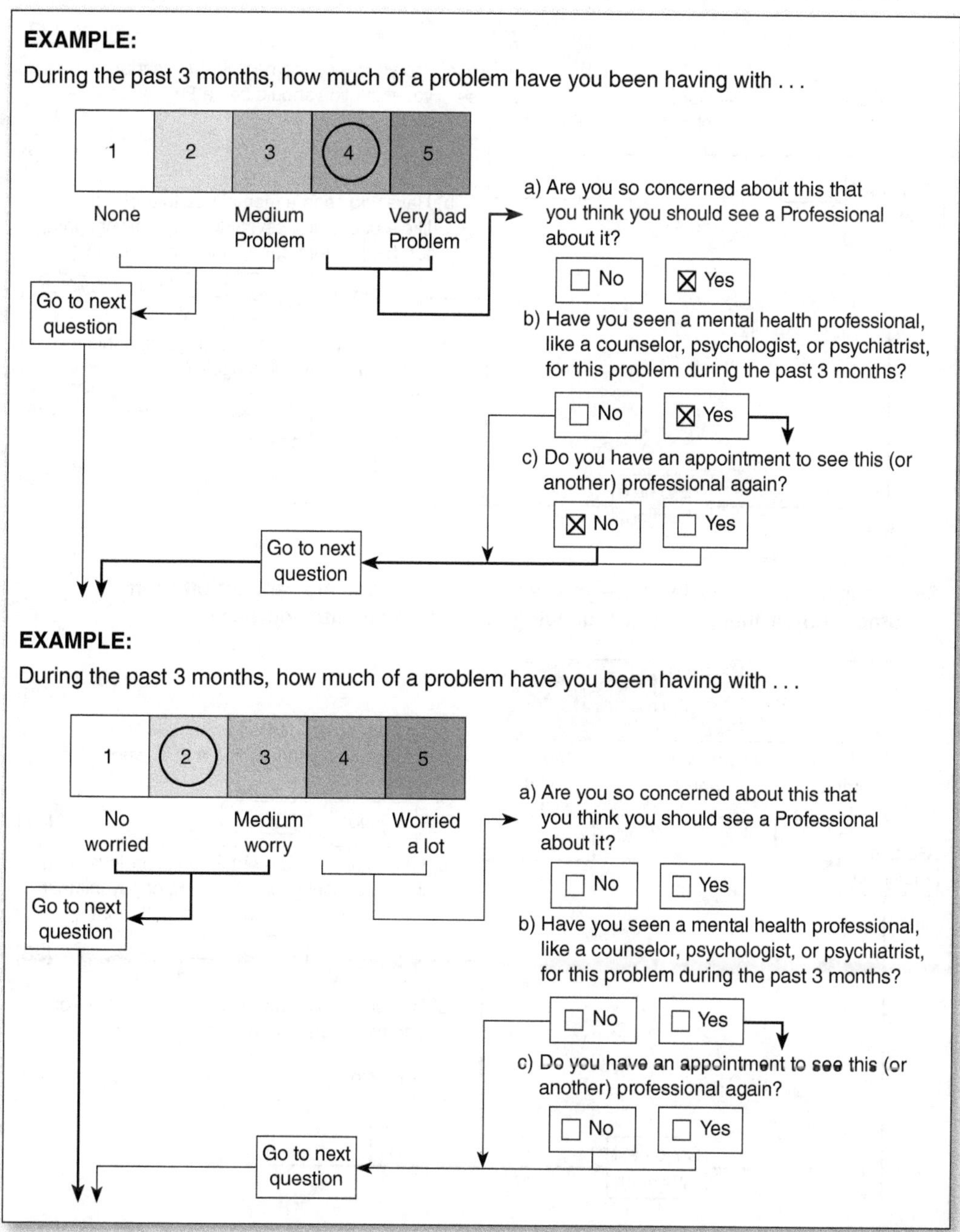

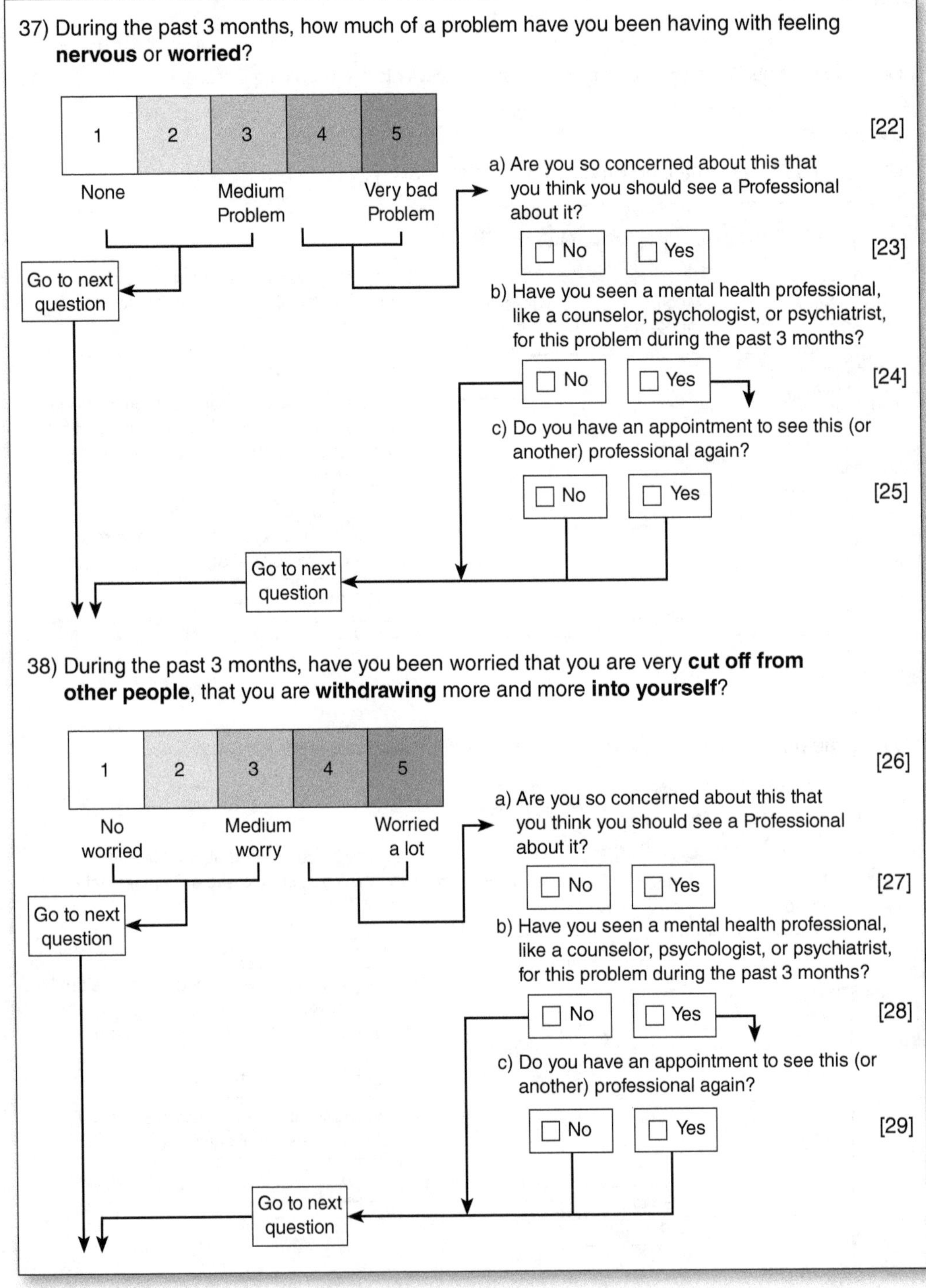

37) During the past 3 months, how much of a problem have you been having with feeling **nervous** or **worried**?

1	2	3	4	5
None		Medium Problem		Very bad Problem

[22]

1–3: Go to next question

4–5: a) Are you so concerned about this that you think you should see a Professional about it?

☐ No ☐ Yes [23]

b) Have you seen a mental health professional, like a counselor, psychologist, or psychiatrist, for this problem during the past 3 months?

☐ No ☐ Yes [24]

No: Go to next question

Yes: c) Do you have an appointment to see this (or another) professional again?

☐ No ☐ Yes [25]

Go to next question

38) During the past 3 months, have you been worried that you are very **cut off from other people**, that you are **withdrawing** more and more **into yourself**?

1	2	3	4	5
No worried		Medium worry		Worried a lot

[26]

1–3: Go to next question

4–5: a) Are you so concerned about this that you think you should see a Professional about it?

☐ No ☐ Yes [27]

b) Have you seen a mental health professional, like a counselor, psychologist, or psychiatrist, for this problem during the past 3 months?

☐ No ☐ Yes [28]

No: Go to next question

Yes: c) Do you have an appointment to see this (or another) professional again?

☐ No ☐ Yes [29]

Go to next question

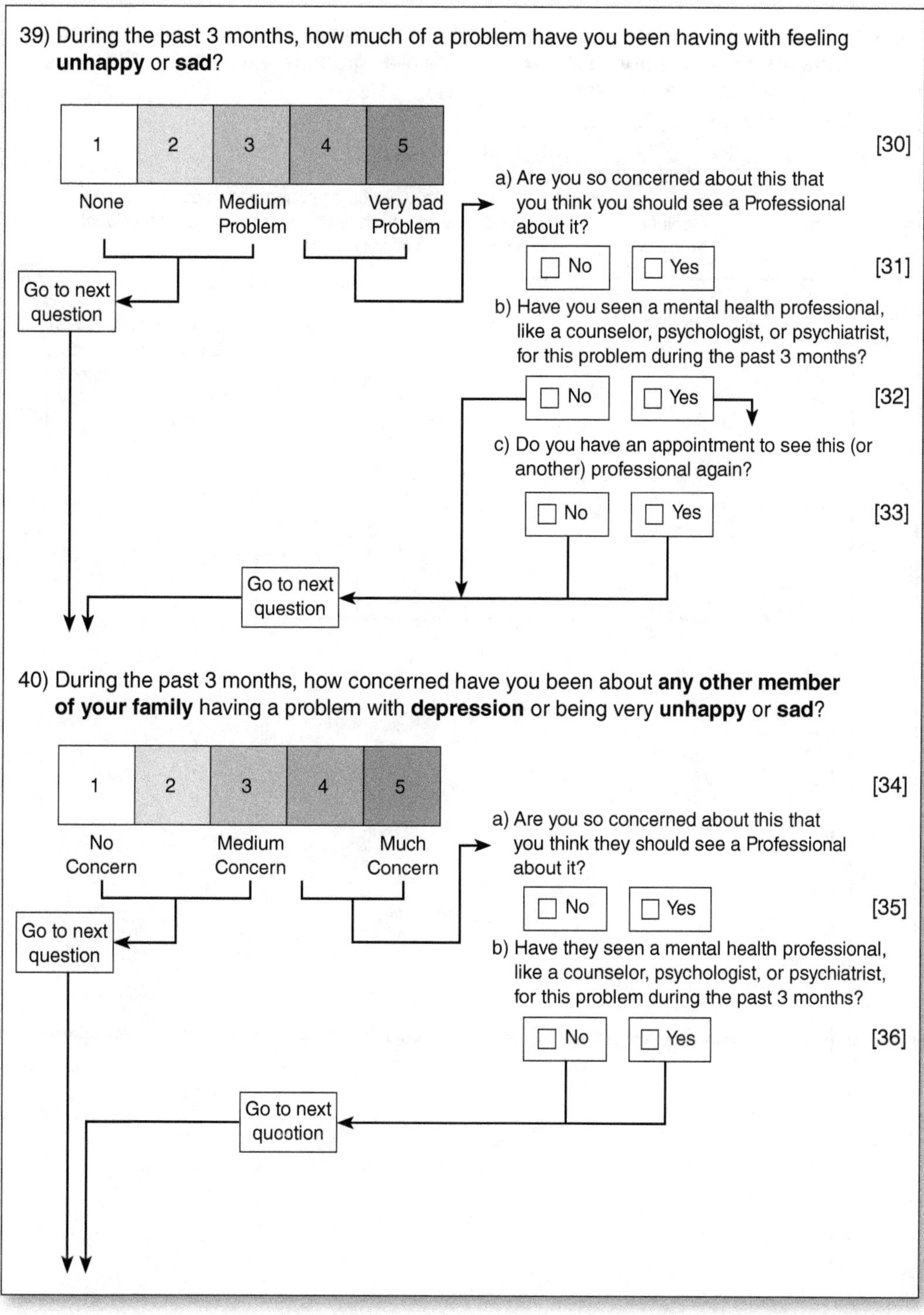

39) During the past 3 months, how much of a problem have you been having with feeling **unhappy** or **sad**?

1 2 3 4 5 [30]

None — Medium Problem — Very bad Problem

Go to next question

a) Are you so concerned about this that you think you should see a Professional about it?

☐ No ☐ Yes [31]

b) Have you seen a mental health professional, like a counselor, psychologist, or psychiatrist, for this problem during the past 3 months?

☐ No ☐ Yes [32]

c) Do you have an appointment to see this (or another) professional again?

☐ No ☐ Yes [33]

Go to next question

40) During the past 3 months, how concerned have you been about **any other member of your family** having a problem with **depression** or being very **unhappy** or **sad**?

1 2 3 4 5 [34]

No Concern — Medium Concern — Much Concern

Go to next question

a) Are you so concerned about this that you think they should see a Professional about it?

☐ No ☐ Yes [35]

b) Have they seen a mental health professional, like a counselor, psychologist, or psychiatrist, for this problem during the past 3 months?

☐ No ☐ Yes [36]

Go to next quoction

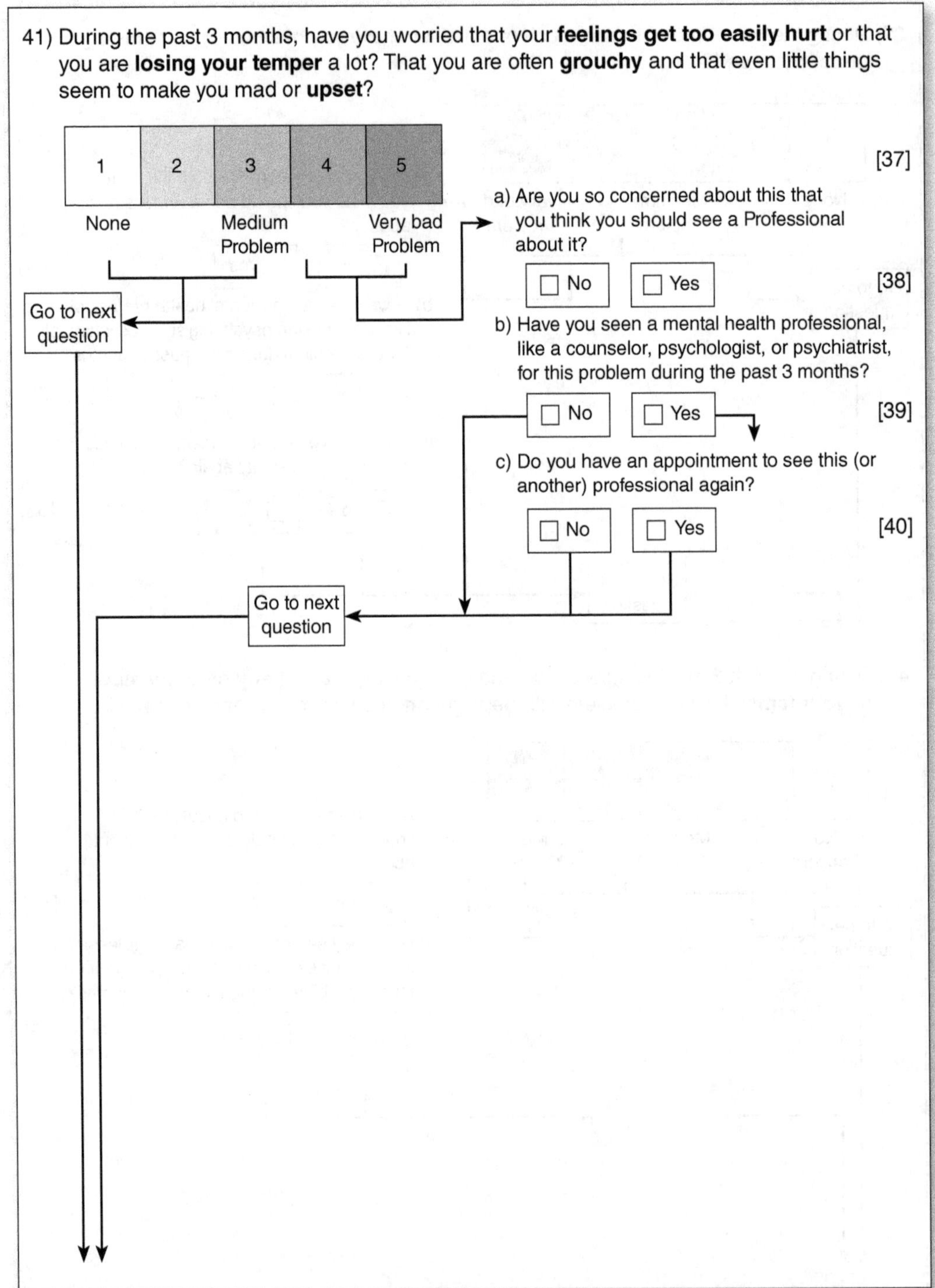

41) During the past 3 months, have you worried that your **feelings get too easily hurt** or that you are **losing your temper** a lot? That you are often **grouchy** and that even little things seem to make you mad or **upset**?

[37]

a) Are you so concerned about this that you think you should see a Professional about it?

☐ No ☐ Yes [38]

b) Have you seen a mental health professional, like a counselor, psychologist, or psychiatrist, for this problem during the past 3 months?

☐ No ☐ Yes [39]

c) Do you have an appointment to see this (or another) professional again?

☐ No ☐ Yes [40]

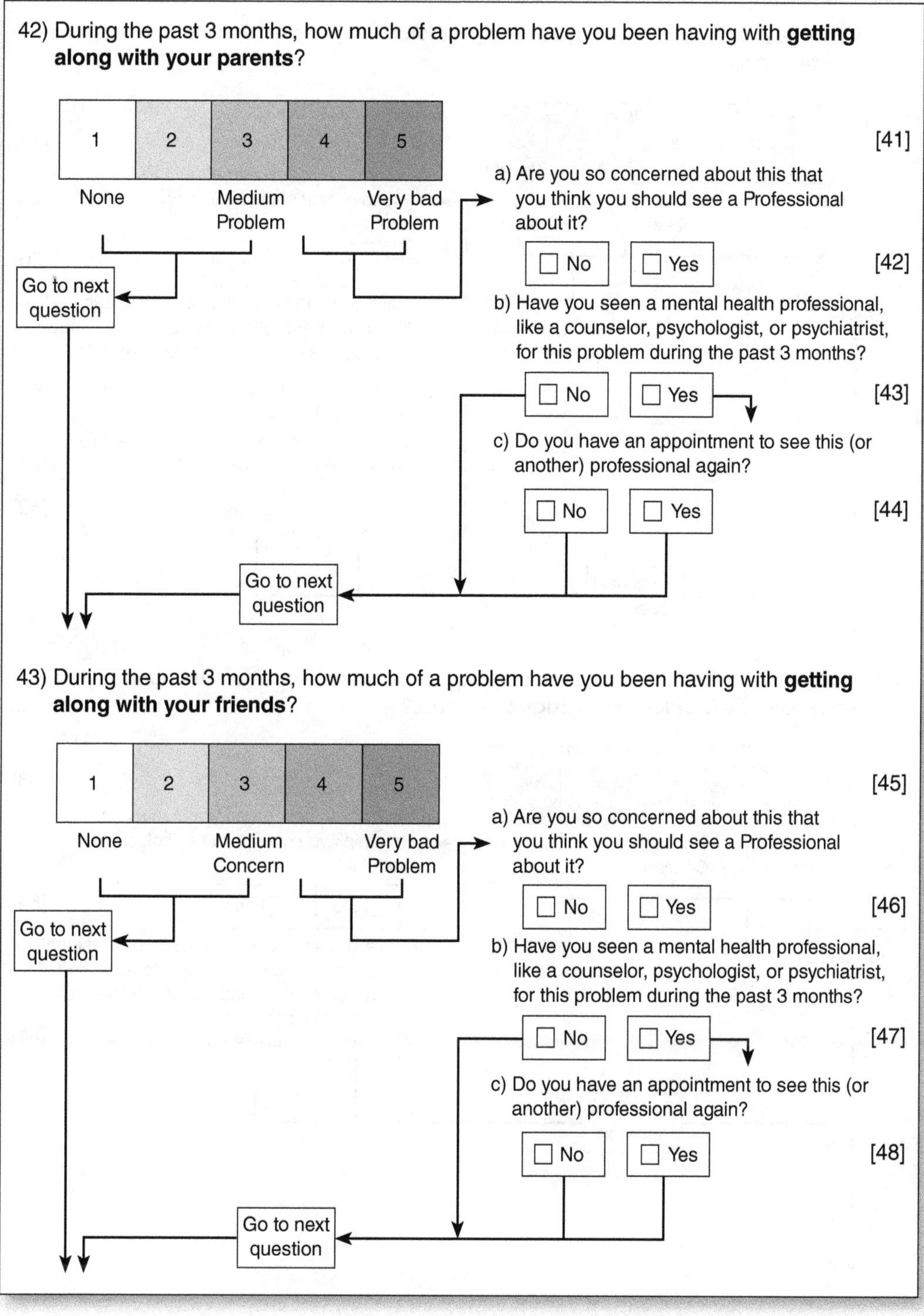
42) During the past 3 months, how much of a problem have you been having with **getting along with your parents**?

1	2	3	4	5
None		Medium Problem		Very bad Problem

[41]

None to Medium Problem: Go to next question

a) Are you so concerned about this that you think you should see a Professional about it?

☐ No ☐ Yes [42]

b) Have you seen a mental health professional, like a counselor, psychologist, or psychiatrist, for this problem during the past 3 months?

☐ No ☐ Yes [43]

c) Do you have an appointment to see this (or another) professional again?

☐ No ☐ Yes [44]

Go to next question

43) During the past 3 months, how much of a problem have you been having with **getting along with your friends**?

1	2	3	4	5
None		Medium Concern		Very bad Problem

[45]

None to Medium Concern: Go to next question

a) Are you so concerned about this that you think you should see a Professional about it?

☐ No ☐ Yes [46]

b) Have you seen a mental health professional, like a counselor, psychologist, or psychiatrist, for this problem during the past 3 months?

☐ No ☐ Yes [47]

c) Do you have an appointment to see this (or another) professional again?

☐ No ☐ Yes [48]

Go to next question

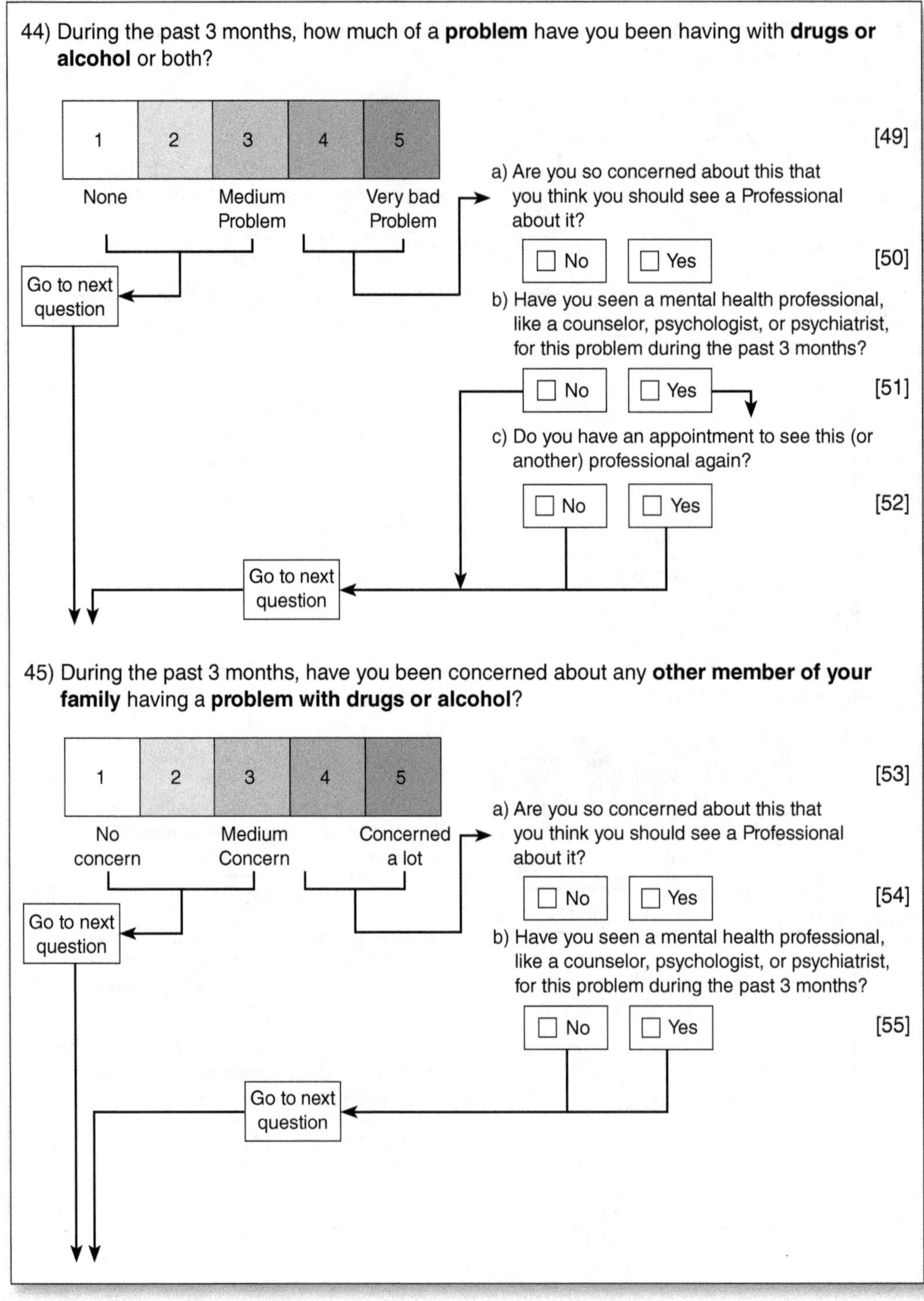
44) During the past 3 months, how much of a **problem** have you been having with **drugs or alcohol** or both?

1	2	3	4	5
None		Medium Problem		Very bad Problem

[49]

Go to next question

a) Are you so concerned about this that you think you should see a Professional about it?

☐ No ☐ Yes [50]

b) Have you seen a mental health professional, like a counselor, psychologist, or psychiatrist, for this problem during the past 3 months?

☐ No ☐ Yes [51]

c) Do you have an appointment to see this (or another) professional again?

☐ No ☐ Yes [52]

Go to next question

45) During the past 3 months, have you been concerned about any **other member of your family** having a **problem with drugs or alcohol**?

1	2	3	4	5
No concern		Medium Concern		Concerned a lot

[53]

Go to next question

a) Are you so concerned about this that you think you should see a Professional about it?

☐ No ☐ Yes [54]

b) Have you seen a mental health professional, like a counselor, psychologist, or psychiatrist, for this problem during the past 3 months?

☐ No ☐ Yes [55]

Go to next question

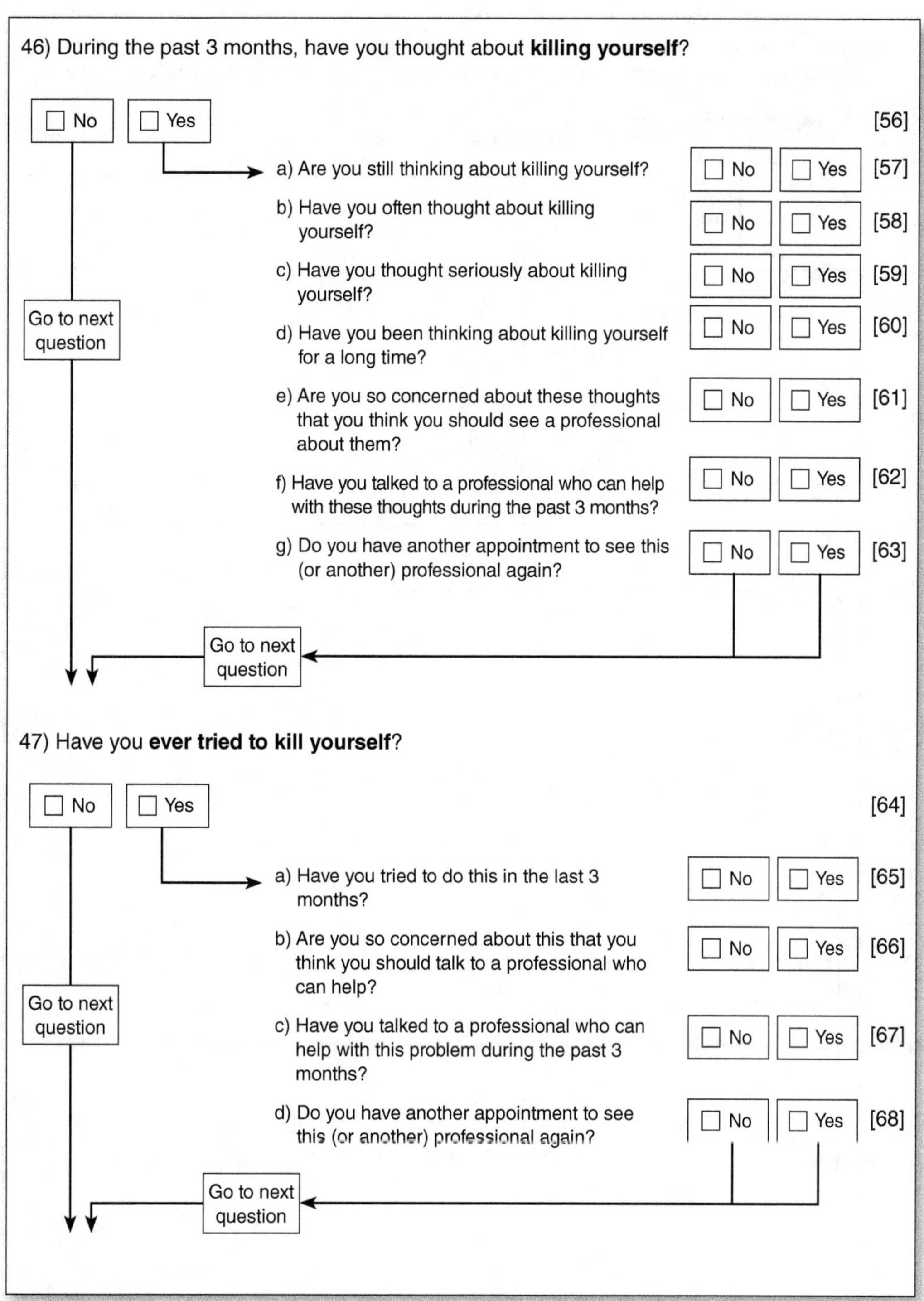

46) During the past 3 months, have you thought about **killing yourself**?

☐ No ☐ Yes [56]

a) Are you still thinking about killing yourself? ☐ No ☐ Yes [57]

b) Have you often thought about killing yourself? ☐ No ☐ Yes [58]

c) Have you thought seriously about killing yourself? ☐ No ☐ Yes [59]

d) Have you been thinking about killing yourself for a long time? ☐ No ☐ Yes [60]

e) Are you so concerned about these thoughts that you think you should see a professional about them? ☐ No ☐ Yes [61]

f) Have you talked to a professional who can help with these thoughts during the past 3 months? ☐ No ☐ Yes [62]

g) Do you have another appointment to see this (or another) professional again? ☐ No ☐ Yes [63]

Go to next question

Go to next question

47) Have you **ever tried to kill yourself**?

☐ No ☐ Yes [64]

a) Have you tried to do this in the last 3 months? ☐ No ☐ Yes [65]

b) Are you so concerned about this that you think you should talk to a professional who can help? ☐ No ☐ Yes [66]

c) Have you talked to a professional who can help with this problem during the past 3 months? ☐ No ☐ Yes [67]

d) Do you have another appointment to see this (or another) professional again? ☐ No ☐ Yes [68]

Go to next question

Go to next question

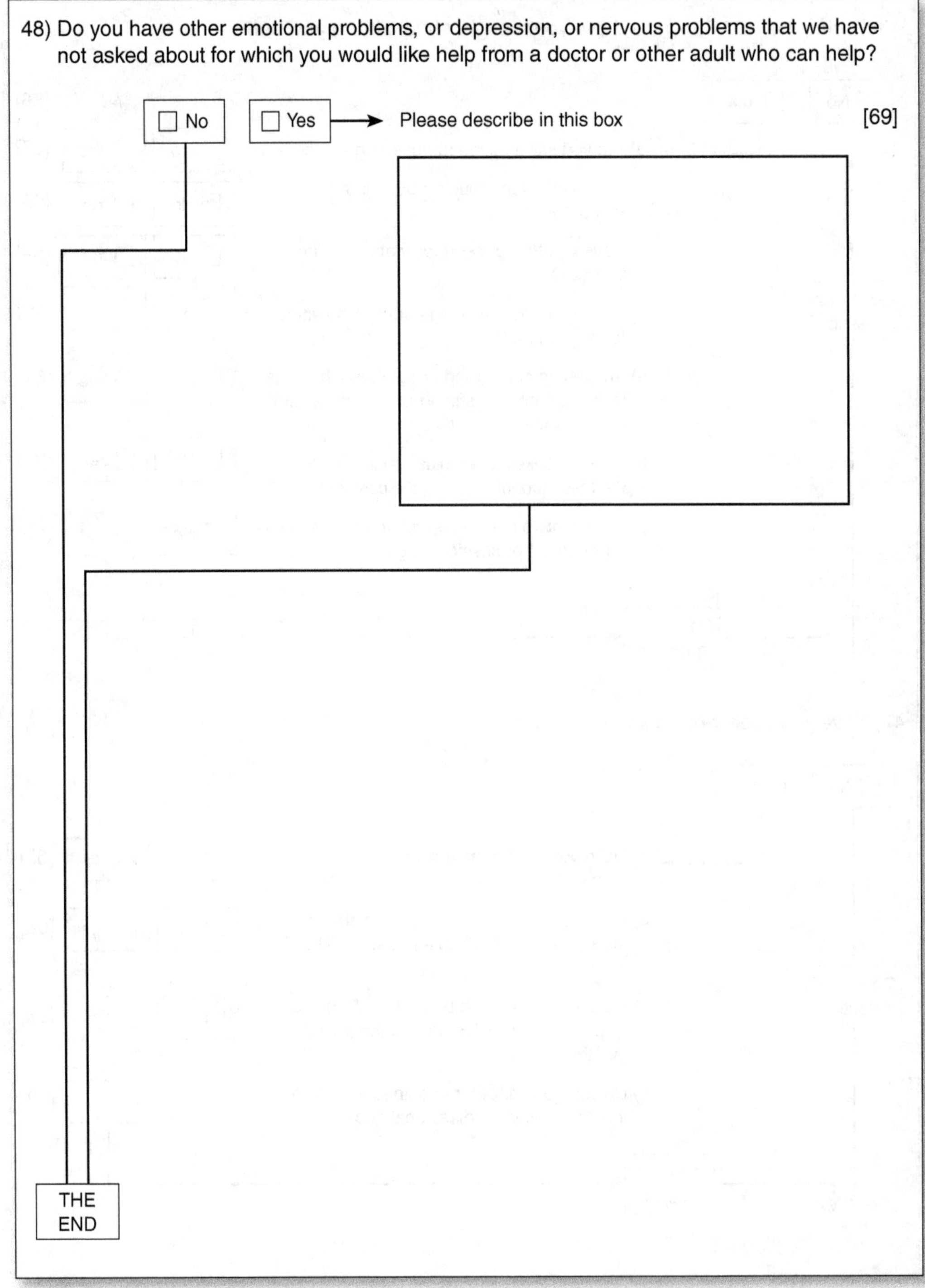

48) Do you have other emotional problems, or depression, or nervous problems that we have not asked about for which you would like help from a doctor or other adult who can help?

☐ No ☐ Yes → Please describe in this box [69]

THE END

APPENDIX F

SIX STEPS

1. OPEN THE SESSION
2. GATHER INFORMATION
3. FOCUS ON COMMON INTERESTS
4. CREATE OPTIONS
5. EVALUATE OPTIONS AND CHOOSE A SOLUTION
6. WRITE AND SIGN A MUTAL AGREEMENT

BENEFITS OF A MEDIATION PROGRAM

- Enhance communication skills
- Prevent or decrease conflicts, violence, and suspension rates
- Develop problem-solving skills
- Create a more peaceful school environment

Program coordinator

DR. JOANN JAROLMEN
Room 109
1999–2000

PEER MEDIATION

WHAT IS PEER MEDIATION?

Peer mediation is a school-based program that uses conflict resolution as a means to settle disputes in a peaceful manner. The mediation processes focuses on problems, not people.

A MEDIATOR IS . . .

a student who has been trained to help people in conflict find ways to resolve their problem. Mediators encourage people to work through the problem and reach agreements that are workable for them.

A MEDIATOR IS NOT . . .

a person who is there to give advice or act as a judge to decide who is right or wrong. Mediators do not take sides. They will not gossip, because they must keep all information confidential.

MEDIATOR QUALIFICATIONS

All mediators must be trained in the skill of . . .

Active Listening

Communication

Problem solving

Brainstorming

Each of our mediators has participated in over 20 hours of mediation training and practice.

TYPES OF DISPUTES MEDIATED

1. Rumors
2. Name calling
3. Fighting
4. Threats
5. Loss of property
6. General disagreements

DISPUTES NOT MEDIATED

1. Serious or repeated acts of violence
2. Issues involving drug or alcohol abuse
3. Issues involving physical or sexual abuse

REQUESTS FOR MEDIATION

A mediation request can come from a student, parent, teacher, or administrator. A *mediation request form* can be found in the General Office and should be completed by the person making the request. This form should be placed in the Peer Mediation mailbox in the General Office. Students involved in certain types of disciplinary action may be required by the school administration to participate in mediation.

WHAT HAPPENS AT A MEDIATION?

If both parties agree to settle their dispute through mediation, then a meeting will be arranged. Two peer mediators will meet with the disputants.

Mediation is a six-step process. The assigned mediators will take the students in conflict through the steps so that a mutually agreeable resolution may be reached. At that point, a contract is drawn, and both disputants sign it.

PASCACK VALLEY REGIONAL H. S. DISTRICT

PEER MEDIATION PROCESS WORKSHEET

STEP I: Open the session

_____1. Make introductions

_____2. State the ground rules

- Mediatiors remain neutral
- Mediation is confidential
- Interruptions are not allowed
- Disputes must cooperate
- No name-calling or put downs

_____3. Get a commitment to follow the ground rules

STEP II: Gather information

_____1. Ask each disputant (one at a time) for her or his side of the story

_____2. Listen, summarize, and clarify

_____3. Repeat the process by asking for additional information

_____4. Listen, summarize, and clarify

STEP III: Focus on Common Interests

_____1. Determine the interests of each disputant

_____2. State the common interest

STEP IV: Create Options

_____1. Explain that a brainstorming process will be used to find solutions that satisfy both parties

_____2. State the rules for brainstorming

- Say any ideas that come to mind
- Do not judge or discuss the ideas
- Come up with as many ideas as possible

_____3. Help the brainstorming process along

_____4. Write the disputants' ideas on a Brainstorming Worksheet

STEP V: Evaluate Options and Choose a Solution

_____1. Ask each party to nominate ideas that seem best

_____2. Circle these ideas on the Brainstorming Worksheet

_____3. Evaluate options circled and invent ways to improve the ideas

_____4. When an agreement is reached, check to make sure it is sound

STEP VI: Write the Agreement and Close

_____1. Write the agreement on the Peer Mediation Agreement form

_____2. Ask each party to sign and then sign yourself

_____3. Shake hands with each person and congratulate their work

_____4. Ask both of the disputants to shake hands

_____5. Close by saying, "Thank you for participating in mediation."

Adapted from Peer Mediation: Crisis Resolution in Schools

PEER MEDIATION

BRAINSTORMING WORKSHEET

List all the possible options:

- What could be done to resolve this dispute?
- What other possibilities can you think of?
- In the future, what could you do differently?

1. ____________________
2. ____________________
3. ____________________
4. ____________________
5. ____________________
6. ____________________
7. ____________________
8. ____________________
9. ____________________
10. ____________________

Adapted from Peer Mediation: Crisis Resolution in Schools

PASCACK VALLEY REGIONAL H.S. DISTRICT

PEER MEDIATION AGREEMENT

Peer mediator____________________ Date__________

Briefly describe the conflict:____________________

____

____

____

Type of conflict (check one) _____Rumor _____Threat _____Name Calling
_____Loss of property _____Fighting _____Other (specify)__________

The students whose signatures appear below met with a peer mediator and with the assistance of the mediator reached the following agreement.

DISPUTANT__________________	DISPUTANT__________________
Agrees to____________________	Agrees to____________________
____________________________	____________________________
____________________________	____________________________
____________________________	____________________________
____________________________	____________________________
____________________________	____________________________
____________________________	____________________________

We have made and signed this agreement because we believe it resolves the issue (s) between us.

____________________________	____________________________
DISPUTANT SIGNATURE	DISPUTANT SIGNATURE
____________________________	____________________________
PEER MEDIATOR SIGNATURE	LENGTH OF MEDIATION (MINUTES)

Adapted from Peer Mediation: Crisis Resolution in Schools

Observing a Conflict

1. How do you know that what you saw and heard was a conflict?____________

____

2. Briefly describe what happened (the facts)____________________________

____

____

3. Who is it between?____

4. What is it over?____

5. What is the problem for **A**?______________________________

____

A Feels______________________ **A** Needs______________________

6. What is the problem for **B**?______________________________

____

B Feels______________________ **B** Needs______________________

7. How did the conflict end?______________________________

____

8. How could this conflict have ended differently?______________________

____

____

Writing Your Own Conflict Scenarios

What are . . .

- the basic facts surrounding the conflict?

  ____

  ____

- the perspectives of the major participants in the conflicts?

  ____

  ____

- the nature of the relationships between the participants?

  ____

  ____

- the causes of the conflicts?

  ____

  ____

- details about the conflict's development?

  ____

  ____

Conflict Dialogues

Chose to write about a conflict you have observed or a conflict you have experienced. You will be writing a dialogue between two characters. Before you write your dialogue, address the following:

Two people are fighting over/about ________________________________

____

Setting (time and place.) ________________________________

Character **A** (first name, age) ____________________________

Character **B** (first name, age) ____________________________

Which character is most upset? Why?__________________________

____

What do the characters do and say that makes each of them more angry and ready to fight?

____

______________ **A** ______________________________

______________ **B** ______________________________

______________ **A** ______________________________

______________ **B** ______________________________

______________ **A** ______________________________

______________ **B** ______________________________

______________ **A** ______________________________

______________ **B** ______________________________

______________ **A** ______________________________

______________ **B** ______________________________

WHAT'S YOUR STYLE IN A CONFLICT?

The sayings listed below suggest different ways of dealing with conflict. Read each of the sayings and indicate how closely each one describes how you feel toward or act during a conflict.

Key: 5—very typical of the way I think in a conflict

4—frequently typical of the way I think in a conflict

3—sometimes typical of the way I think in a conflict

2—seldom typical of the way I think in a conflict

1—never typical of the way I think in a conflict

SAYING	1	2	3	4	5
1. Give him an inch and he'll take a mile.					
2. A bad peace is better than a good quarrel.					
3. Come, let us reason together.					
4. You have to give some to get some.					
5. It is better to give than to receive.					
6. When you are among the blind, shut your eyes.					
7. Don't wake up sleeping sadness.					
8. Better a diamond with a flaw than a pebble without one.					
9. Two heads are better than one.					
10. He who humbles himself too much gets trampled on.					

YOUR SCORE

The numbers in the columns (5–1) represent the score for each item. Fill in the following blanks for an analysis of your style.

Scores for item 2 plus item 7 ____________________ Avoidance
Scores for item 1 plus item 10 ____________________ Competition
Scores for item 5 plus item 6 ____________________ Accommodation
Scores for item 4 plus item 8 ____________________ Compromise
Scores for item 3 plus item 9 ____________________ Collaboration

TEN WAYS STUDENTS CAN HANDLE CONFLICTS

In addition to the open-ended type of problem-solving discussion suggested earlier, it's helpful to teach and reinforce the following specific conflict management strategies:

Share

Figure out a way that everyone can do it or use it, either simultaneously or . . .

Take Turns

Each person gets a chance to do it or use it. Either discuss who will go first or . . .

Use Chance

Flip a coin, draw straws, or use a rhyme or some other random technique to choosing who goes first. This might be a way to . . .

Compromise

Each person gives up some of what they want to work out the conflict. Instead of giving up, they may try to . . .

Expand the Pie

Perhaps there's a way to find more resources to fill people's needs in the conflict. This is one choice when people . . .

Negotiate

People can work together to come up with a win-win solution. If there is too much emotion to talk things out now, then they might . . .

Put it Off

It might be necessary to wait until tempers cool before the people can collaborate. They may even decide to . . .

Skip it

Not all conflicts are worth spending the time and energy to resolve. If it is worth it and the disputants are really stuck, then they may . . .

Ask for Help

A third parry can help the disputants get unstuck by acting as a mediator or an arbitrator. Sometimes all that's needed to get things moving is to . . .

Say "Sorry"

"Sorry" can mean "I was wrong." It can also mean "I'm sorry we're having this problem."

USES AND LIMITATIONS OF DIFFERENT CONFLICT MANAGEMENT STYLES

1. Directing

Potential Uses: when immediate action is needed; when safety is a concern; and when you believe you are right.

Potential Limitations: intimidates people or leads to rebellion; and doesn't allow others to participate in problem solving.

2. Collaborating

Potential Uses: leads to decisions that address everyone's needs; improves relations between disputants; and parties learn from each other's point of view.

Potential Limitations: takes time; and won't work unless all parties agree to the process.

3. Compromising

Potential Uses: quick and easy, and most people know how to do it; when parties of equal strength have mutually exclusive goals; and when all else fails.

Potential Limitations: may avoid real issues in the conflict; and may displease all.

4. Accommodating

Potential Uses: when the relationship is more important than the issue.

Potential Limitations: you may never get your needs met; and "doormat" mentality.

5. Avoiding

Potential Uses: when confronting is too dangerous or damaging; when an issue is unimportant; when a situation needs to "cool down"; and when you want to "buy time" and prepare.

Potential Limitations: important issues may never be addressed; and conflict may escalate, return, or resurface later.

- Every behavior in the conflict is either a step up or a step down the conflict escalator.
- Behavior that makes the conflict worse will take it another step up the escalator.
- Every step up the conflict escalator has feelings that go with it. As the conflict escalates, so do the feelings.

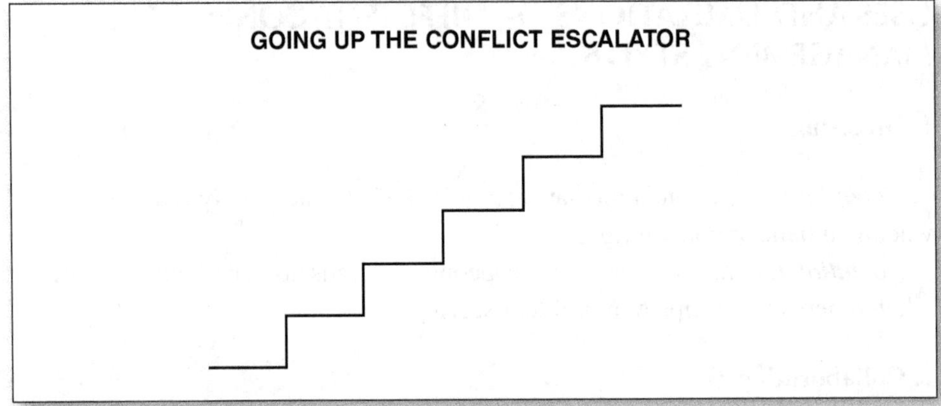

- No one gets on the escalator empty handed. They always have a suitcase. That's the baggage they bring to the conflict. Baggage can be filled with:
- past relationship with the person
- current feelings about the person
- past experiences with conflict
- current feelings about conflict
- feelings about self
- mood that day
- and more: ______________________________

The higher you go on the escalator, the harder it is to come down.

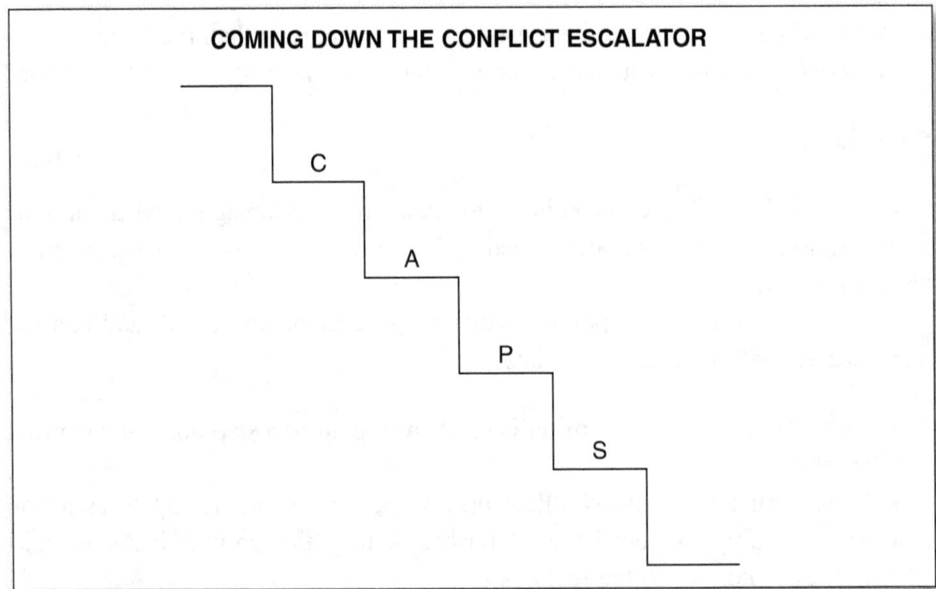

C = Cool Off

Deep Breaths
Relax Muscles
Talk to Yourself
Count Backward
Leave

____

____

A = Agree to Work It Out

Don't Escalate Further
Show Willingness
"Let's Talk It Out"

____

____

P = P.O.V. on the Problem

Each Gives Point of View
Use "I" Statements
Use Active Listening

____

____

S = Solve the Problem

Brainstorm Solutions
Choose a Win-Win
Decide How to Implement It

____

____

BASIC CONFLICT RESOLVING TECHNIQUES

The simplest way to learn to handle conflict more effectively is to practice the basic conflict resolving technique often.

The Basic Conflict Resolving Technique is:

Step 1: Define the problem.

Step 2: Brainstorm possible solutions.

Step 3: Evaluate the solutions, choose one, and act on it.

Step 1

Define the problem in a way that does not assign blame or start to solve the problem. In this step, say what you think the problem is. With practice, defining the problem becomes easier.

Step 2

Brainstorming a technique for coming up with ideas. The goal of brainstorming is to generate as many ideas as possible in a short amount of time.

The rules are:

- work quickly
- try to come up with as many ideas as possible
- defer judgment on the ideas until the brainstorming is finished

Silly or farfetched ideas are okay. Sometimes they can lead to more realistic solutions.

Step 3

Once the brainstorm is complete, evaluate and choose a solution. One approach is to review the list twice. First, decide which ideas are obviously inappropriate solutions and draw a line through those. Any idea that has even a slight possibility of being a solution is left on the list. Then go through the list again looking for the best solution or combination of solutions. Throughout the process, think about why a particular solution is a good idea or not. Is it workable? Are the consequences likely to be positive or negative?

FIND SOMEONE WHO

1. Is a morning person ____________________
2. Moved in the last year ____________________
3. Has planted a tree ____________________
4. Prefers to rent a video to going to the movies ____________________
5. Exercises regularly (at least 3 times a week) ____________________
6. Has expressed appreciation to someone this week ____________________
7. Speaks more than one language ____________________
8. Plays a musical instrument ____________________
9. Was born in another country ____________________
10. Has screamed at someone in the last week ____________________
11. Is an artist ____________________

12. Has cried in the last week ____________________
13. Wonders often about the meaning of life ____________________
14. Was born by cesarian ____________________
15. Does something regularly for peace of mind ____________________
16. Has had anger directed at them in the last week ____________________

READING NONVERBAL CUES

How would you interpret the following body language?

1. Drumming fingers on a desk

   ____

2. Leaning forward in a chair

   ____

3. Crossing arms tightly

   ____

4. Pointing a finger at you

   ____

5. Shrugging shoulders

   ____

6. Lowering eyes when spoken to

   ____

7. Pulling at ears or hair

   ____

8. Slapping one's forehead with the heel of one's hand

   ____

KINESICS

Your sister, head lowered, shoulders slumped, drags herself off the basketball court after her team's last second defeat in the playoffs. What does her body language tell you?

____

____

Your teacher rolls his eyes, places his hand firmly on his hips, taps his foot, then folds his arms and waits because the class is disruptive. What does his body language say?

____

____

Your mother quickly glares in your direction, wrinkles her forehead, and frowns when you tell an inappropriate joke at a family gathering. What does her body language indicate?

____

____

While talking to your friend, he looks around, shifts his position constantly, and taps his fingers. What does his body language tell you?

____

____

While the teacher is talking, you slouch in your seat, yawn, and look at your watch. What does your body language indicate?

____

____

STATEMENTS ABOUT ME

MY FRIENDS SAY THAT I. . . .

____

I FEEL BEST WHEN. . . .

____

TWO WORDS THAT WOULD DESCRIBE ME ARE. . . .

____

I THINK A FRIEND IS. . . .

____

WHEN I TRUST SOMEONE I. . . .

____

I FEEL DISAPPOINTED WHEN. . . .

____

WHEN I FEEL ANGRY I. . . .

____

Feelings	Feelings	Feelings	Feelings
afraid	foolish	mischievous	tenacious
aggressive	friendly	miserable	tense
agonized	frightened	mixed up (confused)	timid
angry	frustrated		
annoyed	funny	negative	
anxious		nervous	uneasy
apologetic	grateful	nice	unworthy
argumentative	greedy		
arrogant	grief-stricken	obstinate	vengeful
ashamed	grieving	optimistic	victimized
at peace	guilty		vindictive
		pained	
bashful	happy	paranoid	wary
belligerent	hateful	peeved	worried
blissful	heartbroken	perplexed	
bored	helpless	persecuted	
brave	hopeful	pleasant	
	horrified	proud	
cautious	hurt	puzzled	
cheerful	hysterical		
cold		regretful	
conceitful	impatient	relieved	
contemptuous	independent	remorseful	
crabby	indifferent	righteous	
cruel	inferior		
	insulted	sad	
depressed	intimidated	satisfied	
determined		secure	

(Continued)

(Continued)

devilish	irritated	sedate	
disappointed		self-conscious	
disapproving	jealous	self-pitying	
disdained	jolly	sheepish	
disgusted	joyful	shocked	
dumb		shy	
	kindly	silly	
embarrassed		smart (cocky)	
empty	left out	sorrowful	
enraged	lonely	sour	
enthusiastic	lovely	spiteful	
envious		strange	
exasperated	mad	superior	
excited	malicious	surprised	
exhausted	mellow	suspicious	
		sympathetic	

ROADBLOCKS TO COMMUNICATION

Ordering:	You must . . .	You have to . . .	You will . . .	
Threatening:	If you don't, then . . .	You had better or else . . .		
Preaching:	It is your duty to . . .	You should . . .	You ought . . .	
Lecturing:	Here is why you are wrong . . .	Do you realize . . .		
ProvidingAnswers:	What I would do is . . .	It would be best for you . . .		
Judging:	You are bad . . . lazy!	Your hair is too long . . .		
Excusing:	You'll feel better . . .	It's not so bad . . .		
Diagnosing:	You're just trying to get attention . . .	I know what you need . . .		
Prying:	Why?	What?	How?	When

ATTACKING AND AVOIDING

BEHAVIOR	RARELY	SOMETIMES	FREQUENTLY
NAGGING			
SHOUTING			
INTERRUPTING			
EXPLODING			
WARNING (If you don't do this!)			
CORRECTING (Look at the facts!)			
PERSISTING (I am right!)			
INSULTING (You're pathetic!)			
SARCASM			
REVENGE (I'll get you for this!)			
WITHDRAWAL			
SULKING IN SILENCE			
TAKING IT OUT ON ANOTHER			
DECLARING "ITS UNFAIR TO ME!"			
TALKING BEHIND ANOTHER'S BACK			
TRYING TO FORGET THE PROBLEM			
FEELING ILL			
NOT WANTING TO HURT THE OTHER			
FEELING LOW AND DEPRESSED			
BEING POLITE-FEELING ANGRY			

LISTENING

Why Listen?

There are two major ways that listening can help resolve a conflict.

- Listening gives us information

Both people in a conflict can be winners if they approach the conflict as a mutual problem to be solved rather than as a contest. However, to define the mutual problem, it is essential to understand how both people see the situation and how they feel about it. Good listening gives the information needed to reach a solid understanding of the problem.

- Listening defuses anger and hostility

There is always feeling when there is a conflict, and usually one of the feelings is anger. It is almost impossible for people to talk things out while feeling very angry and hostile. But once each person's feelings have been heard and acknowledged, the anger subsides, and they can move on to the business of defining and solving a mutual problem.

Active Listening Guidelines

1. Show understanding and acceptance through *nonverbal behaviors:*

tone of voice	gestures
eye contact	facial expressions
posture	nodding

2. *Restate* the person's most important thoughts and feelings.
3. *Empathize*—Put yourself in the other person's place to understand what the person is saying and how she or he feels.
4. *Do not* offer advice, give suggestions, or interrupt. Don't bring up similar feelings and problems from your own experience.

HANDOUT 8.7

INFORMATION SHEET: "I" STATEMENTS

AN "I" statement is a way of expressing clearly your point of view about a situation. It includes an expression of how it is affecting you, and how you would like to see it change. The best "I" statement is free of expectations and blame. It opens up the area for discussion and leaves the next move for the other person.

Aim for your "I" statement to be *clear* (that is, to the point) and *clean* (that is, free of blame and judgment).

Beware of "You" statements which place blame on someone else, hold them responsible, demand change from them, or hold a threat. For example: "When you deliberately clump around the house when everyone else is asleep, you are being defiant and disrespectful and you have got to stop doing it before things get really out of hand."

"I" statement formula

The action A statement of fact. Make it as objective and specific as possible: "When you run down the stairs with boots on" rather than "When you're banging around the house." The objective information carries no blame and allows no possibility of denial from the other person.

My response This should be worded in such a way as to acknowledge the subjectivity of your emotions ("I feel angry, hurt, put down, ignored") or the way you want to act ("I feel like giving up").

It should be clear that these feelings carry no blame and impose no expectations on the other person. Say "I feel hurt" rather than "I feel that you're being mean." Add a reason if it helps clarify the situation for both of you: "I feel hurt because I enjoy seeing you."

What I'd like is. . . . A statement of a desired change or preferred outcome but without expectation of change from the other person. It is OK to say what you want, but not to demand it. Say "What I'd like is to make arrangements that it's possible for us both to keep" rather than "I'd like you to stop cancelling meetings with me."

Examples of clean "I" statements

1. When fed up about others not washing up their coffee cups at the end of each day: "When I arrive in the morning and see dirty coffee cups on the table I feel frustrated, and what I'd like is to organize a washing-up rota."

2. When feeling irritable about sharing a double desk with a colleague who isn't tidy: "When your papers spread over to my side of the desk I feel cramped, and what I'd like is for us to decide where the separating line is so I know how much space I've got."

3. Youth worker annoyed by club members taking drugs on the premises: "When you break the rules I feel anxious about the welfare of the club as a whole, and what I'd like is for everyone to share responsibility for keeping the rules."

4. Youth worker to young people continually interrupting a girls' football session: "When you walk into the room in the middle of a session I feel disappointed at not being able to finish the work I want to do, and what I'd like is to arrange a time when you could have the room to yourselves."

5. Youth worker annoyed about colleague arriving late and having to run the club single-handed in the meantime: "When I'm alone in the club at the start of the evening I feel anxious and uneasy, and what I'd like is not to open the club until there are enough youth workers to cover it."

Notes

This is a structured format and may seem strange to start with. It takes time to absorb new skills and begin to use them unconsciously. Adapt the language to suit your situation. Use it to extend your understanding of situations you are unhappy about, even if you don't want to say it.

Name ______________________________ Date ______________________________

"I" STATEMENTS (RC-50)

DIRECTIONS: An "I" statement is a statement of your feelings that does not blame or judge the other person. The statement starts with "I feel . . . ," "I want . . . ," or "I'm upset because . . . " Change the "You" statements below into "I" statements.

"You" Statements	"I" Statements
You never call me when I ask you to!	I wish we could talk on the phone more often.
Will you turn down your stereo? I can't hear myself think!	
Will you clean your room? I've asked you to do it five times!	
You are so annoying when you tease me!	
Why don't you grow up and stop acting like a baby?!	
Will you stop interrupting me?	
You're such a loud mouth!	
You can't play basketball, you stink! Go play on another team.	
It's your fault I got in trouble! Why did you have to tell on me?	

You never listen when I give you directions!	
You always ignore me when your other friends are around!	
You never let me do anything!	
Why don't you do your own homework and stop copying mine?!	
You are so moody sometimes!	
You never told us the assignment was due today! That's not fair!	

"I" STATEMENT WORKSHEET

Write an "I" statement for each problem.

1. You loan your library back to your friend and He or she loses it.	I ____________ when ____________ because ____________
2. Your best friend shows your boyfriend (or girlfriend) a note you wrote about him (or her)	I ____________ when ____________ because ____________
3. The student next to you looks at your work during a test and gets you into trouble	I ____________ when ____________ because ____________
4. Your mother makes you wash the dishes, which makes you late for the movies.	I ____________ when ____________ because ____________
5. Your teacher always calls you by your "real" name, Francis. You hate this name. Everyone else calls you Frank.	I ____________ when ____________ because ____________
6. Even though there is no dress code, your parents won't let you wear sneakers to school. Everyone else does.	I ____________ when ____________ because ____________
7. The student who sits behind you in class distracts you by constantly tapping your chair and throwing paper wads at you.	I ____________ when ____________ because ____________

Source: Adapted from Conflict Management Training Guide.

ACTIVE LISTENING TECHNIQUES (HANDOUT)

Statements that help the other person talk.

Statement	Purpose	To do this . . .	Examples
Encouraging	1. To convey interest	. . . don't agree or disagree	"Can you tell me more . . . ?"
	2. To encourage the other person to keep talking	. . . use neutral words	
		. . . use varying voice intonations	
Clarifying	1. To help you clarify what is said	. . . ask questions	"When did this happen?"
	2. To get more information	. . . Restate wrong interpretation to force the speaker to explain further	
	3. To help the speaker see other points of view		
Restating	1. To show you are listening and understanding what is being said	. . . restate basic ideas and facts	"So you would like your parents to trust you more, is that right?"
	2. To check your meaning and interpretation		
Reflecting	1. To show that you understand how the person feels	. . . reflect the speaker's basic feelings	"You seem very upset."
	2. To help the person evaluate his or her own feelings after hearing them expressed by someone else		
Summarizing	1. To review progress	. . . restate major ideas expressed including feelings	'These seem to be the key ideas you've expressed . . . "
	2. To pull together important ideas and facts		

	3. To establish a basis for further discussion		
Validating	1. To acknowledge the worthiness of the other person	. . . acknowledge the value of their issues and feelings . . . show appreciation for their efforts and actions	"I appreciate your willingness to resolve this matter."

ACTIVE LISTENING TECHNIQUES

1. **Finding out more information**

   Examples

   "What are you concerned about?"

   "When did this begin?"

   "How long have you known each other?"

   "Where did you last see your books?"

   "How much money do you think it was worth?"

2. **Repeating back the information**

   Examples

   "So you would like her to stop giving you dirty looks."

   "You're saying that you don't know when you first noticed it happening."

   "So you feel like he owes you $9.00."

   "So you would still like to be her friend if she wants to be yours."

3. **Repeating back the feelings**

   Examples

   "You seem angry about all this."

   "I get the feeling that you are sad about what has taken place."

   "You seem frightened about what is going to happen."

   "You seem mad about the situation."

4. **Encourage the party to speak**

Examples

"Please go on."

"Thanks for taking the time to explain this to us. We appreciate your patience."

"Tell me more; I really want to make sure that I understand what you want."

"You are really working hard to resolve this. Thanks."

5. **Summarizing what the party says**

   Examples

   "So you are saying that you are concerned about these three things: the money, your friendship, and getting your books back."

   "So overall you seem to be saying that you like her, but you don't really want to be friends anymore."

   "The things that you want from him are . . . "

   "You're saying that the problems you want to talk about here today are . . . "

PASSIVE AND ACTIVE LISTENING

Check one:
Listener _____
Narrator _____

DID YOU/THEY…………(Check all that apply)

Passive Techniques	Active Techniques
_____ Make eye contact	_____ Use verbal responses (Really? I see. What happened next?)
_____ Nod your head	
_____ Lead forward	_____ Comment directly on what was said
_____ Reflect your feelings with facial expressions	_____ Restate the speaker's ideas in your your own words (Do you mean . . .?)
_____ Use short encouraging verbal responses (uh-huh. . . .)	_____ Encourage the person to express feelings (I guess you must have felt. . . .)
	_____ Encourage more information (Tell me about. . . .)
	_____ Don't pass judgment

LISTENERS……..

1. Did you find it hard to remain quiet and be an active listener, not a narrator?

2. Did you have to concentrate to be a passive-active listener'?

3. Did you:	LISTEN	_____	OR	INTERRUPT_____
LOOK AT THE SPEAKER		_____	OR	GET DISTRACTED_____
ASK QUESTIONS		_____	OR	ASSUME YOU UNDERSTAND_____
BE OPEN-MINDED		_____	OR	MAKE SNAP JUDGMENTS_____
HEAR THEM OUT		_____	OR	CHANGE THE SUBJECT_____

SIX STEPS OF MEDIATION

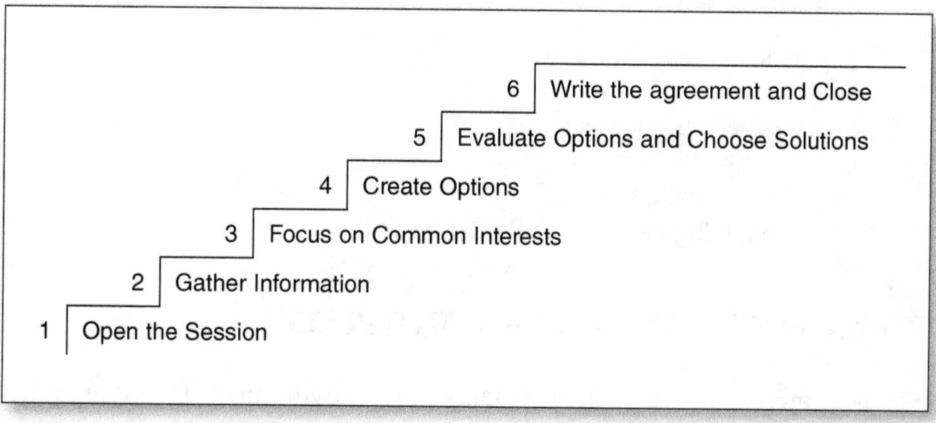

Adapted from PEER MEDIATION, Conflict Resolution in Schools, Fred Schrumpf, Donna Crawford, and H. Chu Usadel

STEP 1: OPEN THE SESSION

1. Make introductions and welcome the disputants:
2. Mediator states the ground rules:
   - Mediators remain neutral
   - Mediation is confidential
   - Interruptions are not allowed
   - Disputants must agree to cooperate
   - No name-calling or put downs allowed
3. Disputants are asked whether they agree to the ground rules.

4. The mediator states that they are present only to help the disputants reach their own solutions.

STEP 2: GATHERING INFORMATION

The purpose of this step is to understand each disputant's point of view about the incident.

1. Ask each disputant (one at a time) for his or her side of the story.
2. Listen, summarize, and clarify.
3. Repeat the process by asking for additional information. (Is there anything you wish to add?)
4. Listen, summarize, and clarify.

Ask open-ended questions such as:

- How did that make you feel?
- Is there anything else you would like to add?

STEP 3: FOCUS ON COMMON INTERESTS

The peer mediator guides the disputants in identifying their underlying interests. Often the students are locked into rigid positions. When the mediator asks them to look behind their opposing positions, they often share certain interests.

1. Determine the interests of each disputant by asking one or more of the following questions:
   - What do you want?
   - If you were in the other person's shoes, how would you feel?
   - What would you do?
   - Is (example: fighting) getting you what you want?
   - What will happen if you do not reach an agreement?
   - Why has the other disputant not done what you expect?
2. State the common interests by saying something like the following:
   - Both of you seem to agree that. . . .
   - It sounds like each of you wants. . . .

STEP 4: CREATE OPTIONS

Mediator helps disputants create, through brainstorming, a number of options that could solve the problem.

1. Explain to disputants that a brainstorming process will be used to find solutions that satisfy both parties.
2. State the rules for brainstorming,
   - Say any ideas that come to mind.
   - Do not judge or discuss the ideas.
   - Come up with as many ideas as possible.
3. Help the brainstorming process along by using the following questions:
   - What could be done to resolve the dispute?
   - What other possibilities can you think of?
   - In the future, what could you do differently?
4. Write the disputants' ideas on a Brainstorming Worksheet.

STEP 5: EVALUATE OPTIONS AND CHOOSE A SOLUTION

The main task in this step is to help the disputants evaluate and improve on the ideas they brainstormed in Step 4. It is also important to be sure the solution is sound.

1. Ask disputants to nominate ideas or parts of ideas that seem to have the best possibilities of working.
2. Circle these ideas on the Brainstorming Worksheet
3. Evaluate options circled and invent ways to improve the ideas by using one or more of the following questions.
   - What are the consequences of deciding to do this?
   - Is this option a fair solution?
   - Does it address the interests of everyone involved?
   - Can it be done?
   - What do you like best about the idea?
   - How could you make the idea better?
   - What if one person did_______? Could you do________?
   - What are you willing to do?

4. When an agreement is reached, check to be sure it is sound by answering the following questions:

   - Is the agreement **effective?**

     (Does the agreement resolve the major concerns and issues each disputant has? Will it help if the problem reoccurs?)

   - Is the agreement **mutually satisfying?**

     (Do both disputants think the agreement is fair?)

   - Is the agreement **specific?**

     (Can you answer who, what, when, where, and how?)

   - Is the agreement **realistic?**

     (Is the plan reasonable? Can it be accomplished?)

   - Is the agreement **balanced?**

     (Does each person agree to be responsible for something?)

5. Summarize the agreement

   ("You are both agreeing to . . . ")

Provided by Peer Mediation Programs Inc.

Biographical Information

I worked as a school social worker for 27 years in elementary, junior high, and high schools. After that period, I was a therapist in a school for emotionally disturbed children for 3 years. This was a high school situation, and most of the students were classified as emotionally disturbed for educational purposes. They ran the gamut from acting out behaviors to severely withdrawn. Suicidal attempts and hospitalization had occurred for many of these students. After that experience, I decided to teach at the college level in the hope of contributing to the social work profession. I taught as a visiting professor, adjunct professor, senior lecturer, and assistant professor (tenure track). As a senior lecturer, I taught at Columbia University School of Social Work in New York. My teaching specialty has been in the area of school social work and direct practice. I taught the school course as an advanced practice course in the fall, 2005, then took a tenure track position at Dominican College (Blauvelt, NY). I was able to teach at NYU (Rockland Campus) as an adjunct during this time. I taught school social work there as well. At Dominican, I was field director and taught macro level courses. I am very aware of the needs of social work interns in the schools and have therefore endeavored to add my text as an essential auxiliary tool. Until recently, I was an adjunct professor at Columbia University.

In 2006, I had a book published by Jessica Kingsley Publishers, London, England. The name of the book is ***When a Family Pet Dies: A Guide to Dealing with Children's Loss.*** Its purpose is to help parents deal with their children's needs when they lose their pet.

References

Addams, J. (1910). *Twenty years at Hull House.* New York, NY: Macmillan.

Ainsworth, M. & Bowlby, J. (1991). An ethological approach to personality development. *American Psychologist,* 46, 331–341.

Allen, J. P., Philliber, S., & Hoggson, N. (1990). School-based prevention of teen-age pregnancy and school dropout: Process evaluation of the national replication of the teen outreach program. *American Journal of Community Psychology*, *18*(4), 505–524.

Allen-Meares, P. (1999). The contribution of social workers to schooling. In R. T. Constable (Ed.), *School social work: Practice, policy, and research perspectives* (pp. 24–32). Chicago, IL: Lyceum Books.

Allen-Meares, P. (Ed.). (2004). *Social work services in schools.* Boston, MA: Pearson Education.

Allison, S., Roeger, L., & Abbott, D. (2008). Overcoming barriers in referral from schools to mental health services. *Australasian Psychiatry*, *16*(1), 44–47.

Ambrosino, R., Hefferman, J., Shuttlesworth, G., & Ambrosino, R. (2000). *Social work and social welfare.* Belmont, CA: Wadsworth/Thomson Learning.

Anagnostopoulos, D., Buchanan, N. T., Pereira, C., & Lichty, L. F. (2009). School staff responses to gender-based bullying as moral interpretation: An exploratory study. *Educational Policy*, *23*(4), 519–553.

Andersson, G., Poso, T., Vaisanen, E., & Wallin, A. (2002). School social work in Finland and other Nordic countries: Cooperative professionalism in schools. In M. Huxtable & E. Blyth (Eds.), *School social work worldwide* (pp. 77–92). Washington, DC: NASW Press.

Angaran, S., & Beckwith, K. (1999). Elementary school peer mediation. *The Education Digest*, *65*(1), 23–25.

Anonymous. (2004). Suicide rate lower among children, adolescents. *Psychiatric Annals*, *34*(7), 508.

Ardoin, S. P., Witt, J. C., Connell, J. E., & Koenig, J. L. (2005). Application of a three-tiered response to intervention model for instructional planning, decision making, and the identification of children in need of services. *Journal of Psychoeducational Assessment*, *23*(4), 362–380.

Astramovich, R. L., & Harris, K. R. (2007). Promoting self-advocacy among minority students in school counseling. *Journal of Counseling and Development*, *85*(3), 269–276.

Austrian, S. G. (2002). *Developmental theories through the life cycle.* New York, NY: Columbia University Press.

Bailey, S. L., Flewelling, R. L., & Rosenbaum, D. P. (1997). Characteristics of students who bring weapons to school. *Journal of Adolescent Health, 20*(4), 261–270.

Banergee, M. (1997). Hidden emotions: Preschoolers' knowledge of appearance-reality and emotion display rules. *Social Cognition, 15*(2), 107–132.

Banks, R. (2005). Solution-focused group therapy. *Journal of Family Psychotherapy,* 16(1), 17–21.

Barnett, A. (2010). Legislative updates: A blueprint for reform—the proposed overhaul of the No Child Left Behind Act. *Children's Legal Rights Journal, 30*(2), 65–66.

Becker-Weidman, A. (2006). Treatment for children with trauma-attachment disorders: Dyadic developmental psychotherapy. *Child and Adolescent Social Work Journal, 23*(2), 147–171.

Behavioral Intervention Plans. (2002). Retrieved from Maine Parent Federation, Farmingdale, ME. website: http://www.mpf.org/SPIN/FAQ%20Sheets/BehInterPlans.html

Berg, I., & DeJong, P. (1996). Solution-building conversations: Co-constructing a sense of competence with clients. *Families in Society: The Journal of Contemporary Human services, 77,* 376–391.

Bernes, K. B., & Bardick, A. D. (2007). Conducting adolescent violence risk assessments: A framework for school counselors. *Professional School Counseling, 10*(4), 419–427.

Berzin, S. C., O'Brien, K. H., Frey, A., Kelly, M. S., Alvarez, M. E., & Shaffer, G. L. (2011). Meeting the social and behavioral health needs of students: rethinking the relationship between teachers and school social workers. *Journal of School Health, 81*(8), 493–501.

Bowen, N. K. (1999). A role for school social workers in promoting student success through school-family partnerships. *Social Work in Education, 21*(1), 34–47.

Bowlby, J. (1973). *Attachment and Loss, Volume II: Separation.* New York, NY: Basic Books.

Bowlby, J. (1977). The making and breaking of affectional bonds. *British Journal of Psychiatry, 130,* 201–210.

Bowlby, J. (1980). *Loss: Sadness and depression.* New York: Basic Books.

Bowlby, J. (1988). *A secure base.* New York, NY: Basic Books.

Braswell, L. & Bloomquist, M.L. (1991). *Cognitive-behavioral therapy with ADHD children: Child, family, and school interventions*. New York: Guilford Press.

Bricker, H., & Rosen, N. (2010). What is the difference between refugees and other immigrants, and how are those differences reflected in policy and practice in the U.S.? Retrieved from http://www.immigrant connect.org

Brock, S., & Edmonds, A. (2010). Parental involvement: Barriers and opportunities. *EAF Journal, 21*(1), 48–61.

Bronstein, L., & Abramson, J. (2003). Understanding socialization of teachers and social workers: Groundwork for collaboration in the schools. *Families in Society,* 84(3), 323–330.

Burrow-Sanchez, J. J. (2006). Understanding adolescent substance abuse: Prevalence, risk factors, and clinical implications. *Journal of Counseling & Development,* 84(3), 283–290.

Bursztein, C., & Apter, A. (2009). Adolescent suicide. *Current Opinion in Psychiatry, 22*(1), 1–6.

Bye, L., & Alvarez, M. (2007). *School social work: Theory to practice.* Belmont, CA: Thomson Brooks/Cole.

Casey, J. (2005). Diversity, discourse, and the working-class student. *Academe, 91*(4), 33–36.

Cash, J., Garland, C. W., & Osborne, S. (1991). *Understanding the individualized family service plan: A resource for families*. Lightfoot, VA: Childhood Development Resources.

Cheney, D., Flower, A., & Templeton, T. (2008). Applying response to intervention metrics in the social domain for students at risk of developing emotional or behavioral disorders. *Journal of Special Education, 42*(2), 108–126.

Cicchetti, D., & Toth, S. L. (2005). Child maltreatment. *Annual Review of Clinical Psychology, 1*, 409–438.

Ciffone, J. (2007). Suicide prevention: An analysis and replication of a curriculum-based high school program. *Social Work, 52*, 41–49.

Clarke, A., Foster-Drain, R., Milligan, C., Shah, I., Mack, D., & Lowe, B. (2011). Engaging high-risk adolescents in pregnancy prevention programming: Service delivery in low-income housing developments. *Journal of Children and Poverty, 17*(1), 7–24.

Clayton, S., Chin, T., Blackburn, S., & Echeverria, C. (2010). Different setting, different care: Integrating prevention and clinical care in school-based health centers. *American Journal of Public Health, 100*(9), 1592–1597.

Comer, J., & Haynes, M. (1991). Parent involvement in schools: An ecological approach. *Elementary School Journal, 91*, 271–278.

Commission on Secondary Schools: Middle States Association of Colleges and Schools. (2006, August 6th). Retrieved from http://www.css-msa.org/about/accredit.html

Committee on School Health. (2004). School-based mental health services. *American Academy of Pediatrics, 113*(6), 1839–1845.

Connell, R. W. (1994). Poverty and education. *Harvard Educational Review, 64*(2), 125–150.

Constable, R. T., Massat, C. R., McDonald, S., & Flynn, J. P. (Eds.). (2006). *School social work: Practice, policy, and research.* Chicago, IL: Lyceum Books.

Constable, R. T., McDonald, S., & Flynn, J. P. (Eds.). (2002). *School social work: Practice, policy, and research perspectives* (5th ed.). Chicago, IL: Lyceum Books.

Corcoran, J. (1998). Solution-focused practice with middle and high school at-risk youths. *Social Work in Education, 20*(4), 232–243.

Corcoran, J. (2006). *Cognitive-behavioral methods for social workers.* Boston, MA: Pearson.

Corcoran, J., & Walsh, J. (2006). *Clinical assessment and diagnosis in social work practice.* New York, NY: Oxford University Press.

Corcoran, K., & Fischer, J. (2000). *Measures for clinical practice: A sourcebook. Volume I.* New York, NY: Free Press.

Corey, G. (2004). *Theory & practice of group counseling.* Belmont, CA: Thomson Brooks/Cole.

Corey, M. S. (2006). *Groups: process and practice* (7th ed.). Belmont, CA: Brooks/Cole.

Corey, M. S., & Corey, G. (2002). *Groups: process and practice* (6th ed.). Pacific Grove, CA: Brooks/Cole.

Cottone, R. (2001). A social constructivism model of ethical decision making in counseling. *Journal of Counseling & Development, 79*, 39–45.

Council on Communications and Media. (2010). Policy statement: Children, adolescents, substance abuse and the media. *Pediatrics, 126*(4), 791–799.

Crespi, D. T. (2009). Group counseling in the schools: Legal, ethical, and treatment issues in school practice. *Psychology in the Schools, 46*(3), 273–281.

Dallaire, D., Ciccione, A., & Wilson, L. (2010). Teachers' experiences with and expectations of children with incarcerated parents. *Journal of Applied Developmental Psychology, 31*, 281–290.

Dane, B., Tosone, C., & Wolson, A. (2001). *Doing more with less: Using long-term skills in short-term treatment.* Northvale, NJ: Jason Aronson.

Degenhardt, L., Bucello, C., Calabria, B., Nelson, P., Roberts, A., Hall, W., Lynsky, M., Wiessing, L., & GBD Illicit Drug Writing Group. (2011). What data are available on the extent of illicit drug use and dependency globally. *Drug and Alcohol Dependence, 117*, 85–101.

Dibble, N. (1999). *Outcome evaluation of school social work services* . Retrieved from www.dpi.wi.gov/sspw/pdf: http://www.dpi.wi.gov/sspw/pdf/outcmeval999.pdf

Diehl, D., & Frey, A. (2008). Evaluating a community-school model of social work practice. *School Social Work Journal, 32*(2), 1–20.

Direct Services. (2009). Retrieved from Care Plus: http://www.careplusnj.org/pages/3043/index.htm

Ditrano, C., & Silverstein, L. (2006). Listening to parents' voices: Participatory action research in the schools. *Professional Psychology: Research and Practice, 37*(4), 359–366.

Diversity among Latinos. Retrieved from www.chadwickcenter.org.

Dubuque, S. E. (n.d.). *Turtles and dragons in the classroom: A teacher's guide to childhood depression and what can be done to help.* [Brochure]. Dubuque, IA: Four Winds Hospital.

DuMez, E., & Reamer, F. (2003). Letters. *Families in Society, 84*(3), 449–450.

Dupper, D. R. (2003). *School social work: Skills & interventions for effective practice.* Hoboken, NJ: Wiley.

Engle, P. L., & Black, M. M. (2008). The effects of poverty on child development and educational outcomes. *Annals of the New York Academy of Sciences, 1136*, 243–256.

Epstein, M., & Sharma, J. (1998). *Behavioral and emotional rating scale: A strength-based approach to assessment.* Austin, TX: PRO-ED.

Erikson, E. (1963). *Childhood and society.* New York, NY: W. W. Norton.

Eyberg, S., Nelson, M., & Boggs, S. (2008). Evidence-based psychosocial treatments for children and adolescents with disruptive behavior. *Journal of Clinical Child & Adolescent Psychology, 37*, 215–237.

Fagan, J., & Pabon, E. (1990). Contributions of delinquency and substance use to school dropout among inner-city youths. *Youth & Society, 21*(3), 306–354.

Fantuzzo, J., Grim, S., & Hazan, H. (2005). Project start: An evaluation of a community-wide school-based intervention to reduce truancy. *Psychology in the Schools, 42*(6), 657–667.

Feindler, E., & Engel, E. (2011). Assessment and intervention for adolescents with anger and aggression difficulties in school settings. *Psychology in the Schools, 48*(3), 243–253.

Ferguson, C. M., San Miguel, C., Kilburn, J. C., Sanchez, J. R., & Sanchez, P. (2007). The effectiveness of school-based anti-bullying programs: A meta-analytic review. *Criminal Justice Review, 32*(4), 401.

Fieldman, J. P. & Crespi, T. D. (2002). Child sexual abuse: Offenders, disclosure and school-based initiatives. *Adolescence, 37*, 151–161.

Finkenbine, R., & Dwyer, R. G. (2006). Adolescents who carry weapons to school: A review of cases. *Journal of School Violence, 5*(4), 51–62.

Finley, L. (2004). School violence: Issues of teacher voice and domination. *Journal of School Violence, 3*(1), 63–77.

First Results from the 2010 Census. Retrieved from www.prb.org

Fishel, M., & Ramirez, L. (2005). Evidence-based parent involvement interventions with school-aged children. *School Psycology Quarterly, 20*(4), 371–402.

Franklin, C. S. (2001). Onward to evidence-based social work practice. *Children & Schools, 23,* 131–134.

Franklin, C., Harris, M. B., & Allen-Meares, P. (Eds.). (2006). *The School Services Sourcebook: A guide for school-based professionals.* New York, NY: Oxford University Press.

Franklin, C., Moore, K., & Hopson, L. (2008). Effectiveness of solution-focused brief therapy in a school setting. *Children & Schools, 30*(1), 15–26.

Freeman, E. M., Franklin, C. G., Fong, R., Shaffer, G. L., & Timerblake, E. M. (1998). *Multisystem skills and interventions in school social work practice.* Washington, DC: NASW Press.

Freud, A. (1965). *Normality and pathology in childhood.* New York, NY: International University Press.

Gabbard, C., & Hart, S. (1996). A question of foot dominance. *Journal of General Psychology, 123*(4), 289–296.

Gastic, B. (2010). Students and school adults: Partners in keeping schools safe. *Journal of School Health, 80*(6), 269–270.

Gazda, G. M. (1984). *Group counseling: A developmental approach.* Boston, MA: Allyn & Bacon.

Gerler, E. (2006). Peer mediation and conflict resolution. *Journal of School Violence, 5*(1), 1–3.

Gingerich,W. J., & Wabeke, T. (2001). A solution-focused approach to mental health intervention in school settings. *Children & Schools, 23,* 33–47.

Glew, G., Fan, M., Katon, W., & Rivara, F. (2008). Bullying and school safety. *Journal of Pediatrics, 152*(1), 123–128.

Goldstein, E. G. (1999). *Short-term treatment and social work practice.* New York, NY: Free Press.

Gonzales, R. (2009). On the rights of undocumented children. *Sociology, 46,* 419–422.

Green, D., & Twill, S. (2006). Special education advocacy: An intervention program. *School Social Work Journal, 30*(2), 82–91.

Greydanus, D., Pratt, H., & Patel, D. (2007). Attention deficit hyperactivity disorder across the lifespan: The child, adolescent, and adult. *Disease a Month, 53*(2), 70–131.

Griswold, K. S., Aronoff, H., Kernan, J. B., Kahn, L. S. (2008). Adolescent substance use and abuse: Recognition and management. *American Family Physician, 77*(3), 331–336.

Guttmann, D. (2006). *Ethics in social work: A context of caring.* Binghamton, NY: Haworth Press.

Hachett, R. (2003). Discourses of demonization in Africa and beyond. *Diogenes, 50*(3), 61–75.

Hanlon, J. (2009, May). A tragic lesson in anti-gay bullying. *Education Week.* Retrieved from http://www.edweek.org/ew/articles/2009/05/27/33hanlon.html

Hao, L., & Cherin, A. (2004). Welfare reform and teenage pregnancy, childbirth, and school dropout. *Journal of Marriage and Family, 66,* 179–194.

Hare, I. (2002). School social work in Hungary and other countries in Central and Eastern Europe: Supporting children in a period of societal transformation. In M. Huxtable & E. Blyth (Eds.), *School social work worldwide*, (pp. 175–200). Washington, DC: NASW Press.

Harrison, K., & Harrison, R. (2009). The social worker's role in the tertiary support of functional assessment. *Children and Schools, 31*(2), 119–127.

Hicks-Coolick, A., Burnside-Eaton, P., & Peters, A. (2003). Homeless children: Needs and services. *Child and Youth Care Forum, 32*(4), 197–210.

Huxtable, M., & Blyth, E. (Eds.). (2002). *School social work worldwide.* Washington, DC: NASW Press.

Igoa, C. (1999, April). *Language and psychological dimensions: The inner world of the immigrant child.* Opinion Paper presented at the annual meeting of the American Education Research association, Montreal, Canada.

Individuals with Disabilities Education Act (2004). Retrieved from http://www.cde.ca.gov/sp/se/lr/ideareathztn.asp#regu

Iowa State Education Department. Retrieved from http://www.idph.state.ia.us/licensure/laws.asp?board=sw

Ivey, A. E., Pedersen, P., & Ivey, M. (2001). *Intentional Group Counseling: A Microskills Approach.* Belmont, CA: Wadsworth/Thomson Learning.

Jonson-Reid, M. (2000). Understanding confidentiality in school-based interagency projects. *Social Work in Education, 22*, 33–35.

Jonson-Reid, M. (2009). An ounce of prevention: Connections to school. *Children & Schools, 31*(2), 67–69.

Jonson-Reid, M. (2011). Looking toward the future. *Children & Schools, 33*(1), 3–4.

Joo, M. (2011). Effects of federal programs on children: Absolute poverty, relative poverty, and income inequality. *Children and Youth Services Review, 33*(7), 1203–1211.

Kadusen, H. (2006). *Short-term play therapy for children* (2nd ed.). New York, NY: Guilford Press.

Kayama, M. (2010). Parental experiences of children's disabilities and special education in the United States and Japan: Implications for school social work. *Social Work, 55*(2), 117–125.

Kayser, J., & Lyon, M. (2000). Teaching social workers to use psychological assessment data. *Child Welfare, 79*(2), 197–222.

Keel, P., & Haedt, A. (2008). Evidence-based psychosocial treatments for eating problems and disorders. *Journal of Clinical Child & Adolescent Psychology, 37*, 39–61.

Kenosha Unified School District No. 1 School Board Policies.

Kenosha, Wisconsin Rules and Regulations. (1995-2006). Retrieved from http://www.kusd.edu/media/pdf/policy/5000/5438.pdf

Kim, H., Ji, J., & Kao, D. (2011). Burnout and physical health among social workers: A three-year longitudinal study. *Social Work, 56*(3), 258–268.

Kim, K. W. (2002). School social work in Korea: Current status and future directions. In M. Huxtable & E. Blyth (Eds.), *School social work worldwide* (pp. 201–216). Washington, DC: NASW Press.

Koerner, M., & Hulsebosch, P. (1996). Preparing teachers to work with children of gay and lesbian parents. *Journal of Teacher Education, 47*(5), 347–354.

Kohl, J. (1993). School-based child sexual abuse prevention program. *Journal of Family Violence, 8*(2), 137–150.

Kolb, S. M., & Griffith, A. C. S. (2009). "I'll repeat myself, 'Again?!'" Empowering students through assertive communication strategies. *Teaching Exceptional Children, 41*(3), 32–36.

Ku, I., & Plotnick, R. (2003). Do children from welfare families obtain less education? *Demography, 40*(1), 151–170.

Lambert, S. (2005). Gay and lesbian families: What we know and where to go from here. *Family Journal: Counseling and Therapy for Couples and Families, 13*(1), 43–51.

Lanning, B., Ballard, D. & Robinson, J. (1999). Child sexual abuse prevention programs in Texas elementary schools. *Journal of School Health, 69*(1), 3–8.

LaRocque, M., Kleiman, I., & Darling, S. (2011). Parental involvement: The missing link in school achievement. *Preventing School Failure, 55*(3), 115–122.

Lauria-Horner, B. A., Kutcher, S., & Brooks, S. J. (2004). The feasibility of a mental health curriculum in the elementary schools. *Canadian Journal of Psychiatry, 49*(3), 208–211.

le Roux, J., & Smith, C. S. (1998). Causes and characteristics of the street children: A global phenomenon. *Adolescence, 33*(131), 683–688.

Leiby, J. (1978). *A history of social welfare and social work in the United States.* New York, NY: Columbia University Press.

Leslie, L., Lambros, K., Aarons, G., Haine, R., & Hough, R. (2008). School-based service use by youth with ADHD in public-sector setting. *Journal of Emotional and Behavior Disorders, 16*(3), 163–177.

Levy, C. S. (1976). *Social work ethics*. New York: Human Sciences Press.

Liddle, H. A., Dakof, G. A., Parker, K., Diamond, G. S., Barrett, K., & Tejeda, M. (2001). Multidimensional family therapy for adolescent drug abuse: Results of a randomized clinical trial. *American Journal of Drug and Alcohol Abuse, 27*(4), 651–687.

Loewenberg, F. D., Dolgoff, R., & Harrington, D. (2000). *Ethical decisions for social work practice.* Itasca, IL: F. E. Peacock.

Loughborough, J., Shera, W., & Wilhelm, J. (2002). School social work in Canada: Historical themes and current challenges. In M. Huxtable & E. Blyth (Eds.), *School social work worldwide* (pp. 57–75). Washington, DC: NASW Press.

Lynch, T. R., Chapman, A. L., Rosenthal, M. Z., Kuo, J. R., & Linehan, M. M. (2006). Mechanisms of change in dialectical behavior therapy: Theoretical and empirical observations. *Journal of Clinical Psychology, 62*(4), 459–480.

Marchant, M., Anderson, D., Caldarelli, P., Young, B., & Young, K. R. (2009). Schoolwide screening and programs of positive behavior support. *Preventing School Failure, 53*(3), 131–143.

Massat, C. R., Constable, R., McDonald, S., Flynn, J. P. (2009). *School social work: Practice, policy, and research.* Chicago, IL: Lyceum Books.

Massey-Stokes, M., & Lanning, B. (2004). The role of CSHPs in preventing child abuse and neglect. *Journal of School Health, 74*(6), 193–194.

Mayer, R., & Mitchell, L. (1993). A dropout prevention program for at-risk high school students: Emphasizing consulting to promote positive classroom climates. *Education and Treatment of Children, 16*(2), 135–147.

McAllister Swap, S. (1993). *Developing home-school partnerships: From concepts to practice.* New York, NY: Teachers College Press.

McAloon, N. (1994). Advocacy in the schools. *Journal of Reading, 38*, 318–320.

McConville, M. (2000). A global war on drugs: Why the United States should support the prosecution of drug traffickers in the International Criminal Court. *American Criminal Law, 376*, 75.

McGuinness, T. (2007). Dispelling the myth of bullying. *Journal of Psychosocial Nursing and Mental Health Services, 45*(10), 19–22.

Meloy, L. (1999). Implementing IDEA 97: Manifest determination. *NASP Communique, 8*(4), 8.

Miller, K. (2006). The impact of parental incarceration on children: An emerging need for effective interventions. *Child and Adolescent Social Work Journal, 23*(4), 472–486.

Minnick, D., & Shandler, L. (2011). Changing adolescent perceptions on teenage pregnancy. *Children & Schools, 33*(4), 241–248.

Miranda, M. (2011). Dream Act, part II. *Diverse Issues in Higher Education, 28*(6), 8.

Mishna, F. (2003). Peer victimization: The case for social work intervention. *Families in Society, 84*(4), 513–523.

Molyneaux, M. (1950). The principal-liaison between faculty and social worker. *Understanding the Child, 25*(3), 26–28.

Moore, S., Bledsoe, L., Perry, A., & Robinson, M. (2011). Social work students and self-care: A model assignment for teaching. *Journal of Social Work Education, 47*(3), 545–553.

Myers, J. (2008). A short history of child protection in America. *Family Law Quarterly, 42*(3), 449–463.

NASW Standards for School Social Worker Services. (2002). Retrieved from www.naswdc.org/practice/default.asp

National Association of Social Workers. (1999). *NASW code of ethics.* Washington, DC: NASW Press.

National Center for Education Evalaution and Regional Assistance. (2009). Retrieved from http://ies.ed.gov/ncee/

National Center for Learning Disabilities. (1999–2006). Retrieved from http://www.ncld.org/parents-child-disabilities/idea-guide/chapter-1-pre-referral-services

National Research Center on Learning Disabilities. (2005). *Response to intervention in the SLD learning process*. Retrieved from http://www.osepideasthatwork.org/toolkit/pdf/RTI_SLD.pdf

Neacsiu, A., Rizvi, S., Vitaliano, P., Lynch, T., & Linehan, M. (2010). The dialectical behavior therapy ways of coping checklist: Developmental and psychometric properties. *Journal of Clinical Psychology, 66*(6), 563–582.

Nelson-DiFranks, N. (2008). Social workers and the national code of ethics: Belief, behavior, disjuncture. *Social Work, 53*(2), 167–176.

Norton, C. (2007). Experiential play therapy. In C. A. Schaefer (Ed.), *Contemporary play therapy: Theory, research, and practice* (pp. 28–54). New York, NY: Guilford Press.

Olweus, D., & Limber, S. (2007). Bullying questionnaire. Center City, MN: Hazelden Publishing.

Olweus, D., & Limber, S. (2010). Bullying in schools: Evaluation and dissemination of the Olweus Bullying Prevention Program. *American Journal of Orthopsychiatry, 80*(1), 124–134.

Olweus, D., Limber, S. P., & Mihalic, S. (1999). *Blueprints for violence prevention: The bullying prevention program*. Boulder, CO: Center for the Study and Prevention of Violence.

Ornstein, E., & Moses, H. (2002). In search of a secure base: attachment theory and school social work. *School Social Work Journal, 26*(2), 1–13.

Ouellette, P., & Wilderson, D. (2008). "They won't come": Increasing parent involvement in parent management training programs for at-risk youths in schools. *School Social Work Journal, 32*(2), 39–53.

Pace, G. (2002). School social work in Malta: Empowering children for citizenship. In M. Huxtable & E. Blyth (Eds.), *School social work worldwide* (pp. 157–173). Washington, DC: NASW Press.

Peer Mediation Training Manual. (1998). Hillsdale, NJ: Pascack Valley High School.

Pelham, W., & Fabiano, G. (2008). Evidence-based psychosocial treatments for attention-deficit/hyperactivity disorder. *Journal of Clinical Child & Adolescent Psychology, 37*, 187–214.

Pelham, W., Wheeler, T., & Chronis. (1998). Empirically supported psychosocial treatments for attention-deficit/hyperactivity disorder. *Journal of Clinical Child and Adolescent Psychology, 27*, 190–205.

Pennekamp, M., & Porschke, H. (2002). School social work in international context: Two colleagues learn from each other. *Journal of School Social Work, 12*(2), 62–70.

Perry, B. (2001). School violence: Why it happens, what you can do. *Scholastic Action, 24*(12), 16–17.

Piaget, J. (1967). *Six psychological studies.* New York, NY: Random House.

Pieper, M. H., & Pieper, W. J. (1990). *Intrapsychic humanism: An introduction to a comprehensive psychology and philosophy of mind.* Chicago, IL: Falcon II Press.

Poresky, R. (1990). The young children's empathy measure: Reliability, validity and effects of companion animal bonding. *Psychological Reports, 66*(3), 931–936.

Pryor, C. (1996). Techniques for assessing family-school connections. *Social Work in Education, 18*(2).

Raab, B., & Pratt, C. (2010). *Student evaluation form for field instruction.* Orangeburg, NY: Dominican College.

Raatma, L. (2004). *Jane Addams.* Minneapoli, MN: Compass Point Books.

Raines, J. (2008). *Evidence-based practice in school mental health.* New York, NY: Oxford University Press.

Raines, J. C. (2004). To tell or not to tell: Ethical issues regarding confidentiality. *School Social Work Journal, 28*(2), 61–78.

Raines, J., & Alvarado, T. (2007, April). *Evidence-based practice in schools*. Paper presented at the School Social Work Conference. Orlando, FL.

Raphael, B. (1983). *The anatomy of bereavement.* New York, NY: Basic Books.

Reamer, F. G. (2001). *Tangled relationships: Managing boundary issues in the human services.* New York, NY: Columbia University Press.

Reamer, F. G. (2006). *Social work values and ethics.* New York, NY: Columbia University Press.

Reid, K. (2010). Finding strategic solutions to reduce truancy. *Research in Education, 84*, 1–18.

Robbins, S. P., Chatterjee, P., & Canda, E. R. (2006). *Contemporary human behavior theory: A clinical perspective for social work.* Saddle River, NJ: Pearson Education.

Roberts, A. R. (2000). *Crisis intervention handbook: Assessment, treatment, and research.* New York, NY: Oxford University Press.

Roberts, M., Vernberg, E., Biggs, B., Randell, C., & Jacobs, A. (2008). Lessons learned from the Intensive Mental Health Program: A school-based, community oriented program for with serious emotional disturbance. *Journal of Child and Family Studies, 17*, 277–289.

Rogers, S., & Vismara, L. (2008). Evidence-based comprehensive treatments for early autism. *Journal of Clinical Child & Adolescent Psychology, 37*, 8–38.

Ryckman, R. (2004). *Theories of personality.* Belmont, CA: Thomson/Wadsworth.

Sackett, D. L., Rosenberg, W. M. C., Gray, J. A. M., Haynes, R. B., & Richardson, W. S. (1996). Evidence based medicine: What it is and what it is not. *British Medical Journal, 312*, 71.

Saleebey, D. (2001). *Human behavior and social environment.* New York, NY: Columbia University Press.

Saleebey, D. (2008). Commentary on the strengths perspective and potential applications in school counseling. *Professional School Counseling, 12*(2), 68–75.

Santhiveeran, J. (2009). Compliance of social work e-therapy websites to the NASW Code of Ethics. *Social Work in Health Care, 48*(1), 1–13.

Schafer, C., & Kaduson, H. G. (2006). *Contemporary play therapy: Theory, research, and practice.* New York, NY: Guilford Press.

Schaffer, D., Scott, M., Wilcox, H., Maslow, C., Hicks, R., Lucas, C. P., Garfinkel, R., & Greenwald, S. (2004). The Columbia suicide screen: Validity and reliability of a screen for youth suicide and depression. *Journal of the American Academy of Child and Adolescent Psychiatry, 43*, 71–79.

Schmidt, C. (2010). Vocational education and training (VET) for youths with low levels of qualifications in Germany. *Education and Training, 52*(5), 381–390.

School Social Work Association of America. (2001, March 15, 2001). School social workers and confidentiality. Retrieved from www.sswaa.org/displaycommon.cfm

School violence threat risk assessment using Acute Petra. (n.d.). Retrieved from http://www.psych-insight.com/threat-assessment.html

Schrumpf, F., Crawford, D., & Bodine, R. (1997). *Peer mediation: Conflict resolution in schools.* Champaign, IL: Research Press.

Scott, T., Nelson, C., & Zabala, J. (2003). Functional behavior assessment training in public schools: Facilitating systemic change. *Journal of Positive Behavior Intervention, 5*(4), 216–224.

Seiber, J. (2007). Family Educational Rights and Privacy Act (FERPA). *Journal of Empirical Research on Human Research Ethics, 2*, 101.

Seipel, M. M. O. (2003). Global poverty: No longer an untouchable problem. *International Social Work, 46*(2), 191–207.

Shannon, W. (1999, July). Special report: Anger: Anger springs from complex combination of traits, events. *The Brown University Child and Adolescent Behavior Letter*.

Sheppard, S., Malatras, J., & Israel, A. (2010). The impact of deployment on U.S. military families. *American Psychologist, 65*(6), 599–609.

Shiller, V. (2007). Science and advocacy issues in research on children of gay and lesbian parents. *American Psychologist, 62*(7), 712–713.

Silverman, W., Ortiz, C., Viswesvaran, C., Burns, J., Kolko, D., Putnam, F., & Amaya-Jackson, L. (2008). Evidence-based psychosocial treatments for children and adolescents exposed to traumatic events. *Journal of Child & Adolescent Psychology, 37*, 156–183.

Silverman, W., Pina, A., & Viswesvaram, C. (2008). Evidence-based psychosocial treatments for phobic and anxiety disorders in children and adolescents. *Journal of Child & Adolescent Psychology, 37*, 105–130.

Simpson, R., LaCava, P., & Graner, P. S. (2004). No Child Left Behind Act: Challenges and implications for educators. *Intervention in School and Clinic, 40*(2), 67–75.

Singer, D. G., & Reverson, T. A. (1978). *A Piaget primer: How a child thinks.* New York, NY: A Plume Book.

Singer, J. B., & Slovak, K. (2011). School social workers' experiences with youth suicidal behavior: An exploratory study. *Children and Schools, 33*(4), 215–228.

Sisneros, J., Stakeman, C., Joyner, M. C., & Schmitz, C. L. (2008). *Critical multicultural social work.* Chicago, IL: Lyceum Books, Inc.

Social Work Code of Ethics. (2008). Retrieved from http://www.naswdc.org.

Somers, C., & Piliawsky, M. (2004). Drop-out prevention among urban, African American adolescents: Program evaluation and practical implications. *Preventing School Failure, 48*(3), 17–22.

Sossou, A. M. (2002). Corporal punishment in schools in Ghana: A social concern. *Journal of School Social Work, 12*(2), 83–94.

Sossou, A. M., & Daniels, T. (2002). School social work in Ghana: A hope for the future. In M. Huxtable & E. Blyth (Eds.), *School social work worldwide* (pp. 93–108). Washington, DC: NASW Press.

Special Education in the United States (2006). Retrieved from http://en.wikipedia.org/wiki/Special_Education_in_the_United_States#Classification

Spencer, M. S., & Clarke, J. S. (2006). Engaging with culturally and racially diverse families. In C. Franklin, M. B. Harris, & P. Allen-Meares. (Eds.), *The school services sourcebook: A guide for school-based professionals* (pp. 785–792). New York, NY: Oxford University Press.

Sprague, A., Thyer, B. (2002). Psychosocial treatment of oppositional defiant disorder: A review of empirical outcome studies. *Social Work in Mental Health, 1*, 63–72.

Stahmer, A., Hurlburt, M., Horwitz, S., Landsverk, J., Zhang, J., & Leslie, L. (2009). Associations between intensity of child welfare involvement and child development among young children in child welfare. *Child Abuse and Neglect, 33*, 598–611.

Stallard, P. (2002). *Think good, feel good: A cognitive behavior therapy workbook for children and young people.* Hoboken, NJ: Wiley.

Standards for Accreditation for Schools. (2009). Retrieved from Middle States Association of Colleges and Schools: http://www.css-msa.org/pdfs/2009SchoolStds.pdf

Steps to Respect Overview. (n.d.). Retrieved from http://www.cfchildren.org/Portals/0/STR/STR_DOC/Research

Strasburger, V. (2010). Children, adolescents, substance abuse and the media. *Pediatrics, 126*(4), 791-799.

Strekalova, E., & Hoot, J. (2008). What is special about special needs of refugee children? *Multicultural Education, 16*(1), 21–24.

Swaim, R. C., Beauvais, F., Chavez, E. L., Oetting, E. R. (1997). The effect of school dropout rates on estimates of adolescent substance use among three racial/ethnic groups. *Journal of Public Health, 87*(1), 51–55.

Teasley, M. (2004). Absenteeism and truancy: Risk, protection, and best practice implications for school social workers. *Children & Schools*, *26*(2), 117–128.

The Rural and Appalachian Youth and Families Consortium. (1996). Parenting practices and interventions among marginalized families in Appalachia: Building on family strengths. *Family Relations*, *45*(4), 387–396.

Tienda, M. & Haskins, R. (2008). *The future of immigrant children.* Cambridge, MA: Harvard University Press.

Tienda, M., & Haskins, R. (2011). Immigrant children: Introducing the issue. *Future of Children*, *21*(1), 1–16.

Titelman, G. (1996). *Random House dictionary of popular proverbs and sayings.* New York, NY: Random House.

Toglia, T. (2007). How does the Family Rights and Privacy Act affect you? *The Education Digest*, *73*(2), 61–65.

Toro, P., Dworsky, A., & Fowler, P. (2007, March). Homeless youth in the United States: Recent research findings and intervention approaches. In D. Dennis, G. Locke, & J. Khadduri (Eds.), *Toward Understanding Homelessness: The 2007 National Symposium on Homelessness Research*, Washington, DC.

Toseland, R. W. & Rivas, R. (2005). *An introduction to group work practice* (5th ed.). Boston, MA: Pearson Education.

Trainin Blank, B. (2005, Summer). Safety first: Paying heed to and preventing professional risk. *The New Social Worker*.

Turnbull, H. R. (2005). Individuals with Disabilities Education Act reauthorization: Accountability and personal responsibility. *Remedial and Special Education*, *26*(6), 320–326.

Turner, F. (1986). *Social work treatment: Interlocking theoretical approaches.* New York, NY: Free Press.

Tyson, K. (2000). Using the teacher-student relationship to help children diagnosed as hyperactive: An application of intrapsychic humanism. *Child & Youth Care Forum*, *29*, 265–289.

U.S. Department of Education. (2011). *Dropout rates*. Retrieved from http://nces.ed.gov/fastfacts/display.asp?id=16

Utah State Office of Education. (2006). Retrieved from 2006 www.usoe.k12.ut.us/data/glossary.htm

Van Dyk, A. (1995). *Sandplay therapy*. Retrieved from www.sandplay.net

vanVelzen, C., Bezzina, C., & Lorist, P. (2009). Partnerships between school and teacher education institutes. In A. Swennen & M. van der Klink (Eds.), *Becoming a teacher educator* (Part I, pp. 59–73). New York, NY: Springer.

van Wormer, K. (2006). *Introduction to social welfare and social work.* Belmont, CA: Thomson Brook/Cole.

van Wormer, K., McKinney, R. (2003). What schools can do to help gay/lesbian/bisexual youth: a harm reduction approach. *Adolescence*, *38*(151), 410–420.

van Wormer, K., Roberts, A. R. (2009). *Death by domestic violence: Preventing the murders and murder-suicides.* Westport, CT: Praeger.

Vazsonyi, A. T., Belliston, L. M., & Flannery, D. J. (2004). Evaluation of school-based universal violence prevention program: Low, medium, and high-risk children. *Youth and Juvenile Justice*, *2*, 185–206.

Velazquez, S., Earner, I., Lincroft, Y. (2007). Child welfare and the challenge of new Americans: Growing immigrant populations are creating questions for child welfare policy and practice. *Children's Voice Magazine*, *15*(4), 20–26.

Vernberg, E., Roberts, M., & Nyre, J. (2008). The intensive mental health program: Development and structure of the model of intervention for children with serious emotional disturbances. *Journal of Child and Family Studies*, *17*, 169–177.

Waldron, H., & Turner, C. (2008). Evidence-based psychosocial treatments for adolescent substance abuse. *Journal of Clinical Child & Adolescent Psychology*, *37*, 238–261.

Walsh, J. C. (2006). *Clinical assessment and diagnosis in social work practice*. New York, NY: Oxford University Press.

Weber, K., & Killu, K. (2005). The status of functional behavioral assessment (FBA): Adherence to standard practice in FBA methodology. *Psychology in the Schools*, *42*(7), 737–744.

Whittaker, C., Salend, S., & Elhoweris, H. (2009). Religious diversity in schools: Addressing the issues. *Intervention in School and Clinic*, *44*(5), 314–319.

Wing Sue, D. (2006). *Multicultural social work practice*. New York, NY: Wiley.

Wright, P. W. D., & Wright, P. D. (2007). Wrightslaw II: *Special education law*. Hartfield, VA: Harbor House Law Press.

Wright, T. (2000). Resisting homelessness: Global, national and local solutions. *Contemporary Sociology*, *29*(1), 27–43.

Wulfers, W. (2002). School social work in Germany: Help for youth in a changing society. In M. Huxtable & E. Blyth (Eds.), *School social work worldwide* (pp. 121–134). Washington, DC: NASW Press.

Yamashita, E. (2002). School social work in Japan: A partner for education in the 21st century. In M. Huxtable & E. Blyth (Eds.), *School social work worldwide* (pp. 217–231). Washington, DC: NASW Press.

Yerger, W., & Gehret, C. (2011). Understanding and dealing with bullying in schools. *Educational Forum*, *75*, 315–326.

Young, H. I., & Jung, K. M. (2002). A pilot project for school social work in Korea. *Journal of School Social Work*, *12*(2), 36–46.

Zur, O. (2007). *Boundaries in psychotherapy: Ethical and clinical explorations*. Washington, DC: American Psychological Association.

Index

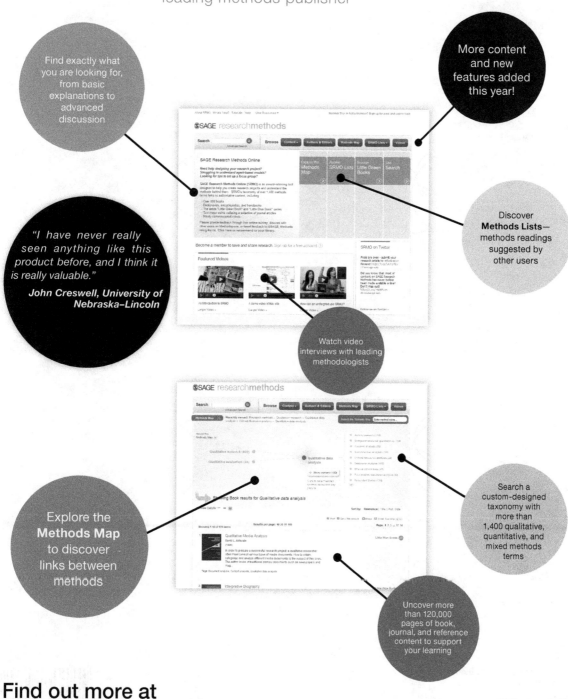

CPSIA information can be obtained
at www.ICGtesting.com
Printed in the USA